A Journey from Within

A Journey from Within

The Love Letters
of Charlotte Perkins Gilman,
1897–1900

Edited and Annotated by
Mary A. Hill

Lewisburg
Bucknell University Press
London: Associated University Presses

Associated University Presses
440 Forsgate Drive
Cranbury, NJ 08512

Associated University Presses
25 Sicilian Avenue
London WC1A 2QH, England

Associated University Presses
P.O. Box 338, Port Credit
Mississauga, Ontario
Canada L5G 4L8

The paper used in this publication meets the requirements
of the American National Standard for Permanence of Paper
for Printed Library Materials Z39.48-1984.

Library of Congress Cataloging-in-Publication Data

Gilman, Charlotte Perkins, 1860–1935.
    A journey from within : the love letters of Charlotte Perkins
Gilman, 1897–1900 / edited and annotated by Mary A. Hill.
      p.   cm.
    Includes bibliographical references and index.
    ISBN 0-8387-5293-4 (alk. paper)
    1. Gilman, Charlotte Perkins, 1860–1935—Correspondence. 2. Women
authors, American—19th century—Correspondence. 3. Love-letters.
I. Hill, Mary A., 1939– . II. Title.
PS1744.G57Z48 1995
818'.409—dc20
[B]
                                          94-24905
                                             CIP

PRINTED IN THE UNITED STATES OF AMERICA

for
David and Noelle Porter

whose friendship and love
have inspired and sustained me

Contents

Abbreviations

AESL   Arthur and Elizabeth Schlesinger Library, Charlotte Perkins Gilman Collection

CAP   Charlotte Anna Perkins

CPG   Charlotte Perkins Gilman

CPS   Charlotte Perkins Stetson

CWS   Charles Walter Stetson

GHG   George Houghton Gilman

Acknowledgments

There are many people who have supported me, both intellectually and spiritually, in making this book possible. I want to thank my parents, Thomas English Hill and the late Sara Prather Armfield Hill for their encouragement and inspiration. My heartfelt thanks also to the many unnamed friends and family members who listened to countless Gilman stories and helped me to develop the interpretations offered here. Some colleagues read the manuscript in whole or in part and offered important insights. I am particularly grateful to Catherine Blair, Susan Bowers, Gale Duque, Elaine Hedges, Laurie Kutchins, Charlene Stoner, and Martha Verbrugge. Special thanks go to Sharon Gerarge who typed and corrected numerous versions of this manuscript, and to a number of Bucknell students who also provided assistance—particularly to Leo Maley, Patricia Sohns Molenaro, Christine Segal, and Michelle Yenser.

I very much appreciate the generous financial assistance for this project provided by Bucknell University, the National Humanities Center, and the National Endowment for the Humanities. I am also grateful to the Arthur and Elizabeth Schlesinger Library on the History of Women in America, Radcliffe College, for permission to publish this edition of the Charlotte Perkins Gilman letters.

Finally, for their patience, inspiration, and affection, I thank David and Noelle Porter, to whom this book is dedicated.

Editorial Note

A word about editing procedures. Although my first priority was always to remain loyal to the style and flavor of the letters, I nonetheless have made some changes. Most important, I have reduced the available material by more than one half. I have included those sections of the letters that focus on Charlotte Gilman's intellectual perceptions, her reading, her friendships and acquaintances within the contemporary political community, and her evolving reflections on herself and her relationship with Houghton Gilman. I have omitted sections of the letters—always indicated by ellipses—which seemed less important or repetitious. Moreover, I have made occasional minor changes in spelling and punctuation. Rather than use the offensive *"sic,"* I have corrected rare misspellings and added punctuation where it seemed to enhance readability. Although the dates and chronological headings are entirely Charlotte Gilman's, the chapter divisions and chapter titles (either quotes or paraphrases from the letters) are my own.

A Journey from Within

Introduction

The focus of this study is Charlotte Gilman's letters to her second husband, Houghton Gilman, during the four years prior to their marriage, 1897–1900.[1] Twenty- to thirty-page letters she wrote him on an almost daily basis—love letters some might call them, passionate, revealing, intensely private, and very different from the published writings for which she justifiably has received national, even international, acclaim. Publicly Gilman was a brilliant theorist for the women's movement, a charismatic "new woman" lecturer and writer, the author of "The Yellow Wallpaper," of *Women and Economics,* of countless other essays, short stories, poems, articles, and books. But privately she also left a prolific record, a story of the underlying battles with almost every women's issue she publicly discussed. In *Women and Economics* she theoretically analyzed and exposed the destructive effects of sex-based inequalities. And in her private letters she acknowledged that many of her perceptions had emerged from agonizing gender conflicts in herself. As she explains in *Women and Economics,* "We ourselves, by maintaining this artificial diversity between the sexes, . . . have preserved in our own characters the confusion and contradiction which is our greatest difficulty in life."[2] And to Houghton she described an enigmatic conflict in herself: "To prove that a woman can love and work too. To resist this dragging weight of the old swollen woman-heart, and force it into place—the world's Life first—my own life next. Work first—love next. Perhaps this is simply the burden of our common womanhood which is weighing on me so."[3]

* * * * *

In an effort to explore the background of Charlotte Gilman's emergence as a woman's movement leader, I have written two books thus far. In the first volume, *Charlotte Perkins Gilman: The Making of a Radical Feminist, 1860–1896,* I focused on the origins of her feminist perspectives, on her family background, on the passion and excitement of her female friendships, on her experiences of marriage and young motherhood, and on the public context that also inspired her life and work. Charlotte's early years, I argued, were painful and perplexing. Her parents were separated. Her father was distant and unsupportive. And her mother, as single head of household, was overworked, economically hard-pressed, and stern. As a young adult, Charlotte's life was plagued by major crises. She faced a miserable depression after her marriage to Walter Stetson in 1884, a "nervous breakdown"

17

following the birth of her daughter Katharine in 1885, a divorce necessitated by the "insanity" of a loveless marriage, and a painful separation from her daughter necessitated by an itinerant public career. And yet by the mid-1890s, Gilman had emerged as a major writer for the women's movement, a critic of many of the destructive gender expectations she had experienced dramatically herself.

In my second volume, *Endure: The Diaries of Charles Walter Stetson,* I again explored the origins of Charlotte Gilman's feminist convictions, this time from her first husband's point of view. Walter Stetson's diaries, carefully written in a leather-bound notebook, begin just months before he met her. They end at the time of their separation and divorce. And they present for the intervening years, 1881–87, a fascinating fictionlike portrait of a remarkable relationship, though by no means according to Walter's original intent. He hoped, of course, that his diaries would show the truth and beauty of his love for Charlotte. But in my view they provide instead a dramatic illustration of the destructiveness of nineteenth-century gender norms. "[M]y love of her has conquered," Walter proudly noted in the early years of courtship. She no longer has "the daring and independent manner of the Charlotte that I first knew." She is "more like what is best in other women—thoughtful, bland, gracious, humble, dependent." "[S]he is as dough to the kneader or clay to the potter, to be fashioned as her lover wills." "O, how that spirit is broken. The false pride is melting before love rapidly." "She wants to be treated more as a child now than a woman."[4]

It took a rebellion, of course, and a long hard tough one, to move beyond the standard expectations, and in her early years its form was largely self-destructive: the childlike doll becomes self-hating and gradually develops the "hysteria," the "spasms of horror," which Charlotte Gilman's autobiographical short story, "The Yellow Wallpaper," so grimly and starkly describes. As she put it in her diary, Walter "would do everything in the world for me; but he cannot see how irrevocably bound I am, for life, for life. No, unless he die and the baby die, or he change or I change, there is no way out." Or as Walter put it, she was suffering because her "old ambitious 'freedom'-loving nature [was] rising in rebellion against the 'weakness' of tenderness and love." She was afraid "that her whole usefulness & real life was crushed out of her by marriage and the care of the baby," he wrote. Her "fierce rebellion at the existing state of things" must be symptomatic of her "brain disease."[5]

And yet however confused and depressed Gilman felt in the context of her marriage, she was strong enough to make some independent choices. She decided to leave Walter Stetson in September 1888 to travel with her mother and child to California, and then she began to lecture and to write. The transition years were tough—Gilman worked as a single mother and simultaneously nursed her own mother through dying and finally death. Yet, through all of this, perhaps in part because of all of this, Charlotte Gilman found herself emerging as a women's movement leader. She had very little academic training. But she was well read. She had her intellectually rich New England heritage. And she had life itself as her most demanding teacher. Also, she received important training from turn-of-the-century socialists and Nationalists, from suffragists and women's movement activists, and from a community of women, like herself, whose survival struggles had shaped a rather different view of truth.

Although my own published work on Charlotte Gilman ends at this important juncture, I very briefly want to summarize the reasons for her subsequent acclaim. First, in 1898, some ten years after divorcing Walter, and at the age of thirty-eight, Gilman published *Women and Economics,* which almost immediately thrust her into the limelight as a women's movement leader. The *Nation* called it "the most significant utterance on the subject since Mill's 'Subjection of Women.'" *The North American Review* praised its "originality, the scientific soundness, and moral efficacy." And, according to the London *Chronicle,* "Since John Stuart Mill's essays . . . there has been no book dealing with the whole position of women to approach it in originality of conception and brilliancy of exposition."[6] *Women and Economics* would be translated into at least six languages, go through more than half a dozen printings, and serve as a bible for suffragists and feminists for years.

For the next several decades, Gilman would continue publishing and writing. According to one writer, she was "the leading intellectual in the women's movement during the first two decades of the twentieth century." Or, in the view of Carrie Chapman Catt, she was the "most original and challenging mind which the movement produced."[7] *Women and Economics* was followed by *Concerning Children* in 1900, by *The Home* and *Human Work* in 1903, and in later years by six novels, seven *Forerunner* volumes of articles, essays and poetry, as well as several other works. By 1935, the year she died, she had to her credit not only countless nationally and internationally applauded lectures, but the equivalent of some twenty-two volumes of published work besides.

* * * * *

Turning now to Charlotte Gilman's theories, I want briefly to review some of the arguments for which she is most frequently remembered. Basically she pointed to five major forces that she thought created and perpetuated gender inequalities. The first and most important was also very simple: women were almost always economically dependent on the men with whom they lived. Women's work, she argued, has a use value but not an exchange value: "[W]hatever the economic value of the domestic industry of women is, they do not get it. The women who do the most work get the least money, and the women who have the most money do the least work." As a socialist, she argued that economic dependence, wherever it occurred, was almost necessarily destructive. She saw it in the factory workers' vulnerability, in the urban poverty accompanying American industrialization, in the fact that the average income in the 1890s was below subsistence level. But she saw the economic issue as central to the woman's movement also; in fact, she saw women's lack of economic independence—both historically and in her own time—as among the most destructive and pernicious obstacles to social change. She argued that most women were essentially the property of men, that their marriages were a form of economic beggary, and that the family itself, as a social and economic institution, perpetuated woman's virtual enslavement. As the child of a divorced woman, and later as a divorced woman herself, she knew from experience that marriage was simply not an equal economic partnership, that if a man loses his wife, he continues to receive an income, but if she loses him, she often has no means of livelihood at all. Thus woman "is the worker *par excellence,* but her work is not such as to affect her economic status." Instead, she obtains her "bread by use of the sex-functions," and her "economic profit" by "the power of sex-attraction."[8]

Thus the first problem, as Gilman saw it, was women's lack of economic independence. The second was their nonvoluntary, often kinship-based, domestic service, the division of labor along gender-based lines. Most women, in effect, were domestic servants for their private families, or, if poor or black, did domestic work in other people's homes.[9] Keep in mind that by far the largest percentage of women—80 percent of working age women in 1890—were not in the paid labor force at all. "In large generalization," as Gilman put it, "the women of the world cook and wash, sweep and dust for the men." Confined to private labor, they were denied free expression of their own productive talents, and then celebrated and romanticized for their loving, selfless, wageless work. As Gilman put it, "It has been amusing heretofore to see how this least desirable of labors has been so innocently held to be woman's natural duty. It is woman, the dainty, the beautiful, the beloved wife and revered mother, who has by common consent been expected to do the chamber-work and scullery work of the world." For by "giving to woman the home and to man the world in which to work, we have come to have a dense prejudice in favor of the essential womanliness of home duties, as opposed to the essential manliness of every other kind of work."[10]

The third factor that restricted women, Gilman argued, was their psychological dependence on men. "Of women especially have been required the convenient virtues of a subject class: obedience, patience, endurance, contentment, humility, resignation, temperance, prudence, industry, kindness, cheerfulness, modesty, gratitude, thrift, and unselfishness." Taught from childhood to respond to other people's needs and interests, to believe their function is to love and serve, women were denied the opportunity to develop autonomous perspectives, the prerequisites for strength and self-respect. In fact, "built into the constitution" of the human personality, she argued, were "irreconcilable elements" of "psychic development." Psychologically as well as economically, the family structure had divided humanity into two fundamentally different types—masculine (human) and feminine (sexual)—thus undermining the quality of human interaction in every other sphere of life.[11]

Gilman's fourth argument focused on what Adrienne Rich and others later called the "institution of motherhood," the notion that as long as women are defined primarily as mothers, there can be no equality or significant advance. She was not, she reassured her readers, criticizing the "essential relations of wife and mother." Rather she believed that women's child-rearing efforts—the main source of women's pride—were often fundamentally misplaced. Barred from "socially productive labor," confined to an "atmosphere of concentrated personality," they pass on to their children the limitations they had suffered themselves. "Nothing in the exquisite pathos of woman's long subjection goes deeper to the heart than the degradation of motherhood by the very conditions we supposed were essential to it."[12]

Fifth and finally, Gilman talked about the oppressiveness of "love." The "sex-relation" had become a "frightful source of evil," she wrote, but "hasty thinkers of all ages" had misconstrued the blame. They had concluded that the "whole thing was wrong, and that celibacy was the highest virtue." And yet it was not the "sex-relation" that had "so tangled the skein of human life," but the "economic relation of the sexes," the "peculiar arrangement of feeding one sex by the other," the system whereby women are "bought and bribed through the common animal necessities of food and shelter, and chained by law and custom." Sexuality, she wrote, is "the deepest force in nature." It is a natural instinct which "developes into that wide, deep, true, and lasting love which is the highest good to individual human beings." And yet too often women were condemned to "mercenary marriage," to a prostitution of themselves for economic gain, to a search for "love" at the "price of liberty." For the young girl, marriage was her "proper sphere, her divinely ordered place, her natural end. It is what she is born for, what she is trained for, what she is exhibited for." "Hence the millions of mis-made marriages with 'anybody, good Lord!' Hence the million broken hearts which must let all life pass, unable to make any attempt to stop it"—the death of the spirit in the name of love.[13]

* * * * *

Although I originally intended in this volume to focus on Gilman's public contributions as a theorist, lecturer, and writer, I turn instead, for reasons which I hope will be persuasive, to a close reading of her private letters during a brief but personally prolific span of time, 1897 to 1900. By 1897, Gilman had in many ways shaped her life according to the convictions she was preaching publicly. She had secured modest economic independence. She had challenged the commonly accepted roles of womanhood—the dutiful daughter, the loving wife, the "natural" mother. Professionally she was urging other women to strengthen their confidence, to break free from their home-based isolation and dependence. And personally she was securing greater freedom for herself: the opportunity for travel, for self-reflection, for creative public work.

And yet for Gilman the years 1897 to 1900 were still ones of vitally important struggle. They were the years she wrote and published *Women and Economics*. But they were also the years of her rich, traumatic correspondence with Houghton Gilman, the man who, in 1900, became her second husband. Starting in 1897, she wrote him almost daily—exposing her insecurities and contradictions, trusting her passions, and exploring what some might call a "different way of knowing."[14] At the time she urged Houghton not to keep her letters: "If you save all this stuff it'll be trotting out biographically some day—and then you'll be sympathized with. I pray thee, mark these letters 'Please Destroy.'"[15] But she did not insist even then, and Houghton did not comply. And in later life she saved them purposely. It was almost as though she realized her published writing would be one type of legacy. Another would be the record of her life—compelling, disquieting, and very real.

*   *   *   *   *

Charlotte had known Houghton Gilman as a child, as an affectionate first cousin seven years younger, as her wholeheartedly admiring, innocently following, unashamedly adoring little "friend I hold so dear." She had enjoyed vacation visits with him a number of times—romping about the hills behind his sprawling New England home, playfully sharing adolescent anecdotes and whistlike games. "Chow Perkins," or "Sis Perkins," Houghton used to call her in energetic notes and scribbles passing back and forth between them in their teen years—the rhymes, jingles, and comic sketches, the warmly flirtatious appeals. "Write again old fellow," she'd prod him gently, "I like to hear you chirp." At age nineteen (Houghton was only twelve), she wrote him, "I'm ravenously busy," but when "this busy time is over I will send you once again, epistles so extensive that you will howl with pain." "I never want you to write until you feel like it," she assured him. "By thus doing our pleasing correspondence will remain a consolation & a joy, and never become, like the grasshopper 'a burden.'"[16]

Charlotte's early correspondence suggests that from the very outset Houghton served as a delightful if somewhat distant outlet for the personality she most preferred. She could be energetically ambitious but also warm and loving. She could be assertive but not combative, gentle but not dependent, straightforward without attracting opposition, childlike without inviting condescending protection and control. With Houghton she could test her skills in safety. She was the elder cousin, after all, seven years more worldly wise, and thus could gorge herself on fun-filled banter—flirting, boasting, teasing—Houghton standing wide-eyed and believing on the sidelines. As she described one January 1880 outing:

> What joys were mine! I went sleighing, I went to the theater, I went to parties, and I received calls. Bye and bye, when you "are old and hideous, and the hairs of your beard are mostly grey," as the poet says, you will understand the joys of such an existence.[17]

In some respects, Houghton's family in Norwich, Connecticut, seemed a welcome contrast to her more restricted Providence environment, and from her point of view, at least one reason was clear: Houghton's mother was starkly different from her own. Aunt Katherine Gilman (her father's sister) was more confident and cheerfully supportive than her mother Mary Perkins was—Katherine was less vulnerable, less anxious, and less unhappy. She did not constantly complain and disapprove as much as Mary did, or care as much about conventions, or rules, or money-matters, or meal-fixing, or dirt-chasing, or a thousand other "petty" worries of "petty" women who were ignorant of the passion and beauty they could find in art, in nature, in books. Years later, Charlotte would appreciate some reasons for the difference. In her elegant, servant-run home, Katherine could afford to be more life-affirming than Mary, and less irritable and demanding. She had the time and energy, the social and economic status that Mary, as a single mother, lacked. But memories of Katherine nonetheless intensified the kinship ties with Houghton—her easy tolerance, her generous appreciation, her kind of motherly warmth that didn't suffocate. "I think that it is your mother's look," Charlotte later wrote to Houghton, that "carries me back to that impression of heavenly tenderness—a very passion of mother love. . . . Strange that a young man's eyes should call up a never-satisfied longing for mother love!"[18]

In her early years Charlotte also found the fascinating mazelike rural structure of the old Gilman homestead utterly appealing: its huge mahogany-filled bedrooms and parlors; its old Beecher-style dining room with "hand hewn beams and beautifully carved corner cupboards"; its odd passages and halls—leading literally "upstairs and downstairs and in my lady's chamber," as one visitor described it. Even Houghton's hometown (Norwich, Connecticut) had a quiet atmosphere of "dignity and beauty and peace": the long, tree-lined streets, the columned and majestic old New England homes, the wide sweeps of lawn under the great elms. What a contrast to Providence, Charlotte flippantly complained to Houghton, and particularly to her own mud-filled street.[19]

> [Next door there] is a snub-nosed cottage inhabited by two women & a dog. There is a cat, too, and a man, but they don't show. . . . Opposite us is a vast expanse of lot where once were trees. Below the street dwindles, and becomes decidedly inelegant as to dwellers thereon. And all about in the foreground are—Hens! Horrid, disagreeable, lowdown, hens. Nasty, unmentionable, villainous hens. . . . When I get rich we shall move.[20]

Although Charlotte was attracted in part to the upper-class atmosphere of Norwich, and also to the upper-class types who could afford to live there, even more importantly, she loved the sheer beauty of the natural landscape: "the cool blue background of far hills across the valley, and the warm foreground a vivid color, great moss-embroidered rocks, the loaded blue-berry bushes, the balsam firs that shot up everywhere, the multicolored carpet of moss and grass and all manner of small underbrush."[21] Even the gardens outside the Norwich home were delightfully appealing, paths and wooden steps weaving through well-balanced flower beds—iris, johnny-jump-ups, yellow alyssum; then on to a rustic grape arbor, some berry bushes and trellised vines; and finally ending in a secluded nook complete with old-fashioned garden furniture of a faded darkish red, some profusely growing roses and clematis, and an open view of the Lathrope meadows beyond. Partly it was the quietness Charlotte loved, and the simple beauty. And when occasionally she tried to capture it in her water-color sketches, according to one observer, she succeeded splendidly: "As carefully detailed as Audubon prints, the little sketches were yet so full of the personality of the flowers, their very poise and texture, that pansies, quince blossoms, cardinal flowers and wild roses seemed to stand out from the paper like living things."[22]

Charlotte and Houghton had found their playful early correspondence—almost as much as the periodic visits between—a welcome contrast to problems pressuring them at home. For Charlotte, the tensions of family life in Providence had, at times, seemed overwhelming: an exasperating brother; an emotionally distant father; a mother who was unhappy, disapproving and cold. And for Houghton also, family life was sometimes stark and painful, particularly in the winter of 1879. First, he faced the death of his elder sister, Elizabeth Coit Gilman (Bessie) in November 1879. Then, weeks later, 2 December 1879, his mother, Katherine Gilman, died. Charlotte and Houghton no doubt shared some short grieving times together, some back and forth wordless comforting, some tears glimpsed briefly. But for the most part they had instinctively used their friendship energy for playful cheer and banter, as though to fortify themselves against anxiety and grieving, as though to secure the needed shelter for a last-chance romp through childhood.

*   *   *   *   *

Almost twenty years had passed since those early friendship/cousin ties with Houghton. By 1897, both Charlotte and Houghton were fairly well established, she as a speaker and writer traveling cross-country on her lecture tours, and he as a Wall Street lawyer, a relatively successful, if not a particularly ambitious man. In the early months of 1897, Charlotte had been resting from a lecture tour in England. She had been staying with her recently adopted family, with Frankie Perkins, her father's second wife; and she also had been lecturing, meeting with New York political reformers, and planning the next year's work. Finally, in early March, she noted in her diary: "Go down town. . . . Look up Houghton Gilman."[23] Years later, she drolly sketched the day's event:

> On the eighth of March I called at an office on Wall Street to look up a certain Cousin Houghton Gilman I had been fond of in 1879. He sat, extremely busy, writing, suspecting the approaching female to be a book-agent. I stood beside him and remarked, "You haven't the slightest idea who I am." Then he gazed sharply at me and replied, "Yes I have, you're my Cousin Charlotte."[24]

Only briefly did Charlotte sense from Houghton the kind of coldness that momentarily she may have feared. He seemed elegant and dignified to be sure, immensely "beautiful" in fact. But given the warmth of his personality—and also the nature of her surprise attack—he must have seemed instantly and utterly familiar: the little boy grin surfacing beneath the imposing Walrus mustache; the ears just a bit too big, almost comic on the frail oval face; the sensitivity of manner strangely reminiscent of his mother; the fun-loving eyes meeting Charlotte's gently yet playfully as though some joke of years before were instantly replayed and shared.[25]

In some respects Houghton could be described as an androgynous kind of character. Gentle, kind, and sensitively responsive to other people's needs, he was patient enough to endure her contradictions and confusions and confident and generous enough to support her public work. The "personal impression you make on me is of intense Beauty," she wrote him. "The harmony—simplicity—restraint—the clear Greek quality of being the thing you are, perfectly, . . . it is Beautiful." Besides, she continued in another letter, "You seem very near somehow," "a kind of background to most of my thinking when I'm not at work." Or again, "It is astonishing how many times a day I incline to write to you."[26] And write she did—more than enough to equal several of her books.

In important ways, Charlotte's conflicts with Houghton differed from the ones with Walter Stetson. Whereas with her former husband she had struggled against *his* efforts to impose the standard female expectations— the dutiful mother, the ideal wife—what these later letters show, in part, is her struggle not to impose them on herself. Despite her theories, and despite a supportive, easygoing Houghton, she had still to battle the destructive lessons her culture had imposed.

Take the issue of women's need for work and economic independence, for example. On the one hand, Gilman was determined to continue lecturing and writing, to act according to her theory: She argued that meaningful work is not only essential to human life; it *is* human life. It is a basic impulse, a social passion as natural as breathing. Obviously women should not content themselves only with domestic service. Women need, or rather people need, professionalized housekeeping, and kitchenless houses, and satisfying work commitments, which for the most part she insisted on having for herself. "I wish you could have heard me last Sunday night," she wrote after one particularly successful lecture. "I never spoke better in my life. A full church. A big platform all to myself. And it *came*! It just poured in a great swelling river and all those people sat and took it in." "What a wonderful life it is—to go everywhere—to meet everyone—to eat and drink so largely of human life."[27]

So on the one hand Gilman enthusiastically continued with her lecturing and writing. But because she also valued a nurturing, satisfying love relationship, she struggled with the social definitions which said that femininity and creativity were mutually exclusive and that while for men, professional success was positive and self-affirming, for loving women it was a mark of aggressiveness and selfishness instead. She thus wrote apologetically to Houghton:

> . . . Don't you see dear how much at a disadvantage I am beside you? Try and feel like a woman for a moment—put yourself in their place. You know what a woman wants to bring a man—a boundless wholesouled love, absolutely and primarily his own—all his own.
> I haven't that. . . .
> A long life of beautiful service and devotion, given wholly to his interests.
> I haven't that. . . .
> I can only give you a divided love—I love God—the world—my work as well as I love you. . . .
> O my dear—do you not see what poignant grief and shame it is to a woman to have no woman's gifts to give![28]

Or again, in a somewhat later letter, "I'm sorry that I can't add my life to yours—woman fashion . . . the usual style of immersion of the wife in the husband." But "[I need to] work out such plan of living as shall leave me free to move as move I must. . . . *I must not* focus on 'home duties'; and entangle myself in them. Remember it is not an external problem with me—a mere matter of material labor and time. . . . it is practical enough to be a question of life or death with me."[29]

Although Gilman was determined to continue working, she could do so only reluctantly, apologetically, and often with enormous guilt about the "feminine" responsibilities society had always claimed were hers. It was almost as though she sometimes felt compelled to use typical "feminine" disclaimers, deceptions some might call them, playing coy, or emphasizing her childlike weakness to protect Houghton's sense of strength. By elaborating on her fears and limitations, occasionally she would try deflecting his attention from her professional successes, and thereby manage to disguise her power. Sometimes she dealt with Houghton's more laid-back personality by pushing him to be assertive: "It is a woman's business to wait, not a man's. It is for a woman to be patient and still—not a man. If you are truly lover and husband—show it. If not—God bless you and Good-bye."[30] But, if she occasionally tried to quell her fears by pushing Houghton to adhere to standard gender expectations, more frequently she had to struggle with the tendency to impose them on herself. As she would later put it in her published writing, that while "*men, man, manly, manhood*" meant the "world and all its activities," "when we say *Women,* we think *Female,* the sex."[31] Or as she wrote privately to Houghton, "I suppose all this flamboyance of mine makes it seem as if you weren't getting on so fast by contrast. But Bless you! Mine is all talk—a mountain in labor. You have seen the mice I bring forth." And this disclaimer came after *Women and Economics* had been published and nationally acclaimed. Or again, "You talk about being 'overshadowed' by your wife—I suppose there will be some people who will think so—but if they only could know how I *feel!* Why when I think of you I feel like a thin forlorn hungry cold little kitten . . . that you had taken in and done for." Or as she also put it, she wanted to be treated as the "dear foolish tired little girl" who needed to come into his "arms and rest."[32]

What we have in Gilman's letters are contrasts that are repeatedly disturbing. The strong public advocate of woman's full equality felt a "compelling desire . . . to complain and explain—to whimper . . . and seek for sympathy which don't do me any good if I get it."[33] She was looking for, and hoping for, a "right relation," as Carter Heywood calls it, an intimate, centering, "love" relationship in which she could express her needs and passions and fully be herself.[34] But repeatedly she floundered. She wanted satisfying work, but she apologized for needing it. She wanted a passionate, intimate relationship, but for that she felt a "tidal wave of shame." "I feel wicked," she wrote Houghton, "shamelessly wicked—as if some one had caught me eating an angel—or plucking the poor thing in preparation for the feast." "My love for you drags me, tears me, pulls me toward you. My reason stands up like a rock, when the waves drop back—and always says the same thing—. . . *You are not fit to marry him.*" "I cannot fully harmonize you with the rest of it. I suppose it is only the essential pain of the woman nature forced out into world service."[35] Or, as she put it another letter, "I wish I could make a picture of the thing [herself] as I see it—sulky, frightened, discouraged, 'rattled' to a degree; one foot forward and the other back, ready to rush forward in tumultuous devotion one minute, and run away shrieking in the next—fingers in ears!"[36]

"Unreasonable," "disagreeable," "absurd"—repeatedly Gilman viewed herself as a "vacillating wretch" swinging back and forth between painfully conflicting needs. "I don't wholly like to be held—and yet I do!" "Makes me kind of angry too. Seems a weakness. To be so tangled up in another person." She described herself as a broken goblet "that everything spills out of—I can't *keep* any feeling—they flow over and through me, and you never can be sure of what you are going to find." "O Houghton—I am so *tired* of all this restless doubt and hope and fear and flickering joy. . . . I've got to the place I wanted. I can write what I please and say what I please and the world is ready to listen. And here I am floundering helplessly among my own affairs—doing no work at all. It is shameful—shameful."[37]

* * * * *

For years I have struggled with Charlotte Gilman's letters. I have found myself frustrated and disappointed by her contradictions and confusions, and by the "feminine" self-hatred that she disguised beneath her firm, impressive public stance. At times it seemed that she could understand causes of women's victim status but could not succeed in overcoming them. Publicly she would call for women to be strong and independent; but with Houghton—as though unable to sustain the courage of her own convictions—she would become the "forlorn" and squalid "little kitten," the "babblesome and childish" little girl.[38] As is so often the case in women's history, we thus confront a disturbing pattern. Taught from childhood to accept "feminine" self-abnegation, to "love" in dependent and self-denying ways, women find it hard to respect themselves, much less to recognize, accept, and respect authenticity and purpose in their work. Like so many professional women even today, Gilman was unable consistently to feel the self-respect she publicly projected. Impressive though she clearly was, she could not free herself completely of the "burden of our common womanhood" that through her published works she helped us understand.

When I first studied Gilman's letters, I thus argued sympathetically (and rather condescendingly), that she was a victim of destructive patriarchal norms, that publicly she launched a persuasive rational attack on the forces that restricted women, yet privately waged war against herself, and far more brutally, more emotionally and passionately. And yet gradually I have come to read these letters differently: as a reflection of her pain and struggle, but not of her capitulation; as an exploration of her labyrinth of fears and insecurities, but as a demonstration also of an absolute determination to resist. In fact, in some respects Gilman's letters are more radical even than many of her published writings, more powerful and also more courageous. For while her published works stand as important statements of resistance in the more abstract, theoretical arena, her private letters expose the underlying "feminine" realities of war. Struggling for self-respect and professional commitment in the context of a "love" relationship, she had to fight against the fear that she was too forceful and ambitious, or too emotional and passionate, or too strong and confident, or too "rebellious" and "unfeminine." In any case, like so many women, she occasionally absorbed the social message and momentarily believed that she deserved the worst of punishments. Or to use the metaphors more frequent in her letters, she was a "monster" threatening to swallow or destroy her lover, and thus needed to be crushed, shattered, or drowned.[39]

The violence of Gilman's metaphors is striking—as is her courage, her determination to resist conventional heterosexual norms. As she put it in one letter, she was like the "old campaigner"—sometimes "crippled" by the battle, but also proud to have survived the war. "I *feel* most like a soldier in a seventy year's war. Sometimes bitterly depressed, often defeated, long imprisoned, scarred and wounded beyond recognition but not crippled past all usefulness."[40] It was almost as though, like Persephone, she was willing, in fact she was uncompromisingly determined, to explore the dark side, to travel to the underworld, to take Houghton to her "catacombs."[41] "Blind" and "creeping," she still kept moving forward, still kept turning up old "gravestones" or "trap-door-stones," and finding "all these buried things, dead and alive." She would experience an "awful landslide," severing her "way down to the bones," "all the flesh and blood" removed. Yet even then she still continued. Terrified of "madness," of what she called a "grey fog darkness"—at "its long worst it meant pitch blackness— unillumined and unilluminable"—it was almost as though she were using "illness" as a spur, "grave stones," or "trap-door" stones serving to intensify her search.[42]

And yet in her relationship with Houghton, Charlotte was not only exploring "dangerous" and threatening emotions, she was also learning to respect them, to trust her feelings, and thus to tap important sources of her energy and increasingly to trust herself.[43] In fact, she often used her letters as her "morning prayers," she wrote Houghton. Confronting and working through the "monster" feelings, she began to move from metaphors of violence to images of birthing, of spiritual awakening, of re-affirming her own power. It "doesn't feel like quicksand anymore," but like rowing on the "open ocean . . . —the oars dipping or not dipping as the waves may rise—. . . and withal the tremendous elation of that very power beneath—the vast rise and swell." Or again, it is as if "some system of irrigation were gradually spreading in a desert country, reclaiming more ground daily, and making the wilderness to blossom as the rose." "I feel as if I had been only playing—before— that *this* is life and I am but just born!"[44]

Proudly but surreptitiously, Gilman used her letters as a source of healing, of empowering, a bridge back and forth between equally important human needs. Enthusiastically and passionately she could describe the satisfactions of her work commitments: the sense of "uniting power," of "constructive power," "rich and sweet with the response of hungry hearts." And increasingly she could delight also in her relationship with Houghton. He was inspiring a "mended strengthened re-born feeling," she wrote him, a sense of "heavenly wonder, so utterly unknown, undreamed of in my life."[45]

. . . surely you can read it in my eyes—hear it in my voice, feel it in my arms about your neck—taste it on my lips that lean to you. You make me so happy— so happy my darling! I love you—love you—love you![46]

Or even more passionately,

Sweetheart! You shall kiss me anywhere you want to and all you want to as soon as ever there is a chance. I will wait till you are exhausted and begin operations on my own account.[47]

With Houghton standing as her lover, friend, and witness, and with correspondence serving as her "morning prayers," Gilman began to move toward an affirmation of the "wild woman" forces, the erotic, the "goddess" energies that so often she had effectively disguised. For a time, Gilman had internalized an antiwoman image. And in sheer self-protection, she often would continue to sustain it in her public life. But privately—since the relationship with Houghton was "the secretest secret I ever had"—she was trusting and enjoying the energizing sensual and spiritual dimensions within herself. "Ceaselessly hungry" for life, she was a "voracious comet," she wrote Houghton, a "wild floating soul," a "flouncing kite," a "cold queer rebellious unnatural sex-failure" that is "well, is not bad to take!"[48]

well, sometimes I feel like "a heathen goddess come again"—a wonderful struggling mixed feeling, half shame, half pride, of being—to most people's knowledge a stern cold thinker, a calm pleasant friend of men, dearly loved by women, the favorite of children—a widow—a celibate, a solitary—and inside—Ashteroth![49]

Secretly and forcefully, Gilman had used her letters as a battleground. Instead of acquiescing either as the evil monster or the needy victim, instead of succumbing to the "essential pain" of the divided self, more often she was emerging as the "transition" woman experiencing the "miracle" of wholeness, the warrior woman, the "old campaigner," the "prophetess" inspiring other women with her work. "Now that I've told you so much—shown you so much of my—catacombs," she wrote Houghton, "You seem at once nearer and more healthfully remote." She was so much "the richer, the sweeter, the wiser, the stronger," so "*much* better able to understand life, to know love, to teach and write," much more ready to turn "naturally" and "with less effort," to "the power of settled work."[50]

Come now! This is what women have got to learn to do, if my new world is to come true! It may be part of my work to accomplish just this thing! To do world's work and live large and glad in it; to love and wed and be great mothers too— this is before the women of the world; and I must at least try at it.[51]

* * * * *

In the late 1890s, Charlotte Gilman was emerging as a women's movement leader, and in those same years, or so I argue here, she was emerging privately as well. And yet that is not to claim that through her letters she managed completely to resolve the issues or that she found consistent answers or solutions. "When the wheel turns round, as my wheel always does," she wrote—as though reminding us that life is never linear or static.[52] At best it is a process of becoming, spirals of creative growth, forms circling, revolving and returning, each time the same yet also new. There is thus an unresolvability in Gilman's letters. Experiencing and reexperiencing the problems, "resolving" a dilemma only to find it reemerging once again, it was as though through letters she was mirroring the lives of generations that had come before her or anticipating struggles that many future daughters would courageously repeat.

Understandably, some readers might prefer that Gilman's letters formed a neat, logical progression toward safe and satisfying answers. My goal instead has been to "hear her into speech," as Nelle Morton might have put it. I have tried to rename what she would sometimes trivialize or ridicule, to facilitate the telling of her story, and thus to help break through the mask of shame and silence that has traditionally surrounded women's private lives. By providing brief introductions to her letters, my goal has been to chart her journey, to supply a road map through her "wilderness," but then to let readers experience the terrain themselves: the "terrors" of the quicksand, the "elation" of rowing on the open ocean, the beauty of the "island" lifting from the "stretch of waves."[53]

And yet, of course, this volume has its limitations. First, it lacks the voice of her respondent, Houghton Gilman, who, for the most part, remains enigmatic and unknown. "I find it increasingly difficult to destroy your letters," she wrote him. "Such agreeable letters." "Over which I smile, and chuckle, and look out of the window and wonder—various things." "But iron necessity compels me—I *can* not carry nor store them!" "It is a wise habit which I will recommend to you forthwith." Or again, as though to tantalize us further—"There! I've read 'em all over and torn 'em all up—which was really an effort."[54]

Second, this volume stands only as a partial story, a four-year slice of life, 1897 to 1900, and not the whole of one. And while some of her important works were published in these correspondence years—*Women and Economics,* most notably—the vast majority were written after 1900, for which very little corresponding private data has as yet been found.

Third, Gilman's letters reflect a private journey rather than a public one. They provide a backdrop for many of her ideas and later feminist perspectives, but only rarely and obliquely do they talk about the specifics of her public life: the books she read, the places she visited, the meetings she attended, the many people who had important impact on her life and work— Jane Addams at Hull House, for instance, or Alice Stone Blackwell, or Susan B. Anthony. For this reason I have tried to summarize important aspects of the public and historic context in my brief chapter introductions to these letters. But readers necessarily will want to move beyond this volume if they hope to understand the whole of Gilman's life and work. Not only should they consult her public writings, most of which have been republished—*The Home,* for instance, or *Women and Economics, Herland,* and many of her articles, short stories, poems, and essays. But they should review the rich biographical and critical analyses as well: those by Carl Degler, for example, or by Ann Lane, Elaine Hedges, Carol Kessler, and Gary Scharnhorst.

Fourth, Gilman's letters focus on issues that were largely middle class and white. African-American, Native American, Hispanic, immigrant, and working-class women—not only were these often quietly ignored in Gilman's writings; theoretically as well as personally, they also often were presented in starkly racist/classist terms. Clearly Gilman's biases were shared by most people of her class and generation, but the resulting irony nonetheless remains: while she had brilliantly denounced the tendency of *men* to universalize their own experience, she ignored the voices and survival struggles of her sisters and too often universalized her own.[55]

Although a volume focusing on Gilman's private correspondence necessarily has its limitations, from my perspective it has historic value of a kind that has been traditionally ignored. The standard historical approach has long been: to ignore such personal and "feminine" discussions; or to ridicule them for being trivial or unimportant; or, as though guilt were a constructive or effective remedy, to categorically dismiss them for being white and middle class; or to offer condescending sympathy; or to emphasize their private contradictions and confusions and thereby help obscure the courage that inspired their fight.

And yet in recent years historians have moved beyond this kind of blame-the-victim history, suggesting that such private battles, though by no means universal, deserve affirmation and respect, and for several reasons which I will review briefly. For one thing, Gilman's letters document the pragmatic implications of many social expectations. Although her published works focus on her formal theories, her letters focus on ideas and how they were reflected in her life. Readers see not just the conclusions of a major theorist but also a theorist's confrontation with the problems themselves. Moreover, Gilman's problems were not simply private ones. Reexperienced with variations in the lives of many, they reflect obstacles that many women faced—in the institutions of the mind, in the institutions of the spirit, in politics, law, and government. Also, they document the courage it took to sustain the battle. After all, if a theorist like Gilman faced such struggles, what about the many other women who never had a chance to see another view? In fact, if we keep in mind the toughness of the problems, what seems to me surprising is not the fact that she and many other women sometimes waffled but rather that they managed to resist at all, that they had the courage to stand up to the opposition, the ridicule, the condemnation so often directed at women with their point of view. Women demanding economic independence, or nondomestic labor, or emotional and psychological autonomy—these women were attacked for their collective fanaticism, their want of foresight, their morbid vanity, their selfish foolish thinking—so amateurish, so beside the mark.

Besides, it was not just public courage that Gilman and many other women showed. It was not just the courage to confront *outside* attitudes and expectations, or to condemn *other* people's narrowness. It was also the courage to confront antiwoman views they had within themselves, to experience the vacillations, even to experience the suicidal swings toward "madness." As Gilman put it in one letter, "As to death—that's nothing. But I do think it takes some gumption to speak calmly of losing one's mind."[56]

So why bother with the private letters? Another critically important reason is that Gilman's written confrontations with her "madness," her private explorations of the "catacombs," document the process by which she deepened her ideas. For while her public works were visible and thus more obviously important, necessarily they had their limitations. *Women and Economics,* for example, was a milestone of resistance and a brilliant use of contemporary theory to promote the women's movement. And yet by borrowing from contemporary theorists (Patrick Geddes and Lester Ward, for example), by using their language, their male-centered frameworks and perspectives, by paying tribute to their God of logic, reason, and abstraction, Gilman sometimes wrote as though women's voices were "too" emotional and feminine, and as though their perspectives had less value, less meaning, less truth.[57] In the letters, by contrast, Gilman tested and learned to trust her own and other women's voices. She was exploring "feminine" self-hatred, but in the process she was deepening her awareness of the pervasiveness of sexual definitions, the longevity of sexual myths—woman from Adam's rib, or woman as the temptress, the self-sacrificing Mary or the seductive Eve, or the many other myths so apparent in art, literature, philosophy, and religion through most of our recorded past. Personally as well as theoretically she knew full well that it was not enough to have economic independence and satisfying work. Given the depth of patriarchal attitudes, the definitions of womanood were themselves fundamentally insulting. It was as though womanhood were something one must work to overcome, which is a bit like saying that blacks should work to overcome their blackness, or that women should strive to be like men.

Gilman's letters, in part, reflect a healing process, a woman-centered journey, a push toward an affirmation of her womanhood and a rejection of dichotomous gender norms. Take the assumption, or stereotype, for instance, that masculine is rational and therefore positive, while feminine is emotional and therefore weak. Whereas Gilman's published writings are for the most part very logical and rational, her private letters are more emotionally courageous and direct. They explore deeply rooted layers of psychological conditioning, and they acknowledge realistically that abstract truths can't always cure. The letters are thus rational *and* emotional, not emotional and therefore weak.

Or take the assumption that masculine means strength and forcefulness and feminine means indecisiveness. Again, Gilman offered public arguments that were firm and clear and confident. By contrast, in her letters she did not even try to offer definitive conclusions—"nugget[s] of pure truth" Virginia Woolf would call them. She was working with the "oil of truth" instead—spontaneous, richly flowing, attached directly to the energetic current of our lives.[58] So, instead of dismissing or criticizing Gilman's indecisiveness, I respect the fact, as she most certainly was forced to do, that truth can be elusive and that complex human motivation does not fit so neatly into confidently stated rules.

Or finally, take the work versus love dichotomy, the notion that "masculine" means cultural achievement and preeminence, while "feminine" means a personal emphasis on love. On this issue Gilman's letters once again are forceful and courageous. For not only did she argue that the need for love is basic, even more importantly she attacked the assumptions that so often stifle and subvert it. By insisting that human love is *incompatible* with inequality, that heterosexual love *requires* mutual respect, she was thus not only challenging dichotomies central to the heterosexual relation— masculine/feminine, mind/body, reason/emotion, work/love—but in the process she was also challenging parallel political dichotomies—superior/inferior, ruler/ruled, owner/owned, user/used—and thereby resisting the fragmentation, the polarization on which our society depends. In that sense I thus would argue that Gilman's correspondence, her search for Eros, for intimacy, was itself a subversive political endeavor.[59] Or as Alicia Ostriker puts it, "Relationships between friends and lovers become paradigmatic for the conduct of political life"; what "resists the self-surrender of love and the commitment to human tenderness in the microcosm of personal relations is also what resists it in Vietnam, Africa, Harlem."[60] For if we begin to understand the breakdown of trust on the private level, if we examine and improve the way we *live* as well as how we *think,* perhaps we thereby help to heal the sense of social separation; perhaps justice in the political arena depends on the capacity for "right relation" in our private lives.

In conclusion I would argue that Gilman's letters are important because they direct attention to important issues, issues that have defined so many women's lives and shaped so many women's destinies and yet still too often are ignored.[61] For until very recently most women have lived in "story-less time," as Carolyn Heilbrun reminds us; for generations, most women were "either trapped in, or have wasted energy opposing, the only narrative available to them: the conventional marriage or erotic plot," the ready-made and constraining stories, the patterns of dominance that are so pervasive yet so elusive, so complex, so well-hidden beneath romantic myth and trite cliche.[62] We thus need stories, as contemporary women writers have so often argued, stories that retroactively make sense of the past, that project meaning toward the future, that knit past and future together, and thus create, suspended between the two, a more just and equal present world. Particularly we need stories that help us understand the institutions of marriage and the family, institutions that give some people, usually men, the opportunity to impose their will—as well as their imaginative vision—and to make it prevail. People have known for centuries that the family is a basic unit in society. What writers have emphasized more recently is that in fundamental ways, possibly in ways that affect the very core of the human personality, the family teaches us that power and dominance are legitimate and just; that it is appropriate for one group to have the opportunity for meaningful work, for economic independence, for a creative and active life, and that it is appropriate for another group to serve man's needs; that it is fine for Emerson's wife (and servants) to be endlessly pursuing domestic chores while Emerson lectures eloquently on self-reliance.

In my view, Gilman's letters help us to focus on an issue that stands at the very core of women's history and on an issue that is also rapidly emerging as a core humanities concern: that we simply have to read beyond the classics, that it is crucial to consider whose tales get told, that this so-called probing of women's private lives is not just gossip, or trivial or subjective. Our stories are not simply personal or individual; they are part of larger patterns. They are part of a socially, economically, intellectually patterned world that profoundly affects many people's lives. As Hannah Arendt has put it, "If we do not know our own history, we are doomed to live it as though it were our private fate."[63] Or to paraphrase Leslie Silko's poignant admonition on the need for healing stories: They aren't just for entertainment. Don't be fooled. They are all we have, you see, for healing the disease.[64]

1

"Open the Doors of Your Heart": 18 March–25 May 1897

On 10 March 1897, Charlotte noted in her diary, "Houghton Gilman calls. Like him."[1] Several days later another visit, then a straightforward note or two, then a blasting of proprieties and a whirlwind response. "Pleasing and most Desirable Cousin," Charlotte wrote to Houghton. "Your letter gives me a most disproportionate pleasure—same as you do! Not till I am again surrounded by numbers of pleasing and desirable relatives shall I know whether I 'love you for yourself alone' or as an epitome of the family! . . . What a good time I did have the other night! You now float and hover in my brain in a changing cloud of delectable surroundings."[2]

Not since her intensely warm and loving friendship years before with Martha Luther, and then later with Adeline Knapp, had Charlotte felt the rush of enthusiasm she now directed Houghton's way. They started going to the theater together, dining "gorgeously" at the Imperial Hotel, spending Sundays at the Bronx Park, the Statue of Liberty, the New York Aquarium. "*Delightful* time" or "Nice talk" are the weeks' most common diary entries; other entries conveyed the same mood: "Houghton comes, rather late, and spends the evening up stairs with me. . . . Get very friendly."[3]

Yet Charlotte made no changes at all in her prescheduled lecture plans while she developed these early friendship ties with Houghton. In fact, as she set off in April for her lecture tour—to Philadelphia, Chicago, Harrisburg, Wilmington—she seemed not at all reluctant to leave. In part it was because she loved to travel, to feel the sense of usefulness and power that her work inspired. But partly, too, it was because she needed space and quiet for centering herself. It was almost as though she needed distance to focus on the meaning of the friendship, to explore its possibilities, and to sort through conflicting feelings and intentions: "In some ways paper is freer than speech," she wrote him. "Especially when you want to talk to a most elegantly polite and proper person, and are mortally afraid you'll shock him!"

In point of fact, Charlotte must have been shocked herself by the "exuberance of joy and loving kindness" that increasingly she felt and talked about with Houghton, especially since in so many ways he differed from her loved ones and companions of the past: from her intense, ambitious former husband, Walter Stetson, for example; or from her energetic and creative California friends—swashbuckling Joaquin Miller, or the poet Edwin Markham, or the sensuously attractive Adeline Knapp. And although Houghton was honest, kind, and thoroughly reliable, for a man of his opportunity and background, he was not particularly ambitious in shaping his career. During the seventeen-year hiatus in their friendship, he had graduated from the Norwich Free Academy in 1883, gotten his B.A. from Columbia in 1887, and his law degree from the New York Law School in 1892. After doing some postgraduate work at Johns Hopkins (where his uncle Daniel Coit Gilman was president), he became a Wall Street lawyer, a military enthusiast in the New York Seventh Regiment, and from her perspective he was rather politically naive. Well-fed, well-educated, well-entrenched (or so she temporarily assumed) in his Wall Street office, he was aloof from most contemporary issues that concerned her—child labor and unemployment, factory conditions and below-subsistence wages—and thus, as she explicitly admitted, was by no means "on the most *growing* road" in political awareness or intellectual ideals. "So you think I over-estimate you," she wrote him, "and that I'll be disillusioned! I don't over-estimate you at all."

> [T]ake you altogether—you fall short of my ideal through your peaceful conservatism. You are content with life as it is, and fail to see the great new duties of today. As I might esteem some highly admirable King—but wish in my heart that he were never so poor a democrat!

Charlotte thus openly acknowledged enormous differences between them—in "ideals—methods—habits—acquirements." She was the committed national reformer; he was less assertive and successful. She had fire and drama and ambition; he was content with a far simpler style of life. And while occasionally she may have felt some condescension toward him—attending baseball games with mainstream America, reading calculus for his evening's entertainment, generously responding to his family's needs—for the most part she found Houghton a delight. "Don't you ever get tired of being so everlastingly virtuous and want to be a pirate?" she wrote him. But what "I rate highest in you is your steady quiet earnest *life,* . . . and that I take simply as I see it."

Having noted and debated some potential problems with this tender, gentle friend and correspondent, Charlotte relaxed and simply stated how happy he made her feel. With shared memories, a sense of "safety" in the kinship basis of their friendship, he left a "pleasant sunlighty sort of feeling," she wrote him, "warm and cosy and safe." It was almost as though he helped her to reconnect with energies of childhood, with a youthful sense of wholeness, with the possibility of integrating a rich variety of needs—for work and travel, for love and intimacy, for professional development as well as for affirmation of her private life. "Half the time I don't realize what it is till I see your eyes—and then I say 'Why it's Houghton—bless him!'" "O life is fine! . . . So big and bright and healthy, and it moves so fast!"

> A great splendid play, and we all have front seats, and the curtain rises and rises eternally, falling also with the night, with the old year, with each brief pause of death,—but rises always.
> And such acting! Such plots and counterplots! Such adorable and interesting and abominable characters! And the heavenly scenery and general magnificence of setting! And it's free! And my own particular time to view it is not half done yet!

In the context of such "abounding happiness," Charlotte began to name and claim some of the sources of her energy. Not only was she "exultantly rich in such unhoped for pleasure of agreeable cousinship," she reassured him, but the "triumphant sense of *living*" was emerging also from her "utter freedom—returning health and increasing grasp of work." Moreover, the warmth and stimulation of her women's movement contacts helped to boost her spirits, as did the affirmation of her professional associates—of Jane Addams and other Hull House workers; of Marietta Dow, who was currently her "Chicago mother"; of Helen Campbell, her "real mother, 'after the spirit,'" who "is a good professional judge and . . . says that I have taken a new grip and am doing splendidly." And while characteristically Gilman tried to blunt her claims with a playful mix of apology and bluster; she nonetheless teasingly suggested that Houghton might serve as her jack-of-all-trades editorial assistant and read contemporary authors who would help him understand her work.

Charlotte's playful, sometimes childlike, explanations of her work commitments suggest an almost conscious, if not entirely successful, effort to achieve a sense of wholeness: to integrate her "feminine" capacity for warmth and caring with her "masculine" ambition and to integrate her youthful sense of spontaneity with confident professional attention to her work. In April, for instance, when she was offered a job at the Kansas State Agricultural College, she wrote immediately to Houghton: "*I have been offered a Chair in a College with a Salary thereto attached of Fourteen Hundred Dollars per annum!!!*" The college officials had written a "most flattering letter" saying they meant to "keep their institution abreast of the leading thought of the time. Apropos of which they want one woman at least on their faculty. . . . Meaning me. And would I care to come. And what would I undertake to teach. (Note the confidence in my varied abilities!) . . . Talk about glory!"

Clearly Charlotte had enjoyed the offer hugely—"There'll be no living with me if these things go on. . . . Look on my works ye mighty and despair." And yet her cheerful wit and banter only momentarily obscured some all-too-common female needs: to disguise and even neutralize her professional achievements and to acknowledge to herself and Houghton that

professional success was profoundly undeserved. "You see if there is anything under the sun I could teach that would not be a fake and an imposition
I'd be glad of a year's stop, a solid occupation, and $1400.00 to settle my
debts. . . . But—bless me! I don't know enough of anything to teach it for
six months." "I couldn't honorably undertake this work. It would have been
obtaining the money on false pretenses."

After all, as she explained it in some other letters, she had never had a
formal education, or college training, or high school even; only sporadically
had she attended the Rhode Island School of Design. She had done a lot of
"private" reading, to be sure. "As a girl I did read, long and earnestly, and
with a clear strong brain, whatever I could lay hands on as to the life of
man. Also as to life in general, that I might understand its laws." But as
though to stamp out any misconceptions about her intellectual credentials,
she mentioned nothing at all of the intellectual Beecher background she and
Houghton both were raised in and nothing also of the socialist/suffragist
contacts she had been developing for years. Instead she focused on her lack
of rigorous or systematic study: only the "vaguest and most general," only
"what little I could assimilate," bits and pieces here and there, "all together
very little," and often "found without recognition in my mind."

What is striking about these autobiographical reflections, however, is not
simply that they document some rather standard female insecurities. Rather
they illustrate the intensity of Gilman's struggle to dismiss them and to
attain the insights she so powerfully would offer in her published works.
Several months later, she would be drafting her *Women and Economics*
explanation of the problem: "[that with] our steady insistence on pro-
claiming sex-distinction we have grown to consider most human attributes
as masculine attributes, for the simple reason that they were allowed to men
and forbidden to women."[4]

A "simple reason" indeed. If the reasons were so simple, why such reluctance to acknowledge and affirm them? Why denigrate her own achievements? Or blame herself for educational deficiencies? Or fail to see them
as a product of social attitudes and expectations that lay outside herself?
Politically and theoretically she could offer more self-affirming explanations,
that women's "reading disabilities," for instance, might be a form of "mental
nausea," a spontaneous rejection of male-centered Truths they had been
trying to swallow and digest for years. But privately and apologetically she
wrote to Houghton: "I haven't been able to read, I keep telling you." "I
can't seem to make you understand that I have nothing to offer the world
but what I *think*—not what I have read." "My poor head has curled up and
swooned away over other people's thought. But my own have sprouted fast,
and it is those I teach"—a self-congratulatory apology if there ever was
one—the "mindless" genius, the brainless intellectual—comic if it were not
so sad.

Although publicly Gilman would expose the injustices of gender-based dichotomies—"masculine" intellectual achievement versus "feminine" emotionality and sex—privately she struggled with the insecurities such expectations often bred. "I'm . . . trying to be reasonable" and "to speak intelligently from time to time," she wrote him. But there must be "elements of genuine dismay as well as weariness in this inordinate behavior of mine."

> You see I've been writing you the most effervescent warm joyous free personal sort of letters; and yours have been so mild and quiet and guarded and cool that I felt sure—after some time—that I really was annoying you.

Disclaimers notwithstanding, Charlotte's letter writing pace nonetheless continued, and with repeated though not consistent affirmations of its worth: "Your letters would be a credit to a discreet curate," she would write Houghton bluntly. "Mine would serve as opening chapters to a novel." And "if you like 'em—for goodness sake *answer* 'em! I don't mean write a letter which acknowledges the receipt of mine of a given date, but answer what I say and the way I say it, as if I was talking to you. As I am!"[5]

> I like . . . to know what you are thinking and feeling—and of this you say little. Now if I wrote you only what cars I took and speeches I made and what people I was introduced to (!) I know you wouldn't like it half as much as you do all this gabble. . . . *Would* you! Would you! Because if you would just say the word, and I'll write you like an itinerant automaton. I've a mind to try!

Work versus love, "masculine" reason versus "feminine" emotionality—and yet if Charlotte often spiraled back and forth between them, she also forcefully and aggressively affirmed her right and need for both. Not always happily, of course. She would experience a sense of "morbid miserableness" as she tried exploring and explaining the contradictions and confusions that arose between them, alternately denying and then affirming her professional achievements, her letters meanwhile serving to affirm her "female" style. As she wrote advisedly to Houghton, "A letter is a visit—a touch—a mingling for a little of two minds," a "talk of thought and feeling," a chance to "open the doors of your heart and mind."

> I am most interested in *you* rather than in what you do. In what you do mainly as it expresses or impresses you. What I hope for is that you will open the doors of your heart and mind to me—let me in where you live—but if that doesn't come easily I don't want it at all.

Although at times Charlotte was afraid that Houghton could not meet her expectations, or that she would overwhelm him with demands, her correspondence nonetheless was rapidly becoming a central, energizing process—central to the "irradiating force" of her professional commitments, and central, too, she readily acknowledged, for sorting through important conflicts in herself. "So. How do you like being a scape-goat for all this bottled emotion?" she wrote him. "You may wonder in the light of these revelations, how I keep so many friends and seem to be generally liked among 'em. Bless you that's different. They don't touch all this evil behavior I reserve for such victims of fate as reach me personally." Besides, she continued, "[I] have absolutely no other correspondent of a purely spontaneous, natural variety." "Wherefore whatever friendliness and cousinliness and nice general affectionateness you feel for me, prithee lay it on with a spade!" "Ply me therewith laboriously on all occasions; and as you desist, to catch your breath and wipe your heated brow, you will have the pleasure of hearing me inquire, 'Do you *really* like having me around?'"

And so the "fight" continued, Charlotte repeatedly insisting on her own impossible behavior and then greedily demanding that he give her more support. "I defy anyone, by the most strenuous exertions—the most incessant assiduity—to keep me convinced that I am a desirable companion!" "This, O my cousin, is one of the most disagreeable qualities of yours truly. Which I knew you wouldn't like. Guess I'll put it in a book sometime."

Letters: March 18 through May 25, 1897

20 W. 32—N.Y. 3-18-'97

Pleasing and Desirable Cousin,
Your letter gives me a most disproportionate pleasure—same as you do! Not till I am again surrounded by numbers of pleasing and desirable relatives shall I know whether I "love you for yourself alone" or as an epitome of the family! . . .
What a good time I did have the other night! You now float and hover in my brain in a changing cloud of delectable surroundings.
That Imperial dining room has been one of my aesthetic delights all winter—to look in at. I felt a Cinderellaish satisfaction in entering it.
As for the rest—Space!—entrancing, exciting, wildly tempting space! And Curves—great cool restful many times repeated curves; and the changeful glitter of those great masses of walking accoutrements—and—very distinct in my mind—long lines of well matched waving legs—like a heavy fringe blowing in two winds!. . . .

217 W Logan Sq.
Philadelphia Pa.
[undated letter, April 1897]

Most Excellent Cousin, . . .
In some ways paper is freer than speech. Especially when you want to

talk to a most elegantly polite and proper person, and are mortally afraid you'll shock him! . . .

Mostly, these years, when I stop doing things and my mind settles and things come up into view, most of those are of so painful a nature that I have to rush around and cram them back. . . . But now—when I'm quiet—there's a pleasant sunlighty sort of feeling—warm and cosy and safe—like sitting on the doorstep in the sun and eating bread and milk and huckle-berries—a purring kind of feeling. Half the time I don't realize what it is till I see your eyes—and then I say "Why it's Houghton—bless him!"

Truly cousin, you are one of the pleasantest people I ever knew—I don't think of any pleasanter—and I feel personally grateful to you for being so agreeable. And I want such a lovely life for you!

With my usual year-stepping imagination I am looking ahead and wishing most earnestly and tenderly that you may have such a home as you deserve and one of the very *charmingest* of wives. And I shall love her and be so glad for you—and she won't *quite* love me—and I shall have to disentangle again and skillfully hold such distance as shall—I hope—make me a desirable "Aunt Charlotte" for long familiar years!

(This suggests to me the image of an overgrown cuckoo, laboriously stepping out of one exhausted nest after another; and anxiously advising other possible nesters to get at it—so he can board with 'em!!!) Never mind—I can be as absurd as I please—can't I. And you won't mind it. While I'm at it I wish to say in cold print as it were, *why* you are such a comfort.

People don't usually get told how highly they are held in the esteem of their friends till after they are dead—which is a pity I think.

Now I propose to state clearly how I honor you for the simple nobility of your life. Not only the negative virtue of not doing anything wrong—but for the royal way you have faced a heavily handicapped life—and are stead-ily forging ahead and going to win. It is beautiful. It is splendidly strong. It gives me the same sense of shivery admiration all down my back that a race or a fight or anything like that does.

Manhood—at its highest. What can one admire more? Besides this I have an artistic admiration for you.

Different as are our ideals—methods—habits— acquirements; and with-out thinking that you are on the most *growing* road—the personal impression you make on me is of intense Beauty. That is the best word I know for it. I don't mean your look[s],—though you a[re] beautiful enough that way—I mean *you.*

The harmony—simplicity—restraint—the clear Greek quality of being the thing you are, perfectly,—your presence, real or imagined, gives me the same pleasure that a work of art or the right piece of nature does—it is Beautiful. Of course you must have some weak spots and bad qualities somewhere, but so far that is why you are such a deep comfort to me;

because of the rest it is to me to look up to a good man and feel the power of a strong one. . . .

Besides—you are such fun! And besides you are my very own cousin and I have a right to be fond of you.

Now I feel better to have all this written out and off my mind. . . . And now I'll stop bothering and write my business letters as I should have at first. Only I do hope I don't make you uncomfortable and feel horridly and wish I would behave like other people! Because I *don't*—never did—and never shall. And it won't surprise me in the least when you get over liking me as they all do—nor alter my opinion either!

> Your affectionate Cousin
> Charlotte

Jersey City on train for Harrisburg
. . . Wed. April 21st. 1897.

My dear cousin . . .

New York looked most attractive as I left it. Leaving on a boat so you see the whole city behind you in a pictorial sense, as you don't in a train. The towering buildings and spires bristled and loomed most attractively, and the thousand blowing plums of snowwhite steam made all feathery and soft. Directly before me and last in sight were two massive chimneys bearing the magic words—"Eat H-O!" Ah what tender emotions these words excite! Not that I wish to eat you, pleasing youth—though you're quite good enough—but there is a friendly frequency about this inquisition which is warming to the heart. "Eat H-O" said the big square chimney. "Eat H-O" said the slim round one. And I grinned appreciatively and thought I would. . . .

Now I will draw this amiable babble to a close with a few remarks as to how well I feel—how *good* I feel is more what I mean.

Partly just being well again—that's a world in itself. After being a cripple—an invalid [?]—for so long—so very long—it *does* feel good to be well. Partly because of my [?] satisfaction with my clothes! That is something. Never in my life before was I so—suitably dressed. It's not an extravagant outfit certainly, but it's new, its just what I want, and it's *mine,* I bought it, I made it, and I made it masterfully. It isn't anybody elses old clothes, and it isn't a weary dragging half foiled effort. And partly because I'm so exultantly rich in such unhoped for pleasure of agreeable cousinship! So there!

Goodbye till I get 'round to you again. Your happily-for-the-present-removed-to-a-distance cousin.

> Charlotte

Mich. Cent. Sta. Detroit . . .
Sunday April 25. '97

My pleasing Cousin,

Here is a testimonial of esteem as 'twere—delicately adapted to the circumstances. I flatter my self 'tis not a bad product for a railroad train. . . . I am still in a calm serene content selfgratulatory frame of mind.

'Tis true I did not do at all well in Harrisburg, but that is already past history.

You see I was to speak on Woman Suffrage pure and simple, and that never did interest me. I can only fire up on that subject when I apply it to other things in life. And this was a cold stiff unsatisfactory speech. Nonetheless some were pleased therewith; and out of it grew a little 500 word "tract" for the Suffragists' which will probably do more good than the speech by far. . . .

My gown is a great success. Also the bonnet goes well. Mrs. Corbett, a discerning woman, (my hostess) said I spoke 75 per cent better than last year when I was here before. And added that though she knew I had "points" of beauty she never had thought me beautiful before!

That was partly gown and partly being well and happy. (Eat H-O!) I told her I was familiar with these diverse opinions, that some thought me beautiful and others did not; but that I knew all about it; ordinarily I was a fairly good looking woman, but I had seen my self look startlingly beautiful. (The legal mind can here present an opinion, if so moved.). . .

Your letter awaited me here, which was very pleasant. I expect to be judging by my present intentions—as much of a nuisance by letter as I was in person; but experience reminds me that I shall probably move swiftly. So don't worry if you get too many at first. I can write letters in the cars— easy ones that I don't *have* to do; and as I am in the cars a good deal and have absolutely no other correspondent of a purely spontaneous, natural variety, you are likely to come in for lots of gablett.

Kate's letters must be adapted to her—bless her! You wouldn't believe how hard I work at her letters. You see its all the hold I have now—and I just lay myself out in delicately adjusted literature—sitting forcibly on my heart meantime. To Grace and Walter it is always a certain strain to write— there are so many things to be held in mind when I set the gauge for them. There are many friends to whom I am bound to write occasionally—it is part of my religion to keep hold of all I can—I who have let go so much. . . . But you are just play time—ease—indifference of effect—a drawing assurance that you'll like it anyhow—and the keen pleasure of *kinship* as I never have realized it before.

So—look out from under for the present. . . .

. . . As to Margaret—come now, why not! I approve of Margaret with something of the same awed admiration I have for you. She is so exquisitely all she ought to be! And if it were Margaret I should feel real comfortable and happy about you—which I want to.

I think I shall present you with my blessing in advance like a Papal Indulgence—a blank blessing, to be filled out later. . . .

As I have remarked before you're a dear boy!

Serenely,
Cousin Charlotte

473 Orchard St. Chicago
April 28th. 1897.

Ha! What Ho! Minion! And other expressions of a similarly lofty and contemptuous nature. I have been offered a Chair in a College with a Salary thereto attached of Fourteen Hundred Dollars per annum!!!

Which being simmered down to hard facts . . .—means this: The Kansas State Agricultural College has written me a most flattering letter saying that they . . . meant to keep their institution abreast of the leading thought of the time. Apropos of which they want one woman at least on their faculty who is in the enviable position with regard to aforesaid zeitgeist. Meaning me. And would I care to come. And what would I undertake to teach. (Note the confidence in my varied abilities!) Cookery and Hygiene would suit them if it would me, etc., etc.

Talk about glory! Wait till you have a boarding institution of learning like the Kansas State Agricultural College come humbly and ask you to teach anything you want to in it—for a fabulous salary like that!!! There'll be no living with me if these things go on. . . . Look on my works ye mighty and despair!

Well—I wrote to this person, modestly enough and explained the bald fact that I was "not prepared" on Cookery and Hygiene; but as to Ethics and Sociology and little things like that—why I should be in Kansas in June and we'd see!

So here is a new factor to consider as to my winter in New York. Lest the legal mind now show its powers and advise me—honestly—as to this important step.

You see if there is anything under the sun I could teach that would not be a fake and an imposition I'd be glad of a years stop, a solid occupation, and $1400.00 to settle my debts. . . . But—bless me! I don't know enough of anything to teach it for six months.

Wouldn't it be fun though! And haven't I a right to feel proud of my six year old reputation built out of *nothing* but my own feeble brain!! . .

. . . As for me I'm very comfortable welcome here, and invited elsewhere, continuing well, and happier everyday as I realize my utter freedom—returning health and increasing grasp of work. . . .

473 Orchard St. Chicago
May 4th. 1897.

Pleasure before business!

Wherefore, with quite a stack of letters to answer, I set me calmly to answer yours first, so as to give you "the top of the morning" and the cream of my redundant happiness.

Life is so *good!* So big and bright and healthy, and it moves so fast! A great splendid play, and we all have front seats, and the curtain rises and rises eternally, falling also with the night, with the old year, with each brief pause of death,—but rises always.

And such acting! Such plots and counterplots! Such adorable and interesting and abominable characters! And the heavenly scenery and general magnificence of setting! And it's free! And my own particular time to view it is not half done yet! Then, best of all, when I can't stand the helpless excitement of seeing it go on, I too can start right in and act—act up to any standard of daring and cumulative achievement I choose; and then when breathless and temporarily exhausted I have to stop acting—why I can sit and see it just the same. And even when I sleep I know that the big beautiful performance goes on just the same!

O life is fine!———As for me I feel so good I just want to hug somebody, and sit and hug myself—literally—for lack of a better.

Now perhaps you will understand why, feeling this exuberance of joy and loving kindness as I mostly do, and your defenceless head having popped up within my range of late, I shower so much affection on you—quite passing the mild limits of cousinliness. Hasten therefore and supply me with some half a dozen other desirable cousins, male and female, that I may distribute my regard and give you a rest occasionally! . . .

You talk of my "threatening" you—! Why man, I'm holding out faint gleams of hope, trying to be reasonable and remember that *you* may have some feelings as well as I, and that there are elements of genuine dismay as well as weariness in this inordinate behavior of mine.

So I try to speak intelligently from time to time; to explain, as I did at first that it's partly on account of my lack of family ties—of near persons to consume some measure of my affection; and as now, that it's partly because I am so aboundingly happy and full of the triumphant sense of *living,* and that an irradiating force which is strong enough to keep me going as I do and inspiriting hundreds of people at a time, day after day, must needs be rather strong when turned full on to one unprotected young man. Were Mrs. G[ilman] in her proper place *she* would protect you! But she isn't, and I feel bound in a general motherly manner to do it myself! So it is not threatening at all when I tell you the honest truth about myself. I am prone to love people as the sparks are to fly upward—all people, near and far; and when they are near the effect is like that of using a search light for a reading lamp!

But all things have their compensations; and you may be able to sustain with patience this concentrated glare if you realize that it is not everlasting. I do not mean that I shall not always be "your affectionate cousin"—I shall. . . .

But I do not want you to picture yourself saddled for life with a female relative in the attitude of unmeasured and delighted devotion I seem to hold now. Such prospect is enough to daunt the stoutest heart.

To which it might be said, "If you know all this, why do you not moderate your behavior to that of a rational and ordinary cousinliness?" Because I don't want to—that's why. Just at present you are the only Person—(save Katharine,) who comes warmly and strongly into my thoughts without concomitant reasons why I must not think about you. And I say, "Hang it all! I'm going to think of him as much as I please! I'm going to be as fond of him as I please! He's well worthy of such affection and I guess it won't hurt him for a while!" Then I have compunctions, and explain at length—as you see. So. How do you like being a scape-goat for all this bottled emotion? . . .

My gracious! Consider the amount of family feeling—the undrawn bank account—with which I am stuffed! Father—Mother—Brother—Sister—all comparatively untouched capital. Lover—an immense amount here—scarcely opened. Husband—child even—why the whole lot are more or less thwarted and sealed up. (admirable metaphor there?). . . .

Now I don't want you to imagine that I am taking from the full share of honest admiration and equally honest love which is yours from me and all the jolly *liking* which count's so much; but do not imagine either that you are to be perpetually saddled with poems of praise and letters a mile long!

Now after six pages of conscientious explanation I'll answer your letter. Do I like long descriptions. Per Se—no. As being about you, yes. They give me not only an account of what you are doing, which interests me as being your life; and an account of interests and affairs which adds to my knowledge in ways not easily obtained, but in what you say and how you say it I learn to know you; and shall be the better able to be of real use to you some day.

All human life is mine—I am ceaselessly hungry for it; and its details are inseparably important.

So go ahead and write just what naturally comes to you to write. As far as personal preference goes I like best the talk of thought and feeling; of personal relation; of plans for further action. A letter is a visit—a touch—a mingling for a little of two minds. I am most interested in *you* rather than in what you do. In what you do mainly as it expresses or impresses you. What I hope for is that you will open the doors of your heart and mind to me—let me in where you live—but if that doesn't come easily I don't want it at all. . . .

But that is the way I stand in life. Close as your own heart—far as the sun.

I am near—thrillingly near—to the folks that I touch; but not near anyone as most people are near each other—to live steadily at an equal distance. That kills me. That is why "wife" is a word unknown to me, and must be always.

Let me suggest—apropos of the stenographer's remarks about reading love letters in the office—that you pocket 'em for a more convenient season. For there will be a lot—for some time yet I judge. . . .

Now to come clear down to common ground—common feminine ground I mean—I am fiercely desirous to know when you saw me startlingly beautiful! When? When? And I'm ever so glad you find me pleasant to look at— it makes me feel good. . . .

. . . I experience a certain relief to know that it isn't Margaret. But again am struck acold by the thought of the Unknown Damsel you came within a day of asking no long time past. Heavens. I say to myself. It might have happened several times already—and it may any time it appears! Really, Houghton—you must give me a few weeks notice to prepare my mind! . . .

Now the best part of all your letter is the closing paragraph, where you speak of my visit as affecting your life for the—well not for the worse at all events.

If knowing me is going to be a good thing for you—that's what I want to feel! That's what I'm for. It makes me feel happy way through. . . .

473 Orchard St. Chicago
May 11th 1897. . . .

This May 5th [letter] is depressing in the extreme. As an upholder of the merits of New York, and a supposed desirer of my company, you don't do worth a cent. . . . Now let me explain to you what your attitude should be.

As a youth of great natural modesty, coupled with that humility which always accompanies a liberal education; you should not assume that either your personal attractions or the weight of your arguments would coerce my own judgement in this matter. You should on the contrary assume that I am perfectly well able and all too likely to stay somewhere else; and then, unhampered by any vain presumption as above described, throw all your energies into the arguments for my return—merely as an expression of good will! . . .

For, say I, if he really wishes I'd come back he must be strangling this desire in a masterly manner. Why should he do this? Only on the assumption that if he said all he wanted to it might alter my plans. . . . No need for such a "vain presumption." "No," she concluded, "he don't much care."

And then I rather drearily say to myself—"Why on earth—or Why in thunder—or Why in the name of reason—should he care? I'm an old nuisance anyhow. A tagging unavoidable elderly relative, open even to awful suspicions of being a Bore! . . .

Now isn't that about as unreasonable and disagreeable as you ever knew me to be?

But truly Houghton, for all the invulnerable self-belief and self-reliance which I have to have to live at all, you've no idea how small potatoes I think of myself at heart, how slow I am to believe that any one's kindness to me is other than benevolence, how ready to seize upon the vaguest hint that I'm—presuming too much. This I suppose is partly being born so, and partly the result of circumstances—lots of circumstances. Being so many times marked n.g. [no good] it has sort of stuck in!

Again I am amused at you asking me what text book—if any—I would recommend you to read on my line of work. I can't seem to make you understand that I have nothing to offer the world but what I *think*—not what I have read. My reading on social economics is the vaguest and most general. As a girl I did read, long and earnestly, and with a clear strong brain, whatever I could lay hands on as to the life of man. Also as to life in general, that I might understand its laws. . . .

I read quite a little at one time on temperance—and took a stand thereon;—again on free trade, and took a stand on that. Matters of health, theories of diet, methods of character building—such things as these I thought out deeply and fully as a girl. My sociological reading is later, and a very vague memory, being what little I could assimilate during those mindless years. . . .

I think *Looking Backward* was the first of the forecasting books I happened to touch. Caesar's Column too. O, and the whole trend of the French Revolution spirit—all the old peasant uprisings—it is the *whole* of this thing that I have been watching.[6]

Of late years I have read some of the Fabian Essays—I can recommend you them, with unction[?]; some of Ely's economics, articles here and there—but altogether very little. I haven't been able to read, I keep telling you. My poor head has curled up and swooned away over other people's thought. But my own have sprouted fast, and it is those I teach. I think it certain that you have read far more than I on these subjects; all that I have and more. . . .

473 Orchard St. Chicago Ill.
May 18th. 1897.

Now my dear Cousin, I will try to write you as nice a letter as you deserve—or at least begin one, for I have but an hour. Yours of the 15th came yesterday, and gave me much joy. Yours of the 9th is here also, and has hung around unanswered, because I couldn't muster up spirit enough to answer it—I felt so depressed—so sort of snubbed as it were.

You see I've been writing you the most effervescent warm joyous free personal sort of letters; and yours have been so mild and quiet and guarded and cool that I felt sure—after some time—that I really was annoying you. Now I'll sail in again and write just as I feel like writing—that being the only way it is worth while to write letters at all—and if you, like 'em—for goodness sake *answer* 'em! I don't mean write a letter which acknowledges the receipt of mine of a given date, but answer what I say and the way I say it, as if I was talking to you. As I am! I remember I wrote you one most exuberant thing about how good life was and so on, and you never even said "I don't care much for that sort of stuff"—but simply passed it over as one does an irrelevant remark when one wishes to crush the speaker. So I got real scared, and felt sure you couldn't abide my state o'mind, and then my state o'mind became depressed and I stopped writing in sheer doubt and discouragement.

But I feel so good today—partly because this last letter of yours tastes good—makes me feel as if you were really alive at the other end and did want me to write— and to come back—and partly because Mrs. Helen Campbell, my real mother "after the spirit"—is here, and has been praising my recent work—that perhaps I can write and not be cross! . . .

. . . So you think I overestimate you—and that I'll be disillusioned! I don't overestimate you at all. What I rate highest in you is your steady quiet earnest *life.* . . .

I think your main weakness is on the line of—well secretiveness—evasiveness. I never feel as if you were over frank. Perhaps I'm wrong and do you injustice here. I mention it to show that I'm not in a state of unmixed and unreasoning adoration.

And then—take you altogether—you fall short of my ideal through your peaceful conservatism. You are content with life as it is, and fail to see the great new duties of today. As I might esteem some highly admirable King—but wish in my heart that he were never so poor a democrat! This of course is from my own point of view—you have yours and have a right to it—again, I mention it only that you may cease your fear that I overestimate you!

I doubt sometimes if I give you full justice—perhaps you see farther than I think you do. Perhaps you'll grow. Well now comes your very satisfactory letter of yesterday. But my time grows short and I think I'll not begin on it. Instead, a few remarks about Kansas. I'm not going there this time. Partly because Helen Campbell, who is admirably fitted, may take the place—I begged them to ask her as soon as I heard of it—and partly because I am not fitted for the work, and know better than to risk my new health in any such strain and effort.

Also because I am simply bursting out into literature. Also because it would take a good deal to make me willing to lose next winter in New York.

That last, honestly, would not have counted if the thing had been right to do—I am well used to giving up what I like—thoroughly well trained in it. . . .

9.5 a.m. Wed
[May 19, 1897]

Good morning, dear Cousin!

Before I plunge into my story I'll finish my talk with you. For a long time after I left I talked with you often—would find myself constructing conversation at a great rate. But my recent mood of meekness and apologetic withdrawal has been a check to conversation. I suppose you are grumbling, man-fashion, "Confound the girl! She *knows* I like her! Have I got to say so in good set terms every five minutes?"

This, O my cousin, is one of the most disagreeable qualities of yours truly. Which I knew you wouldn't like. Guess I'll put it in a book sometime. I defy anyone, by the most strenuous exertions—the most incessant assiduity—to keep me convinced that I am a desirable companion! . . .

Why if were I married ten years to a ceaselessly adoring lover—it wouldn't take a week of—well of the mildest preoccupation—to make me need convincing all over again! This is a vice nearly as bad as jealousy—of which sin by the way I am wholly guiltless. . . .

Wherefore whatever friendliness and cousinliness and nice general affectionateness you feel for me, prithee lay—it on with a spade! Ply me therewith laboriously on all occasions; and as you desist, to catch your breath and wipe your heated brow, you will have the pleasure of hearing me inquire, "Do you *really* like to have me around?" You may wonder in the light of these revelations, how I keep so many friends and seem to be generally liked among 'em. Bless you that's different. They don't *touch* all this evil behavior I reserve for such victims of fate as reach me personally. Mercifully they are few. . . .

That Special Delivery letter came Sunday. . . . As I think about it it reminds me of how kind your eyes are. . . . you looked at me in a way that stays. I told you how I vividly dreamed of it one night thereafter.

I think that it is your mother's look and carries me back to that impression of heavenly tenderness—a very passion of mother love. . . . Strange that a young man's eyes should call up a never satisfied longing for mother love! . . .

As to my writing, Mrs. Campbell, who is a good professional judge and fond of me, says that I have taken a new grip and am doing splendidly. . . . I doubt if you care much for most of my work. It doesn't come to your standard of excellence technically, and I don't think—well, never mind. . . .

. . . I hope I haven't been too cross—or too silly—or too anything. If I wasn't nervously anxious to have you keep on liking me I probably shouldn't act so foolishly about it. . . .

. . . May 25th. '97 . . .

. . . This is a good letter of yours. Not *quite* so good as the last one though. Still you show capacity for improvement and I have hopes that by judicious chastisement. . . . I shall in time make a complete letter writer of you! . . .

. . . It may reassure you somewhat . . . to know that I speedily destroy my letters—because I can't carry 'em around. It is a wise habit which I will recommend to you forthwith. . . .

If you save all this stuff it'll be trotting out biographically some day—and then you'll be sympathized with! . . .

In this letter you speak of the Staten Island day—and it pleases me. You speak of more days we'll have together—and that pleases me . . . it makes me feel as if it were really *you,* and you were really *there.* I like to know what you are doing. But I like better still and also to know what you are thinking and feeling—and of this you say little. Now if I wrote you only what cars I took and speeches I made and what people I was introduced to (!) I know you wouldn't like it half so much as you do all this gabble. . . . *Would* you! Would you! Because if you would just say the word, and I'll write you like an itinerant automaton. I've a mind to try!

. . . Your line of argument respecting my going to Kansas—(which you should have brought out in your first letter on the subject) is exactly wise. I couldn't honorably undertake this work. It would have been obtaining the money on false pretenses. . . .

I think well enough of myself,—better than is just perhaps, but I don't think I have power to draw and hold people close. Because visibly there are none! . . .

2

"The Fanatic and the Great Discoverer": 4 June–29 August 1897

On 1 July 1897, Charlotte Gilman recorded in her diary: "Still weak, but fall to work. . . . Get hold of a new branch of my theory [the economic basis of the woman question]. . . . Now I can write the book."[1] And on 10 July, while traveling on the lecture circuit, she wrote to Houghton:

> I have . . . made an enormous new step in my sociological theories. So large and valuable a one that I am now quite clear and determined about the rest of the summer's work, and mean to have a book ready to read to you when I get back!
> . . . It is quite possible that you will see little in it, and consider me another crackbrained enthusiast; but all the same I am banking on your sympathy and kindliness for assistance.
> The fanatic and the great discoverer have much in common. Of course I fondly believe that I am the latter—and you may fondly believe that I am the former—and conceal it from me.[2]
> But I am solidly committed to my course of thinking, and shall out with it to the best of my ability. . . .[3]

Although Gilman included the appropriate "feminine" disclaimers—about her "palpable deficiencies," her need for Houghton's "invaluable assistance"—the letter nonetheless enthusiastically continues: "The line of thought is on The Economic Rela[tionship of Woman] to Man As a Factor in Human Development. That's too long for a title, but that's what it's about."

> . . . And the big thing I'm hugging myself about just at present is this:
> All human progress is natural[l]y collective organic. [H]umanity is an organic relation, and all its processes develop on organic lines—industry—religion—government—everything human. Now the sex relation is not a distinctively human one at all, but held its place as a process of race preservation before humanity was. It is a purely individual relation—an individual and private instinct—in no way organizable.
> Human industry is a social process, and as such naturally organic in its tendencies. But!—and here is one of the biggest buts that ever was!—by combining the sex-relation with an economic relation we have combined a process purely individual with a process progressively collective—and *that* is what ails us! In economics I mean.

53

There is a strange sense of counterpoint and contrast in this letter: its intensely private introduction—"the big thing I'm hugging myself about just at present"—and the abstract theoretical approach; the emotionally charged nature of the sexuality and marriage issue and the formality of her appeal to evolutionary and economic law.

But then again, perhaps the contrast isn't quite so strange, abstract theory eliciting such sheer emotional delight. Just consider, even momentarily, the transforming possibilities—not just of integrating women's issues with prominent contemporary theories but also of demonstrating that a distorted sexual relationship lay at the very heart of social malaise. And because women's issues usually were considered so personal and private, excruciatingly so at times, just consider the thrill, the relief, and ultimately the power if women finally could demonstrate that a fundamental obstacle to progress was an economic system based on the dominance of men—in violation of the evolutionary process, in violation of natural law itself.

In some respects, Gilman would simply borrow and adapt some of the major theoretical contentions of her contemporaries, of reform Darwinists and utopian socialists most particularly, as though they were accepted "Truths": that there was a biological or evolutionary base to human progress; that competition in the sex-selection process contributed to progressive change; that economic "instincts" within the more specialized society would be naturally inclined toward cooperative and peaceful ends. Like the reform Darwinists, she argued that the sex-selection process (the competitive survival-of-the-fittest laws) prompted variation and improvement, thus assuring progress. Like the utopian socialists, she emphasized economic instincts as a central force for progressive social change. And like both, she used the organic analogy to explain the transition from the animal (and competitive) to the social (and "naturally" more cooperative) human world: It is "biological law," she would write in *Women and Economics,* "that all the tendencies of a living organism are progressive in their development," that "cells combine, and form organs; organs combine, and form organisms; organisms combine, and form organizations," thus assuring "the gradual subordination of individual effort for individual good to the collective effort for the collective good."[4]

But if all this was standard fare for turn-of-the-century reformers, quickly and briefly summarized for Houghton, there was nonetheless a twist in Gilman's argument that she felt was strikingly new: "By combining the sex-relation with an economic relation we have combined a process purely individual with a process progressively collective," thus subverting social progress at its very roots. As she explained it, the biological sex-selection instinct is essentially individual and competitive, the economic instinct potentially social and cooperative, but the two combined unnaturally when women became the property of men. By nature woman was meant to do the choosing; but when man became the one to choose instead, "sex-functions to her" became "economic functions" (she had to find a mate who could support her); and "economic functions to him" became "sex-functions" (he worked not to help society but to keep his wife). Thus, as Gilman later put it, "there is a radical distinction between sex-competition and marriage by purchase. In the first the male succeeds by virtue of what he can do; in the second, by virtue of what he can get." "Legitimate sex-competition brings out all that is best in man. To please her, to win her, he strives to do his best." But the sexuo-economic relationship inspires the "intensified desire to get" instead, thus assuring "the inordinate greed of our industrial world." Without marriage to impede them, men would work with one another in human ways, i.e., cooperatively, peacefully, constructively. But by allowing the sexual relationship to dominate economic relationships as well, "by making it a sex-characteristic of our species that the male 'support' the female," men's attention turned from social to private family needs, from "natural" social service inclinations, to greedy efforts to expand their property and power instead. The goal then was to "disentangle these incongr[u]ous forces" so that the "natural economic tendencies" could work for "peace and plenty," and the "natural sex tendencies" could ensure that marriages were based on love.[5]

Gilman was justifiably pleased with what she was attempting: the theoretical reach of her hypothesis, its social justice implications, and the skillful use of contemporary arguments to show the centrality of women's claims. But understandably she approached her work with caution. To lend intellectual dignity to the women's movement efforts, to demonstrate the injustice of women's subjugation, she framed her views according to expectations of contemporary canon, and purposefully, if not entirely successfully, developed a formal methodology and style. Focusing on clarity of principle, on authority of tone and voice, she claimed her "truth" in the name of justice, rationality, and natural law.

Unfortunately, in writing Houghton, underlying tensions reappeared. She was acknowledging her ambition as a "great discoverer" for women when she had not even had a high school education. She was claiming status as a theorist when intellectuality itself was still defined as male. She was borrowing and adapting contemporary androcentric theories when her goal was clearly to subvert and undermine their power. And she was offering a radical critique of masculine/feminine dichotomies when she was tormented by those dichotomies herself.

No wonder Charlotte's private letters evidence ambivalence and insecurity, a shifting back and forth from confident assertions to agonizing doubts beneath. As the "discoverer" she was confident of her insights and her mission. But when confronting and exploring the more spontaneous and passionate roots of her convictions, she sometimes condemned herself as too emotional and thus unstable, or, in the light of her "illness" and depression, as the volatile "fanatic" who might in fact be "mad." No, it's not "dizziness" or "vertigo," she emphatically insisted. It is an "infirmity," a "brain-sinking melancholy," which "would be of little consequence if it did not stop my literary work and make me very unhappy. But as it does these things and more," its "effects are baleful." It's "a good honest disease which I have carried off and on for fourteen years," she told him, and although she tried to recognize and warn him of the symptoms, more often it was so "hard to discriminate between it, and facts" that too often the "mean quarrelsome" effects of illness would erupt in letters unawares.

> . . . you need not be surprised to get most melancholy letters, or cross unreasonable letters, or mean quarrelsome letters, or no letters at all. I am already in the mood to hold that it is no sort of use to write to you—that you do not "understand" nor "care," etc. etc. That I won't be a tax on any man's patience and all the rest of the morbid miserableness. . . .
>
> You see nobody *can* be near me when I've fallen through a hole; I *have* to be alone because I've gone there! And I have to be miserable because that is the condition.

Obviously Charlotte *was* "alone" as she tried working through the "miserable . . . condition," because according to her letters, other friends provided insufficient opportunity for healing or exploring it. For even as she traveled on the lecture circuit—and in the summer of 1897 it was to Illinois, Michigan, Kansas, and Wyoming—she apologetically and far too flippantly proclaimed her friendship needs: "Never was there a more babblesome and childishly confidential person than I; and as the passing years give me strength to refrain from unwise confidences to strangers, I am the more like to burst for want of some one to tell everything to." Besides, she continued in another letter, "One thing that makes me hold you very near is that you knew *me*—me before I died. Truly—wasn't I strong and of good promise? It is hard to keep faith in one's self—through long years—when your brain goes back on you *and there's no one to corroborate your memory.*"

"Knew me—me before I died." Through family circuits Houghton was familiar with her grisly tale. It dated back to her early years with Walter Stetson, to her marriage, to her daughter Katharine's birth, to the separation and divorce she finally felt were necessitated by her "illness." "Madness," she sometimes called it, the "Wolf at the Door" terrors that her autobiographical short story, "The Yellow Wallpaper," had poignantly explored. Recently she sometimes hoped the "illness" was behind her, but rather quickly the all-too-familiar symptoms reappeared: "I'm not feeling very lively these days," she would write to Houghton. "I wake up tired and feel my own weight."

> I wish I had somebody—young old or middleaged—male female or neuter— to whom I could just say *everything!*. By what absurdity a flopsy-wopsy hair-sieve of a disposition like mine ever got stood up alone [in] this fashion I should like to

know! And you are just near enough to arouse all this foolishness and not near
enough to—assuage it as it were!

O well—I'm mightily thankful for you all the same. You've helped me over a
most barren and baldheaded summer!

However foolish Charlotte sometimes felt about her "flopsy-wopsy" disposition, she was increasingly aware that her correspondence served a fundamental need. The "fanatic and the great discoverer"—it was as though
through letters she could openly admit to feeling she was both. As the "discoverer" she could test her more formal, rational convictions, and as the
"fanatic" she could explore the passions and resulting conflicts that in part
inspired her work. Every letter, it seems, expressed her sense of isolation,
her longing for more understanding and affection, for a respite from the
loneliness that too rarely was mitigated by the warmth and hospitality of
other friends. She was exhausted, that was clear, from attempting to sustain
a cool objective public image. Constantly responding to other people's needs
and problems, observing, sometimes sharing in their joys and sorrows, but
always keeping safely distant, she felt she had become the solitary peripeta-
tic woman's movement pioneer. Later, she would note the private cost of
such a mission: "those who do resist" conventions find it costs so much in
"loneliness and privation," and "they lose so much in daily comfort and
affection that others are deterred from following."[6] But compared to statements in her letters—"I never was so lonesome in my life"—that was a
rather abstract indication of her "miserably unhappy" feelings in the here
and now.[7]

Gilman's correspondence served not only as an important antidote to
isolation, however, but also as a bridge between conflicting needs: for accepting ambiguity as well as striving for conclusive understanding, for experiencing intimacy as well as independence, and trusting emotion as well as
reason as a source of truth. And yet, not surprisingly, the correspondence
produced some fears. Because she recognized how frequently her rebellious,
woman-centered efforts were undermined by bouts of "madness," how her
struggles had repeatedly been painful and alarming to her closest friends—
it was no wonder she felt ambivalence about writing so openly to Houghton.
Sweet, proper, and conventional, would he understand? "Sometimes I wish
you cared more for my kind of things," she would write him; "and then
again I think it is just as well you don't. And I'm so sulky and cantankerous
about it that I suppose no one ever can."

My thought and work were so alien to all about me when I began—it was such
a struggle to think out and do the things I believed, I was so utterly unused to
help or wise appreciation, and so utterly unused to opposition—derision—all that
a family can do to check thought; that I don't suppose I shall ever bring forward
an idea to a close friend without my elbow up. Of course the public is different.

Gilman's letters present a striking contrast to her published writings. Formal and confident at times, they are alternately playful, coy, and deferential. Intellectually assertive, they are simultaneously emotionally exhausting—all suggesting a complex struggle to continue with her explorations while trying also to keep the relationship intact.

One way, and at this juncture the one most comfortable for Charlotte, was simply to blast through conflicts and confusions with wit and repartee. And even that, of course, she seemed to need to denigrate. "Why on earth I should gabble on as thus on all occasions, in season and out of season, of small personal concerns, to an elegant youth in New York City, I cannot for the life of me see." And yet how else, except with playful humor, to face some obvious differences between them? How else, for instance, as a pro-labor socialist, was she to handle Houghton's loyalty to the strike-breaking New York Seventh Regiment? Or his summer stints in military camp?

> Since you close [your letter] with [an] alluring promise to write to me from camp I shall look for letters presently of a swashbuckler character, written on nothing less military than the head of a drum; and interspersed with "strange oaths and warlike instances." In this I shall probably be disappointed, so prone is man not to do what one expects of him.

Given her feminist and socialist perspectives, one important challenge of the early correspondence was to find effective ways to deal with Houghton's conservative perspectives, his gentlemanly concern about priorities, his deliciously quaint and cautious ways. For instance, as they planned some excursions for her next New York visit—swimming, boating, sundry outdoor treks—she teased: "Go to!—Is it Proper?" "Is it the custom in New York for elegant youths—Elegant Youth I should say (which is you!) in company with Distinguished Age (which is me!) to secrete itself for whole days as we purpose?" "How can you bear it, well bred youth that you are!" And with "a reputation to sustain! Far be it from me to inveigle you into performances compromising to the dignity of a Grace Church Usher!"

Whatever insecurities the letters thus acknowledge, Houghton had become a delightfully supportive friend with whom to work them through. She could articulate her theoretical convictions, but she could attend to paradox as well and to the "fanatic" undercurrents and complexities that intellect and reason could not readily resolve. Thus Gilman's letters show a kind of playfulness and humor, which, in fact, both grounded and enriched her rational discussion. And they also show—with spontaneous and almost mocking delight—a self-affirming recognition that truth might be elusive, and that even well-trained academic fathers might not have the kind of intellectual monopoly they claimed. In the same letter that introduces her *Women and Economics* theories, she wrote to Houghton:

> Now see here. If you want more things to do for me—if you still thirst to "prepare" for the demands I propose to make on your intellect, suppose I outline

the kind of thing I am writing about, and you just skirmish around in sociological literature and [see] what is already there on similar lines. Then you can give me some reference notes and make up for my palpable deficiencies on those lines. And then I can put in a nice introductory note explaining that any signs of erudition observable in this book; any reference to collateral literature etc. etc. are due to the invaluable assistance of my learned friend G.H.G. Ph.D., A.b.c., P.L.Y., R.X.Y., etc. etc.!

Repeatedly the playful, almost mocking quality in Charlotte's letters suggests a confidence that familiar "feminine" disclaimers might momentarily obscure.[8] Casually, for instance, she requested that Houghton browse around and find the "stuff" she recently had published in *The American Fabian,* a series entitled "First Class in Sociology." "Altogether your opinions are so favorable that I am simply rolling about in them—like a nice kitty in the grass! It makes me feel good all over," she wrote him. But side by side with the almost childlike pleasure in his affirmations is a sheer delight in assuming the teacher and adviser role—"go [to] it—you're doing finely," she wrote him, and of this there will be "more, in that heavily mortgaged winter of ours. One evening a week and pleasant Sundays—Gracious! How we shall have to talk! . . . Just wait till you hear *my* arguments on Socialism! Or at least my views!"

It was almost as though Houghton were providing Charlotte with a testing ground for theory, and with a challenge to shape them into accessible and commonsense appeals. She tried offering him a homespun version of "The Law of Supply and Demand," for instance. "Our usual assumption is that these things are only produced by one man in order to get something of another," pure "animal individualism"—"To make—to swap—to eat"— as though one man's griddle cakes could be exchanged for another man's syrup on "comparatively simple lines." "Now that's not very clear—I know it." But out "of many fumbling efforts to express, comes finally the clear expression"—which for her meant everyday directness. She revised her argument for women's economic independence, for instance:

> Why man—if there was only just so much work in the world (which isn't true) and just so much wages to go with it, it would be better for man and wife each to do half a day's work and get half a day's wage than for him to do all the work and she none—him to get all the money and she none. They'd have just as much money as now and have spare time to see each other in!

Or, she offered a commonsense explanation of the presumed "inferiority" of women's brains:

> The reason women aren't smart about "two-masted sloops" and such like, is from lack of associative ideas. They have nothing to tack the information to, and it slips out easily; as perhaps it would with you if you were given names of feminine decorations or crochet stitches.

Yet such casual playfulness was not useful simply for explaining women's disadvantages. In confronting Houghton with her question—what are the reasons women aren't considered "smart"?—she was confronting indirectly a core dilemma of her own: how a woman could affirm her intellectual accomplishments and not be threatening to a man she loved. Just recently, for instance, Charlotte had been talking to Jane Addams, founder of Hull House in Chicago. "And I . . . told her of my recent development in economic theory, and she was much impressed and approved thereof—which did me good." But when, in response, Houghton admitted he knew nothing of Hull House or Jane Addams, she used wit to curb her disappointment, nonetheless delighting in the opportunity to poke some fun at the weakness of men's purportedly well-trained brains:

> Behold the deficiencies of a college education! Why Jane Addams is one of the noblest, wisest, strongest, sweetest women in the world, and Hull House is the greatest Social Settlement in America. Get "Hull House Maps and Papers" right off, and improve your mind. When I come back I'll improve it more. . . . How good it feels to know something you don't!!!

What is striking about these letters is not simply that they document some of Gilman's insecurities. They also illustrate emerging strategies for effectively resolving them. She decided to introduce Houghton to her academic mentor, Lester Ward, for instance, and suggested that he "skirmish" around and find Ward's book *Dynamic Sociology,* or his recent article, "Our Better Halves." "It gives me *such* a pleasant feeling of—of common ground I guess; of some sort of standing room somewhere—to have you care to read and talk with me." But then, after pausing for some reassurance—"Are you sure you like it?"—she also not only reclaimed her own originality, she suggested he needn't bother reading Lester Ward at all. "I wrote The Brood Mare long before I read Ward." "I've been thinking those things—and much more—for many years." So why even bother "recklessly" to "purchase that big book [*Dynamic Sociology*] of Ward's, O Youth? 'Tis a rash project. Read it first and then you'll not want to buy it."[9]

Although Gilman's letters suggest her hungering for Houghton's affirmations, she nonetheless emphatically resisted a condescending kind of help. Repeatedly she apologized for needing him. "Who wouldn't apologize!" "It's as if you offered your hand to help me down from something, and I fell all over you." In fact, an insistence on equality already was emerging as a core issue in the friendship. Which one of them was more open and expressive? Whose letters were the longest? Who cared the most? Sometimes she would worry that she had taken too much initiative, that she was writing too effusively. But then again she would worry that he was taking too much initiative on practical affairs. He began attending to her legal correspondence, visiting her father, and scouting about for "collateral" material she felt the need to read. With Houghton becoming so considerate and giving, two ironically conflicting worries unexpectedly appeared: either that he would assume the role of male protector or, alternately, the role of dutiful and self-sacrificing wife. "I cannot get over the sense of entire onesidedness," she wrote him, "of accumulated obligation. Do fix up some request or other—if it's as queer as an election bet!" As to the personal implications of her *Women and Economics* arguments, she refused to be an "incessant drain" on his "spare time and spare cash," and like it or not he would have to "count on [her] assistance."

> The cash part of it bothers me in a degree you have no idea of. You must invent cheap things to do—or I won't do 'em! If I have any money I shall insist on sharing in the larger schemes. If I don't—I shall insist on keeping the schemes within limits. Now don't be unruly!

Besides, she continued in another letter,

> Isn't there any kind of thing I can do for you some time to kind of even up things? I shall have to send you some blank checks—payable on demand—some drafts on my goodwill for you to present when you want things. . . .
> The letter continues:
> I agree to pay to George Houghton Gilman, on demand, such services and good will as he may consider due in return for obligations rendered, unless such claim be deemed extortionate or untimely; as for instance should he require me to darn his stockings while lecturing! In case of dispute the claim [is] to be submitted to a court of arbitration composed of three persons, one to be selected by each disputant and a third whom they shall agree on.

*   *   *   *   *

In late August 1897, Charlotte made a three-week visit to Prestonia Mann's Summer Brook Farm cooperative. Located some twenty narrow twisting miles into the heart of the Adirondack Mountains, it not only was a reformers' meeting ground, a small-scale experimental imitation of the "Brook Farm" transcendentalist community of some fifty years before. It was also a sensuous, magnificent natural kind of setting that inspired and energized her writing. Prestonia Mann, its founder, was an *American Fabian* editor, the daughter of Mary Peabody and Horace Mann, abolitionists, educators, and Brook Farmers themselves. And most of its residents were college-educated, urban-based activists and writers who prided themselves on their political commitments and on their genuine respect for the old Brook Farm values:

> Whoever is satisfied with society as it is, whose sense of justice is not wounded by its institutions and its spirit of commerce, has no business with this community; neither has any one who is willing to have other men give their best hours and strength to bodily labor, in order to secure himself immunity therefrom.

Although Gilman shared the philosophy and spirit of the Summer Brook Farm community—it was one of her many training grounds—she described it in delightfully nondeferential ways. For instance, she recounted how the residents—the "inmates?—co-residents?—brethren and sisters?"—would begin their loosely scheduled "work" day gathering for breakfast on the magnificent outdoor veranda. With white clouds touching her feet and sunshine all about, Prestonia Mann would start reading "somebody's 'History of Institutions,'" or "Darwinism in Politics," or "something bionomical"; then, after attending lectures by the distinguished and not so distinguished, or after having "earnest" discussions on "'cause and effect,' 'idealism and materialism,' 'monism and dualism,' 'the universal and the particular,' and all the other fascinating and insoluble verities," they would go berry-picking, or hiking, or frolicking about with like-minded socialist friends.

As Gilman described the regulations, residents were expected not only to share in the expenses of the place (roughly three dollars a week), but also to draw chore assignments from a hat, to put in two good hours of work a day, and then to recount their "deeds of valor" in a little book which is "passed round at supper." All this confirms the socialist contention that "incentive will act collectively—common labor for common gain," she wrote Houghton with amusement, especially on communal washing days: "the cheerful good-will and colossal ignorance of these co-laborers," these "gallant college professors and high-minded poets toiling at the wringers while buttons flew away and spots remained."[10] Admittedly most gender-based roles were fairly standard—women cleaning, sewing, washing dishes while men were gardening, chopping wood, or tending to "Aristophones," the mule. Nonetheless, Gilman enjoyed the atmosphere immensely. "O if you could but be here and see," she wrote Houghton. "This place is *fine* for me. Splendid air. Lots of genuine exercise and some useful work, and a lot of people to play with! Some of 'em I can help perhaps."

> You should see me eat! You should see me sleep! You should see me vault fences and skip up mountains! . . .
> A Community life is evidently well suited to my style of beauty; and presently when I am wooed to enter lots of them, I can flit agreeably from point to point and maintain my equanimity without difficulty.

Based in part on her Summer Brook Farm experience, Gilman spent the last two weeks of August visiting and lecturing in Sarah Farmer's camplike retreat in Greenacres, Maine, another natural scenic setting for "advanced" reformers (her good friend Helen Campbell would be there).[11] "I have walked and wandered about, sat in the sun and shade, enjoyed the beautiful river with the far off slim white mountains across it," she wrote to Houghton, albeit this time some unpredicted complications interfered. Charlotte had been invited to lecture on "New Motherhood," a theme she was particularly fond of. But before she arrived, Miss Ida Hultin, a Unitarian minister from Illinois, had voiced objections: Gilman was not a "fit person" to lecture on such topics because she had "given up [her] child."[12] "Great

Fun," Charlotte wrote to Houghton, since as it turned out, the Hultin slurs and censures backfired and turned to her advantage. This "is the first time since I left California that I have stepped into this sort of thing," yet the "joke of it" is that "I [have] achieve[d] instant popularity," and "to my secret delight" have "made 'The New Motherhood' a subject of thrilling interest." "I have . . . won golden opinions and made friends, have set on foot other engagements;" and have "had a triumphant feeling of having at last had a chance" to "promulgate my deadly views at my leisure."

Letters: June 4 through August 29, 1897

473 Orchard St. Chicago.
June 4th. 1897 . . .

I'm not feeling very lively these days, and go to bed early. . . .

Why I was simply buoyant when I reached here—just *happy,* and lively as a cricket; and now I wake up tired and feel my own weight. . . .

You see my brain is all mixed up with other internal machinery, and when anything happens at either end of the line it's bad for me. Mostly the brain is the ground of attack. . . .

. . . It's not "vertigo." It is just that I'm not happy—things are grey, and I have no strength and get tired easy, and my head isn't clear. That's the mischief. I lose my grip mentally. And I have such a good head when I have it—that I hate awfully to have it cloud up and weaken.

. . . I have told you before how high I rate you. You are a good man, and I know no higher praise. A good man. It helps me to be better and stronger to know you. . . .

And I do hope, earnestly hope, that I may be wise and strong enough to keep your friendship for long years, and to serve you sometime, as I would like to do. . . .

. . . You see one advantage of your writing these nice replyable letters, is that you get longer ones from me! But when you write fine big ones like this, number your pages dear Cousin—it gives a "rich effect."

You get nicer all the time. . . .

. . . June 5th. 1897. . . .

I'm feeling better. Had quite a buoyant day. Finished article on the Servant Question and modelled the poem of yesterday a little. It is good poetry—somewhat great.

Sometimes I wish you cared more for my kind of things and then again I think it is just as well you don't. And I'm so sulky and cantankerous about

it that I suppose no one ever can. My thought and work were so alien to all
about me when I began—it was such a struggle to think out and do the
things I believed, I was so utterly unused to help or wise appreciation, and
so utterly well-used to opposition—derision—all that a family can do to
check thought; that I don't suppose I shall ever bring forward an idea to a
close friend without my elbow up. Of course the public is different.

I wish you could have heard me last Sunday night. I never spoke better
in my life.

A full church. A big platform all to myself. And it *came!* It just poured
in a great swelling river and all those people sat and took it in.

Some day I do hope you can hear me when I'm at my best—and I don't
know you're there. This last is not essential however; for I forget everyone
in an audience when I speak.

If you like heavy reading why don't you sail in on Ward's "Dynamic
Sociology" & "Psychic Factors of Civilization" etc. Perhaps you have. I
mean to read 'em, when my head is equal to it.

By the mail—or sooner or later—it's all stamped to go—I send you a
thing [Lester Ward's] just sent me, on "Collective Telesis." Isn't it good of
him to bring my poems in in that shape. He has always thought well of
them. Says I'm the only scientific poet! But he's no judge of poetry; so I
never was set up by it! . . .

[June 6]
Sunday A.M.

While I think of it—I'm great on boats. New York is an island. If I'm
there any in September—or in October which is more likely—why not take
a train to some place and then row! . . .

Faint misgivings assail me. Is it the custom in New York for elegant
youths—Elegant Youth I should say (which is you!) in company with Distinguished Age (which is me!) to secrete itself for whole days as we purpose?

Go to!—is it Proper?

Personally I don't care. But you no doubt have a reputation to sustain!
Far be it from me to inveigle you into performances compromising to the
dignity of a Grace Church Usher! . . .

7.50 A.M. Monday [June] 7th. . . .

Am feeling lots better—thank goodness! Whatever be the nature of the
infirmity which has accompanied me so long its effects are baleful. And for
all my experience it is still hard to discriminate between it, and facts. When
so affected in [the] degree proportioned to the severity of the thing, *the
same facts* that before gave sensations of pleasure, now cause pain.

This little waft of the last few weeks was only a shade of pale blue over the landscape—a thing I could reason around and see through. At its long worst it meant pitch blackness—unillumined and unilluminable.

Cheerfully will I run around the world the rest of my life—a tentless Arab—living in a pair of handbags and a sleeping car—!—cheerfully will I forego "the comforts of a home" including the whole gamut of family affection—yes, rather would I never see again a face I knew—than to suffer again as I have suffered years on years. . . .

7.25 P.M. Monday

Well. I'm tired. . . .

. . . I ate dinner between a crossfire of what—crime though it be!—is of all noises the most trying to me—the outcry of the young. I'm sorry—but it drives me wild. Even goodnatured noise. . . .

Tues. 8 A.M. June 8th

I am certainly forming the Houghton habit—an insidious and powerful assailant.

Why on earth I should gabble on as thus on all occasions, in season and out of season, of small personal concerns, to an elegant youth in New York City, I cannot for the life of me see.

It is as dangerous, apparently, to make never so cautious an inroad on my friendliness as to make a hole in a levee—I proceed to come through in great volume!

Thus where you naturally expected a tinkling rivulet of pleasant though superficial intercourse, behold you! . . .

> sketch of Houghton drowning in
> "Sea P. Stetson"

This baby down stairs makes me think of Kate so. Kate when she was little and O so lovely!—and I *knew* it, but couldn't *feel* it! And it aches and aches. I wish—no I don't wish a thing.

It's all right.

Aforesaid Katharine has sent me a letter this morning which I value exceedingly. . . . See if it does not impress you as indicating a sense of nearness and confidence. To be so full of a special interest and to take the trouble to write it all out—a full letter—to me. O it's no use—I have to stop and cry. This little mother here is so young and fair and pretty! And the children are so fat and handsome . . . and so I come up stairs and bawl, and favor you with choice selections from my state of mind! . . .

Wed. June 16. 1897.
Eureka. Kansas. . . .

A week ago last night I posted you a letter in Chicago, a letter so voluminous, so trivial and so guerulously confidential that I was seized with morti-
fication thereafter, and resolved to give you a rest. . . .

It is a large undertaking, to keep an ingenious young man out of mischief;
but as far as an incessant drain on your spare time and spare cash will
achieve that worthy end you may count on my assistance. The cash part of
it bothers me in a degree you have no idea of. You must invent cheap things
to do—or I won't do 'em! If I have any money I shall insist on sharing in
the larger schemes. If I don't—I shall insist on keeping the schemes within
limits. Now don't be unruly!

I am greatly amused—and not displeased—at your elaborate criticism
of the blank verse thing I sent you—the long one. I had no idea you would,
but am glad you were moved that way. It seems so funny to me—the point
of view. I never should pick out phrases like that and roll them like a sweet
morsel under my tongue. I think only of what I'm trying to say, and how—
clearest —to say it. Still I admit the bits you quote are good. You see I
write 'em as fast as I write this—with no consideration whatever. And,
having my own vanity, I think it means a good deal of practical feeling to
think poetry as freely as that. . . .

It tastes real good to have you talk about my stuff—do it some more! . . .

Now, coming to your second letter, I resent its opening. "I find I am
becoming weakminded," say you—because you are moved to write to me
frequently! Goodness! What a drivelling idiot you must think me! Shall I
become strongminded and write once a month, to punish you? . . . Your
remark makes me think of those lovers who open a proposal by exclaiming
"vainly have I struggled against this mad passion!" etc. "Having no news to
tell."—do you really think I value your letters for the qualities of the daily
press? "Without any excuse"—hm! How much exoneration do you require
for this wild folly?

My excuse for writing to you at this inordinate rate is that I like to. I
like you—and I'm lonesome—and you treat me well—and so I pour out
volumes. . . .

Never was there a more babblesome and childishly confidential person
than I; and as the passing years give me strength to refrain from unwise
confidences to strangers, I am the more like to burst for want of some one
to tell everything to! Poor cousin! I tremble for you! There is yet time to
repent and have another engagement for next winter! . . .

My age has nothing to do with the appearance of our actions, bad boy!
An ungenerous world is always ready to exclaim that there is no fool like
an old fool! But if it is customary with you to permeate the countryside in
the company of a fair friend I say no more. . . .

And here I've written all this and not a word of my adventures so far in Kansas! Well, it'll have to go. I spoke Thus. in Mankato, preached Sunday in Topeka, and am here now—so far about five dollars out of pocket. . . .

It's a tedious thing to have a brain of unequal consistency! I'm not sure at all which is *me!* But so far I have always hopefully supposed that the strong and jolly one was—and I guess I'm right. One thing that makes me hold you very near is that you knew *me*—me before I died. Truly—wasn't I strong and of good promise? It is hard to keep faith in one's self—through long years—when your brain goes back on you *and there's no one to corroborate your memory.*

It comes horribly close sometimes—the feeling—"What's the use of fussing—*This* is you—and all you'll ever be!"

Well—You're a comfort. . . .

Eureka. Kansas.
June. 17. 1897. . . .

I'm sorry, but I do not remember one thing about the house in Norwich. It was a vague hurried visit to me, thick with intense feeling, and I recall little except the persons,—not all of them. . . .

Eureka, Kansas
June 22nd. '97.

. . . Since you close [your letter] with alluring promise to write to me from camp I shall look for letters presently of a swashbuckler character, written on nothing less military than the head of a drum; and interspersed with "strange oaths and warlike instances." In this I shall probably be disappointed, so prone is man not to do what one expects of him. . . .

Sat. A.M. [June 26, 1897?]. . . .

. . . Meanwhile I continue to be "low," and I think lower.

If it goes on you need not be surprised to get most melancholy letters, or cross unreasonable letters, or mean quarrelsome letters, or no letters at all. I am already in the mood to hold that it is no sort of use to write to you—that you do not "understand" nor "care," etc. etc. That I won't be a tax on any man's patience and all the rest of the morbid miserableness.

I guess if it comes on heavy I'll just drop you till I get over it, and come back, companionable and smiling, in the Fall.

You see nobody *can* be near me when I've fallen through a hole; I *have* to be alone because I've gone there! And I have to be miserable because that is the condition.

Don't worry—nothing is the matter with my "health"—and I'll get out of this bye and bye. And perhaps it isn't going to be any worse and I've scared you for nothing. . . .

. . . But just now it feels discouraging.

Your dilapidated cousin
Charlotte

The Addison Ranch
Star. Kansas
11 A.M. Tues. June 29th. 1897. . . .

Yours of the 23rd, from camp, arrived Saturday, last mail, after I had posted mine. Tis a pleasing letter, replete with information. . . .

Why do you persist in talking about "dizziness" and "vertigo" in connection with my not being well? Have you materialistically misconstrued my description of symptoms to that effect? So that when I say "things grow dark to me" you think I mean chairs and tables? Let me then explain more specifically that it is my mental atmosphere that darkens—not the scenery. I'm not dizzy nor anything of that sort—I am simply low spirited and weak. This would be of little consequence if it did not stop my literary work and make me very unhappy. But as it does these things and more to the same effect it is serious enough. So now you will have to cook up a new lot of sympathy and apply it to the right spot—this won't do! . . .

Wed. A.M. [June 30, 1897]

Now I have a favor to ask of you, involving the expenditure of fifty four cents, which sum you are to peacefully accept at my hands when I return. Please get a copy of "In This Our World" of Miss Mann . . . and send it to Mr. Ripley Hitchcock of Appleton's Pub. Co. Only I want you to correct certain errors in it please: those I marked in yours, and what others you may have seen. . . . For this grace will I bless you, and owe you much gratitude beside fifty cents and two stamps!

In view of my recent outbursts of further verse—which I hope to add to materially before winter—and the coldness of "our leading magazines" to these productions, I have decided to take Mr. Howells' hint and get out a good American edition this winter—if I can! So I wrote to him about it, and he replied at once, sending the kindest of notes, and advising that I try Appleton's via Mr. Hitchcock their literary reader. He says "and I beg you to quote me as cordially in its favor as your selfrespect will allow." . . .

El Dorado. Kansas
July 10th '97. . . .

Tuesday morning I spoke to a sort of mother's meeting; on Childhood and a mother's duty. It was what I call a successful lecture. I succeeded in saying what I wanted to, and several of the women were really impressed. When one is propagating truths deeply radical and desperately unpalatable one can not expect an eager and convinced audience. . . .

. . . But I have done some good both public and private; have written a little, and, what makes me more than happy, I have . . . made an enormous new step in my sociological theories. So large and valuable a one that I am now quite clear and determined about the rest of the summer's work, and mean to have a book ready to read to you when I get back! I think that with all my lack of proper training I simply must write it; and I shall look [for] invaluable assistance from you in the way of criticism. You see my head is so weak still that I may make a poor book of it, but I must get it down somehow—so that it is revisable—and then can work it over in the Fall. It is quite possible that you will see little in it, and consider me another crack-brained enthusiast; but all the same I am banking on your sympathy and kindliness for assistance.

The fanatic and the great discoverer have much in common. Of course I fondly believe that I am the latter—and you may fondly believe that I am the former—and conceal it from me.

But I am solidly committed to my course of thinking, and shall out with it to the best of my ability. . . .

Now see here. If you want more things to do for me—if you still thirst to "prepare" for the demands I propose to make on your intellect, suppose I outline the kind of thing I am writing about, and you just skirmish around in sociological literature and [see] what is already there on similar lines. Then you can give me some reference notes and make up for my palpable deficiencies on those lines. And then I can put in a nice introductory note explaining that any signs of erudition observable in this book; any reference to collateral literature etc. etc. are due to the invaluable assistance of my learned friend G.H.G. Ph.D., A.b.c., P.L.Y., R.X.Y., etc. etc.!

. . . The line of thought is on The Economic Rela[tionship of Woman] to Man As a Factor in Human Development. That's too long for a title, but that's what it's about. The main sub heads are the effect of this Economic Relation on Sex—Character—Economic Progress. And the big thing I'm hugging myself about just at present is this.

All hum an progress is natural[l]y collective organic. [H]umanity is an organic relation, and all its processes develope on organic lines—industry—religion—government—everything human. Now the sex relation is not a distinctively human one at all, but held its place as a process of race preservation before humanity was. It is a purely individual relation—an individual and private instinct—in no way organizable.

Human industry is a social process, and as such naturally organic in its tendencies. But!—and here is one of the biggest buts that ever was!—by combining the sex-relation with an economic relation we have combined a process purely individual with a process progressively collective—and *that* is what ails us! In economics I mean.

Men as individuals tend to socialize industry as naturally as they have socialized warfare or government. But where the sex-instinct comes in there remains individualism. By putting the sex-relation on an economic basis—by making it a sex-characteristic of our species that the male "support" the female, we have brought all the ferocity and bel[l]ligerence of sex combat into the field of economic competition.

Men, single, organize as naturally as bees. Men, married, individualize on the instant—as far as their marriage touches their other work.

Now as soon as we disentangle these incongruous forces, we shall leave the natural economic tendencies of the race to work out peace and plenty for us all; and shall leave the natural sex tendencies to work out a purer happier monogamy than is possible at present.

Guess I won't go any further. But anything that is written on these lines I should like to see. Personally I have never seen it touched on—nor heard of it. . . .

Bebel's "Woman" doesn't treat it from this point of view, though he goes a long way. Ward I don't fully know—I wish I did, but I have looked at his chapters that touch woman and this is not his position at all. I wish you'd read (if you haven't) Ward's paper in The Forum—August '88 I think—on "Our Better Halves." . . .

Sunday, July 11th 11.20 A.M.

Now then—Let me proudly state that I feel lots better! . . . Was hungry for breakfast this morning—and a charming breakfast we had, too—oranges, poached eggs, creamed potatoes, graham muffins, and exquisite waffles. These be good folk to visit! . . .

Now see here! My sort of apology for writing so much is *not* similar to your sort—alleged weakmindedness! The thing I've been apologizing for is not the writing but the *kind* of writing. Your letters would be a credit to a discreet curate. Mine would serve as opening chapters to a novel. . . . I need apologizing for. It's as if you offered your hand to help me down from something, and I fell all over you. Who wouldn't apologize! It's as if you said "call and see me some day," and I came and stayed six months.

I know you are strong enough . . . and good enough to carry it all right; but it mortifies me just the same to have to be carried. . . .

Now you have no such tale as this to tell. You can write all you want to and you know I like it. You have plenty of margin all the time—owing to my awkward profusion of expression. . . .

The heat here has pulled me down a good deal, I know that well enough. It makes me weak and lazy. But that brain-sinking melancholy business is a good honest disease which I have carried off and on for fourteen years. . . .

About 9 A.M. Tues. July 20th. '97
"Hillside." Wyoming. N.Y.

Agreeablest of Cousins;

Behold me within a stone's throw as it were, even here in New York State! And behold me *exceedingly* comfortable! A big big room, cool, light, high, creamcolored, three windowed, wide-bedded, big-closeted, running-watered—all that is lovely.

A comfortable wicker rocker—(my ideal writing desk!) a table immediately contiguous to lay out papers on and eke the ink; my lap table, long hidden in the trunk, a new pen perfect quiet, a cool breeze—ah! But no letters, no letters since *Thursday!* (or Fri.) This is very bad. But I expect some down from Rochester, perhaps even today. I wrote you ad libitum—I fear almost to the reader ad nauseam. . . .

I look out through mighty maples elms and locusts, across dripping wooded valleys and steep rounded hills—way—way off—green, and blue-green and blue, and checkered golden with the ripe wheat. M-m-m! It's lovely. . . .

Chicago I left at 3 P.M. on Friday, and reached here Sat. about noon. It is a nobly beautiful place. A house of vast proportions—big as a Sanatorium, but simple and true in line and color, and just a home of comfort and love. Jane Addams was here till last night, . . . with a Miss Mary Smith of tall stature and serene beauty; a damsel wealthy and philanthropic also.

This was a great pleasure to me. To be with Jane Addams for two days is a memorable incident. And I had a chance to talk to her too, and told her of my recent development in economic theory, and she was much impressed and approved thereof—which did me good. For she is a most "practical" person, of large wisdom and experience. . . .

What do you suppose I've been doing since I began this letter? For two hours and three quarters? Picking currants with Mrs. Coonley-Ward. Such huge currants! Big globy scarlet berries, so thickset that you held clumps of them in your hand like grapes—absolutely—. . . . Red white and black currants—two long rows, with peach trees set between bushes and a grass path between the rows. And there are black white and red raspberries too— huge ones, in overwhelming numbers.

And cherries also, in the same colors. O it's a fine place to visit! . . .

Here it is Wednesday—and I have had no mail since last Thurs! It's a shame. You see letters are family and home to me. If I don't get any I feel homesick—all the kind of homesick I know!

Yes—in England I was homesick for America—nothing less. And I used to be homesick for dear Pasadena.

But usually my homesickness can't find the place! . . .

12.15 Thurs. July 22nd. 1897.
Wyoming N.Y.
c/o Mrs. L.A. Coonley-Ward. . . .

Never was ship wrecked mariner more pleased by a solitary sail than I was this morning by a solitary letter. My first in a week! It was from you, too; which, next to being from Mr. Ripley Hitchcock of Appleton, was calculated to gratify and please. . . .

So I, being famished for "the personal touch"—living letterless so long—will now proceed to extract all the companionship I can out of this epistle. Tis not, so to speak, of a tender nature, but shines warmly in contrast with not having any! . . .

I derive great satisfaction from your determination to seize a day or so in September for Norwich—and me! The more I see of your methods of spending your time and your spring of action, the more convinced I am that you find in me precisely the most sacrificial field of philanthropy you can compass! . . .

Well there, I've read that letter dry. I've tried to read things into it that I know you never thought of; and I warrant I've read out of it all you ever put in—and more.

I wish I had a stack of love letters—wildly ardent ones—from six desperate adorers! I wouldn't have believed how I should miss my mail! It's almost a fortnight since I've had any. . . .

11 A.M.
[July 22nd. 1897]

. . . As to the lecture on the Responsibility of the Purchaser. . . . [I]t's nothing you ever read or thought of I warrant!—and by no means a legal maxim. . . . It treats of the power of the consumer to modify the product of the world—the effect of "the market" on any art or industry, and then, showing how women are the main purchasers of the world—the consuming class *par excellence,* shows how their present status—their tastes and education, their judgement and methods, affect the output of humanity.

It isn't calculated to make women feel very good, either. . . .

I'm so glad you've got my dear Impress. Only I wish I could have been there and read things to you. I am pleased that you agree with the Editor on the Ethical Problems. . . .

But most am I pleased with your remarks on the short stories. I take no small credit to myself on those efforts. It is the only "literary work" I ever did; and I think some of it is good. . . .

Yes, I just sit here and purr to have you recognize so many and so easily—the George Eliot even by the title (you see I couldn't take a short story of hers—she never wrote anything short—not even a sentence! And to think out a whole novel and imitate a piece of a chapter that way—it seems to me to indicate good critical and constructive power!!! . . .)

Altogether your opinions are so favorable that I am simply rolling about in them—like a nice kitty in the grass! It makes me feel good all over. . . .

As to Better Halves—good. It gives me *such* a pleasant feeling of—of common ground I guess; of some sort of standing room somewhere—to have you care to read and talk with me. Are you sure you like it? . . . I hope you are not being merely benevolent, in your usual self-immolating way! I wrote The Brood Mare long before I read Ward. I've been thinking those things—and much more—for many years. . . .

Do you know Bebel's "Woman" [Woman and Socialism]? There's a good deal in that too. But I've got more than any of 'em—as far as I've read. . . .

I hate to get to the end of this letter. It is such a good one. . . .

I wish I had somebody—young old or middleaged—male female or neuter—to whom I could just say *everything!*. By what absurdity a flopsy-wopsy hair-sieve of a disposition like mine ever got stood up alone [in] this fashion I should like to know! And you are just near enough to arouse all this foolishness and not near enough to—assuage it as it were!

O well—I'm mightily thankful for you all the same. You've helped me over a most barren and baldheaded summer!

Dear Mother Campbell is about as close as anyone I have—but as usual she doesn't care as much for me as I do for her. And I will not intrude— that is I don't mean to, and try not to, and hate myself when I do. . . .

Wyoming N.Y.
July 27th. 1897. . . .

And now let me break the Jeremiad of the past two months by instantly stating that I feel a little better. Not very much, nor very long; but it tastes very good—just a day's lift of the spirits, and I record it gratefully. . . .

Are you tired of my errands? . . .

I wish I didn't have to bother you so often. Isn't there any kind of thing I can do for you some time to kind of even up things? I shall have to send you some blank checks—payable on demand—some drafts on my goodwill for you to present when you want things. . . .

. . . And the dear little stepmama [Frankie Perkins] writes me a most tender letter[;] says "she'd better come home and cuddle up on her mother's shoulder for a little while"—it just makes me cry again. Bless her loving heart! I shall be very glad of the cuddle, and she won't mind the cry.

I never was so lonesome in my life as I've been this summer.

I envy the girl you're going to walk with on Staten Island! [A]nd wish I were a girl again so as to try for the place! (Now *isn't* that a hateful one!) Never mind. I'll be as good as pie when I come.

Yes, I do wish I were the girl—I do, I do, I do.

Please, mayn't I be the girl on occasion—if I'll be very good and wear the blue suit? . . .

Not know Jane Addams! See what it is not to live in Chicago!

Jane Addams of Hull House! Not know Hull House & Jane Addams! Behold the deficiencies of a college education! Why Jane Addams is one of the noblest, wisest, strongest, sweetest women in the world, and Hull House is the greatest Social Settlement in America. Get "Hull House Maps and Papers" right off, and improve your mind. When I come back I'll improve it more.

How good it feels to know something you don't!! . . .

4.20 P.M.
[July 27, 1897]. . . .

I rejoice to dismiss the benevolence theory in regard to your plans for my entertainment. But unless you let me somehow do something for you I cannot get over the sense of entire onesidedness—of accumulated obligation. Do fix up some request or other—if it's as queer as an election bet!

Buy a board all you want to, but don't you go to practicing chess with any more powerful person than a great grandmother!

You see if I can really and truly beat you it will be not only a pleasure, but do more to reassure me as to my brain than any other one thing I can think of. You have a strong trained mind—especially mathematical.

I have a strained and shattered mind—untrained entirely, and anything but mathematical. If I *could* beat you it would reassure me beyond words. I don't want any handicaps. And if I once thought you were *letting me beat* I should never enjoy playing with you again. But I do build much on your inexperience—if all your statements are as accurate as they are modest—and I have hopes. Now you wouldn't go and spoil all that gain to me for the sake of a cheap victory over a feebleminded female—would you? . . .

This is *such* a good letter. And look at the miles of gabble wherewith I am answering it! Why recklessly purchase that big book of Ward's O Youth?

'Tis a rash project. Read it first and then you'll not want to buy it. At least I shouldn't think you would. . . .

Wyoming, N.Y. July 27th. 1897.

I agree to pay to George Houghton Gilman, on demand, such services and good will as he may consider due in return for obligations rendered, unless such claim be deemed extortionate or untimely; as for instance should he require me darn his stockings while lecturing! In case of dispute the claim [is] to be submitted to a court of arbitration composed of three persons, one to be selected by each disputant and a third whom they shall agree on. . . .

Summer Brook Farm,
Hurricane P.O. Essex Co. N.Y.
Sun. Aug. 1st. 1897. . . .

As to women as purchasers—consumers. Most ultimate consumption is done at home. Most women live at home all the time—(and consume like silk worms!) Production is for human use, and most of the stuff is made—directly or indirectly—for ultimate home consumption. Take architecture—more of it is dwelling houses than anything else.

Furniture & decoration—houses again. Crockery—glassware—silverware—ironware—etc. etc. etc. etc.—used mainly at home. Drapery hangings, bed & table linen—towels etc. etc. household use mainly.

Dressgoods—the vast majority for women & children—and even some choice in men's wear—all [?] by women.

Pictures and ornaments—mostly for the home & *novels* etc. Of course women don't buy steel rails—or rolling stocks and the whole interchange system is in men's hands mostly; but women are the ultimate spenders of most of the money earned, the governing purchasers of the world. . . .

Of this, more, in that heavily mortgaged winter of ours. One evening a week and pleasant Sundays—Gracious! How we shall have to talk!

O, but it's the second Fabian Essays you are reading—and I've not read 'em myself! I mean the first series; and even those I've not read all of!

But go [to] it!—you're doing finely. Shaw's work is always clever and good reading. But I do not love the man. He has an evil spirit.

[Just] wait till you hear *my* arguments on Socialism! Or at least my views! Can you read Marx? I can't, now: *Maybe never* could. . . .

As to me—and the apostles! Why of course. That is exactly what I am. I have neither purse nor scrip—barring enough to get around with—and that I pick up as I go. And I am absolutely giving my life to what I consider to be preaching the gospel. So naturally, necessarily, I get taken care of. . . .

And yet I am ashamed to be so ungrateful. It is a deep steady ever-growing joy to be so widely loved. I *am* thankful. And I guess it *is* rather unusual—come to think of it. Yes, new town—or new country—I struck 'em just the same in England and Scotland—dear loving homesharing friends. . . .

I have come down from the charming *chalet* adjoining, wherein is my room, and wandered around the house, looking at its environs. Large and thrilling adjectives flock to my pen. All the other—inmates?—co-residents?—brethren and sisters?—are about their various businesses, or pleasures. . . . You see, we have our names down in the small hallway—and our "specialities," and we all lecture and teach to such of us as wish to hear and learn.

I am at a loss to select a speciality. What do I know among learned folks like these? Naught truly. But I will hang me up my lecture list, and offer to lecture to anybody at any time! . . .

Speaking of landscape—Ah! Mm! I should say so! And O if you could but be here and see this *beautiful* building—solid logs with the bark on, caulked tightly—that's the wall, inside and out. A brick chimney—not a chimney *piece* but a whole out—goes up through the roof. I shall have to sketch some of it, I simply must. [sketch included here]

That's rather vague—but it gives a sense of dimension. I'm cuddled up in the hither comes, my inkstands on sill no. l. Pillows and seat dull crimson, streakily shaded by the sun. Outside a corner of the piazza we eat on. Then bright grass. Then a mighty gulf, with bright trees reaching up out of it.

Then a far sweep of farm land. Do you find the speck of a home? *Then* mountains.

And we eat right out on that piazza, looking all down Keene Valley.

near 10 A.M. Monday [August 2, 1897]

The washing is done and a-drying. Some fifteen or twenty of us in all. Two washing machines, two wringers, two tubs, many pails, dippers & basins, and a lot of jolly jokey friendly people all in it. The men work the machines & wringers, mostly, and empty and fill tubs etc. The women do the lighter things. Great fun. . . .

Tues. 8.30 A.M. . . .

You must remember that the same incentive to labor as now exists will then exist—corn will not grow with out the sower, nor flour be made without the miller. But the difference is that the incentive will act collectively—common labor for common gain.

The Socialist does not have to prove that man will work without "reward," but that men will work for a common reward. And that is not difficult to show, even now. Moreover, there remains the individual reward in honor and power—things always dearer than gain.

There'll be no trouble about people's working, especially when all children are rightly fed and trained. . . .

. . . Are you reading my stuff in The Fabian from month to month? If you find holes in them make note thereof, and we'll talk thereon this winter. . . .

c/o **Miss Prestonia Mann.**
Summer Brook Farm
Hurricane P.O.
Essex Co. N.Y.
Aug. 3. '97. . . .

O but this letter of yours is so nice! Skimpy? Not it! It is not the amount of paper covered that makes letters—it's what's *in* 'em.

And there's a heap of friendliness and—O I don't know—personal touch in this. I like it. . . .

Wed. 8.35 A.M. [August 4, 1897]. . .

I've only got about fifteen minutes for you now, between the table work, (my modest share in it as one of eight or ten) sweeping the dining hall, and ironing. You see we are each bound to put in two hours work a day, somehow; and a book is passed round at supper in which we recount our deeds of valor. . . .

. . . Thursday—at 9.—A.M. [August 5, 1897]. . . .

At eating I would cheerfully undertake to race you. *We* eat here! On an open piazza—a dull green floor and tree trunk pillars, and a mountain sunset with our supper! 'Way down Keen Valley and over the hills and far away.

Friday. 1.30 P.M. [August 6, 1897]. . .

[After going berry picking on Mt. Hurricane, she wrote] I picked more than he did, an unparalleled feat so far. Indeed he confided to some one that I was "equal to two men." Now there's a compliment after my own heart. . . .

Enclosed is a clipping Walter sent me yesterday: Isn't it fine. Send it

back please. I rejoice to have so grand a person as this Broadus—whoever
he may be—to champion my cause! O but it is good to feel better again!
This place is *fine* for me. Splendid air. Lots of genuine exercise and some
useful work, and a lot of people to play with! Some of 'em I can help
perhaps. . . .

9.05 A.M. Sunday Aug. 8th. 1897.
Summer Brook, Essex Co. N.Y. . . .
(Hurricane P.O.). . . .

You perceive that our community hath its sports and pastimes. Well—
let me see.—Sunday I arrived. Monday I washed. Tuesday I ironed—also
Wednesday. Thursday we went up Hurricane. Friday I berried—blueber-
ried—four hours and enjoyed it much. Saturday I raspberried, three hours
and a half, and enjoyed it little.

Every afternoon I have rested a little.

I have talked—my kind of talking—to Sister Rodman, Sister Sewall &
her mother, Mr. Whitehead and Brother Vatralsky. . . .

You should see me eat! You should see me sleep! You should see me
vault fences and skip up mountains! You should see me clear tables and
careen about in the laundry! This is doing me *heaps* of good. We eat the
table clean at each meal and never have enough. And I have entirely gotten
over being lonesome.

A Community life is evidently well suited to my style of beauty; and
presently when I am wooed to enter lots of them, I can flit agreeably from
point to point and maintain my equanimity without difficulty. . . .

I read over with renewed pleasure your remarks as my welcomings and
detainings in many homes. Maybe I *am* agreeable for a while—it does look
so, doesn't it? It even seems like a pretty good evidence thereof. But you
see I don't wear well—I'm not good to live with, and they don't know that.

I said many years ago—in girlhood—that I was like a big bird without
legs. As long as I could fly it was all right; but when I attempted to sit down
it was painful and awkward. Nothing but complete prostration brings me
down, and then it is a painful spectacle. . . .

Mon. about 7 A.M. [August 9, 1897]

This is breakfast time, but the bell has not rung yet. . . . Some delay first
(———bell!) for people to gather, then for Miss [Prestonia] Mann to read
to us from Ruskin, or Bellamy, or somebody's 'History of Institutions,'" no
"Darwinism in Politics," I think is the name of it—something bionomical
any way. . . .

4.40 P.M. Mon. [August 9, 1897]. . . .

The reason women aren't smart about "two-masted sloops" and such like, is from lack of associative ideas. They have nothing to tack the information to, and it slips out easily; as perhaps it would with you if you were given names of feminine decorations or crochet stitches. . . .

*   *   *   *   *

[*Following her two weeks' at Summer Brook Farm, Gilman made a brief visit to New York. Part of the time she would spend with Houghton, but an important reason also was to see her daughter, Kate. Walter and Grace were on their way to Europe (Walter had wanted to pursue his art career in Rome for years), and before they left, Katharine would spend several days with Charlotte. As she later wrote, "[I was] . . . met at the station by my Cousin Houghton and—Katharine! . . . Rules or no rules, she fled past the gatemen and came flying down the platform to meet me. . . . Twelve years old, and a darling." "A few days" they would have together, vacationing, sightseeing, getting reacquainted. "Houghton and I took her to Bedloes Island . . . where she went up the inside of the Goddess of Liberty, then to the aquarium. Monday we went shopping together, Katharine and I."*[13] *Or as Gilman's diary reports:*]

Tuesday: A fine long day in the park with Katharine. We do everything pretty much, and she has a very good time. Is especially delighted to learn to row, which she does in astonishingly quick time.

Wednesday: Put a few stitches on Kate's pongees, pack her valise and take her down to Hotel Albert.

There I saw my dear Grace, and had a chance to do a few errands for her. They sailed on the *Westerland.*[14]

[*For Gilman, this New York visit was brief but strenuous: the emotionally charged contact with her former husband, Walter; the renewal of her long-term friendship with Grace, Katharine's second mother, and also Walter's second wife; the tangles of short-term mothering with Katharine; the juggling of family members' needs and schedules while ensuring that her courtship with Houghton remained a secret to them all. Very likely this visit marked a turning point: it was almost certainly their first extended face-to-face discussion of her work. And although she was in some ways pleased with the encounter, there are some niggling worries that the letters allude to but do not explain.*]

9.50 A.M. Mon. Aug 23rd 1897
On "Pier" for Boston
Central Depot—N.Y.

Excellent Cousin Living in New York! . . .

Having conversed with you at great length for ten hours Sat. and twelve Sunday, I now experience deep satisfaction in sitting down to write you a letter.

This shows how monotonous and tiresome I find your company. Yesterday was a good day. A very good day.

And last evening was a good evening.

I went to sleep with a pleasing sense of having been kissed and comforted by my entire family! And, being thus cherished, slept the sleep of the happy.

. . . As to our discourse, past and future, I am greatly relieved in my mind. Having plunged in with great difficulty and effort, and poured forth such material as I could hastily lay hold of and vaguely arrange; and finding you so far neither alienated nor a scoffer; I now contemplate with equanimity—yea, with a rising sense of pleasure, the prospect of certain other opportunities, wherein further to divulge and reinforce my "views."

'Twas a parlous task—trying to cover so much ground in two days; but you will understand its limitation and hold judgment on the gulfs and gaps which yawn in the landscape so hastily presented.

It heartens me much to have you, so far so favorably impressed. And it comforts me much—O very much, to have you patient and kind and sympathetic.

I still somewhat resent my piteous state of mind—preferring much to preserve to all men my cheery and vigorous aspect.

But I suppose we all have to leak somewhere: and 'tis your hapless fate to stand on the leaky side. Lucky there are no more of you!—I couldn't get around and do business! But under the resentment I am conscious of a vague impression that if I heartily and cheerfully accept your kind offices and am not ashamed to be plaintive and weepful occasionally, that I may come into a far healthier state of mind.

It surely is not wholesome to be closecorked *all* the time! . . .

[*Following her ten-day New York visit, Charlotte was invited to spend the last two weeks of August visiting and lecturing in Sarah Farmer's camplike retreat at Greenacres, Maine, another cooperative community for political reformers.*]

. . . 9.35 A.M. Greenacre [August 24, 1897].]. . . .

Beautiful trip up the still gleaming river—banks wooded—grassed— rocked—ferned—anything you like. . . .

. . . Arriving here—Greenacre is a wide stretch of pretty rivershore farm land, with a hotel, tents, cottages, and adjacent farmhouses—. . . .

I am put in an adjacent farmhouse. Nice clean little room. Bed of slats, straw & feathers. Meals in the Inn. And the people! O! O!! O!!! Such people! . . . The occultists of the place stick out all over it. There goes the Swami Saradananda, even as I write a portly broadshouldered black man. I am not occult. . . .

12.30 P.M. Tues. [August 24, 1897]. . . .

All this eastern thought business gives me a mental nausea—always did. It is one of the most sharply defined instincts I have. Anything occult—Psychic—Metaphysical—quite sickens me. If I persist in receiving it I forthwith become angry and unjust. And yet my own work touches closely on their ground—on one side. . . .

Yes, Saturday and Sunday were *fine*—and I love to sit here and read the words that say you liked 'em. I'm not speaking for the world at large, nor even for all women; but for myself absolutely, and pretty generally for my sex.

I think there is in it something of the power and pleasure of art—as beyond nature. . . . To see a person live loving and serving you—that is best of course, as to live on the green earth is better than on mere pictures. But of the green earth the painter takes a little and gives it to you for your own—and you are glad. Life is all about us, to see and study at our leisure. Comes the writer and makes a story of it, and we read with joy and see life with new eyes.

The thought put into words, spoken or written, speaks more directly to the mind; and to those who live most in thinking and feeling—*it seems more real than reality.* . . .

. . . ha! I see a story—a good story. Thus.

Girl. Lover. Adventurer. Accessories.

Lover the dumb servant kind, but not a fool.

Adventurer comes. Girl wavers.

Lover considers—studies—analyzes—makes up his mind.

He does not desert from serving—(which the practical minded female always values), rather adds to his labor; but with deliberate purpose he sets himself to compete with the adventurer! Though inferior in address he steadily improves; and having always the steady weight of his usefulness to back him—comes in a winner! Nice story! . . .

9.45 or so. A.M. Fri. Aug. 27th. 1897.
Greenacre. Eliot. Maine. . . .

I have walked and wandered about, sat in the sun and shade, enjoyed the beautiful river with the far off slim white mountains across it, and made friends among the other boarders. . . .

[*She then describes her theory of supply and demand*]: . . . Each generation takes part in the process of material development which is essential to social growth; and shares in the advantages given to society by preceding generations. Some individuals . . . produce things of unusual and more permanent value, in which more people and more generations share. As, for instance, many must make bread, and make it often. A few can make great musical compositions—and they keep. We all share today in the complex good gain produced by previous generations—peace and liberty, law and order—religious freedom, education—art—science—good roads—rapid transit—improved utensils and tools. All this is true of value. Now as to exchange.

Our usual assumption is that these things are only produced by one man in order to get something of another; . . . they are then exchanged with that other for the something desired—and there's an end. And forthwith we struggle to make plain what is the value of any given product, and how much of something else we ought to give or ask for it. And here, settling it after all by rule of thumb, we simply take all we can get—which is a natural enough process on a line of animal individualism but hardly a thing to be formulated and explained under "The Law of Supply and Demand."

Our notions of exchange and exchange value, might do for a short distance argument, if one man made griddlecakes and another syrup.

To make—to swap—to eat—and there's an end—one might on this basis begin to figure out how much syrup a griddlecake was worth on comparatively simple lines.

But when a man makes a bridge over which thousands will pass after he is dead—or a statue—a symphony—a picture—a poem; when a man discovers an anesthetic or invents an engine—*who* is to pay him?— and how much? He invents, discovers, builds, create[s] as a part of society. He—so to speak—*secretes,* as a given organ secretes; for the uses of the organism to which he belongs. . . .

. . . Now that's not very clear—I know it. But you are in for it, young man! I shall probably use you henceforth . . . and "try it on" you as the spirit moves me. Out of many fumbling efforts to express, comes finally the clear expression. . . .

. . . I do truly think that the principles of Socialism are gaining ground enormously.

"Equality" was selling on the train—O I told you that. See here, how would "Sex in Sociology" do for my title? Too much? It covers the ground beautifully.

The Economic Status of Woman as a Factor in Economics— is pretty long. But that's what it is about. . . .

Greenacre. Eliot. Maine.
Sun. Aug. 29th. 1897.

I was glad to get to my room last night and sit down by the clean lamp in the big red-cushioned rocking-chair, and read your letter—all the letters of this week—three of 'em—good ones all. I would have liked to write to you, but hadn't much productivity left. So I went peacefully to bed and slept the sleep of the weary this time sure. And I dreamed—saints defend us! of C. W. Stetson as he used to be, only far more finished and attractive, and of certain yearnings toward him, checked by a serious contemplation of the rights and preferences of Mrs. S. No. 2. No, said I, this won't do at all, she wouldn't like it! And no more she would! . . .

I know I find it increasingly difficult to destroy your letters—have left three in my trunks at home, and am hanging on to these here with unfeigned reluctance to part with them.

But iron necessity compels me—I can *not* carry nor store them! . . .

. . . Why man—if there was only just so much work in the world (which isn't true) and just so much wages to go with it, it would be better for man and wife each to do half a day's work and get half a day's wage than for him to do all the work and she none—him to get all the money and she none. They'd have just as much money as now and have spare time to see each other in!

3

"When the Wheel Turns Round": 1 September–12 October 1897

On 1 September 1897, Charlotte wrote to Houghton, "Yesterday I began the Book! Not a great beginning, but still a beginning."[1]

Gilman had chosen Belmont, New Hampshire, as the first setting for her *Women and Economics* writing. It was partly the sheer beauty and calmness of the place that had attracted her. She loved the "cool sweet freshness of the morning[s]," the woodland walks, the lovely private room overlooking the "sunsetting—hills blue and green, covered with trees—covered with grass—covered with faint low clouds." Here, in the home of a friend by the name of Isabella Hackett, she could enjoy a loving four-generation family setting, a "familified family," she called it. After her mornings' writing, she could go blackberry picking, or play tennis with the "Titian-haired Miss Hackett," or enjoy story telling in the early evenings when the family "sat on the piazza, . . . watching the dull rich glow die out over the pale hills, and the yellow half moon sink slowly through the violet sky." "Such a good day!" she wrote to Houghton. "I am simply assailed by the desire to write."[2] "Can't fool away time and brain power on letters to aged youths of thirty years while I am turning out [manuscript] at the rate of twelve hundred words an hour." "I want to keep my brains for the morning['s] work and write to you only with my—well, heart I guess. Just brains enough to keep from being silly."

Except she could not, of course, make that kind of separation, her private writings enhancing the creative tension for her public work. "It is astonishing how many times a day I incline to write to you," she told him, especially since he was writing such "fine fat frequent epistles" in response.

It was almost as though Houghton were offering a female kind of caring. He was visiting her father, attending to her daughter Katharine, being "supernaturally nice" in a variety of ways. "I think I am taking more comfort with you than I have since the days of Martha Luther—my dear girl friend of '77–'81," she told him; "the things that you do and the kind of person you are . . . please me over and over, with a funny little sense of satisfaction and delight." "I have not before known a man" who was so "nice" to *every-*

84

one, and "the forlorner they were the nicer you would be to 'em." Still, she continued, "I am satisfied absolutely and forever that you do like *me*—for the pleasure of it, and not as another piece of duty or kindness." Besides, "You seem very near somehow—a kind of background to most of my thinking when I'm not at work."

With the Houghton correspondence as a background to her thinking, on 31 August 1897, Charlotte noted in her diary: "Begin my book on the Economic Relation of The Sexes as a Factor in Social Development. Write only about 1700 words, but do some planning." The following day: "Ha ha! I have finished the first chapter—forty pages! About 4000 words. It feels good."[3] Years later she described the thrill of those early days of writing. The "smooth, swift, easy flow— . . . the splendid joy of it—I went and ran, just raced along the country road, for sheer triumph."[4] Or as she put it in a letter, "My second chapter is done. Thirty-five hundred words I wrote this morning, in three hours!" A book's chapter in one sitting, a steady pace of morning writing, an explosive blending of insights and reflections, with the gradually accumulating pages she was moving toward her goal: "To show how some of the worst evils under which we suffer, evils long supposed to be inherent and ineradicable in our natures, are but the result of certain arbitrary conditions of our own adoption, and how, by removing those conditions, we may remove the evils resultant—." The Preface to *Women and Economics* continues:

> This book is written to offer a simple and natural explanation of one of the most common and most perplexing problems of human life,—a problem which presents itself to almost every individual for practical solution, and which demands the most serious attention of the moralist, the physician, and the sociologist.[5]

* * * * *

According to her diaries and letters, Gilman wrote the first five chapters of *Women and Economics* in this idyllic Belmont setting—very likely the most introductory ones, the most "scientific," the most general and abstract. Giving central place to the views of contemporary theorists, she turned to Reform Darwinist writers to prove the importance of sex-selection in the evolutionary process, to socialist writers to prove the importance of economic instincts as a progressive force for social change, and then to Lester Ward to help her prove the primacy of women's subjugation in understanding and explaining both. As she recently had put it in one letter, "by combining the sex-relation with an economic relation we have combined a process purely individual with a process progressively collective," thus subverting social progress at its very roots.

As Gilman approached her *Women and Economics* writing, she later claimed that two works particularly had influenced her. One was *The Evolution of Sex* by Patrick Geddes and J. Arthur Thompson; the other was Lester

Ward's 1888 *Forum* article entitled "Our Better Halves." Both argued not only that sexual differentiation was a central source of evolutionary progress, but also that progress was dependent on innate differences of sex. As Geddes and Thompson put it, "males live at a loss, are more *katabolic,*—disruptive changes tending to preponderate"; whereas females "live at a profit, are more *anabolic,*—constructive processes predominating in their life, whence indeed the capacity of bearing offspring." To be sure, Gilman must have sometimes winced at the antiwoman implications of their "scientific" statements: among animals and humans alike are "numerous illustrations of the excellence of the males over the females." But she nonetheless recognized the useful purposes such theorists could serve. Geddes and Thomson spoke about the "preponderating passivity of the females, the predominant activity of the males," and yet they also argued that females represent "ideals of ethical progress" in fundamental ways. Through "love and sociality," through "co-operation and sacrifice," through altruistic tendencies, they provide "the highest expressions of the central evolutionary process." After all, Geddes and Thompson confidently concluded, in the last analysis "'creation's final law' is not struggle but love."[6]

Surely it was arguments such as these that attracted Gilman to evolutionary writers. It was gratifying to find such positive, caring values attributed to women, and it became more gratifying still when she "smilingly" and "gladly" adapted and paraphrased the work of Lester Ward. She had met him the year before at a National Woman Suffrage Convention (1896). Subsequently she read his 1888 *Forum* article, "Our Better Halves." And, according to her later writings, she concluded that his "Gynaecocentric Theory" was the "greatest single contribution to the world's thought since Evolution."[7] In explaining the evolutionary force of the sex-selection process, Ward had clearly shown the lessons "true science" had to teach: that "the elevation of woman is the only sure road to the evolution of man," and that "the grandest fact in nature is woman." Because the "female sex is primary in point both of origin and of importance," as Ward put it, any evolutionary or social progress "must be from the steady advance of woman rather than from the uncertain fluctuations of man."[8]

> Woman is the unchanging trunk of the great genealogic tree; while man, with all his vaunted superiority, is but a branch, a grafted scion, as it were, whose acquired qualities die with the individual, while those of woman are handed on to futurity. Woman *is* the race, and the race can be raised up only as she is raised up.[9]

In some respects, there clearly were advantages in drawing on contemporary evolutionary theory. It affirmed women's capacity for altruistic caring and gave scientific proof of the destructiveness of women's status as the second sex. For if men were more aggressive and disruptive, women more cooperative and caring, anything men came to dominate—politics, economics, religion, literature, the arts—necessarily became corrupted by their competitive, self-aggrandizing ways. Thus, while Gilman continued to support contemporary political reformers in their attack on the profit-seeking, individualistic tendencies of industrializing society, she also argued that most reformers failed to understand: that when women became the property of men, masculine competitiveness came to dominate feminine cooperativeness, necessarily assuring that socialist egalitarian values would be virtually destroyed. Thus, as Gilman put it, we should "study the development of human life as we study the evolution of species throughout the animal kingdom." First, we should remember that the "human creature is affected by his environment, as is every other living thing"; second that he is affected "most of all . . . by what he does for his living"; and third, that "[w]e are the only animal species in which the female depends on the male for food, the only animal species in which the sex-relation is also an economic relation." In fact, "man, in supporting woman, has become her economic environment. . . . Man, as the feeder of woman, becomes the strongest modifying force in her economic condition," thus assuring that she, in turn, becomes disproportionately weaker and disproportionately incapable of serving her society in useful or creative ways. As *Women and Economics* phrased it:

> For, in her position of economic dependence in the sex-relation, sex-distinction is with her not only a means of attracting a mate, as with all creatures, but a means of getting her livelihood, as is the case with no other creature under heaven. Because of the economic dependence of the human female on her mate, she is modified to sex to an excessive degree.[10]

Although Gilman was delighted with such scientific "proofs" of women's need for economic independence, both personally and intellectually the process of borrowing contemporary theory had a significant and ironic negative effect: it perpetuated and supported the androcentric vision she was attempting to expel. Because "variation and adaptability" were rooted in biological determinants, all "civilization and progress," as Lester Ward explained it, had "hitherto been carried forward by the male half" of human kind.[11] Men were the achievers; women were more affectionate and sympathetic. Men produced with passionate, "spasmodic bursts" of energy;[12] women passively conserved "the world their sons have made." So pervasive was this kind of androcentric thinking—among men it was almost universal— that too often women not surprisingly adopted it themselves. As Gilman put it, "Economic progress . . . is almost exclusively masculine," whereas women form nothing but an "enormous class of non-productive consumers." They take and take forever and never "think of giving anything in return except their womanhood."[13] "We suffer," as Gilman publicly and apologetically explained it, "from an intense self-consciousness, from a sensitiveness beyond all need; we demand measureless personal attention and devotion, because we have been born and reared in a very hot-bed of these qualities." Hence the "heavy legacy," the limiting of woman's "ideas, her information, her thought-processes, and power of judgment," the lending of "disproportionate prominence and intensity" to "sensations and emotions." "In the ever-growing human impulse to create, . . . to express one's new spirit in new forms,—here [woman] has been utterly debarred."[14] Or, as Charlotte put it privately to Houghton, "You must allow of course for my loose and easy manner of construction; for a method of putting which would not be yours, and which would not perhaps be like any treatment of a serious subject you ever saw."[15]

Clearly Gilman was acknowledging some antiwoman inclinations—her derogatory focus on woman's "sensations and emotions," her underemphasis of women's strength and power.[16] And no wonder, given the presumption and influence of contemporary theorists. In *Women and Economics,* she understandably had drawn on and adapted their reform Darwinist and socialist perspectives; she had borrowed their scientific terminology, emulated their authoritative and "objective" tone, and appealed respectfully to their goals for social change. But in the process of using scholars' tools in a variety of disciplines—in sociology, history, religion, and literature— she seemed not always to remember that her writing had another different but critically important source: the struggles of her mothers, her sisters, her friends. Moreover, many of the vitally important problems she was probing lay outside the scholars' usual endeavor. Male theorists rarely concerned themselves with women's experiences of love and sexuality, for instance, or of marriage and motherhood, or of painful inequalities in most family roles. Understandably such matters would be difficult to package neatly, or to explain with standard principles of proof or logic, particularly since powerful emotions so often interferred with critical awareness of destructive social patterns that were assumed to be women's natural lot. For Gilman also, women's issues were rooted in passion and emotion—anger intermixed with sympathy for women, pride undermined by shame, delight in perceiving women's toughness, but resentment that each woman experienced isolation and estrangement even though so often the stories of their lives converged. Privately and separately each woman had to grope for answers—each confronting debilitating gender definitions, each mapping out her own rebellious course, too often each searching for self-respect alone. In *Women and Economics,* Gilman attempted to provide some explanations and solutions. But to portray the depth of women's hardships, to expose their losses, to applaud their strength—understandably this would occasionally elude the standard principles of scientific theory. It would necessitate an appreciation of complexity and circularity instead, an approach resonating with spontaneous originality and commonsense integrity, and resonating also with memories of conflicts and battles she had experienced herself.

* * * * *

Whereas Gilman's first few days of writing *Women and Economics* were spent in the quiet Belmont setting, her next extended stay was in Providence, Rhode Island. Providence was "home" for Gilman, a place of "happy" memories but a place of some grimly disappointing ones as well. Emotionally she would find herself returning to the sense of isolation in her childhood, to her early loss of Martha's friendship,[17] and to the disastrous years of marriage and young motherhood. And although the uninterrupted peaceful Belmont setting may well have inspired the more logical, scientific sections of the *Women and Economics* manuscript, the family memories of Providence, Rhode Island, posed an intellectually demanding challenge of another sort. Reconfronting close-to-home relationships, she focused less on abstract evolutionary theory to buttress and legitimize her public writing and more on autobiographical conundrums that still bothered and perplexed her.[18]

It was a courageous undertaking, this going back to Providence, giving texture and conviction to her formal *Women and Economics* theories, returning privately to memories that were emotionally more vivid, personally more tangled and complex. Charlotte wrote to Houghton, "Neither I, nor any of my friends, neighbors or relatives had families I thought desirable," except perhaps for "one or two isolated instances," that is, the Roland Hazard family in Peacedale, Rhode Island, or her Aunt Emily Hale's in Boston. These were the "first families that made any impression on my young mind as being agreeable institutions," with "all the sweetness and pleasantness of family life that made me feel as if—well as if I'd missed something."[19] Or, after visiting another set of relatives: "I can remember how I used to come to Xmas times here; and be jolly and bright and keep them all laughing, and then go home to my cold third story room—be at peace at last—and cry." Reexperiencing family memories as a means of sharpening her feminist perspectives, Gilman thus was finding poignant grounding for her public theories, autobiographical experience writ large. Her nightmare was emerging now in formal writing, but to be exposed to public scrutiny, it would be presented in more abstract form. As *Women and Economics* phrased it, some people seem to be "so constituted as not to fit existing conditions" and "cry out against them" in "sharp and painful consciousness." Most people, by contrast, do not even notice. They "become accustomed to the most disadvantageous conditions" and "are not pleased with those who do."[20] Or, as she put it privately to Houghton:

These folks tire me by the absolute limitation of their lives. They always did, when I was a girl. All the people . . . were such—a drag, not a help. And they all thought, and still think me "queer." I am amusing to listen to, and they are good to me—I *think* a little pityingly—with that cheerful condescension of the contented practical person for the theorist. . . . So I don't feel my best happiness with them.

Charlotte was staying, in Providence, at the home of her mother's half sister, a "brave and sweet and steady" woman, who is "paralyzed and lies placid and sweet in her bed." "I quite admire her," Charlotte wrote to Houghton, "meeting age and poverty and weakness and criticism with so strong a face," but "I couldn't do what she does—not a week of it." More importantly, the illness and paralysis revived some all-too recent memories of nursing Mary Perkins in her dying, understandably with some feelings of resentment and regret.[21] As a divorced woman, a single head of household, Mary Perkins had supported two children by running a day school, taking in boarders, sharing expenses with women relatives and friends. And although in early years Gilman had resented her mother's self-protective coldness, her discipline, her restrictive narrowness, more recently she had come to recognize her mother's strength.[22] She admired her sheer survival skills in overcoming problems which a lot of women faced: economic dependence, unsatisfying jobs, a painful shattering of the romantic myth that men necessarily would lovingly support their wives. Theoretically, abstractly, Gilman had talked about the destructive effects of "combining the sex relation with the economic relation." But as she reconnected with the "ingenious cruelty" suffered by so many women, the *Women and Economics* writing became more poignant and direct. Consider the "mis-made marriages," the "million broken hearts which must let all life pass, unable to make any attempt to stop it," she wrote; consider the "long chapter of patient, voiceless, dreary misery in the lives of women." As long as marriage was a woman's "means of livelihood," of course it was not based on love or caring. It was a relation "enforced by law in return for the functional service of the woman, the 'duties of wife and mother.'" For "the young girl, . . . marriage is the one road to fortune, to life." It is her "proper sphere, her divinely ordered place, her natural end. It is what she is born for, what she is trained for, what she is exhibited for."[23]

To make matters worse, most mothers did not prepare their daughters for future disappointments—predictably so because they themselves did not understand themselves. As *Women and Economics* phrased it, "With very few exceptions, the mother gives her daughter no warning or prevision of what life holds for her, and so lets innocence and ignorance go on perpetuating sickness and sin and pain through ceaseless generations." For mothers themselves were "ashamed" even of their motherhood, "unable to explain it, . . . lying to their children about the primal truths of life." No wonder the pernicious "falseness" of the "love" relation, the "marriage of convenience" which "the world has always hated." And no wonder, too, that the ideal goals of marriage— the "wide, deep, true, and lasting love which is the highest good to individual human beings"— had become fundamentally corrupt.[24]

As Gilman's formal writings intermingled with memories of her mother's struggles, they intermingled also with memories of her own disastrous relationship with Walter Stetson and of her own experiences of marriage and young motherhood. "Pain pain pain, till my mind has given way. O blind and cruel! Can *Love* hurt like this?" she had written just months before their separation.[25] Or, as she put it in her autobiographical short story, "The Yellow Wallpaper," he "does not know how much I really suffer. He knows there is no *reason* to suffer, and that satisfies him."[26] After all, as Walter Stetson once had put it, good women were expected to be gentle, sweet and caring—not strong and self-assertive. They were to be as "dough to the kneader or clay to the potter, to be fashioned according to love's will."[27] Male rationality and independence was thus contrasted to "attractive" female tenderness and caring, just as her father's intellectual ambition was "justifiably" contrasted to her "good" mother's more passive, duty-oriented style. No wonder Charlotte finally decided: "I don't like to be here much." "I'm not writing well . . ., and things kind of press on my mind. I'd like to have grown up in a different atmosphere." Or again, "Not feeling very scrumptious this morning," she wrote Houghton. "When the wheel turns round, as my wheel always does, . . . I begin to get uneasy. . . . Which foolishness please excuse—mark it with a big M. for Morbid—and forget it forthwith."

What these letters show, I think, is Gilman's struggle with some ironic implications of her theory. By focusing on the destructive effects of women's subjugation, by emphasizing women's victim status, she had unwittingly circled back to gender definitions that undermined her own confidence and strength. And while at times she was proud and affirming of her own and other women's courageous and resistant spirit, as she remembered now the painful experiences in Providence and as she realized her growing ties to Houghton, she sometimes apologetically concluded that femininity meant weakness, that masculinity meant preeminence and strength, and that as a woman, the price of strength and nonconformity was apparently too high.[28]

> I *feel* most like a soldier in a seventy year's war. Sometimes bitterly depressed, often defeated, . . . but . . . boasting a well earned skill in handling my weapons;— that's the way I *feel*.
> . . . Except of course when I have to acknowledge and wrestle with a woman's weaknesses.

Given pressure of the standard sex-role definitions, Gilman seemed to feel she only had two options: either she must blame herself for wrestling with a "woman's weaknesses" or conclude she was unfeminine and thus not capable of love. In a flash of inspiration she wrote half seriously to Houghton: "I only wish I was your grandma or great aunt or—I have it! An invalid sister that you simply *had* to have around all the time!!!" Understandably, on the one hand she would try to render the relationship less threatening, less passionate, less sexually explosive, and on the other, she felt attracted to the kind of warmth and caring she felt she had lacked for years.

As is true for many women, the choice had been a cruel one: of being independent and thus "repellant," or of loving Houghton and therefore becoming "feminine" and weak. "I feel hot and angry and ashamed," she wrote to Houghton, for "as you may have seen I am getting exceedingly fond of you. . . . And I don't like it. . . . It makes me unreasonable—sensitive—disagreeable—absurd." "I tell you truly Houghton I'm *not* a nice person to be close to."

Letters: September 1 through October 12, 1897

7.20 or thereabouts A.M. Wed.
Sept. lst. 1897
Belmont N.H.

Pleasing Cousin,
    I wish I could send you some of the cool sweet freshness of the morning I have just been out in—the early dewy morning walking down soft woodroads in company with—? a small white bull dog!
    A very friendly and agreeable little bull dog. "Doctor" by name, who regards me with favor.
    I went out with an object—blackberries. Fat shiny big sweet blackberries, droves of 'em. It was fine to wander about and eat 'em—with no demanding six quart pail beside me! The road was soft and good and when it was down hill I ran and galloped and leaped like an ancient horse in unexpected pastures—somewhat stiffly, but with genuine enjoyment.
    Yesterday I began the Book! Not a great beginning, but still a beginning. . . .

10.30 A.M. [Sept. 1, 1897]

    Ha ha! I have finished the first chapter—forty pages! About 4000 words. It feels good. This first one is all to establish the fact of the economic dependence of the human female on the male. Does it too, I think. Now for the rest of it.

8.10 P.M.

    And with that I went out and played tennis with the Titian-haired Miss Hackett! At first I couldn't remember a thing, but soon found myself doing good straight overhand service, and even returning a ball now and then. We both forgot the score, and I was soon tired, but it did seem good . . .

Just think—two straight mornings of clearheaded work! I'm proud. . . .

. . . granting all you say of both Bellamy's books, the fact remains that that kind of laborious detailed explanation of exactly how things are going to be appeals to the mass of American minds. They like it. It makes things seem clear and real to them. . . .

I can not tell you how it delights me to have you good to people. No service to me could ever give me the keen appreciative pleasure that your service to others gives. I love people for what they are rather than for what they are to me. An inferior person devoted to me and neglectful of others, does not warm my heart at all in comparison with a superior person doing what he ought, and utterly regardless of his attitude to me. Some are not thus. I have not before known a man who was at once so absolutely desirous to do his whole duty in the world and so clever and able in the execution of his desires. And I keep finding out new things you do, and know that there are many I never shall find out. You are a comfort. . . .

8.45 P.M. Thurs. Sept. 2nd. [1897]

. . . Such a good day! Such a good good day! My second chapter is done. Thirty-five hundred words I wrote this morning, in three hours! Three hours straight clear brain work—and no ill effects that I can see. Then I went out with Florence and walked a little, eating delicious blackberries. Then dinner. Then sat about and talked some. Then tennis, played two sets— and really got in some very good shots considering. They say I will make a good player. You should see me jump over the net. (It is sagged very low.) Then I rested and talked and told stories with Mrs. Hackett and Florence. Then we all went out blackberrying, and I picked two quarts and was happy. Then supper. Then we sat on the piazza and talked, watching the dull rich glow die out over the pale hills, and the yellow half moon sink slowly through the violet sky. . . .

And now I've a few moments left to talk to you—and am so glad I've got you to talk to! . . .

But you mustn't make fun of me! I said I shouldn't write to you much this week and I haven't. One letter a week is scarce for me. . . . Can't fool away time and brain power on letters to aged youths of thirty years while I am turning out [manuscript] at the rate of twelve hundred words an hour!

. . . You are a most excellent person to go around with. I think I am taking more comfort with you than I have since the days of Martha Luther— my dear girl friend of '77–'81. And as I perceive how good and satisfactory some kinds of companionship are, I marvel backwards at other kinds; and wonder in my secret heart if I am such an incompatible wretch after all. However this is an unprofitable meditation. . . .

. . . I missed you upon leaving, and had hard work not to write to you every time I sat down. You seem very near somehow—a kind of background to most of my thinking when I'm not at work.

8.40 or 50 A.M. Thurs. Sept. 2nd. [1897]

. . . A big corner front room, with four windows; looking on one side over an irregular green with a tennis court; and on the other far far off toward the sunsetting—hills blue and green, covered with trees—covered with grass—covered with faint low clouds.

It's a lovely place to write. An old farm house. . . .

Present family: The Grandmother and a very much attached grey son. His wife, Mrs. Isabelle Hackett. Her daughter, a fair sweet stern young damsel—a la Beatrice as it were—of gleaming abundant tresses, columnar throat and round little figure.

Daughter-in-law-(son absent at present—Prof. of music in Northwestern University at Chicago) and last but not least, the Baby.

Between them all I am simply assailed by the desire to write. A Family—a very much familified family like this—simply sets me wild. . . .

Sun. Sept. 5th. 12.30 P.M.

. . . It is astonishing how many times a day I incline to write to you. (Which being analyzed is reducible to very simple elements.) I am now about to reread a fat little bunch of your letters, and cast them into the basket! No use—I *cannot* carry things. . . .

The book rests—149 pages—about 1500 words. One morning I wrote 4000 words in three hours. That is good fast work. The words seem to hang together very fairly too, but I can't see the forest because of the trees—it may be all wrong somehow. . . .

I think—maybe—when I've got all written that I can I'll send on the mss. to you to read before I see you. Yes, I guess I'd better, for there will be hours of reading aloud in it, and I'm sure I couldn't sit still and watch you read it. And if we "looked over"—well I want you to give an undivided attention to this book—I don't even want to divide it with myself.

(A "situation"—fine—for [a] short story. Woman—intense, self-conscious—jealous. Writes book. . . . Lover—anxious to please. Woman gives lover book to read—*resents* his preoccupation in book. Lover seeks to pacify her and neglects book. *Resents that!* Wouldn't it be funny. Howells could do it finely.)

So some time toward the end of the month look out for a large dose of mss!

You poor young one! I do have qualms from time to time. But you are in for it now.

And having thus far spoken I revert to your letters. There! I've read 'em all over and torn 'em all up—which was really an effort. . . .

Such agreeable letters. Over which I smile, and chuckle, and look out of the window and wonder—various things. . . .

5. P.M. . . .

How I would like to have had you along—various times . . . this summer.

On berryings and such like. I keep thinking on all sorts of occasions, how nicely you would fit in—what a pleasant addition you would be. And what pleases me most is to know that whoever I was with you'd be nice to them *too*—and the forlorner they were the nicer you would be to 'em. . . .

Mon. 10.30 or so. A.M. Sept. 6th. [1897]. . . .

. . . you are just supernaturally nice, and I've given up trying to understand it.

I do not mean that you seem to me as a colossal figure of nobility and virtue—remarkable among men. But the things that you do and the kind of person you are—these facts please me; please me over and over, with a funny little sense of satisfaction and delight.

It is a most novel and charming sensation. I have loved many people, in various ways, mostly because they needed it, but sometimes from other causes. As to men folks I have told you of my having taken them in chapters as it were—a serial story without, unfortunately, any connection to it— mere chapters begun and ended piecemeal.

But with each instance there were heavy disadvantages—things that of course, one loving, loves to bear with and understand. But the astonishing thing about you is that I don't have to "bear" at all—or to make allowance for and try to help.

You seem to be all made as it were, and made to fit, and I regard you with ceaseless wonder. I expect it is the "blood is thicker than water" theory, now first presenting itself to me in pleasing guise. . . .

Perhaps as we know each other longer I shall find wide stretches of disagreement, and relapse into a sense of everyday commonplace half and half sort of comfort. . . .

But as it stands, whatever your relation or lack of relation to me, I shall think of you always with sensations of pure satisfaction—because you are that kind of man. . . .

I never felt that way about anyone before, and it does taste good. I daresay it is a selfish feeling, in no way a noble feeling. I don't brag of it at all. But it feels good anyhow. I regard you with deep and sincere pleasure— am glad you are alive and the man you are.

8.45 A.M. 50 Pitman St. Providence R.I.
Wed. Sept. 8th. 1897.

Before I start anew on The Book, I self-indulgently stop to talk a bit. . . .

. . . I am now moved to begin a new course of lectures on letter writing! You mustn't make 'em so good—so satisfying and pleasant—because it grows increasingly difficult to tear 'em up; and ultimately my interstate progresses will be clogged with accumulated mss. This particular letter has simply got to remain with me awhile—I can't spare it. It means a great deal to me. Not that it is any more affectionate and jolly than many others, but from what it proves.

For instance I am satisfied absolutely and forever that you do like *me*—for the pleasure of it, and not as another piece of duty or kindness. How do I know that now? Because no amount of duty or kindness would make you choose to spend a whole morning, with luxurious dallying over new pens and exultance in solitude and opportunity, in just writing to anybody. In duty or kindness one may write, and even cover much paper; but not gloatingly devote a long spare morning to it. I may further question your judgment and taste, but the fact is established in my mind irrefutably. You like me for your own pleasure. Good. And further you touch me on my tenderest side by the genuine confidence of it. It is just *you*, talking.

I am never finally content with anyone unless I feel that certainty of touch—that it really [is] the personality I feel—not any layers of conduct and manner. I am good enough judge of literature, to say nothing of people, to feel *you*, clear, in this letter; and it makes it very dear to me. I shan't keep it all the same; in fact for that very reason.

Talk like that is between two—whatever two they may be at the moment, and oughtn't to be kept around. At least that is my feeling.

Letters are awful things to bring out at [the] wrong places.

One has a right to present what face one will to the world, and a right to show much more to one's friends; but it isn't pleasant—to my notion—to leave pieces of oneself on paper permanently. Still this doesn't apply to you keeping my letters. You're safe to keep 'em from anyone else; and in course of later years—well the thing they carry is only that I'm fond of you—and I'm not at all concerned about that.

But this letter will keep in my mind if I don't carry it in my bag for more than a month or so.

Truly it counts a lot—means more to me in some ways than all the time we've had together.

I've had always a vague undercurrent of resentfulness . . . because my own situation was so palpably adapted to call out all your good offices in my behalf. I know perfectly well that you would be just as good to me as you could even if you didn't like me much; because I needed it. Just as you'd have been good to Kate even if she wasn't a darling in her own right.

But now I feel real easy. . . .

If I should now become rich and famous and desired of all persons; and my Englishman should turn up and fill that side of things, and I had Katharine and a home—why I now feel sure that you would come to see me tolerably often and we'd play chess and whist and go to things occasionally.—I feel sure of the disinterestedness of your friendliness. And it is a great joy to me; for both as a woman and as a person I am exceedingly sensitive, at heart, about my position. So you may congratulate yourself that in six months time you have succeeded in convincing me that I am pleasant and attractive to you on other grounds than as a needy person—a "distressed female." And with this I must leave you though I don't want to— and write further on The Book. . . .

3. P.M. [Sept. 8, 1897]. . . .

I can't stop to argue out the work and wages thing now—it must keep, for talk. It's too long and solid. I want to keep my brains for the morning work and write to you only with my—well, heart I guess. Just brains enough to keep from being silly.

And I've a strong suspicion that since so much of my limited amount of brain power *has* gone into the morning's work that your letters have had more candy than meat in them! I must reform. Sugar is wholesome but not too much. . . .

I am still feeling well, better for my New Hampshire week. I'd like to have stayed there longer. . . .

I don't like to be here much, but can stand it for a week I guess. Then Hingham and my dear old friend Martha.

These folks tire me by the absolute limitation of their lives. They always did, when I was a girl. All the people I had in Providence were such—a drag, not a help. And they all thought, and still think me "queer." I am amusing to listen to, and they are good to me—I *think* a little pityingly— with that cheerful condescension of the contented practical person for the theorist.

So I don't feel my best happiness with them. . . .

Sat. Sept. 11th. 1897.
50. Pitman St. Prov. R.I. . . .

Not feeling very scrumptious this morning. I do not propose to spend another two days on an inferior chapter, but to postpone the completion of my great work till next week at Hingham. . . .

Feeling well I write—write easily, swiftly, clearly, forcibly, interestingly.

Presently I don't feel so well. Never mind, say I, work you must! and I continue to write—with conscious effort and cumulative exhaustion. And then the stuff written is not good! That's the finality of it. It's not good and I can't make it good—that which is good without effort if I feel right, no effort makes good when I don't.

So I have learned to drift—to wait—not to waste energy and delay improvement by trying when I can't—and generally to be a most irresponsible and lazy person.

And *I* never can tell whether I might have behaved better or whether my patience and adaptability have saved my brain. I am so anxious for your opinion on this book as a piece of mental work. You have a sound clear well trained brain. I want to see—apart from its opinions—how the work strikes you.

If it seems to you clear, consistent, consequent, forcible—well, it will take a load off my mind.

You must allow of course for my loose and easy manner of construction; for a method of putting which would not be yours, and which would not perhaps be like any treatment of a serious subject you ever saw. But, taking the stuff on its own merits, see if it impresses you as strong or weak. *And tell me the truth.*

Well——. Here are two delightful letters of yours to answer. You have caught up and got ahead of me on letters. As I gloatingly peruse these fine fat frequent epistles, I become less sensitive and apologetic over the unlooked for deluge with which I assailed you this summer. . . .

In my improved health and spirits of the end of this summer I have reviving hopes of ultimate bicycling. That you like my fair Kate so well is another feature. And, if not on bicycles, then in canoes—what's to prevent the three of us from having a lovely summer trip together sometime? Down the Connecticut or such like? Truly—I don't see why not. And *wouldn't* it be fun! . . .

Somehow I feel as if I'd carried the joke about my "attractiveness" too far. It is true as I told you, that as a girl I was unattractive—indeed repellent, to men; and that I used to wonder at it and be a bit lonely sometimes.

Once a cousin on mother's side came to see me, and played on a guitar, I remember, and commented (it has always stayed by me) on the clear white of my eyes—where they were white!

Once a brother of this cousin invited me to go to ride.

Once one of two brothers who were regular family callers, took me to the theater.

And once a foolish underwitted sort of boy used to ask me to all sorts of things—he was truly not bright.

Arthur was the only admirer I ever had in girl days.

It is equally true that within the past four years I seem to have changed in some way; and I can feel a difference in men's attitude toward me. But I don't think it's very creditable—I have an uneasy feeling that perhaps I don't behave as I ought to. I never had "an assured touch" on this ground anyhow; have always taken most comfort with women.

I told Walter once I wished he was a woman, and it seemed to hurt his feelings. I can see why now, but I didn't then.

What I do value in myself—always have—is the power to reach right across sex distinction, and be the dispassionate friend and confidant of men.

Some I have been a help to. I hope I shall not lose that power for this other foolishness.

Every time I tell you how I regard you you speak about not having done anything to deserve it—so to say. Can't you see that the things you *do* are only valuable as indication—often [a] small one, but unerring—of what you *are?* It is what you *are* that I like—the kind of man that you were by birth, were made by education, and have made yourself by a strong ceaseless sense of duty.I like that kind of man. Here again I am conscious of overdoing it— saying too much lately along this line. Must stop, lest you find it displeasing.

But I think most people err in not telling their friends how highly they regard them. You never know when anybody'll die, or you not see them again; and you never know either how the most assured person apparently may secretly long for the deep full force of *recognition*. Not approval—but recognition. To be seen, truly, and appreciated for what one *is*.

Therefore when I began to see how nobly you have lived—are living, I began to tell you so. It hasn't anything to do with your good will toward me. If you entirely dropped me I should hold the same estimate of your personal character, just as I should of your physical attractiveness—that you are sound and sweet and strong and generally as a man should be. . . .

I didn't know Aunt Emily hated to keep home.[29] And you never told me anything about Nellie. I remember her as "Sister," a tall sweet lovely girl, the center of a loving devotion from all the younger brothers and herself a fountain of the same to the whole family. I remember her especially as reading a little red stockinged Robbie out of Lane's Arabian Nights; and the boys kissing her good night, and all the sweetness and pleasantness of family life that made me feel as if—well as if I'd missed something. Their family life and that of the Hazards was a revelation to me. Such as I had seen before were not like that. . . .

But truly—your letters are getting nicer than I feel as if I could afford to have things. When the wheel turns round, as my wheel always does, and I don't have 'em any more, they'll leave too big a hole. So I begin to get uneasy and think it's time to quit drinking! Which foolishness please excuse—mark it with a big M. for Morbid—and forget it forthwith.

(My settled determination with you is to take all the comfort I can and be thankful. I always was a fool. . . .)

There—that letter's answered. You certainly are the dearest boy imaginable, and I only wish I was your grandma or great aunt or—I have it! An invalid sister that you simply *had* to have around all the time!!! However, debarred from these advantages, I will be thankful for existing relationship; and the prospect of six months more or less of having you about!

Now here I have got to the 18th page and not said a word about my visit here. I don't like it much but they are good folks and honestly glad to see me. You see my mother had a half sister on the father's side, and she has two daughters, eight & ten years older than I. . . . The half aunt is paralyzed and lies placid and sweet in her bed—cared for by a Companion.

There are two daughters and the younger one—fourteen, and dressed as short as Kate—likes me much. We sally forth of an evening, with our arms interlocked, and hop skip and jump in true infant fashion. She claims that I go faster than she does, and then I tell of how she has to support my tottering and aged steps, and we make merry accordingly. A nice child. Last night Mary & I "took tea with" The Browns, certain cousins of my mother's. A tiresome quarrelsome noisy goodnatured set. I never thought much of 'em but we were always good friends. . . .

. . . I've got to go and see a lot of people. And that's about all.

(I'm not writing well here. It's hot, and things kind of press on my mind. I'd like to have grown up in a different atmosphere.)

I can remember how I used to come to Xmas times here; and be jolly and bright and keep them all laughing, and then go home to my cold third story room—be at peace at last—and cry. I think my life would have been smoother if I'd grown up with my father's side of the home. . . .

10.20 A.M. Sunday the 12th. Sept. 97. . . .

. . . at Dr. [E.B.] Knight's last evening. . . . Dr. Knight was our physician and is Walter's best friend. They like me too. He has most of Walter's pictures at his home, and I saw them. O they are beautiful! There are some there that I really would buy if I could—and that is a great deal for me to say. I love this lot particularly because it is my California; but he has improved greatly in his work, and they are most lovely.[30]

I am so glad of all his growth and gain. If there were no other reason there is Kate—and there are plenty beside that. He is interpreting the mystery and majesty of California as no one else has—or will I guess. I am so glad. . . .

50 Pitman St. Providence R.I.
Tues. Sept 14th. 1897. . . .

The little mother requires to be "babied" rather than "jollied" I find—requires lots of it. And usually does what she wants to all the same.

But she is so brave and sweet and steady—meeting age and poverty and weakness and criticism with so strong a face, that I quite admire her. I couldn't do what she does—not a week of it. . . .

Wed. Sept. 15 [1897] 4.10 P.M. Parker House. Boston. . . .

Monday—(and also Sun. eve.) I went to see people; and to see more of Walter's pictures in the Art Club, and School of Design. They are great.

I was dilating on them to one of my cousins, Sunday night. "Ah!" said she: "it makes the old love come back after all, doesn't it!" I was wroth, but then she is that kind of a cousin. . . .

8.25 or 30 P.M. Sat. Sept. 18th. 1897.
Hingham, Mass. . . .

It seemed very good to get your letter this morning. I had not had one since Tuesday—and it seemed very long somehow. If I don't write to you every few days it seems to leave out something in the way of friendly converse. . . .

Thurs[day] A.M. I started in on Chap. VI, but made little headway. Friday A.M. I went on, but tore up again and again. If my work doesn't run easily it is no good—I simply can't do it at all. But yesterday P.M. and evening I read the stuff to Martha, got a good coherent grip of the whole thing, and started in again this morning with better luck—only 2000 words, but good.

Martha is my dear old girl friend that I was once so happy with. She is fond of me yet, and I of her. And the children like me, especially Margaret— near eleven. How I should enjoy having Katharine here! . . .

The Hales—and the Hazards—were the first families that made any impression on my young mind as being agreeable institutions. My ideals as a child were of fairy places and wondrous powers and privileges (always philanthropic in their use!) but no family ties were included. And my principal personal ambition as I grew older was some day to be able to be alone. . . .

Neither I, nor any of my friends, neighbors or relatives had families I thought desirable, till I went to Aunt Emily's at about fifteen and one or two isolated instances did not much alter my feeling. I do not argue that family snags *must* be—but I have seen them pretty often. . . .

Sun. 19th [September, 1897]. . . .

Yesterday we took a long lovely walk hereabouts, in the bright September weather, Martha and I and a Mr. Blackman. I walked on the stone walls, ran down the hills in shady woodland roads, hopped over fences or squeezed through 'em with nimble speed—behaved in short as becomes an eminent literary person with a load of years and a lame ankle.

The roadside was all beaded with barberries and wild rose hips, the marshes flamed with crimson samphire, and the purple flowers and yellow flowers were so good as to bloom close to each other everywhere. And I just wished you were along side—not excluding the amiable Mr. Blackman, but leaving him to walk with Mrs. Lane! . . .

Tues. Sept. 21st. 1897.
Hingham, Mass. . . .

I came in [to Boston] on the 9.20 with Martha, and met Mr. Sylvester Baxter at Doll & Richards. With him I called on Walter Page at the Atlantic office. Mr. Page was most cordial—most respectful, and gratefully accepted the poem I had altered to suit him—taking my New York address that he might send me a Check! (I suppose.)

You will have to introduce me at your bank so I can get Checks cashed this winter! Also he took a lot of others to look over.

He talked to me as if—as if I really was somebody!

Then Mr. Baxter took me to his publishers—Small, Maynard & Co. And Co. was there. Who do you think Co. is? *Bliss Carman*! Wasn't I pleased to see him! They are all young fellows, Small a mere boy, and they regard my work with the eye of favor and want to publish 'em. At present they are publishing Whitman's works.[31],[32],[33]

I, it appears, come next! I am to call again next Sat. morning, and they will make a definite proposition. Then I can see Mr. Ripley Hitchcock and talk quite big. It all seemed very nice and stimulating—I enjoyed it. Then I called on Mr. Edwin Meade at The New England office.[34] He was delighted to see me—being a fellow Socialist, and having suffered much for my sake in publishing The Yellow Wallpaper—of which he spoke in extravagant terms. The Yellow Wallpaper and Similar Cases—these have made me apparently. He wants anything I'll send him, so if I can turn out some small stuff that I'm willing to part with for $2.50 a page—there's a market. Bring on that bank—I'll open an account![35]

Then I said goodbye to Mr. Baxter and went into the Woman's Journal office and had a fine visit with Alice Stone Blackwell—who thinks highly of me.

Altogether a fine morning. . . .

Friday A.M. Oct. 1st '97.
Norwich Conn.[36]

[*She is currently staying with Mrs. Rudd in Norwich, Conn.*] . . . I intended to go on with the book, but found more important business in talking with Mrs. Rudd.

That afternoon she and I walked abroad, and again yesterday. . . .

Evenings I converse in a varied and improving manner with the awe-stricken family assembled.

The youngest members have given me no peace, crying "kiss the wall!" at intervals, usually right after a meal; until finally at a proper time I did "lean over backward and kiss the wall"—which is one of my feats.

How they knew of it I cannot tell, but they clamored for it as soon as I came.

I shall be glad however when this visit is done, and I return to the bosom of my family in New York. (This refers to my step family—not to my Entire Family! Not that I wish to deny some pleasure at returning to an approximate and respectful distance from my Entire Family's properly starched and silk-lappelled front—but I would not wish to so eagerly express it!)

I am pleased that your Aunts regard me with the eye of favor as to looks. I have however seen no more of them. They have not asked me to tea. I imagine that they couldn't without Mrs. R[oyall] & perhaps don't want to— I know not, I. And also I imagine—in a vague way, that from the point of view of Aunts my being handsome is really no attraction—rather otherwise! And again, it strikes me oddly and freshly—always does—when anybody calls me handsome.

Of course I know, intellectually, that I have good points; but the face I see in the glass does not often give me an impression of beauty, and the feeling I carry about with me—which is what counts most—is so far removed from a sense of personal beauty that as I say I'm always surprised when I give that impression.

I *feel* most like a soldier in a seventy year's war. Sometimes bitterly depressed, often defeated, long imprisoned, scarred and wounded beyond recognition but not crippled past all usefulness; boasting a well earned skill in handling my weapons; rich in the tricks and shifts of an old campaigner weather beatened and coarsened by long exposure and a bit hard on the sensitiveness of new security—that's the way I *feel*. And then when one says "Why what a handsome women you are!" I feel funny—sort of pass my hand over my face and wonder.

The mental attitude—the basis and habit of thought of my life are so far removed from being any kind of woman—let alone a handsome one. Except of course when I have to acknowledge and wrestle with a woman's weaknesses. . . .

I forgot to say that I liked your Aunts immensely. They are so—fit. They belong. They are everything they ought to be and are well placed according to their needs. And it did my heart good to see you sitting there—at home, and loved so well. It makes me feel warm and comfortable about you. You dear boy! . . .

Talk to me of "*my* book by Mr. Ward!" No you don't! Go and plunge into this notion and irrational extravagance and then expect me to accept the responsibility! Why man it may be years before I am able to read such a book! Maybe never! . . .

Yes Tues. P.M. was our best walk. I'd liked to have sat up there on those sunny rocks with you for hours. You are a very pleasing person to be with.

And seeing the places where you used to be and hearing of all the things you used to do and play, brought back the cousin that I knew long ago very clearly, and made me feel most tenderly to him.

As to your next decade—with me in it—God send I may do you no harm my dear Cousin. I have thought of you much and earnestly this last six months; for as I have told you, though my life is full and rich and strong and happy, the foreground is quite empty. You are at present the only figure in it.

Katharine even is not in the foreground in the sense I mean—of intimacy and interrelation. For [to] keep open and thrillingly responsive to the thought of her would be, to my temperament, death. Or a mind unhinged. I cannot bear any more leaks and losses and pains.

But you are pleasantly and naturally close. You have a right to be by relationship and old association.

Perhaps I shall be of some good to you in opening up things you had not thought to think about. Perhaps some good also in a most genuine and tender affection—it is nice to have people fond of one! I know you are a very great comfort to me.

And I have most faithfully prayed that no harm may come to you from me, but that I may be useful to your life and live to see you "well homed" and happy, a husband and a father and the steady noble soul you will be anyway—a big bright pleasant spot for me to think on wherever I may be.

So here goes for our decade—or another six months of it anyhow! . . .

Brewer, His Room
18 West 32nd St. [New York]
10.15 P.M. Sunday Oct. 3rd. 1897. . .

[*The following letter is written after Charlotte and Houghton have had an evening together in New York*]

I feel somehow as if I had been behaving abominably—as if I owed you an apology—or somebody did. Surely things weren't as bad as this last winter.

Am I grown wickeder—that things look worse to me? Or, having come from a series of visits among gentlefolk of sorts, does "home" seem a little—queerer, than it did last year.

I'm glad to be back . . . but tonight I feel hot and angry and ashamed and disappointed.

I don't want to be hasty, but it seems to me that I can hardly spend the winter in this environment.

I fancy it is you who make part of the difference.

Last year I simply lived in my room, and when I came down stairs did it to make myself agreeable to others—caring little what they did. Now, having a sense of personal relation to you, and liking to meet you on levels quite other than these, I feel as I had been tripped up and thrown down stairs; amiably enough 'tis true, but none the less grovelingly.

I'm cross. I'm puckered on the inside and it doesn't feel good.

Now the cause is, as it usually is when one is uncomfortable, a personal feeling—the wanting of something for oneself.

But I see no reason why I should not want to spend rational evenings with you—and with others.

I should be ashamed to ask any friend to share such entertainment. And here I sputter it all off to you; not at all like a guide, philosopher and friend, but like any other irascible person.

No harm I guess to come down from my eminence occasionally. And yet how can the little girl help it—with such training, and such surroundings! The poor child has no place to sleep but that couch in the corner there—cannot go to bed till all are gone—has *no* privacy or peace—ever! I'd die.

I hated to have you shoved out so, as it were—between the sleepy sister and the visibly waiting brother, but I was not sorry after all. . . .

Well—I'll see what I can do about rooms. I may find a neighboring house—with a good room and a decent parlor. . . . Now write me a nice big-brotherly letter, do, and tell me you understand and don't mind.

Truly I feel personally mortified—yet can't quite see why—*I* didn't marry 'em! . . .

Near 10. A.M. Wed. Oct. 12th. [1897]
My Room. 18 West 32nd St.
New York City. . .

I am not quite myself yet—had a very bad night—lay awake for hours, and even wept—so low were my spirits.

I should have mentioned to you that Sat. was a very tiring day to me—and probably that is the reason I didn't hold out better Sunday. You see I went to see Father in the morning—which is always a strain; hurried back, had lunch and nap and went to that very tiresome lecture I told you of—

. . . called on Mrs. Stanton & dined with her, and flew back again to a temperance evening here. . . .

Now as to my horrid behavior last night.

First, please allow a large permanent margin for my behaving unpleasantly, and be thankful when I don't. As I have told you from the first you touch me on my weak side—my defenseless side—my grievously injured side.

To most people, meeting them as I do, I can behave nicely, and as you have observed they mostly like me. I can be wise and kind and patient and steady and cheerful and all sorts of nice things.

But as soon as any one comes near me and takes hold, I wobble awfully. Now as you may have seen I am getting exceedingly fond of you—even more than I had expected to be. And I don't like it. It makes me unreasonable. It makes me feel—where I don't want to feel; and think, where I don't want to think. It sort of wakes me up where I'm dead, or where, if I'm not dead, I ought to be.

Now I can't afford to be fond of anybody in that sort of way—man woman or child. I can't afford to want things. I do not mean that I am flinging the remnants of my aged heart at your head—by no means. I shall go off next spring, Heavens knows where, and peacefully leave you behind—as I have left so many things behind. I'm handy at that.

But being here, and being so undeservedly kind to me all the time—and being, to your sorrow—my "entire family"—why it brings out all that is worst and weakest in me instead of what is best and strongest. It makes me unreasonable—sensitive—disagreeable—absurd. It makes me want to be petted and cared for—me!

And then all this makes me very mad; and I say "Go to! I'll get out of this in short order!" I've been telling you this sort of thing since we began. Of course it would be wiser if instead of talking about it and all the time going right on and being an old goosess(!) I should remain such reasonable distance from my beguiling cousin as to avoid this disagreeable commotion among my fragments.

But there you are—so close and convenient as it were—so increasingly satisfactory and comforting—so I have just helped myself to you and been grateful.

But now I'm beginning to act horridly and am quite likely to go on—worse.

I tell you truly Houghton I'm *not* a nice person to be close to. I do very well at long range. You see—forgive my endless repetitions—forgive me anyway for being such a nuisance—I *am* a wreck on that side of me; the inside, the personal side; and you come dreadfully close to it.

Now if you were an old party, happily married and settled with worlds of patience and experience and so large a background of personal happiness that you could easily spare a little stamping ground for me to have occasional fits in—why that would be different.

But you're not. You're a most pleasing youth, and so more than anxious to do your duty by everybody that I don't see as you have any "background of personal happiness" at all.

And here am I returning your unvarying courtesy and kindness with this offensive spectacle! And then I get madder—and then am more disagreeable—and so on.

Now don't you think you'd better cut me off with a shilling?

You see I can't promise to behave better. I shall probably behave worse. And you'll find it a most trying occupation—getting along with such; you'll get your feelings hurt, and your temper lost more than once.

This being a futile and foolish letter I think you'd better waste basket it at once—I know I'm being foolish but my head's bad and I can't do any better.

I surely don't need to tell you how grateful I am for all your kindness to me. . . .

4

"Letters Are Like Morning Prayers to Me": 29 October 1897–22 April 1898

In *Women and Economics* Gilman had explained the destructive effects of women's subjugation. Yet in her private letters she illustrates the agonizing tensions she and many other women faced in trying to resist them. Because, supposedly, creativity and femininity were mutually exclusive, she experienced a mounting fear as she confronted her growing love for Houghton, and depression as she struggled with the fear. "I'm principally ashamed of myself," she wrote Houghton. From "Child to Mother—Sister—Brother—Father—Lover—Husband—Friend"—she had never had a "satisfied love," except with Martha Luther. They had "all gone wrong somehow—like a stopped sneeze," and left her with a "choked thwarted fiercely unreconciled feeling—an accumulated revolt" against the devastating price of loneliness. "Am . . . miserable," she wrote, and "don't know why."[1] Insanity, some would call it; "madness" was the label she sometimes used herself. It was as though her conflicts had no social causes; she was simply suffering from the "bucks and plunges" of a "misbehaving brain." "The spring is broken," she wrote to Houghton. "I *can* not suffer any more." And with "my serene views of how life works I'm not even worried about my 'work'—if I don't do it somebody else will." "Dying is the blessedest thing I've had to think of since I was twenty one."[2]

Depression notwithstanding, Gilman continued working at a steady pace. She had started *Women and Economics* on 31 August 1897. And on 10 October her diary entry reads: *"Finish book. 356 pages."*[3] Her work had focused on the destructive origins and implications of the patriarchal family structure. Yet courageously, if not intentionally, she had spent almost the entire time of first-draft writing in private family settings which compelled her to test and apply the theories to herself. In addition to her three-week stay in Providence, she had visited her Aunt Emily Hale's family in Boston; she had spent a day with Martha Luther in Hingham, Massachusetts; a week with friends in Norwich; and for the last few days of writing, according to her letters anyway, saw almost no one but her "family" in New York. She was staying at her stepmother's crowded boarding house, but with "*no* privacy or peace," she complained to Houghton. She was making trips to see her father; that, too, always was "a strain."[4] And in the evenings, she was spending time with Houghton, which often made her feel discouraged and confused. It was almost as though for first-draft writing the private struggles necessarily were paramount. To explain the complex forces that had crushed the spirits of so many other women, she had to explore the ways in which they also crushed her own. The result, she wrote to Houghton, had not been "all gravestones, but some, and some kind of trap-door-stones that keep things down. When the will-strength, or brain-strength, or whatever it is that keeps me happy and steady and brave, gives out, up hop all these buried things, dead and alive."

With "brain-strength" combating "buried" needs, theories confronting "fiercely unreconciled" emotions—the power of the letters emerges from Gilman's efforts to explore and document the spontaneous "revolt." In fact, her solace in the midst of this and other crises always was her private writing. "Perhaps you think all these little letters absurd," she wrote to Houghton. But they are "like morning prayers to me": a means of exploring contradictions and a means also of gradually learning not to blame herself. "The world is a great garden full of lovely wonderworking laws," she continued. "But the 'transition woman' of this age has a difficult position, and I've met my share of the difficulties. . . . A few generations more and it will be easier. And I know I've helped it on a little. Every little counts."[5] Or as *Women and Economics* puts it, "The main struggle now" is with our "heavy legacy," and "with the distorted nature" in ourselves.

> The soul of woman must speak through the long accumulations of her intensified sex-nature, through the uncertain impulses of a starved and thwarted class. She must recognize that she is handicapped. She must understand her difficulty, and meet it bravely and firmly.[6]

By mid-November, Gilman was beginning to "recover," beginning, that is, to reaffirm her pioneering role. She quoted at length from Olive Schreiner's *Dreams* to affirm the "transition woman" concept. And the next day she took a trip to Boston to reconnect with her women's movement friends. She felt inspired and energized by those at the Boston *Woman's Journal* office, for instance, by giving lectures in the Boston-Brookline area and by visiting for several days in the home of the woman's movement activist, Alice Stone Blackwell. "Good bed—good meals—good house—good people," Charlotte wrote to Houghton, and they "like me."[7] They "run the paper (*Woman's Journal*), you know.—Lucy Stone (now dead) & Henry Blackwell and their daughter Alice." A "fine visit," Charlotte wrote to Houghton, or, to use the *Women and Economics* phrasing, an inspiring sense of "splendid sisterhood," a reminder or the energizing legacy of "women who have battled and suffered for a half a century, forcing their way, with sacrifices never to be told, into the field of freedom so long denied them—not for themselves alone, but for one another."[8]

According to her letters, Gilman's "recovery" thus accompanied her return to the Boston/New York political community. Instead of the self-imposed isolation of her first-draft *Women and Economics* writing, she began to meet with political colleagues at the New York Women's Penn Club, the Fabian Study Club, the Social Reform Club, and the "Nurse's Settlement" on Henry Street.[9] She met with philanthropist reformer Josephine Shaw Lowell, with William Dean Howells, with settlement house workers Jane Addams and Lillian Wald.[10] In short, she was not only sharing the excitement of contemporary political discussion—on socialism, on suffrage, on antipoverty campaigns—but she was also lecturing for local political and social groups occasionally, revising and rearranging *Women and Economics* chapters, and drafting articles and poems besides. "How Many Poor!" "On the Anti-Suffragists," "His Own Labor," "A Man Must Live," "Inequality," "When Socialism Began"—these were just some of the poems and articles she was writing. And it no doubt helped revive her spirits to find a number of journals enthusiastically accepting and applauding them. In the next few months, not only would her work be published in the Boston *Woman's Journal,* but also in Charles Lummis's *Land of Sunshine,* the *Kansas Suffrage Reveille,* the *American Fabian,* and the Chicago *Social Democrat.*[11]

Even more importantly by this juncture, Gilman had good reason to believe that *Women and Economics* also would be published and well received.[12] During her September visit to Boston, she had taken the manuscript to Sylvester Baxter of Small, Maynard & Company, the original publishers of her *In This Our World* anthology. "They regard my work with the eye of favor and want to publish 'em," she wrote to Houghton. "At present they are publishing Whitman's works. . . . I, it appears, come next!" And in November she wrote: "They've taken it!—the Book—! They'll get it out in the spring for the Fall trade—They are duly impressed." "[W]ho wouldn't feel better to feel the opening of the gates as I begin to now?" "And of course it helps my health—would anybody's." Or as she put it in her "Thoughts and Fingerings" some weeks later:

> As poet—as author—as orator—I am being given a recognized place. . . . This means the same method as before—to see clearly and think boldly and speak wisely and well.
> . . . I must come out forever from the feelings of shame and regret. Must leave off the past more fully than ever before. Must feel and be a strong calm brave happy useful honorable woman . . . and give the world the light and hope and strength, the clear simple pleasant commonsense about life, which it so needs.[13]

During the winter months of 1898, Gilman had been struggling with a precipitous depression. According to her letters, she had been writing and lecturing forcefully and effectively, yet simultaneously she had been using her "morning prayers" reflections, her written dialogue with Houghton, as a means of healing private pains. After all, he was her only correspondent of a "purely spontaneous, natural variety," she told him. He never tried dismissing her worries and forebodings: "Don't you know when one is melancholy how aggravating it is to have people cheerfully insist there's nothing the matter?" Nor had he even helped her directly with the conflicts: "You haven't much of the imaginative faculty that enables one to reach far out and see what another person means," she admitted rather bluntly. Yet his listening had been vitally important. He had attended respectfully to her struggles and had thus inspired, as she put it in a Christmas poem, a sense of "deep" and "absolute release." With Houghton standing "solid like a post—good thing to tie to," she was "letting go" of all her "terrors," all the "remnants of a woman's pride," and thus finding herself healed. "Now that I've told you so much—shown you so much of my—catacombs," she wrote him, "You seem at once nearer and more healthfully remote." Or to use another metaphor, he had rolled "away the stone" from her "poor shamed dead broken heart" and made it "come out new and strong."

With Houghton as her audience, her inspiration, her postlike muse, Gilman had been confronting and exploring some spontaneous and powerful emotions that could not find expression in any other way: gnostic writings, some would call them, an affirmation of private sources of her understanding, a compelling route to important sources of her power. In fact, Gilman had used her letters almost as a bridge between two very different ways of knowing. Continuing to draw on and adapt the contemporary theoretical perspectives, she was also trusting intuition as a source of understanding, and emotional exploration as a source of truth. Thanks in part to the friendship correspondence, she was so "*much* better able to . . . teach and write," she told him. "I shall be a much clearer thinker . . . , a much more consistent, definite, forceful speaker, for knowing you and loving you enough to *have* to talk to you."

According to these early winter letters, Gilman had begun to sense the growing possibility of reconciling two long-term but conflicting needs—the need simultaneously to be loving and professionally effective, caring yet also committed to her work. She was beginning to hope she might have "happiness in personal relationship," she told him, beginning even to see it—"a little bit—as a kind of a permanency." Houghton was helping her professionally and financially. He was a "solid good" to Katharine. Between editing and writing sessions, they were reading Whitman poetry together, dining out occasionally, spending evenings at the theater or the opera. "A great smooth beautiful life before us—why not?" she wrote him. "Every morning I feel so rich, so happy, so proud, so—so *at ease*." And "dearest, you are in it all, under it all, with me continually," friend and inspiration for her newfound "courage and power to live and love and work."

Although Charlotte had been seeing Houghton on an almost daily basis, and perhaps surprisingly, still sending letters at a steady pace, by mid-February, for a variety of reasons, she decided that she would have to leave. For one thing, despite the stimulating opportunities New York offered for her lecturing and writing, she never liked the atmosphere of cities. She preferred a more rural, nurturing environment, the more aesthetic beauty of the countryside, the healing force of nature. She also knew that her health and happiness depended on her traveling and having time and space alone. In fact, she admitted bluntly, "I shall be almost glad . . . to leave you." "Everything is drawing together and concentrating on my work—my two years work," she continued. That "ought to settle things." "What are two years to make clear the way for such a thing as this?"

As Gilman tried explaining reasons for the separation—and to herself as well as Houghton—she focused in part on her work commitments, her need for contacts with a variety of political communities, and for the stimulation that traveling and lecturing would necessarily afford. But she also needed time and space to think through potential obstacles to marriage. For one thing, she rather unpersuasively insisted, Houghton needed the opportunity to reconsider. With no obligation, no guilt, no responsibility, "you [need] the chance, free, utterly free of the insistent pressure of my intense personality, to recover yourself." But even more importantly, she needed time to work through some hesitations of her own.

She was not bothered, as apparently he feared, by his economic status, nor by his conservative political perspectives, though she continued, occasionally, to prod him: "Do with honest prayer and effort try to spread and grow out into the big currents of our social progress" so that "at least I can feel that you *care* about the main interests of my life and sympathize with my purposes if not my actions."[14] More importantly, she honestly admitted, she needed to be certain that marriage would not interfere with the "duty I owe my people and my God, . . . the work I have to do on earth." "[S]omething has come to me which I dare balance for a moment with my work!" And yet "I would choose the work, if I died next day. Just *because* it means so much."

Work versus love, the classic female bind. She was beginning—"just faintly and questioningly" to "dream of happy human life in personal relation." But she worried that she could not, or should not, allow it to be real. Besides, she continued, perhaps this was just "a dream," an "imagination," one of those "cloud castles" she had found comfort in since childhood. "I must be surer than the past has ever been before I dare attempt it." The feeling is "so utterly unknown" that "I sort of *crumble* before it! I've got to go way back and get things straightened out—all the way. I've got to start new—all new."

Letters: October 29, 1897 through April 22, 1898

5.30 P.M. Friday. Oct. 29th. 1897. . . .

Now I was pleased to get your letter, for I too had been meditating on myself as a nuisance—(goodness me! that's not the way to spell it!) And with most dissimilar results—namely, that I wish I were less of one! And mean to be. The idea!. . .

You see I'm not quite so old yet as to be willing to be petted on that basis—nor so unhappy as to be duly grateful on that basis—nor so indifferent as not to mind either way.

And out of the heterogeneous mixture of ideas and emotions which present themselves at intervals, I'm principally ashamed of myself and determined not to do so any more. I should think that you'd think that I was a . . . steadily increasing nuisance.

Only you're so polite and essentially kind that I suppose you won't admit it even to yourself. . . .

You, now, are a comfort, right straight along. . . .

18 West 32nd St.
New York City
Wed. Nov. 3rd, 1897. . . .

I wasn't a bit cordial last night—part of the crookedness. . . .

Please bear in mind that I am not horrid when I feel well—and try and be patient with the drag and flop of my exhausted brain as you would, I know, be inexhaustibly tender and patient if it were an exhausted body.

You are finding, as all my near friends find, that "it is hard work to wait on a crazy man" . . .; and if I didn't feel sure that you would really be more grieved by my entire withdrawal than even by my disagreeable behavior I should be strongly moved to cut all the ropes at once—simply because I HATE to be this kind of trouble. . . . Now sick folks are unpleasant. There is the weakness that drops one out of companionship at once. There is the changed appearance—sometimes to hideousness. There is the suffering—hard to watch—a strain on one's nerves. And there is the plaintive unreasonable behavior. Nobody minds these things when the patient is in bed! Now all these symptoms befall my brain at times—the slowly retiring remnants of years of a terrible disease. It isn't pleasant. It makes me want to go away and hide like a leper. But there is nothing to be done—on any ground that I can see—but simply peg along and bear it and count the slow years of improvement.

As to you and me—surely you've had sensible and pleasant hours enough with me—and letters from me—to know how I feel toward you. Believe that and count on it—always. . . .

But part of the trouble is a compelling desire to talk about it—to complain and explain—to whimper and extenuate and seek for sympathy which don't do me any good if I get it. . . .

Just like the physical illness again—you bear up longer when with strangers than if at home, but you have to give out sometime and then it's worse. . . .

You see all my life I haven't had what I wanted in the way of being loved. . . . From mother up. The whole way is lived with—not all gravestones, but some, and some kind of trap-door-stones that keep things down. When the will-strength, or brain-strength, or whatever it is that keeps me happy and steady and brave, gives out, up hop all these buried things, dead and alive.

I want everything I haven't had—all at once.

It isn't as if I'd had 'em and lost 'em, you understand. I have never had—save in the one girl friend—a satisfied love. The others have all gone wrong somehow—like a stopped sneeze!

It is not clean grief—one of the easiest things to bear; but a choked thwarted fiercely unreconciled feeling—an accumulated revolt—both mental and physical. And they all pile up together—I want them all—from Child to Mother—Sister—Brother—Father—Lover—Husband—Friend.

Now perceive the misfortunes of my elegant and irreproachable Cousin who happens to be about! . . .

Being in the state of mind where it seems as if I simply *must* have somebody—or something—I grab you. Then with a morbid sensitiveness, and an intermittent consciousness of what you must think of me, I try to back out—and hurt your feelings. . . .

I suffered intense shame last week—foundationless, I don't doubt—to think that I had really as good as asked you to kiss me. You see the woman of it is that I don't want to whine around and be pitied by a man.

It makes me ashamed. So I let you go off last night without my usual friendliness even—having lost my real balance and happening to be at the cold end of the swing.

Now your cousin—when herself—likes you steadily and always. Likes to have you as near as you care to come. Likes as much of you as you care to give. And is not a sentimental idiot.

. . . But this is the worst piece of road since England. And I'd *much* rather not have you at all than to hurt your feelings and make you angry perhaps. . . .

Now don't be concerned about me. I'm not—at heart—at all worried. It will pass, and I shall live long enough to do what I'm here for. And even if I don't, I don't care. The *facts* don't worry me at all—only the feelings. When I finally got myself to sleep last night—after a long time of sniveling and sobbing and thrashing around to find an easy position in my mind—it was by sort of dodging down *beneath* all the agony of thinking—refusing to think—and saying over and over—"It's not that these things are true—it's nothing but a pain! It's nothing but a pain! It's nothing but a pain!"

And that's all it is. And the very fact that I could do that shows I'm by no means at the bottom! No. I'll be all right again soon, and able to slide it all back to oblivion and go on to the one thing—work. But when you *want* to be harrowed just think of those four years in Oakland and San Francisco—

with this kind of trouble inside and all kinds of real ones outside—and *nobody* to holler to!!!

Now do I make you feel through all this stuff that you are my dearest cousin and a solid comfort and that I can't see too much of you to suit *me*?

Because that's what I'm writing for. . . .

After dinner. Nov. 4th. 1897.
18 West 32nd St. N.Y. . . .

You seem so solid and firm and permanent somehow—and I feel so wobbly and in the dark. . . .

Through all the bucks and plunges of my recently misbehaving brain, and without at present any very well formed explanation or justification or anything—I temporarily cuddle down and clutch you remorselessly. Later on I shall flop and wobble again. Later still soar off no doubt.

But just for a little time—and with the excellent reason that I can't help it—behold me as it were a sleepy Newfoundland puppy in your overcoat pocket! . . .

10 A.M. or so. Sun. Nov. 7th. '97
18 West 32nd St. New York City. . . .

I can do no better than to quote from a letter of last August—that "being kissed and comforted by my Entire Family I went to bed and slept the sleep of the blessed." I remember that because you wrote about it in your next. A long quiet night. I was awake some—but not unhappy, for I went to sleep with a smile on my lips and woke only to think again of the dear comfort that you are to me—of your unfailing loving kindness; your quiet strength, your patience and wisdom—and your tenderness. . . .

I am really beginning to hope that I can gradually deflect some of the barred currents of my heart—(I wish I could make a picture of the thing as I see it—sulky, frightened, discouraged, "rattled" to a degree; one foot forward and the other back, ready to rush forward in tumultuous devotion one minute, and run away shrieking in the next—fingers in ears!—) . . . You see I can't even let myself go toward Katharine, for the simple reason that it hurts so. And pain—emotional pain—means madness. I *can* not suffer any more. The spring is broken. To think much of her is to want her—that won't do. They think I'm heartless and indifferent—I am, practically. I have to be.

But I've got six months of you—as far as I see. And I'm just going to let go and see if I can't lower the level in the reservoir and save the dam!

If you're quite sure you can stand it—and that "Mrs. G.[ilman]" won't mind! Tell her all about it and I think she'll understand and not care.

I perceive by the difficulty of writing that I'm not out of the woods yet, but I am distinctly better, and shall be all right soon.

I have a very sleepy drowsy sort of feeling about it all. But some way it seems as if I'd got hold of your hand and knew you'd take care of things and it would be all right somehow.

I don't really mind either way. Dying is the blessedest thing I've had to think of since I was twenty one or so. . . .

With my serene views of how life works I'm not even worried about my "work"—if I don't do it somebody else will. If you do truly believe in God it doesn't matter much what happens.

And please remember dear that the major part of my conscious life has been full of faith hope and big far reaching happiness—truly.

The world is a great garden full of lovely wonderworking laws—and I've enjoyed it rapturously.

And people have been heavenly good to me.

But the "transition woman" of this age has a difficult position, and I've met my share of the difficulties.

A few generations more and it will be easier. And I know I've helped it on a little. Every little counts.

[*The letter then continues with an almost exact quotation from Olive Schreiner's* Dreams.]

She said, "And, of those that come first, some are swept away, and are heard of no more; their bodies do not even build the bridge?"

"And are swept away, and are heard of no more—and what of that?" he said.

"And what of that—" she said.

"They make a track to the water's edge."

"They make a track to the water's edge—." And she said, "Over that bridge which shall be built with our bodies, who will pass?" He said "*The entire human race.*" And the woman grasped her staff and I saw her turn down that dark path to the river."

But I feel a cheerful assurance that I *have* helped to build the bridge—quite materially. And that feels good.

So don't feel badly about me, dear boy, even if things do go as I sometimes fear. A sick brain is no more to be dreaded than a sick liver—to break one's leg or one's heart is possible to all of us.

And—in such event—try and tell Kate about me. There's no one else who can so well, I think. Not only the personal part, but I want her to know that when one does realize the great spreading uplift of human life—and our fractional usefulness in it—and the profound dizzying beauty of the thing we call God—the endless soundless peace of it—why even this kind of thing doesn't matter to one. Why should it. . . . God is still doing business and the world's all right. . . .

Hotel Thorndike
Room 112. ($1.50!)
Boston. Mass.
Sun. Nov. 7th. '97
9.40 P.M.

In accordance with your good advice, behold me ensconced in a comfortable room at this worthy house. . . . I have a window on Church St. And it is a good room. . . .

And I'm lots better. I can feel the strength and "balance" flow back—it's lighter in my sky. Light or dark, you're a comfort dear boy—*such* a comfort. If only I can be some good to you! . . .

9 A.M. Mon. Nov. 8th [1897]. . . .

Now that I've told you so much—shown you so much of my—catacombs! You seem at once nearer and more healthfully remote.

In letting go of what remnants of woman's pride remain to me, and telling you the kind of wreck I am, I've lost the uneasy sense of responsibility I had about you; and feel more as if you were a doctor—a nurse—an Aged Relative! So you begin to settle and stand out clearly, not as the advancing and receding vision that I have been plunging at and away from; but solid like a post—good thing to tie to! . . .

I shall be a much clearer thinker, Sweet, a much more consistent, definite, forceful speaker, for knowing you and loving you enough to *have* to talk to you.

Don't think I think you are stupid—I don't, ever. You are not. But I am very slipshod and weak, the more so for my vivid consciousness of your kind of mind; and you haven't much of the imaginative faculty that enables one to reach far out and see what another person means. It's as if I couldn't throw very well and you couldn't catch very well—so we ruin it. But I'll keep a trying, and you'll be very patient I know. Head's tired—must stop writing. Heart's *not* tired—don't have to stop loving! . . .

11.07 A.M. Wed. Nov. 10th [1897]
3 Park St. Boston, Mass.

O my dear Cousin—

They've taken it!—the Book—! They'll get it out in the spring for the Fall trade—They are duly impressed. You see I only left it Mon. A.M. Mr. Small read it, and gave it to a scientific friend to read also—a woman—biological person—(doctor, I think)—wouldn't tell me who. But she knows my work. He told me her criticisms. They were good—fair, I mean, and all as to the errors in execution—marks of haste, etc. Of the matter she thoroughly approved—was impressed. I'm a bit confused but very happy, and had to write a word at once to you, dear boy. . . .

5. 45 or so. P.M.
Thurs. Nov. 11th. 1897
At Mr. Blackwell's—Pope's Hill
Dorchester, Mass. . . .

. . . Went to the W.J. Office. Saw my publisher and left mss. Also talked poems. . . .

. . . Spoke successfully to the W.S.ers. . . . Came home with the Blackwell's to spend the night. They run the paper (Woman's Journal), you know. Lucy Stone (now dead) & Henry Blackwell and their daughter Alice. They like me. . . .

Today I've had a fine time. Went to bed last night at 8 o'clock about—slept till 6.15. Yes, . . . it was fine! A most excellent bed! With copious bedclothes, soft, light, warm. Came in town and regaled myself with your letter. . . .

Well—then I visited Mrs. Hackett of Belmont N.H. Now at 214 West Canton St. Stayed to dinner. Another most desirable dinner. Roast-beef, baked potatoes, white and sweet, macaroni & cheese, boiled onions, celery and cider—lovely cider! Then an "apple dowdy"—sort of copious dish-pie with one crust—fine. . . .

I begin to feel a bewildered sense of gratitude to think that you have happened into my life about this time. I think its going to do a great deal not only to make me happier—but to help my work. . . .

As to death—that's nothing. But I do think it takes some gumption to speak calmly of losing one's mind—to be, so to speak, reconciled. And that's the step I've made lately.

I don't feel to blame about it, so if it comes—why it's none of my business. . . .

9.40 A.M. Friday [Nov. 12, 1897]

Now my dear Cousin, here I am as comfortable as you please with the big house practically to myself for the day; and nothing to do but read and write and loaf. Snow storm outside; a soft fat one—won't last.

To revert to your pleasing letters: Do you mean to be ostentatiously modest in speaking of the small hole it would make if you died? Why Houghton—don't you *know* how your people love you? . . .

You see it is not only that you are a satisfactory, efficient and agreeable young citizen, superficially; but that every one whose life you touch feels the deep earnest spirit of human love and service which seems to animate all you do. I have never seen it stronger in anyone. If you chanced to be a priest instead of a lawyer it would be more understandable perhaps; but it is easy to be seen, by those who can see; and anybody can *feel* it. You would take a very large slice out of all the lives you touch if you should leave. . . .

I didn't find this letter depressing. On the contrary. Don't you know when one is melancholy how aggravating it is to have people cheerfully insist there's nothing the matter? I do think I have cause for my "gloomy forebodings," and it quite heartens me up to have you take them seriously and speak as you do of Katharine and my work.

As soon as I have completed the book—which will be before Xmas I think; I mean to set in order all the stuff I have written, and—if I can—write out "in small" what I think most important that I'm going to say! Then if I live I can say it all; and if I don't why my executor can publish as an interesting posthumous work. "As I was going to say"—by the late C. P. Stetson.

It doesn't make me feel sad to speak of it. It eases my mind—relieves that tangled sense of pressure and culpable responsibility which is the essence of the pain in melancholia. In my kind at least. . . .

No dear boy—it's not the air of Boston that makes me feel better—far from it. It's first a change in the inside state—I don't know what it is—in the physiological or pathological condition. And it's second and very largely the ease and happiness you brought me—to have said it all off my mind—to feel easy about the debts even—as far as my income would go; and a great big wave of comfort about Katharine. I can just *see* what a solid good you will be to her. Also, with this, as I say perhaps too often, the direct rest and relief of your personal presence and tenderness. That's a great deal.

And then, top of all this, who wouldn't feel better to feel the opening of the gates as I begin to now? . . .

18 West 32nd St.
Nov. 23rd. 1897. . . .

After all this week isn't so bad. Today is first-rate because yesterday is so near to it. Indeed the nicest part of yesterday was this morning.(!?!) . . .

Only one day to pine. And the next day is easily passed because it's next door to Friday. And after Friday comes a possible Sunday! I feel rich. Chap. V of the completed work is done. . . .

But you are a great big slice of happiness to me dear cousin—solider and solider. . . .

This majestic Book, my eagerness therein and your most lovely patience therewith, is a great comfort this winter. . . .

18 West 32nd St.
New York City.
Nov. 29th. 1897. . . .

. . . I really begin to believe in you—a little bit—as a kind of a permanency. . . .

. . . Xmas 1897

> . . . I feel so rich Beloved! You
>   have brought
> Such large assurance, such
>   unbroken peace,
> Such promise of a joy that
>   cannot cease
> Such a deep sense of absolute
>   release
> From any terror I could
>   once have thought! . . .

9.20 A.M. Dec. 30. 1897. . . .

. . . But, dearest, you are in it all, under it all, with me continually. And when I put aside the work and really let you in—you are so close! So close! . . . you [have] warmed and brightened my whole life. Everything is so different. I have a home now—in your heart. . . .

. . . 18 West 32nd Street
New York, Feb. 8th, 1898

Heart's Dearest—
It is after eleven; but I cannot go to sleep without a word to you. . . .
You have pulled[?] away the stone from my poor shamed dead broken heart—and it has come out new and strong and glad. . . .
You have made my life . . . stronger than ever before. . . .

. . . 18 West 32nd Street
10 A.M.
New York, Feb. 10th, 1898.

O my Sweetheart!

A great smooth beautiful life before us—why not? . . .

O my dear! My dear! I can't somehow think out life without you any more!

And yet, under all the bewildering sweetness I *know*—you may trust it absolutely, that if you outgrow your present love for me and find that Cousin and Friend is enough and that some other can give you Love and Home and—children—I shall be able to bear it and shall find it right—good—best. Do not let this rushing surrender blind you to the long trained strength beneath. I can live on and do good work without you—if need be; the richer, the sweeter, the wiser, the stronger for this heavenly vision. Do not be afraid for me, dearest if things change places in your mind. . . .

Please remember—no matter how I love you, I often think of late that if this wonder passes—and it is too heaven-sweet to seem always real—how *much* better able to understand life, to know love, to teach and write, I shall be. This great good you have done me already—it is irrevocably mine.

It is too soon to boast, but I feel as if the most painful chapter in my life was closed forever. . . . But the beauty and the power of love is mine now—nothing can take it away. . . .

. . . 18 West 32nd Street
5 P.M.
New York, Feb. 20th 1898. . . .

Everything is drawing together and concentrating on my work—my two years work. . . . And I don't mean to think or feel much— personally—till it's done. . . . months to nod and smile at as they pass—only twenty four or thirty of those!—and soon the half way post of '99—then the home stretch! The home stretch.——I shall be almost glad when it's time to go away. Almost glad to leave you—think of that! Because then I can bury you better, way down deep in my heart, till its time to open the door and look. If you come out—well. If you have really gone—then I shall be glad I buried you. . . .

Whatever else is clear, the work is clear. If you are waiting beyond it— it is the way to you—the quickest way. The only way. If you are not—— well, the work is still the right way to keep on living till its done—the quickest way—the only way. . . .

But this unspeakable heavenly wonder, so utterly unknown, undreamed of in my life—as it grows and grows on my consciousness I am the more overwhelmed with new feelings as to it—to you—to myself—to life. I feel as if I had been only playing—before—that *this* is life and I am but just born! . . .

. . . I sort of *crumble* before it! I've got to go way back and get things straightened out—all the way. I've got to start new—all new. . . .

What are two years to make clear the way for such a thing as this?—if it is to be? But I must be surer than the past has ever been before I dare attempt it. . . .

By the duty I owe my people and my God, by the work I have to do on earth, by that duty which is more than even—I cannot say it! Look you! Something has come to me which I dare balance for a moment with my work!

But I would choose the work, if I died next day. Just *because* it means so much. . . .

So I do not propose to write like this again. . . . To give you the chance, free, utterly free of the insistent pressure of my intense personality, to recover yourself. . . .

. . . 18 West 32nd Street
9. P.M. Sunday.
New York, 1898. . . .

. . . I love you so! You are unspeakably dear to me. . . .

. . . surely you can read it in my eyes—hear it in my voice, feel it in my arms about your neck—taste it on my lips that lean to you. You make me happy—so happy, my darling! I love you—love you—love you! . . .

. . . 18 West 32nd Street
New York, March 10th. 1898.

Dear Love—Dear Friend—Dear Comforting true soul—I did have such a good time with you last night! . . .

I'm afraid I should feel very chilly now without those loving eyes to turn to. Well—I'm thankful for the two years. They ought to settle things.

And if we come to where I truly dare take the big risk there must be a definite understanding that that too is but an experiment—if I can't—I can't! We'll "handfast" it for a while. Say a five year conditional contract to be considered final after that time! . . .

. . . 18 West 32nd Street
New York, March 24th. 1898. . . .

The first word this morning is to you who have given me new life to rise and go on again. . . .

And, dear, do not set your heart on getting money for me, for I want none; but do with honest prayer and effort try to spread and grow out into the big currents of our social progress. You will have your views no doubt, as I have mine; and your methods; but at least I can feel that you *care* about the main interests of my life and sympathize with my purposes if not my actions.

For instance if you had a warm interest in, and worked for, merely local city measures toward municipalization of gas, or street railways, or any one thing that works toward that end—I should be contented. I can't expect your closebuilt well filled orderly mind to stretch itself to follow the loose waving filaments of mine; and I must learn not to. It is not fair to you. It is not a right desire.

Your love and sympathy is for me to come back to after work—to rest on and rise recreated by your blessed love. It has always been hard for me to learn this—to let people be what they are. . . .

. . . 18 West 32nd Street
11:10 A.M.
New York, April 2nd. 1898.

This is right in the middle of the morning, but I have to tell you how happy I am—how peaceful, and how, as other things quiet down and take themselves away from my mind the ideal of sweet home happiness rises up more and more clearly.

You to speak to—you to look at—you to read with—you across the table or the desk—you to go about with. Ah the dear togetherness!

My poor wild floating soul begins—just faintly and questioningly begins—to dream of happy human life in personal relation.

If this feeling stays and grows—why, dearest—perhaps I shan't be so sorry for you after all! . . .

. . . 18 West 32nd Street
New York, 9. A.M. Thurs. April 21st. 1898.

O my own dear love! My very own! More and more and more you are taking me to yourself.

It doesn't feel like a quicksand anymore, but like a warm sweet boundless sea. I do not feel it pull me now because I am in it. So deep and rich and warm and limitless—this ocean of your love! And the home life—our home life—rises clearer and clearer before me, like a shining island lifting itself out of the stretch of waves—a real place—where I can live. Even my fear for your happiness is disappearing, for I grow so happy myself that it seems as if you must be too.

The peace and joy in my heart is gradually covering every other thought. . . .

And over and under and through all that you have made me love you, love you like a child, love you like a girl, love you like a woman who has lived and suffered and to whom such love is heaven after hell.

By and by I shall forget to talk about it perhaps—forget to notice—just settle into the habit of being happy!

But it is still so new, so unbelievably strange and wonderful! So I have to tell you over and over—how happy you make me! How happy you make me! . . .

. . . 18 West 32nd Street
9.23 A.M. by your dear watch
New York, Friday April 22nd 1898.

My own—Perhaps you think all these little letters absurd! But it is like morning prayers to me. Every morning I feel so rich, so happy, so proud, so— so *at ease.* . . .

I am trying to yield myself frankly and wholly to the new influence, feeling since that it will make me in all ways a better woman and a better worker. Surely with this will come the power of settled work which I have waited for so long. As I grow into this sweet placid contentment I turn more and more naturally to my work—with less effort. . . .

5

"Nearly Drown in a Sea of Love":
1 May–30 May 1898

For the month of May 1898, Gilman chose Goldsboro, North Carolina, as her place of work. She planned to do some lecturing and writing, to put the finishing touches on her *Women and Economics* manuscript, and also to renew her friendship ties with Clara Royall, whom she had met in New York several months before. Clara Royall had attended some of Gilman's New York lectures, stayed with her at Frankie Perkins's boarding house, and after sharing some private family worries, had invited Gilman to her Goldsboro home for an extended stay. "Mrs. R[oyall] said yesterday she wished I loved her lots," Charlotte wrote to Houghton. She is "Beautiful, gifted, young, and *so* unhappy!" "Funny, isn't it—here I am already, one of the family, right into all their concerns, as naturally as if I was born here." In fact, Mrs. Royall "wants me to come every year—says she wishes she owned me!" She "says I've done her more good than anybody she ever met. Says a lot more than that—that I have made life easier for her—put her in touch with her own town—and so on."[1]

Almost immediately, Gilman felt a sense of contentment and support in this small-town southern setting. "New York has [its] attractions for a city; but for *living*—O how much one loses there." Here, "Birds sing everywhere; the yards are rich with roses, the woods sweet with wild honeysuckle." "Violets, periwinkles, . . . and dogwood trees in blossom. A wide lawn with big trees, and just across the road a wood, all misty with the new leaves." "The red sun drops softly on one side of the world, and the yellow moon rises on the other." Moreover, she continued, the people are "wonderfully appreciative" here, and "hot to have me come again—to arrange for lectures next fall." "This is what I missed so in New York," she continued, the sense of a "professional call," the "chance to serve." The Goldsboro community might be less "progressive" than northeastern cities, and the women's movement likewise less developed, but that in itself lent excitement to her challenge.[2] In New York, "Nobody wanted me," she wrote, yet here she felt the "personal touch, the 'heart to heart talk,'" the "real *giving* talk," especially with the women, and that "adds much to my always wobbly sense of professional value." To some extent, of course, she hoped to give some of the men "a better feeling toward the woman's movement," and yet "I know women best, and care more for them," she admitted honestly. "I have an intense and endless love for women—partly in reverence for their high estate, partly in pity for their blind feebleness, their long ages of suffering. . . . If women didn't like me I should be astonished. When men do—that surprises me."

By mid-May, Gilman had started a four-part lecture series. The first lecture, "We and The World," introduced her political philosophy. A "great success," she told Houghton; even the "rich & eminently respectable" old banker of the town had apparently enjoyed it. The second was the "woman one"—"The Greatest Movement of Our Times." The third outlined her "new motherhood" ideas—"What We Owe Our Children." And the fourth—"Our Own Duty"—explained the pragmatic "application" of her social theory. "I am honestly pleased to take so well in the South," she wrote to Houghton. "This visit has been a real success in the best way," and has "made me feel genuine and strong and useful again." And besides, "I'm getting very much interested in North Carolina, its circumstances and prospects. Several profoundly interesting character problems lie before me. I may be of some service."

Although Gilman used her letters in part to explain her work to Houghton—"See how modest I am! I complacently cover pages with my own praises!"—she also needed to think through its importance for herself: the sense of satisfaction resulting from the Goldsboro support and recognition, from the modest but still helpful monetary compensations,[3] and most importantly from the "rich and sweet . . . response of hungry hearts." "[A]s I enter again into the current of world interests . . ., I feel the deep assurance that this is indeed my work—and always must be." "If I can harmonize love and home with this great calling I shall be happy beyond my wildest hopes." And yet "if I had to choose today between you and my work—two hearts might break, and I might die of the breaking, but I could not choose other than the one way."[4]

Very shortly, however, Gilman would quite directly confront such "heart break" possibilities; only momentarily, as it turned out, but poignantly. "I feel stunned," she wrote to Houghton. "I've just seen yesterday's [New York] *Herald*. Says the Seventh [Regiment] is to go" to Cuba, to front-line service in Teddy Roosevelt's "splendid little war." Her attitude was "selfish," she admitted. It is "no worse for me to suffer than for the thousands of other women," and yet "you *can't* go to Cuba! . . . you mustn't think of going now!" "Guess I'm a woman all right—just like the rest of 'em. Isn't any fun either."

On 21 April 1898 Gilman had very briefly noted in her diary: "War with Spain becomes a fact."[5] And as she wrote to Houghton some days later, "War has seemed very far away in this quiet country home . . . all the little domestic processes going on peacefully." Yet nationally not only was the

"Yellow Press" whipping up stories about Spain's "atrocities" in Cuba, dramatizing incidents designed to "shock, horrify, titillate or disgust their readers,"[6] but reformers also were acclaiming the "altruistic significance" of this "supremely just" and timely "little war."[7] Elizabeth Cady Stanton wrote that Spain was a "disgrace to the civilization of the nineteenth century." Or as John Peter Altgeld put it, Spanish "atrocities" in Cuba were a shock to "the moral sense of the civilized world."[8] Of course a number of Gilman's contemporaries opposed the military effort, William Dean Howells, for instance, and E. F. Godkin writing for the *Evening Post.* They argued that U.S. intervention would strengthen the capitalistic structure, enhance the wealth of munitions makers, and crush the efforts of Populists and Nationalists at home. Yet many of the political reformers that Gilman also enthusiastically respected unqualifiedly joined the chorus of support. As her friends at the *American Fabian* office put it, "The duty upon this Government of intervention in behalf of Cuba seems to us so clear that we wonder that any human person can object to it." This war in support of our "helpless and oppressed neighbors" "is largely the result of the advanced social teachings so widely diffused during the last decade."[9]

To some extent, Gilman's perspectives in this context differ from those of many of her contemporaries. Whereas Teddy Roosevelt and others celebrated war as an expression of masculine virility, for Gilman, it was also often an expression of "male energy" at its very worst, a result of "blind competition," of a "brutal combative instinct," of the "intense sex-vanity of the male." Or as she would put it in her 1915 utopian novel, *Herland,* "Patriotism, red hot, is compatible with the existence of a neglect of national interests, a dishonesty, a cold indifference to the sufferings of millions. Patriotism is largely pride, and very largely combativeness. Patriotism generally has a chip on its shoulder."[10]

Likewise in her private writings, Gilman expressed some reservations about the American invasion. "This war is not like the last. I see no earthly reason why a man should go—at present—unless he wants to."[11] Yet, in the context of the mounting public pressures, unfortunately she waffled. Without speaking directly to the specifics of the current crisis, she nonetheless stressed the need for patriotic loyalty to America's progressive intent. The United States may not be Utopia, she wrote, and "our democracy" is not yet fully realized. Yet "we owe love and duty, honor and allegiance to the country as it is." Besides, she continued, American history did not read quite so bleakly as angry critics claimed. Despite "the wealth accumulated by the few, the poverty pursuing the many," America's wars had not been entirely destructive. The Civil War, for instance, had "forced people from the condition of slave labor agriculture . . . to a rapidly developing manufacture and commerce" and had also intensified the "consciousness of evils and [the] search for remedies." Thus, in Gilman's view, war sometimes had its benefits. In spite of all of its "black record of pain, loss, and terror," it had been the "first socializer." It had helped man to learn that the "noblest life is that which gives itself most absolutely to the service of humanity," and it had helped women to enter the realm of public work. "In the absence, injury and death of so many of the male population, women were forced into unaccustomed positions of effort and responsibility . . . driven sharply forth into self-supporting effort and complex labor."[12]

*   *   *   *   *

Although Gilman's published writings on this and other topics certainly deserve extended treatment, the private correspondence nonetheless remains the major focus of this study. I return, therefore, to Gilman's "stunned" response to the possibility of Houghton's entering the war. When the New York *Herald* had reported that his regiment would be called to front-line service, she experienced, as she dramatically described it, a devastating "one night's widowhood."[13] "It makes a difference to one's virtues when one loves folks," she candidly admitted. "I'm quite mortified to find myself behaving so badly about this war. I shall be more patient with other women after this."

Although, as it turned out, the nightmare fantasies were needless—Houghton's regiment had not, in fact, been called—the experience nonetheless triggered some reassessments of the friendship: first about the ways it helped to heal her and second about the ways it challenged traditional sex-role expectations that still had a strong and troubling appeal.

According to the letters, Gilman first reacted to the possibility of losing Houghton by returning to the "rigid training in voluntary numbness" she had self-consciously been working on since childhood. Because she was "honestly convinced" that such a "full-felt pain would kill or craze" her, she would build up "breastworks" and "embankments" and prepare for the "assault." Or to use another metaphor, "thought and feeling" must be put "to sleep," she wrote him, "as the hapless baby with the empty rubber nipple."

If the metaphors suggest an effort to return to self-destructive strategies she remembered from her childhood—the "hapless baby" building up defenses, "the empty rubber nipple" serving to fortify and numb the mind—they also suggest that Houghton helped her reconnect with some positive and trusting memories as well. He reminded her of childhood "pleasures" as well as disappointments. In fact, he reinspired a "child love of long ago," she told him, and by using "the old sweet ways of girlish memories and family affection." Gilman still expressed some anxieties about the process: about the vulnerability, the "blind groping hunger," the "naughty girl" sensations when people disapproved of her behavior or ideas. ("It will take more than one lifetime to outgrow that state of mind," she noted.) And repeatedly she worried about some "quicksand" dangers also—as if love would undermine her professional commitment, or even worse, as if intimacy would mean the death of her creative powers. Yet, for the most part, she spoke appreciatively about the sense of "healing" that had accompanied her grow-ing ability to trust. "I think it is one of the sweetest things in life to have a feeling go way back and connect with childhood's heart," she wrote him, and with such a sense of "comfort," of "blessing," of "games and jokes and fun." "Seems like a full cycle somehow," to experience his "excusing mother and father love," his "big sweet brotherly interest," his "approving friend-ship." "I just dive and float and swim in, and reach no bottom to your dear love."

Quite often there is a striking childlike quality in Gilman's letters, almost as though she were appealing for a kind of mothering affection, regressing, some might say, to Houghton's "all embracing sea of love." Except that as so often happens, the "regressive" state was also a creative one, a "healing" environment that inspired her not to abdicate responsibility, but to risk creative work.[14] "Come now," she wrote him. "Devise for me the kind of man whom you honestly think would make me a better husband . . . to know and understand and sympathize and bear with me—to make me happy at home and let me freely go and come as I must—to care for my work and help me do it."[15] "You understand to the full that I am a world-worker and must be—that I simply give you the part that stays at home, and that I shall go right on thinking, writing, lecturing, and travelling when I must." Be-sides, if "I married some kind of a genius—as indeed I did, before,—he would *need* also—I [would] feel it as a drain." Instead, what a "miraculous dispensation of Providence"—to find "myself surrounded by your love" and yet "my freedom of motion guaranteed." In fact, she candidly admitted, some people might suggest there was a role-reversal in their friendship. Since "my work has forced me into what has always been held a man's place," it is "as if you held the woman's place toward me." Or as she teased him in another letter, "I, being of the superior sex, and a noble specimen, am careening about the country alone and unaided, and having a beautiful time . . . funny how we reverse every established program! There you sit and here I go and come."

Given the standard gender expectations—that men should have success and opportunity, that women were meant to serve—understandably Gilman sometimes felt "remorse" about the "selfishness" of accepting Houghton's help. After all, "[o]n all usual human grounds you are the one who ought to have the personal devotion—the life consecrated to your loving service." Just think of the "home he might have had, . . . the advantageous connection he might have had." "O this is most ignominious!" she wrote him. "I seem to be swallowing you," a classic antiwoman metaphor, if there ever was one, the female spider feeding on and swallowing the hapless male. And yet she nonetheless appreciatively continued, "from all I can make out you are the kind of angel that only seeks to be swallowed."

There is a strange sense of spiraling full circle in Charlotte's struggle with the friendship. At times she was delighted to accept the warmth of his

affection, and at others, she saw herself as the peripatetic woman's movement leader who was selfish to want and need his love. It was as though she
envisioned only two potential models for their friendship: either she was
weak and "crippled" and thus needed strong-armed male protection, or,
alternately, she was strong and thus not lovable, independent and thus
"selfish" and oppressive, successful and thus destructively demanding the
kind of love that creative men so often ask from wives.

Yet occasionally, and rather indirectly, Gilman glimpsed another friendship model, and by no means a simple role-reversal one. It was almost as
though his love were like the kind that women often give to one another.
Based on mutual support instead of condescension, on mutual respect instead of domination, it was a friendship that by no means encouraged a
regressive weakness but inspired both partners to be free and active in their
work. "I've been happy before," she wrote him. "I was as happy as I could
hold with my friend Martha [Luther]."

Although Gilman readily acknowledged that Houghton was not particularly ambitious in his work commitments, what helped sustain the mutuality
of friendship were qualities that she in fact admired more: his gentleness,
his "integrity and good will," his "absolute reliability." And while by convention less ambitious men were labeled unsuccessful, nondomineering men
defined as weak, Gilman admired the kind of strengths in Houghton that
were considered quite typical for women, but unfortunately were far more
rare in men. Given his "quiet undiscussed right doing," his "excessive generosity, devotion, [and] unselfishness," no wonder he wasn't "grasping enough
to enrich" himself materially, she wrote him. Precisely that was what she
valued most: his conspicuous unwillingness to dominate, his "feminine" rejection of the assertive power-seeking role. "Such helpfulness, such pleasant
friendliness, such merry companionship, such plain straightforward useful
help—these I had never known." "I confess it grows on me," but "I'm not
yet all the time sure it is right for me to have it." And yet, almost as though
to reconfirm the depth of standard gender expectations, Gilman nonetheless
repeatedly would spiral back to self-destructive fears: "[T]o think that you,
my dear dear love, are not my first and only thought! All the piled up
ancestral womanheartedness cries out Treason!"[16]

Letters: May 1 through May 30, 1898

About 10.40 A.M.
Sunday May 1st, 1898. . . .
    [On route to Goldsboro, North Carolina]

    . . . A summer Sunday in the country. Warm soft and bright—, with
little winds that are warm too, and young leaves all astir.

I am on the porch, alone save for an old old dog, who is quiet and friendly.

Violets, periwinkles, dandelions, cherry bloom nearly gone, and dogwood trees in blossom. A wide lawn with big trees, and just across the road a wood, all misty with new leaves.

And all around in it and through it your face,—your voice, your eyes—dear tender eyes! . . .

5.15 P.M. Mon. May 2nd '98. . . .

. . . I have reasons for wanting to get to Goldsboro—my mail is there! *Perhaps* I shall find a letter from you—or a postal card. Just to say you are well, and have not gone to war! War has seemed very far away in this quiet country home— a sick grandmother upstairs—a healthy baby downstairs—all the little domestic processes going on peacefully. . . .

. . . Goldsboro, N.C. . . .
Half past nine or so A.M. Wed. May 4th.

Good morning Heart's Dearest!

Here I am comfortably settled in my new room, ready for the morning's work. But first, as dearest pleasure, a word with you.

It is a cool cloudy morning—cool for here that is, where they have had roses for a month. . . .

O—you *can't* go to Cuba! . . . you mustn't think of going now! I *am* so comfortable! . . .

. . . No. I saw nothing of Baltimore, except a car and cab ride across it. Another time. With you perhaps. . . .

. . . Yes, our war gets on finely, doesn't it. I continue to rejoice inwardly that you are not in it. Why in the name of reason should you be! Fight for New York if you have to— that you'd enjoy. . . .

. . . Hope you'll enjoy The Quintessence of Socialism. Do get the first volume of Fabian Essays—that is the best I know. And Ely's books are good. . . .

. . . 9.45 A.M.—
. . . May 5th, 1898.

Sweet Sweet Sweetheart—my Precious Darling—My Dear Love! I am just as happy as I can be—without you.

And I have you in my heart all the time.

Everything is so nice. I am getting the sense of time and space and restfulness—no hurry—plenty of room.

This is the largest handsomest home in town, or as good as any at least; these people quite the aristocracy of the place. Mr. Royall likes me. Mrs. Royall wants me to come every year and spend a month with her—says it will do me good!

I have my usual wondering sense of gratitude at being so pleasantly placed.

Blue bells are sent me this morning—a little vine that grows wild here.

People called last night and like me.

Stories begin to stir in my brain. Sewing looks easy. I'm thoroughly glad I came. I fear I shall always have to have a good deal of change, dear heart—in spite of my happiness with you. . . .

I sleep beautifully here, in this big bed, in the great four windowed room.

There are trees, large trees . . . all through the wide streets of this sleepy town. Birds sing everywhere; the yards are rich with roses, the woods sweet with wild honeysuckle. We drive in the cool of late afternoon in a little open buggy with a big gentle horse, Mrs. Royall and I—and a little son perhaps.

The red sun drops softly on one side of the world, and the yellow moon rises on the other. The wagons on the country roads move in rosy clouds of soft dust, and the water-tower stands dark red against the twilight. . . .

. . . 9.30 A.M.
Fri. May 6th 1898
Goldsboro N.C. . . .

A cool sweet morning. Gentle winds blowing through the leaves, and much chirping of little birds. More roses sent me. And hopes of a letter today from the man I love. . . .

Dear—I would give so much if I could be sure I was really doing right by you. There is such a remorseful undercurrent in my happiness—such a painful sense of inadequacy and of owing you more than I can pay. I have always had this, in any love I ever knew, except with Martha. I never was all I should be to mother or brother or child. . . .

4.45 P.M. . . .

I know you like to write to me—and to talk to me and make me happy in all ways. And of course there are times when you just can't. I'll always understand.

But somehow even what virtues I have fail me with you—I'm greedy, and I—yes, I actually worry!

Think you must be sick, or that you have somehow been ordered off to the war in spite of everything.

It makes a difference to one's virtues when one loves folks! . . .

10.15 P.M. Fri. May 6th
1898
Goldsboro N.C.

. . . Your fine long sweet letter of yesterday arrived tonight—to my great joy. I hope it does not mean that I won't get one tomorrow! See how greedy I am! O but this is such a dear one—so full of you so near. . . .

Sweetheart! You shall kiss me anywhere you want to and all you want to as soon as ever there is a chance. I will wait till you are exhausted and then begin operations on my own account. . . .

I do miss you, Sweetheart, for all I am so glad to be out again, free, at large, belonging to everybody. With the world to work in and you [to] play with—the world to go out to and you to come back to. . . .

11.10 A.M. Sat.
May 7th. 1898. . . .

. . . I am so comfortable here! My big rocking chair, my little rocking chair, my big bureau, big mirror—two of 'em, big bed, big big room all bright and clean. Mrs. R[oyall] wants me to come every year—says she wishes she owned me! . . . Mrs. R[oyall] asks me if I always had such a sweet nature?—So—I seem to be working all right in the South so far. . . .

This is a delicious place. I see myself living here— with you, and a flock of the sweetfaced children who abound here.

New York has attractions for a city; but for *living*—O how much one loses there. . . .

4.20 P.M. Sun. May 8th. 1898
Goldsboro N.C. . . .

Yes, four weeks from today I shall be preaching in Longwood, Penn., and the next day ought to see me in New York, or Tuesday at farthest. 30 days is the outside. Unless of course my mercenary nature was tempted by further engagements. It is lucky for my return that I have that definite date engaged, for these people here seem to think I belong to 'em! I am immensely gratified by it. If the south likes me as well as the west, I shall begin to feel that I am indeed an American. I'm getting very much interested in North Carolina, its circumstances and prospects. Several profoundly interesting character problems lie before me. I may be of some service.

And as I enter again into the current of world interests and feel the quick response of human lives, I feel the deep assurance that this is indeed my work—and always must be.

Dear, if I had to choose today between you and my work—two hearts might break, and I might die of the breaking, but I could not choose other than the one way.

If I can harmonize love and home with this great calling I shall be happy beyond my wildest hopes. . . .

This is life, my life, rich and sweet with the response of hungry hearts everywhere, full of stimulus and comfort and glorious enthusiasm and deep peace.

In it I feel that "flushing of the mains"—that full current of swinging throbbing life for which I have always hungered—for which we all hunger in some degree I think.

To fully be—and know that life is well spent—full spent—spent in the right direction. And then I feel so remorseful and ashamed to think that you, my dear dear love, are not my first and only thought! All the piled up ancestral womanheartedness cries out Treason! . . .

. . . 11.10 A.M.
New York, Tues. May 10, 1898. . . .

. . . perhaps I may as well state that, coincidentally with feeling unusually well this morning, I feel unusually well disposed toward you! You come up clearer out of the fog—I see the happiness of being with you—sort of feel and taste it more. I fear my brain is but a shifting sand bank! I've been feeling very murky and remorseful about you lately—feeling myself swing off so with the wider range of life and liking it as well as ever. And though I had your image conspicuously in my mind, and profusely labelled "Happiness," "Love," "Comfort," "Home," and so on; still my *consciousness* was not in it, but far afield. . . .

. . . I guess that's all the trouble with me dear. Patent collapsible brain cells. Capable of great expansion. Warranted to shut down at a moment's notice. . . .

Mr. Bates, worthy lad, has written to me of the loud goodwill of the people at 265 Henry St. Miss Wald says for me to stop there any time when coming through the city. That is very kind of her. . . .

. . . 12.45 or so.
New York, Wed. May 11th 1898. . . .

Last night I lectured—"America's Place Today." A tiny handful of people in the "Opera House." But it went well— was well taken—they want more perhaps.

Mrs. Royall and I get on well together.

I impress her, and her friend Miss Lewis, a teacher here, as being very "great." As Mrs. Rudd felt. Now I don't impress you that way. Singular! I fear I impress you as being comparatively small. You see you are not very big. And yet you can reach all round me—take me right up in your arms and carry me! Quite a limited little country; bounded on the north by your mouth, on the south by your lap, on the east and west by your arms! Well well, what better can one expect of a near relative and "mere human"!

4.30 P.M.

Such a lovely letter from you this noon, my dear one! A love letter of the most entrancing description. . . . Likes to make you feel like that! Maybe wicked but I like it—naughty girl! . . .

It is too bad that you are hungry, dear. I feel it a little, but not much, consciously. But I have stepped out into new currents, and the full swing of my work. You are just left, so much minus. That—(again our paradox!) is usually the woman's part. (*Isn't* it funny!)

. . . I rather resent such tender loving memories of me being denounced as "the animal side of it"! Good gracious man! What did you expect? To love my astral body? Or to pass your days in intellectual pursuits, lit by a mild glow of platonic affection?

I don't think it is "an animal side of it" when I remember the look in your eyes—the pressure of your loving arms—your beautiful strong body. Dear—it strikes me that you don't know what the animal side of life is!

. . . As to what I propose to do about it, that's easy! . . . I shall make it my business to see that you do not have that hungry feeling any more! . . .

But O dear Lover! Dear Brother! Dear Friend! More than all this rich sweetness is the unbroken flood of your strong constant love of *me*—the real whole inner woman, who has longed so long for such a love. . . .

I know it is the biggest part of your feeling for me. That it came first and will last longest. But these other feelings are perfectly natural and right. . . .

. . . Thurs. May 12th. 1898.
Goldsboro N.C. . . .
About noon.

Dear—I feel stunned. I've just seen yesterday's *Herald*. Says the Seventh is to go—and to the front. . . .

Well now—my remarks are these. Either you come back or you don't. If you come back you are either as good as before, or perhaps injured.

As to these chances.

1. If you come back all right. Then all stands as it is, and we presently get married and "live happy ever after."

2. You come back injured. Then (in spite of natural regrets on your account) I feel at last convinced that you won't be materially injured by marrying me; that I can do it with a clear conscience—and I do, promptly. (I'm not sure but it is your duty to leave an arm or a leg or a digestion somewhere, just to relieve my mind of all these troublesome compunctions I have about marrying you!)

3rd. You don't come back. Now dear, I want you to feel absolutely safe and sure in the knowledge that I shall pull through it. I shall not die, nor give up trying—nor break down. The world and the work remains—I'm not excused from living, even if you are! I shall count you as one great unbroken tender joy in my life—its sweetest dearest chapter. . . .

Further, as to this summer, and all the time that you are away.

I shall not be foolish enough to try to go nursing or anything like that. I'm no good at it and am good for other things.

I shall settle right down, build up my health, and work, work, work. . . .

10.5 A.M.
Friday. May 13th. 1898
Goldsboro N.C. . . .

I'm trying to be just as good as good can be. *Not* thinking very hard. Throwing up breastworks and fortifications in my mind as hard as ever I can. One is "The War may be over before he is called out." Another "He may not be hurt—lots of men are not."

Another. "It is no worse for me to suffer than for the thousands of other women"—not so bad, for I know how. . . .

And, biggest and best, the deep deep prayer—Help me to meet whatever comes—to see the Right—to Bear and Do and Live—Whatever comes. Behind these embankments I lie down— prepared for assault. . . .

. . . I can't but think that if you come through this all right it is going to be a splendid thing for you. It will break up and loosen lots of little crusty places that your comparatively changeless life must needs form. It will—so to speak—coarsen you a little—not in any lowering sense—but as against a too intense refinement. You will be the broader bigger man for it, more open to all growth and progress. . . .

4.13 P.M.

Your letter with Mr. R[oyall] at dinner time—2 P.M. . . . I could wish the letter had come yesterday. 'Twould have saved me one night's widowhood. . . .

. . . *Such* a load off my heart! . . . Guess I'm a woman all right—just like the rest of 'em. Isn't any fun, either. . . .

10.25 A.M.
Sat. May 14th '98. . . .

Things go on nicely here. Mrs. Royall thinks this would be a good place for me to spend next winter! . . .

Mr. Royall waxes slowly conversational. She says he likes me. He is a pious popular person; of a strange type. I don't know him at all yet.

My last page proofs are in this morning. That ought to mean at least advanced sheets before I leave. . . .

You would be amused by the flowery exordiums of the local editor. Speaks of me, among other things as "a ripe scholar"! There's for you!

Huge pink roses brought me this morning—great full fat ones. Now I must leave off talking to my beloved and read laborious chapters with blue pencil in hand. . . .

1. P.M. . . .

I've been figuring, if all comes in as I expect, I ought to leave New York for Cold Spring with 50 odd dollars as a starter. That's not so bad. . . .

My first lecture here netted me 3.00 and something! The school nobly forbore to claim any of it, and I magnanimously gave it back to the school. But this series they are running now ought to bring me a clean 25 I should think—almost cover the trip. Perhaps quite. . . .

12.36 P.M.
Sun. May 15th. '98.
Goldsboro N.C. . . .

Funny, isn't it—here I am already, one of the family, right into all their concerns, as naturally as if I was born here. . . .

About 4.50 P.M. . . .

Yes I do receive quite a number of letters. Not enough however that yours is quite prominent. I endeavor to refrain from any marks of joy when I receive it . . . and try when I can to post my own to you so that the parallel frequency may not be observed.

Further than that I philosophize calmly, and let 'em think. They don't know what's in 'em! . . .

9.10 A.M. Mon. May 16, '98
Goldsboro N.C.

Dear—I know it is only because you do care so much that it makes you angry—same as fond mothers who scold the child when he hurts himself. But I wasn't much to blame dear. I did expect you to write me about it as soon as you knew— even to wire if you knew for certain.

But remember the day's mail time. It was Wednesday's Herald which I got Thursday—and Wednesday's letter did not come till Friday. . . .

I fully expected your letter of that day would "break it to me gently"— and it didn't come at all! . . . And, if you please, I think you might say a little less of what I ought to have known and the excellence of my reasoning processes, and a little more of your natural satisfaction at the result of those processes! If you feel it.

And I was trying so heroically to be good! You don't seem to notice that at all! . . .

. . . You see dear, one reason that this has worried me so about you, is that from the first I have not been able to make married happiness fit into my scheme of life. . . .

. . . (I am suddenly called upon by Mrs. Royall—who gives singing lessons—to come down and show these girls my development! Meaning chest space—breadth of rib. I cheerfully accede, and go down and show off my "barrel" with great joy, thumping myself proudly.) . . .

It has never seemed reasonable to me that I should marry you. It seems perfectly reasonable that I should again have to face and carry utter loss— unmeasured pain. This particular scare has done me good in that—I have come nearer to being reconciled to lose you than I have been before—to forcing my spirit to admit the large possibility of losing all this bewildering new hope and joy, and to face the life remaining to me in a just and honorable way. To really admit the pain I do not dare. I am honestly convinced that a full-felt pain would kill or craze me—I haven't brain strength to stand it. . . .

To consistently withdraw my consciousness from that whole field of thought and feeling; . . . to work it hard in those lines and put it promptly to sleep with some set thought in view—as the hapless baby with the empty rubber nipple—that is what I am fixing for. This course, being persisted in, allows the gradual atrophy of the strangled region. In course of time I could uncover it occasionally and it wouldn't scream at all. . . .

Sometimes I wish your letters gave a little more of your thoughts and feeling; but you don't even in talking, say much of those things. Your mind doesn't run to words. And you do write a thousand fold more satisfactorily than when you began. . . .

Now I must leave of[f] babbling to you and fall to sewing. Tonight is the first lecture of my four. And it is only three weeks from today or tomorrow when I see you again! . . .

9.23 A.M.
Tues. May 16th. 1898
Goldsboro N.C. . . .

How good it is to have some one to turn to every day—to touch hearts with for a few moments even when hands and lips cannot meet. And you do care—don't you? You are interested? You care about this little lonely (lonely, *not* lovely!) woman who blows about the world in such queer ways, wishes so much and does so little. I don't mean just to *want* me; but the big sweet brotherly interest; the excusing mother and father love; the approving friendship. I am very greedy. I want all kinds of love and lots of it. And all the time there stands implacable behind it the feeling that it is not for me! . . .

. . . Last night I lectured again—first of series. 'Twas in the courthouse. Good audience in size; super excellent in quality. Professed itself pleased. I didn't enjoy it so well as last time. . . .

About 10.45 A.M.
Wed. May 18th '98
Goldsboro N.C. . . .

I've been wondering a bit lately whether my "numbness" of sensation even to love and joy, is not due to my rigid training in voluntary numbness toward pain. Where one has spent years in denying a sensation—refusing to "answer the bell"—carefully withdrawing all consciousness from the affected part and pursuing other business, I should think it might very naturally affect one's power to feel anything. Now I am going to stop bothering about it. To accept gratefully the little trickling streams and occasional big rushing currents of love that I feel; and, when I do not feel any, to rest assured that it is there—just as my pain is there though I refuse to feel it. . . .

Further, on the same lines, I am beginning to recognize that a life capable of such wide and varied interests as mine; and such a long steady unfailing "set" in the direction of what I believe to be the right, need not expect at the same time to be able to maintain a keen and steady interest in "daily duties"; with the constant change of focus that goes therewith.

I must be more humble—not expect to do everything. If I keep my mind open to see things as it should; and speak when I can—write when I can— why that is my "stint" and I should not resent the comparative vagueness and lack of adjustment in so many of my days. I suppose it is the old woman's temperament, with its exacting routine of hourly and momently duties; failing to adapt its conscience to the eccentric orbit of the work I am set to do. I'd better begin to apply some of my wisdom to my own life and become a more agreeable member of society. . . .

O this is such a good letter! But it is sinfully long, dear boy. You mustn't waste so much of your precious time on me. . . . Why there are about 1800 words in this letter! . . .

Dear Love—Dear dear Love—I do not think you need fear my ever loving any one else better. Of course no one can swear to the future, but I cannot imagine any man on earth catching up after the start you've got. . . . No one else on earth touches my early life as you do. And when I think of all I have been through, and of what it has cost me to tell even you about it; and how, in honor, I should have to tell it all again to another man if I came to love him—why I just want to bury my face in your neck—to feel you wrap me all up in your arms and hold me tight—never *never* to stir away from you. Our friendship, comradeship, cheery intimacy, means so much to me. The games and jokes and fun—that is like my brother and the pleasures of my childhood. . . .

A man might come much nearer to my work, my thought, that is true. I do not feel you near nor particularly sympathetic there. You are sympathetic with *me*—with my intentions; and you are as helpful as you can be to the external work; but we don't think in the same lines by nature. But, bless me! If I find a co-thinker, man or woman, there is nothing to prevent our co-thinking that I know of! I don't have to marry 'em! My one grave doubt has been deliciously settled; I know now that we are fitted to one another in the most important things. . . .

Disappointed in you? I? Why I don't expect anything of you except to be what you are—and I shan't be disappointed in that. . . . You understand to the full that I am a world-worker and must be—that I simply give you the part that stays at home, and that I shall go right on thinking, writing, lecturing, and travelling when I must. Of course I should give up a few years of the travelling in case certain contingencies arose. (Can't you see 'em arising!) . . .

The daily paper here goes to Mrs. R[oyall]'s mother after the family have read it; and I do not like to ostentatiously purchase one—it is against my steady principle. They are only the flowery "journalese" outpouring of the country press. But I am pleased with the impression I have made.

Mrs. Borden took me strawberrying again this morning. She is a Virginian—he the Banker of the town—old, rich & eminently respectable. She told me he was reluctant to go—had never heard a woman speak—but thought he ought to go, once. That he sat through the whole thing with unswerving interest, never complained of the seats (—wooden benches of an unspeakableness!) and has since been telling every one to go and hear me—with many praises. She said also that another man, lawyer, also reluctant to go—said it was the best address he had ever heard anywhere! I asked her if as far as she knew I had shocked or offended any. She admitted that there had been a little fear of that expressed, but that she had heard no one say a word of the sort—that everyone was pleased. . . . The south loves "oratory" and dislikes "progressive women"; and I feel much gratified as a woman and as a speaker. The little old lady said they liked my manner and appearance as well as the matter of the discourse.

It adds much to my always wobbly sense of professional value. I feel a very pleasant sense of right beginning in a new section. . . .

3.18 P.M. Thurs.
May [19]th. 1898
Goldsboro N.C. . . .

. . . I'm only going to write you a little letter (if I can stop!) because I must write to Kate today. . . . And tonight I lecture again.

This morning I forsook you entirely. For what think you? For my black silk skirt, now nearly done. I stitched it, I pressed the seams, I faced it around the bottom, I worked industriously from 8.30 to 1 o'clock! . . .

People continue to be pleased with me, and that last lecture—"We and The World"—was a great success. The aged Mr. Borden continues to exhort the youth of his town to go and hear me. A Jewish Rabbi wants a copy of "An Obstacle" (which I read on that occasion), and a Presbyterian Elder made my lecture, or its theme—which was Love and Unity as the essence of Social Progress—the subject of his Wednesday evening prayer meeting! "I cert'n'y am pleased"—to use a localism.

Mrs. R[oyall] continues to regard me fondly and beg for a yearly visit; and Mr. R[oyall] regards me with the eye of favor—that I can see for myself. I didn't see the paper after this one; but am told that the editor—who introduced me on this occasion—said nice things about it—that "it contained valuable hints to live by"—or something like that. See how modest I am! I complacently cover pages with my own praises! . . . I am honestly pleased to take so well in the South. And I'm not representing anything either—its just me and my ideas—so there! . . .

This is the loveliest letter that ever was. I read it and read it. And the days go very quickly between letter and letter—they seem to come flying like heavenly little birds. You make me *so* happy. . . .

9.15 A.M.
Fri. May 20th. '98
Goldsboro, N.C. . . .

. . . I am pleased to hear about this business that kept you from writing. May you have lots more of it! And I think you will. I do not believe that real learning and integrity and good will; together with that quality which we will kindly call perseverance, can go forever unrecognized. I have the most absolute confidence in your making a very good living by and by. . . .

Dear—I sort of grieve to have you speak of "the children" so confidently. You know it is a slim chance at best— very slim. Please don't hope it too much!

I should feel badly enough and if I thought you did too——! . . . Of course I hope too—but it is really unlikely you know. If we didn't there would be consolations. I should insist on thinking that the combination would not have been a wise one—great risk of a poor product; and that it probably would have upset my health again; and that I could remain freer to be your lover, companion and friend; and that I should not age so soon———O I'd think of lots of comforts if it didn't happen! . . .

The subjects of my lectures—if I haven't sent you them already—are 1. "We & the World." 2. "The Greatest Movement of Our times." 3. "What We Owe Our Children." 4. "Our Own Duty."

They are newly arranged for this little course; the first was about the whole progress of the world, as among men; the second the woman's movement; the third the child question; and the fourth the application to individual character. I'm not doing them very well. Last night was the woman one. I had a good house, and all expected much, but I did not please the men of the place—for which I am truly sorry.

Mr. Royall was very unpleasantly impressed, and thought other men were. I thought so too. . . . I fell short of my "high office"—I know that. But then one cannot always do one's best—I'm not letting it discourage me. Many other trials remain to be better met.

The women liked it however. . . . But I wanted the men to get a better feeling toward the woman's movement—and feel as if I had not succeeded in that at all—rather the other way. . . .

10.40 A.M.
Sat. May 21st. 1898
Goldsboro. . . .

My big comfortable room, just swept this morning. A glass pitcher of richly varied sweet peas against the dark wood and clear mirror of my toilet-table; bureau, rather. A little dark blue and white pitcher of starry jasmine on the other table that stands a little off to the left front of me with one deep crimson rose in the middle of it. (Down stairs a great silver bowl full of splendid roses.) All of them brought me this morning. The jasmine and sweet peas I particularly love. Occasionally a little breeze stirs the soft air and brings me the breath of my neighbor's honeysuckle. Cool—clean—still—room and time and such plentiful sweetness and color—it is lovely.

Furthermore the advance sheets of my book have come! Actually come, this moment—that is this morning's mail. And I can sit and cut it and let the folks here read it and all. I am glad it came while I was here—I wanted it to. The young sister is anxious for it. . . .

And now, darling, last and first and highest and deepest— is the joy of *YOU*. . . .

. . . The happiness of having you to love me just grows and grows in my heart—the healing of it—the sort of mended strengthened re-born feeling. . . .

I believe I wrote you rather dismally yesterday. That lecture wasn't so bad after all. Some think it was the best I've given yet. I guess it was Mr. Royall personally who took it the worst. I've heard many pleasant things about it. So that's off my mind also. O I could just roll over in the grass like a happy cat—I feel so good! . . .

. . . I am more pleased than I can say to have you so genuinely interested in "the social organism". Pleased way through. And I must get to work and into my book on it— maybe that will help.

I do care very much about it; but I love you so well that I don't *think* I should suffer materially if you remain an individualist. It would be a tremendous bar though—to have so utterly opposed a basis for our whole views of life. Well—there's time enough. . . . A conception so new, so large, so utterly different from all preconceived ideas, must take time to possess the world's thought. It's my business to help it, and if I have you to labor on— you, calm, rational, logical, well equipped on the other side—it will do me yeoman service. If I can convince you I have done it for millions. If I can't, the practice will still help. So take heart of grace—you have a long siege before you! I don't care so much for your being a socialist proper—but I do about your seeing the "organic" theory of social development. . . .

I must get to have a clearer understanding of municipal politics—perhaps

I might even be a little use some time in suggesting things. You can teach me so much dear! . . .

Near 10.30 Sunday A.M.
May 22nd. 1898
Goldsboro. N.C. . . .

Two of your letters yesterday!

2.35 P.M. . . . then it was church time. I went to the Presbyterian one, just across the way from us—whose tender organ music has added to my pleasure here.

'Twas a foreign mission sermon—salvation & damnation—I quite suffered. To think that "Christianity" still obtains among us in such a guise! . . .

Mrs. R[oyall] said yesterday she wished I loved her lots. Poor woman! Beautiful, gifted, young, and *so* unhappy! . . .

A whistle blows continuously—I wonder if the rumors of a naval victory are true. I'm sure I hope so. Won't I be glad when it's all done, and I can breathe in absolute freedom again.

I'm quite mortified to find myself behaving so badly about this war. I shall be more patient with other women after this. . . .

As to my being "a very fascinating woman" I do not admit it all. Even for the first time or two. Some people like me, others don't. Your father don't. Your Aunts don't. . . . And the people who don't are apt to be very nice people, and ones that I wish would. Some people in an audience come up and shake hands and say nice things. Many more go out silent. How do I know what they think? No Sir! I am grateful everyday for the liking I get, but it always surprises me. And when I meet disapproval I feel that I am indeed "a naughty girl" and deserve all I get. It will take more than one lifetime to outgrow that state of mind I think.

I don't know why you should be so surprised about the women. Women are human—and so am I. I know women best, and care more for them. I have an intense and endless love for women—partly in reverence for their high estate, partly in pity for their blind feebleness, their long ages of suffering.

If women didn't like me I should be astonished. When men do—that surprises me. If men liked me more than women, that would mean mere sex attraction; and you know I do not rate that very highly—in any one—and still lower in myself. I like to have men like me over and above that—as a friend, and I'm proud to say some do.

If I thought I drew or held you by "fascination" I should be bitterly ashamed. But surely you knew me and love me first as a friend and cousin—and only gradually succumbed to the other influence. . . .

I think that the thing I am here to do is a big thing—the truth I see deep basic truth, and that I have been given unusual powers of expression. I truly hope that my life will count for much good to the world—as Darwin's did, and Galileo, and many another blessed soul who was given high place to serve the world.

But when it comes to the woman of me, and my fitness and desirability for marriage, all this counts against me. Great men are by no means the best husbands. And to be a great woman is as yet so painful and sacrificial a task as to shear and cripple the poor female thing most cruelly.

By virtue of what I have of greatness I am the less desirable wife—even if I were young, beautiful, healthy, and no relation.

As it is you take a "damaged article," "defective" to begin with, and "shopworn." . . .

I truly think, with this clear cold head of mine that goes on thinking under and over every pain and pleasure I ever knew—(except when you make my reason fly!) that you are precisely the most valuable kind of husband I could have—if I have any. It was very strange—the re[c]ognition of that that forced itself on me as I grew to know you. Your qualities fit mine, marvelously. My defects are counterbalanced by your excessive generosity, devotion, unselfishness. I think you will be better able to be content with the scrappy life I can give you than almost any man I ever saw. If I married some kind of a genius—as indeed I did, before,—he would *need* also—I feel it as a drain. Now if we are clever enough to avoid housekeeping complications, I shall not feel that you need much of anything from me except love. And that crop seems coming on finely.

The very fact that your life is, in a way, commonplace, makes me feel easier about you. As my work has forced me into what has always been held a man's place; so it seems in many ways, as we have often noticed, as if you held the woman's place toward me. And yet—surely my lover—my husband—you find no lack of womanliness in me—do you, dear?

I think it is a miraculous dispensation of Providence. I am not yet all the time sure that it is right for me to have it; but I confess it grows on me!

The more I see myself surrounded by your love, backed up by your wide culture and education, the material details of life settled by our business partnership and yet my freedom of motion guaranteed—the more I think it means long life and health and good work accomplished. It still seems to me an awful sacrifice for you. But you don't seem to feel that way! On all usual human grounds you are the one who ought to have the personal devotion—the life consecrated to your loving service. I seem to be swallowing you.

But since from all I can make out you are the kind of angel that only seeks to be swallowed—and since, being a free agent, you frantically insist on my being the swallower—preferring to find pleasure in the process—why here goes! . . .

That's the way I feel about you. You are big hearted enough to take me in, all shattered and crippled as I am; to feel only pity instead of blame for all my wretched years, to ignore every disadvantage and injury to yourself, and to want—honestly to *want* to have me to take care of and give your life to.

For me not to do it—not to let you, however nobly I might mean it, would seem to be a real loss to you—a dreadful pain.

I blame myself still for not having had strength to draw myself away while yet it would have cost you but little—but that time is gone. And I fear still that the years will bring me bitter remorse when you find what a burden you have shouldered.

So. . . . I am accepting the sacrifice of a good man's life—his giving up the home he might have had, the children he might have had, the advantageous connection he might have had: —the good human happiness that he may devote himself to me. Maybe after all I can not bring myself to do it; and shall think it better to break your heart for ten years time even—and still leave you a chance of happiness after that.

But I forget—how about my heart? Wretch that I am! I can't afford another crack, to say nothing of the utter crushing this would be! . . . I'm very much afraid that I am going to marry you just because I love you so I can't help it! O this is most ignominious! I resent it—I do really. I never intended to do any such thing ever!

But this thing grows and grows until it is just a blind groping hunger that will be satisfied with nothing till it can find you—feel you—and then I can shut my eyes and sleep.

I feel wicked—shamelessly wicked—as if some one had caught me eating an angel—or plucking the poor thing in preparation for the feast—but if they took it away I should fight for it desperately. . . .

8.40 A.M.
Mon. May 23rd. 1898
Goldsboro. N.C. . . .

There are, it is true, two other men in the world who would be glad to marry me at any minute—but I do not love them—they don't count. Moreover they are in no way to be compared with you—in birth, breeding, education or looks. They are more suitable in age, and they agree with me in my ideas—fully and cordially; . . . but—they don't compare with you in "eligibility" on the general plane. . . .

The last man I loved—and, I think, would have married, did not love me. No other men have loved me since—or, O yes, there was one more that I might have married,—I had clean forgotten him!

Three, since '93—none since '95—till you came. That was only '96, after all—or 7. Come to think of it it was about one a year since I took that queer turn and became "attractive."[17]

But as to picking you out—why dear, there was no one on the horizon except the slowly dying image of the last—I did honestly love that good man; to a degree. . . . I was steadily strangling out of existence the thought of the last—it cost a good deal, too; and buckling down anew to the prospect of life without personal love, when you came. And you, "by your persuasive flattery and external charms"—you, with a slow and masterly campaign; proceeded to attack me on my utterly defenseless side—a side unfortified—unmanned—where I had never dreamed of attack—by the old sweet ways of girlish memories and family affection.

Such helpfulness, such pleasant friendliness, such merry companionship, such plain straightforward useful help—these I had never known. . . .

9.30–35 A.M.
Tues. May 24th. 1898. . . .

I lectured again yesterday afternoon, on "What we owe our children" at 5 P.M., to accommodate those who lacked escort to come evenings. (Note [the] disability of women!) It went well. There were not very many present—but they were good ones and enjoyed the talk I could feel. It is a subject I get very much excited on. Folks seem to keep on liking me. I am gaining ground I think even with Mr. Royall. Now I must leave off lazily talking to you; and get to work. It is such a pleasure to touch you—even this way. . . . I, who erstwhile felt like a little wet starved stoned street kitten, am become plump and vigorous, a petted saucerling, under the plenteous comfort of your constant love. . . .

9.42 A.M.—
Wed. May 25th. 1898. . . .

The "youth of the town" I spoke of are school children. I have met almost no men here, and those I have, married and staid, show no signs of more than polite tolerance to an eccentric stranger. My welcome is among the women here. They do like me far better than I expected. You, being utterly besotted, imagine that every one else thinks me as handsome and attractive as you do—but they don't. I chuckle inwardly, to think how surprised they'd all be to know that I had a real live lover, as ardent as any of theirs—these sweet young girls. . . .

Goose Angel! Thickheaded Seraph! Come now! Summon the legal mind! Be rational. Devise for me the kind of man whom you honestly think would make me a better husband . . . to know and understand and sympathize and bear with me—to make me happy at home and let me freely go and come as I must—to care for my work and help me do it. . . . Satisfied? Why, Darling, you satisfy wants I did not know I had, as well as filling my cup till it runs over—such cups as I was thirsty for. . . .

Nearly 4. P.M. . . .

. . . I had to learn how to open my heart to it. I have never felt such joy—never. And it grows sweeter and fuller and richer—swells and swells like music—till I feel as if something would break—as if I couldn't hold it! . . .

You know I have told you all along how much words are to me—how much I get through them. And, from you who do not naturally run to words as a medium of expression, they mean even more. So when I see how much you find to say to me—how easily and fluently and gladly you say it, and what dear delicious kindling satisfying love letters you write—why I feel as if for love of me you had worked a miracle. . . . I'm simply swimming in it—near drowned in happiness! . . .

. . . It sort of rises higher and higher till I choke a little—have to get off the ground and float in it.

I've been happy before. I was as happy as I could hold with my friend Martha. And I've been happy for years in the great sunlight of God's love. That sun still shines, and under it has flowed into my life this all embracing sea of love from you. If this goes on I shall lose consciousness of it almost . . .; shall just feel "this is life!" . . .

Dear—it touches me so—to have you tell me again of the love of that dear with the beautiful eyes I knew so long ago. Such a dear boy! I think it is one of the sweetest things in life to have a feeling go way back and connect with childhood's heart! If, when I am loving you so fully now, and by and by—when I am holding you in my arms, quite still and fully satisfied with kisses—when I look deep into your eyes and smile resistlessly from my unbounded happiness—if then it connects in your mind with the child love of long ago—well it must taste good. Seems like a full cycle somehow. . . .

11 A.M.
Friday May 27th '98
Goldsboro N.C. . . .

I'm glad you have taken solid ground about the 7th and your own stand. This war is not like the last. I see no earthly reason why a man should go— at present—unless he wants to. . . .

The poor girls here, and mothers—and sisters—with their boys gone;—

and all the bitter memories of the last war so real and fresh to them—it wrings my heart. And I do feel honestly ashamed of my selfishness about you. . . .

O—I forgot to state that last night was the last lecture—"Our Own Duty," that there was a good house—of "the best people" and it went off very well; and I have been settled with this morning—$37.50!

That's not bad a bit. My total assets just now are 42.50. . . . This visit has been a real success in the best way. . . .

3.10–15 P.M.—
Sat. May 28th. '98. . . .

Mrs. R[oyall] says I've done her more good than anybody she ever met. Says a lot more than that—that I have made life easier for her—put her in touch with her own town—and so on.

The people are wonderfully appreciative here. This is what I missed so in New York. Nobody wanted me—I had no chance to serve—no professional call. These people are hot to have me come again—to arrange for lectures next fall. I'm willing. I'd just as soon be South as anywhere next winter. Truly dear it would not be wise for me to be in the city with you. Letters are better for us now. . . .

This visit has set me up most needfully, made me feel genuine and strong and useful again. I need it—the personal touch, the "heart to heart talk"(!!!) . . . It doesn't shake me a bit about you. . . . I do not think that will interfere. If it did I should tear loose—if I died. We mustn't let any ancient instincts get the better of my present necessities. . . .

9.30 or so. A.M.
Sun. May 29th. 1898. . . .

. . . You are so gentle, so tender, and so exquisitely self-restrained that passion does not show in you as it does in some men—either to plead or to demand; but I am beginning to read it in beneath and behind . . . and I like to see it—as a woman must. I like to feel the force and fire of it—as a woman must. . . .

2.37 P.M.

. . . I shall endeavor, dear boy, to postpone the day when you have been kissed enough as long as I can. But I am such a pig myself that I shall find it hard to cut your rations down. You see it works both ways, and I can't leave you unsatisfied without being unsatisfied myself. But I shall hope that it will be a long long time before you have enough. . . .

9.6 A.M.
Mon. May 30th. '98 . . .

I take such continuous comfort in the kind of man you are—your quiet undiscussed right doing. I have absolute confidence in you. Confidence—reverence—honor—faith—trust—reliance—all the things like that I have for you— loads of 'em. And . . . so exquisite a lover. . . . And—if it isn't too much of a come down—such jolly fun! . . .

6

"What a Mother's Happiness Should Be": 1 June–22 September 1898

In *Women and Economics,* as in her short story, "The Yellow Wallpaper," Gilman explored some of the destructive effects of marriage and young motherhood. "No theme of commensurate importance has been so little studied," she wrote, and yet "Nothing in the exquisite pathos of woman's long subjection goes deeper to the heart than the degradation of motherhood by the very conditions we supposed were essential to it." Because of her economic dependence, because of "the intensely personal limits of the more primitive home duties, interests, [and] methods," the young mother faces the "pain and strain" of unused and wasted powers. "What a supreme and magnificent martyrdom," Gilman wrote, all these "exhausted, nervous and prematurely aged" mothers offering "unreasoning devotion and constant surrender" to their childrens' private needs, bearing and rearing the "majestic race to which they can never fully belong!" Clearly the problem was not motherhood itself. In fact, in her view, the mother-love potential was in many ways a primal source of Eros, of human love, of social caring, and political involvement.[1] Children needed mothers with outside interests and objectives, and mothers needed "wider combinations, more general interest, more organized methods of work for larger ends." As Gilman queried some years later, "Are we so blinded by the beautiful ideal of motherhood as it should be, that we continually overlook the limitations of motherhood as it is?"[2]

In an article entitled "Coming Changes in Literature" (1915), Gilman would call for a new fiction that would offer a true picture of the motherhood dilemma. "No more picturesque vividly dramatic subject was ever offered to the artist," she would write, than the story of this "oldest, deepest, wildest, truest passion." In fact, the "mother-love story is as unlimited as life itself." Showing "every feature of comedy and tragedy," of "humor, pathos, patience, [and] despair," it would offer background reasons for "the tumult" of emotions, the "stress and anguish," the doubt and conflict, the "slow eating disappointment which must never be owned to a living soul."

151

But it would also show the mother's gradual "awakening" and the emergence of that tragically unknown figure—"the Human Mother."[3]

* * * * *

By the summer of 1898, Gilman had already developed many of her motherhood convictions, what she had recently called her "radical and desperately unpalatable" ideas. Yet given the sheer tenacity of motherhood expectations, the deeply layered conflicts in her own as well as many other women's lives, the process of understanding and exploring them could never be linear or sudden. As she put it in *Women and Economics,* there is "no other field of thought [in which] are we so blinded by our emotions," yet none is "more pathological . . . , more morbid, defective, irregular, diseased."[4] Or as she had put it in a letter to Houghton at roughly the same time:

> You see I can't even let myself go toward Katharine, for the simple reason that it hurts so. And pain—emotional pain—means madness. I *can* not suffer any more. . . . To think too much of her is to want her—that won't do. They think I'm heartless and indifferent—I am, practically. I have to be.

For the last several years Gilman had been traveling, lecturing, and writing, and for a number of reasons had decided that her daughter Katharine should live with Grace and Walter Stetson.[5] At the time she had first decided on the separation, the combination of domestic and professional responsibilities had been almost overwhelming: nursing a dying mother, running a boarding house, trying to earn enough to pay the bills. Moreover, as she put it in her autobiography, not only had Katharine's father "longed for his child and had a right to some of her society," but also Grace Channing would make a fine "second mother . . . fully as good as the first, better in some ways perhaps." Besides, she wrote Houghton a bit defensively, "What might have been an ill effect of [my] nervous personality, she is saved; and the best of me I can give her—give her in such wise that she can have it on hand permanently and yet not be fretted by it."[6] So while Charlotte would have some summer holidays with Katharine, some weekend visits, and some occasional days when Grace and Walter Stetson were traveling through New York, for the most part she would keep in touch through correspondence. "Letters have always been a very close companionship—both ways; and in letters I can be a Mother."[7]

For Gilman the decision had been wrenching: the sense of guilt and loneliness, the memories of "Kate when she was little and O so lovely!—

and I *knew* it, but couldn't *feel* it!"[8] It "aches and aches," Charlotte would write to Houghton, "it's no use—I have to stop and cry." Or, as she put in her later fiction, she had to struggle "to hold down her grief, and use it as a spur." She had daily to control the "ceaseless heartache and remorse that motherhood had meant." The process necessarily required some distance, some emotional aloofness. As she had put it to Houghton several months before, "To keep open and thrillingly responsive to *the thought of her* would be, to my temperament, death. Or a mind unhinged. I cannot bear any more leaks and losses and pains."

It had been some three years since Katharine had gone to live with Grace and Walter. In mid-June 1898, however, after months of enthusiastic planning, Charlotte went to Cold Spring Harbor, New York, to spend an almost three-month holiday with her thirteen-year old daughter.[9] Immediately Charlotte wrote happily to Houghton. Everything here "is lovely and still and sweet." The "soft hazy clouds," the "shaded greens and glimmers of the trees," the "drift of gold and white . . . on the still water," the calming mixture of the "sea and the near woods and lakes." The "birds are modestly holding forth, and occasional frogs pipe pleasantly." And "O it is so good to have that dear slim tall barelegged girl with me," swimming, wading, boating, sleeping, swinging, berrying, and walking into the "great metropolis." Katharine "has waded and splashed all day; hunting bullfrogs, turtles, and other game." And at night, "we have splendid times when she goes to bed. I trying to eat her up inch by inch as she comes out of her clothes, and she, the lovely laughing thing, squirming and screaming like a mad thing, in peals of happy laughter. Last night she fairly bubbled over. Said I was such a nice mama!" Altogether, "I'm having a beautiful time with Katharine." She is as "lovely as an angel," and "to my joy, she seems to 'like' me very well."[10]

Yet almost immediately some conflicting feelings emerge in Charlotte's letters: on the one hand, the warm and sensuous mother-daughter passion—"her little body is lovely beyond words—such as you read about—or see in pictures of slim wood fairies with long wings"—and on the other hand, a sense of "stress and anguish," the "slow eating disappointment" which her later public writings so vividly portray. At first she tried to argue that she was simply overtired; or that "internal disturbances" were bothering her;[11] or that she was troubled that Houghton might feel "jealousy of Kate." More realistically, however, she admitted some resentments. The "sharp eyed Kate . . . swarms all over me," she complained to Houghton. "She is a darling . . . and yet it is sort of dreadful someway." "I'[ve] sort of lost my bearings." "I guess it brings up things—makes old wounds ache, or try to."[12] "When I get those little glimpses of what a mother's happiness should be— and think how miserably little I have had of it—. . . it just adds a few more layers to the gloom." It's "very black and it hurts—just squeezes down," "the same old smothering sense of something wrong. It blinds and strangles and sets me wild."[13] "Perhaps this will pass. But I fear me it will not be till life passes; and then I don't expect to wake up!"

Charlotte's first reaction to the "smothering" sensation was to turn to Houghton for protection, almost as though he could help her be more nurturing to Katharine or could dispel the gloom by allowing her to be the nurtured child herself. "I want to come close close to you, creep into your arms, nestle under your chin, be all wrapped and covered and hidden and held," she wrote him. "[Y]ou are my bearings. . . . You *are* there. You *do* love me. You love me, Kate and all! And I can have you both one day—two live people that belong to me." In fact, she stated in one of her more optimistic moments, "I sort of feel as if you made [Katharine] mine the more—made it more possible for me to have her," and to anticipate a "sweet home" happiness as well. "I have sort of settled down to it, as if she was permanent," and was even "trying this morning . . . to plan some way in which I could dare marry you on the good old housekeeping terms—earn my bread as a capable home-maid & cook—and have the joy of serving you."[14] And yet she almost immediately continued, and as though the "fault" were entirely hers, "I daren't undertake even that." "No—the machine won't work." "I love you . . . in a most piggish and reprehensible manner—I can't get along without you," and yet "the essential duties of the day drag and grind like juggernaut wheels." In fact, it doesn't "make me happy even to think of you," she continued. "I must get out—get away—get into new conditions somehow." "[N]othing touches" this grinding smothering sensation—"not Love even." "And as I no longer have the power to leave you . . . there's only the quick sharp step possible to me."

On the one hand, Gilman seemed to have an intensifying need for Houghton—"Not to have you to live with—not to have you to die with . . . why I can't seem to think of it"— and on the other an intensifying recognition of a resulting possibility she always feared: that she would lose touch with the strength and power within herself. It's a "full blurry sort of feeling. . . . I collapse all over . . . *feel my own weight*—feel it hang on you." "I wonder," she continued, "if a big love carries its own weakness with it— in its longing dependence? No, I don't believe it. Love is strength. Love is . . . not this helpless yearning." And if this "sickness holds I trust I shall be able to refuse even your love." For if "there is a prolonged return of this steady eating sense of gloom and weakness—I sincerely doubt if I could bear it very long. . . . Partly couldn't. Partly wouldn't." "I grieve so dreadfully to have brought you to this hurt," but "if there is no way of making you get over it but by my being out of the world—why that is not a long step." "I shall devote my borrowed funds to gathering strength enough to get away from you. . . . And if you can't get over it while I'm alive—it is easy to be dead. I can't stand this, simply can't."

* * * * *

On 1 September 1898, Gilman's diary entry reads: "See Katharine off. . . . Go home and collapse."[15] Katharine returned to California with Grace and Walter, because by midsummer it was clear that Gilman could not stand the strain. "Such a tidal wave of grovelling abnegation I never dreamed myself capable of feeling," she wrote to Houghton. Or, as she autobiographically explained the reasons for the reinstated separation:

> If I had any settled home, any settled income, any settled health, it would have been "my turn" now—how gladly my turn!—but I could hardly keep myself, even with many visits, much less keep two, so it was another good-bye.

* * * * *

For several weeks following Katharine's departure, Charlotte stayed in Cold Spring Harbor. "The whole place seems sort of new, seeing it now alone," she wrote. "I went out into the lovely water. . . . Warm, yet soft as silk, glittering and clear," as though the moist and sensuous force of nature were helping now to nurture and to mother her. "I swam on my back, looking up at the tall locusts and the clean blue sky." "O it *was* so fine," she continued. The "soft green bright apple leaves against a warm clear sky," the "[s]weet fresh smells of the moist earth and grass, the tender shade and protection of young trees, the warmth, the stillness." It was "like the passing of a black cloud," a "sudden change," a reemergence of the strength and confidence she temporarily had lost. "I shall have to write a tragedy and call it The World and The Woman," she wrote Houghton, as though already imagining her "new literature" on motherhood. "What needs most to be done now by those who can is to point out the connections so as to establish solidly what ought to be done," to develop a "plan of living" free of "hampering" domestic duties, to develop "a new power—a man's power" that separates professional commitment from the "insidious tyrant" of "home duties." "This comes nearer to the way I've been feeling this year than I've had power to put it before," she continued, and it all "points one way": the need to get back into the "lift and swing of my world feeling again," to reimmerse herself into "the great ceaseless stream immortal," to "breathe easily" again as one does while "swimming easily on ocean swells." "I don't exactly see why the present victory of the heart should so age and weaken me," but since it "is that big range of thought and feeling that has kept me alive," young and eager, "I'm going to swing off as wide as I can and see how it works." "Come now! This is what women have got to learn to do. . . . To do the world's work and live large and glad in it; to love and wed and be great mothers too." "Remember," this is not a "mere matter" of time and labor. It is a "question of life or death with me."

Letters: June 1 through September 22, 1898

[*The first few letters of June 1898 were written while Charlotte was on route from Goldsboro, North Carolina, to Cold Spring Harbor, New York.*]

8.30 P.M. Wed.
June 1st '98
SS "Charlotte"
York River Line

Allow me to recommend the steamer "Charlotte!" Of all agreeable changes! To get off that shabby stuffy dusty hot train of cars; . . . away from the weariness, thick headedness, and carsickness—and on first a little tug, and then this great white steamer. . . .

. . . Walked and walked and walked—sat and sat and sat—had the deck all to myself; and just basked in the sunset light and the big moon. It is a long time since I have had a whole unbroken sunset all to myself, *and* a moon! Let alone all that blue and rose and saffron and lavender sky, and the weltering silvery water, and a few splendid stars. I did just revel. . . .

7.25 A.M.
Penn. R.R. Stat. Baltimore MD.
Thurs. June 2nd. '98

You, no doubt, are in bed and asleep at this writing! (wouldn't be asleep long if I could reach you!) I, being of the superior sex, and a noble specimen, am careening about the country alone and unaided, and having a beautiful time. . . .

Isn't . . . funny how we reverse every established program! There you sit and here I go and come.

8.17. . . .

You are the solidest comfort. . . . And you're going to be such a superior lawyer that folks will flock to you when you are in the city and stand in line waiting for you to come back! . . .

. . . 9.30 A.M. Wed. June 8th [1898]
18 West 32nd St. N.Y.

O Sweetheart! . . . I am so happy! So calm and rich and peaceful and satisfied and full of gratitude! And yet—greedy and insatiate wretch that I am!—so eager for more and more and more of you! . . .

You are so personally sweet and satisfying to me. And you are getting to have a power over me that I almost resent. It stirs the primitive woman, with her desire to deny—to conceal—to escape. And here I sit—not writing—thinking deliciously and dangerously of you.

Till tonight, my *love*.

6.10 P.M.
Sun. June 12th '98
Cold Spring Harbor

[*After visiting in New York for several days, Houghton took Charlotte to Cold Spring Harbor, where they spent the Sunday afternoon together.*]

Under the tree by the lake, My Heart, where we spent one happy hour or two this noon. You may be at the station yet for aught I know, or under the trees near it—waiting for the 6.38. I shall be glad to hear if you made your train. . . .

. . . It is very very pleasant here. The air is good. Sort of mixture of the not distant sea and the near woods and lakes. . . .

9.05 A.M. . . .

Now I am out under a tree by the pond side. Not ours of yesterday, but a giant walnut in a little lawn of its own. . . . An oriole's nest hangs from a bough over the water. I can hear the soft rush of the water . . . the birds are modestly holding forth, and occasional frogs pipe pleasantly. I'm glad I came. . . .

That drift of gold and white is on the still water again this morning. Soft hazy clouds help make it cooler. Everything is lovely and still and sweet. . . .

. . . 9.05 P.M.
Tues. June 14th, 1898.

The fair Kate is in bed. This feat we accomplished in the dark, with faint glimmer from the three windows—not wishing to invite our friends the mosquitoes. . . .

Katharine has waded and splashed all day, hunting bullfrogs, turtles and other game. . . . O it is so good to have that dear slim tall barelegged girl with me.

The damsel Lizzie, being inspired of the evil one, sitteth opposite me and playeth shrilly upon the mandolin. I must be lots stronger than I was. All last night I didn't get cross, and once, to be kept awake that way would have made me wild. But it was a tempestuous night. The whole thing was so sudden you know—the letters, the telegrams—the dusky ride behind that old animal . . . the not having any chance to speak to you alone and relieve my mind—and there I lay and counted hours, and was pulled in two.

Out of the turmoil of "mingled emotions" one shapes itself vaguely—a queer absurd little feeling—a sort of jealousy of Kate—for you! How's that for a sentiment? I wanted to get close to you and hold you tight and assure you that having her only made me love you *more!* . . .

And tonight your letter has come and brought me such peace and comfort. In this upheaval inside I'd sort of lost my bearings. A daughter I find a very intoxicating thing.

But you are my bearings—and now I've sighted you again and feel steady. You *are* there. You *do* love me. You love me Kate and all! And I can have you both one day—two live people that belong to me. . . .

6.35 P.M. [June] 15th [1898]. . . .

O I am going to take such comfort with you. More and more I realize what a good thing it is to have a strong man to help one along. I shall become a clinging vine—I feel it coming! You will spoil me, you surely will. . . .

. . . This letter is such a dear one. Someway I was so upset by all this wonderful arrival you were some how shaken loose in my mind. I felt as if I had lost you—as if you weren't quite *real*. . . . There was she—but where were you? . . .

. . . 8.40 or so. A.M.
Cold Spring Harbor
June 16th 1898. . . .

It is a fine cool clear morning. . . .

The fair Kate is joyously searching for wild strawberries in the fields up behind the house—and finding some. . . .

She is so lovely and good. And she likes to cuddle and hug and frolic as much as she ever did. We have fine times of mornings.

This visit is far better than the other one. I have sort of settled down to it, as if she was permanent. And, to my joy, she seems to "like" me very well. . . . But in and through it all the thought of you grows more insistent rather than less. I sort of feel as if you made her mine the more—made it more possible for me to have her. . . .

. . . Now I must get to work. . . .

. . . 7.58 A.M.
17th June. 1898. . . .

Yesterday I essayed a Criterion article—with small success. [H]ope to do better today. . . .

. . . Cold Spring Harbor
June 20th [?] 1898. . . .

Please, I'm very far off, and quite lonesome, in spite of Katharine. I suspect this is due to the approach of internal disturbances presently— no harm!

But the sense of wrong in my having you comes back strongly—the feeling that I have meanly taken advantage of your loving cousinship and let you love me to your own harm—and a deep aching contrition in the thought of it.

To think that I shall always feel apologetic before all your relatives and most of your friends;—(this is only selfish cowardice—but it hurts) shall always be feeling contrite and deprecatory—and I do hate to feel so!

And—to be fully honest—there comes back the sense of strain in that I fear I shall be too heavy for you—that I must not bear my full weight.

As long as I am good—am well and strong and happy, I have no doubts of our getting on well together, and your being tolerably contented in spite of my defects and deficiencies; but when I feel helpless and want to let go and just blindly drop on something—crouch down and cry and be carried— then I feel as if you weren't strong enough—as if I should break you.

I've felt that all along you are so sensitive yourself, so tender of me— so easily distressed on my account. And when I see you suffer I shall suffer so much more. Now. What are you going to do when this great ungainly bird comes flopping down on you! I want a large calm smiling faith and hope to brace me up when mine fails. I want to feel your life so well founded and widely buttressed that when mine isn't any good I can shut my eyes, snuggle down on your breast, feel your arms around me, and *rest*—knowing that you can stand it for a while. . . .

Meanwhile I'm having a beautiful time with Katharine. She is really fond of me. Says "Mothers are nice things to have." . . .

. . . Cold Spring Harbor
June 21st. 1898

O my dear Love!

I'm very doleful indeed. I dreamed about you all night. You were being just as good—taking me around everywhere and so on,—and I—well, my head gave out in a sudden spot as it does sometimes, and I forgot you were waiting for me and stayed to dinner somewhere! Stayed to dinner, and you outside waiting for me!

Then you were very angry and stayed away from [me] all the rest of the day— . . . and I was very miserable, and am yet. I think my head must be bad, I am so blue.

I can't think of pleasant things even, except ridiculous fairy things, such as my turning into a paragon of loveliness all at once—as blooming and vigorous as a Greek Goddess, and being suddenly possessed of vast wealth, so that I could come to you right away and be worth your taking.

And there's not much satisfaction in that sort of dreaming!

I suppose you are wondering how I can be so unhappy while Katharine is with me. I'm sure I don't know. It is all foggy and dark somehow—I can't think it out. . . . She is a darling and I am taking comfort with her and yet it is sort of dreadful someway. I do not understand it at all. I guess it brings up things—makes old wounds ache, or try to. . . .

I've written a short poor thing for the *Criterion:*—and another for the Y[outh] C[ompanion]. Must copy and send off. . . .

Partly I want you to comfort me, and partly I want to crawl away and hide. My head is very thick. But I love you, blindly, helplessly just love you. . . .

. . . c/o Mrs. P. P. Jarvis
Cold Spring Harbor
June 21st. 1898[16]

A letter from you today, Heart's Dearest, that made me wish Kate wasn't around! But she was, and wondered why I didn't read it aloud to her. She knows your letters instantly, and is warmly interested in when you are to come again. Alas! alas! I fear me she is "on to us!" Nothing so sharp as a child's eyes—so keen as a child's tongue. . . .

Once in a while it occurs to me that there are two of us in this bargain, and that you are not so easy to get away from! Not that I want to get away! Only—when I feel ill—it does seem such a shame to saddle you with me. . . .

The nearest I come to not wanting you is this dreadful limpness. I collapse all over—don't hold anywhere—there's no "want"—no pull—no grip to me. And then I sort of *feel my own weight*—feel it hang on you—and being sympathetic to the verge of idiocy—it makes me ache to feel you lift it! . . .

I have never had any desire to lose or leave you. . . . You are always so good to me. There have been times when I feared that you would interfere with my work—but I got over that.

Only when I'm miserable and things hurt—I want to get away from *everything*—to run away and hide—utterly unknown. But I do love you, my own—and only wish it was more worth your while to have me. . . .

. . . 9.45 A.M.
. . . Wed. June 22nd. 1898. . . .

I am feeling better this morning. Your letter did me lots of good—lots. I read it over and over. I like so to feel the solidness of you, and that you hold me tight no matter how I wiggle. All night I thought of you—when I wasn't asleep, and some of the comfort began to come back with the thought. I wonder what it is that happens to me dear—can you think? It must be in the brain stuff somehow. For the facts don't change any, surely.

Anyway it is getting better, and as I held the thought of you close to my heart, it got sweeter and sweeter, till I could smile all to myself in the dark for pure pleasure in your love. . . . If you were willing, just for once, I should like to take you with me down the dark hole I slip into. It wouldn't do you any permanent harm, and then you'd see just how it was. *Such* a poor wretch as I feel! . . .

I want to come close close to you, creep into your arms, nestle under your chin, be all wrapped and covered and hidden and held—and just feel the warmth and comfort steal through and over me. . . . Only I couldn't have your letter in my heart because of the sharp eyed Kate, who swarms all over me. . . .

It feels so funny! It is so long since I had the blessed child in my arms. . . . It almost seems as if the child were trespassing! Isn't that absurd. . . .

I wonder if a big love carries its own weakness with it—in its longing dependence? No, I don't believe it. Love is strength. Love is all growing and bearing and doing—it is not this helpless yearning—that is weakness and selfishness—not Love. . . .

9.15 or so P.M.
Thurs. June 23rd.
Cold Spring Harbor. . . .

Yours of the 22nd is under my hand. . . .

And you'll be pleased to know that I am feeling better—much better. . . .

But my trip up north, lecture at Longwood—three days of convention and nights with a strange bedfellow—no end of talk all day and no aloneness at all—and our dear week in New York with its hurried going about— . . . all this tired me a good deal. . . . (By the way, there's such a lovely new moon tonight, bright as silver—between the green tree tops.) . . .

However its well over now—the bad two days; and I'll be all right by Sunday.

As I feel better I enjoy Kate more, naturally. She is as lovely as an angel. The young ones here are big-eyed with astonishment to see us play together. "What do you do?" asks little John, who sleeps next door. "Tickle each other?"

I guess we do. We have splendid times when she goes to bed. I trying to eat her up inch by inch as she comes out of her clothes, and she, the lovely laughing thing, squirming and screaming like a mad thing, in peals of happy laughter.

Last night she fairly bubbled over. Said I was such a nice mama! And that she did feel so happy. Perhaps I wasn't pleased! . . .

. . . 9.15 A.M.
Cold Spring Harbor
Tues. June 28th. 1898. . . .

Hark ye!—we have a new boarder! Man. Nice Man. Columbia man I *think*. Biologist name of Sumner. I am greatly pleased. Some one at the table to talk sense. Someone who can swim; and walk about, and play chess a little! . . . He is but a lad in sooth, but I rejoice in a room taken by a single gentleman, instead of a bawling young family. . . .

. . . c/o Mrs. P. P. Jarvis
Cold Spring Harbor
9.16 A.M.
June 30th 1898. . . .

. . . and this new youth is really an acquisition. He has travelled, studied read, and even thought. Rows, swims, and so on. Night before last we took a short walk in the moist moonlight after the rain, and last night he took Kate and me rowing down the harbor. Such a night! Such color of waning sunset and waxing moon! It was great. But Katharine got pretty tired. She prefers you to these new persons. (So do I.) Still it is comfortable to have a gentleman about—at the table and all. . . . "Are you the author of that remarkable paleontological poem?" quoth he with further specification; and I owned I was. Now he's reading the rest of 'em, and wants "the book."

Walter is reading the book and speaks well of it. . . .

All right! All right! I'm not damaged nor yet defective, but a blooming vigorous woman in the prime of life, well balanced and strong, wise, kind and tender. Having passed the period of capricious exaction and childish complaint I shall open before a rich pasture as it were—a calm sweet steady life. . . . O— and also—a woman of marked personal attractions and great charm of manner—nimbly statuesque (!) and of some note as an author and lecturer. Well! Well!! Well!!! It all depends on how you look at it, doesn't it? I suppose these are the things you see—but what I see is the lonesome weary crushed and withered heart that is opening slowly and timidly in the soft warm river of your love. And each poor crinkled petal has its apology as it dares unfold. And what I want to be is such a great deep glowing rose— all color and fragrance and rich yielding warmth—for you to be enfolded in! . . .

. . . **Cold Spring Harbor**
10.30 A.M.
Friday July 1st. 1898. . . .

The place continues a delight in every way. My appetite is good, and though I do not sleep as well as if I was alone, still the joy of having that dear child in my arms again is worth lots of sleep! And she clings and cuddles as if we had never been parted—bless her sweet heart!

I wish you could see us rioting together when I forcibly undress her and kiss her all over in spots—she struggling and gurgling in mingled anguish and delight. And her little body is lovely beyond words—such as you read about—or see in pictures of slim wood fairies with long wings. . . .

. . . **Cold Spring Harbor**
Sun. July 3rd 1898.
[Charlotte's birthday]

Thirty eight years old today, Dearly Beloved, and feeling very lively thank you. . . .

There are [lots] of Boarders, besides Katharine and I. . . . I have constituted myself head of the table and mistress of ceremonies, and keep them all jovial. . . .

About 9.30 A.M. July 4th.

Now yesterday I was writing in a jovial mood, and was about to tell you that your property was looking up. . . .

I eat cheerfully and don't feel so low spirited. Moreover I'm thirty eight and you are only thirty! So I'm well ahead of you now, and you have to behave and do what I say! All this cheerfulness was going on yesterday. But alas! Before bedtime I was horribly tired—just limp; and last night was as hot and sleepless as any I ever remember. A glorious night too. Full moon—big one. The pond a cool glitter of silver light and the trees pulsating in it. (There's a piece of Whitman that does it well—but you don't like Whitman.) . . .

Yesterday just before supper I seized upon Mr. Sumner and took him up to the tramp road and back—for a rest and change. "I am going with you"! announced Miss Dorothy aged nine, and possessed of a shrill insistent voice and assertive disposition.

"Indeed you are not!" said I with great cheerfulness. "I'm tired of the whole of you!" So I went off with my prey. Katharine objects to our conversation—says it isn't interesting—that we always talk about "eras." . . .

I think I'm going to get just what I want down here—enough biological thought to stimulate me to better writing—closer thinking, more accurate knowledge. Mr. Sumner has books too—some of which I shall enjoy. He has begun mine. . . .

As for you, you continue to be a frequent subject of thought—an unfailing source of satisfaction . . . Please don't think me foolish. My heart is yours—contentedly yours—settling down so gladly to the peace and power of your love. . . .

My body is yours—that you know fully—and O so happy! But my mind has never been satisfied—and it counts. When the waves of feeling that *make* me content sweep over and lessen and lessen a little, the facts loom up again like rocks at low water. . . .

. . . 9.12 A.M..—
Cold Spring Harbor–
Wed. July 6th 1898.

Good morning, Heart's Dearest,
The top of the morning to you!

I must forthwith set to work, especially as my Fabian article is not yet sent in! I can write those so much easier—because it is not for money. Necessity is no incentive to me—at least a very poor one. . . .

About 3.45

Well——I wrote the Fabian thing this morning, ten or eleven hundred words, on "Does the War Impede Social Reform?" or some such phrase. Said it didn't.

That was ten dollar's worth anyway, so I'll feel that I've earned my board this week even if I do not get it. Have heard naught of any other ventures so far. . . .

A family of seven—or ten—variously represented, two husbands, two wives, two babes, two maids, and a single gentleman, for two months—I think that is the array. . . . Still they will not *always* be here; and Mrs. Jarvis has some rights I suppose. . . .

Letters today & various. Small & Maynard write of splendid advertising in Denver, and that the Boston Pub[lic] Li[brary] has ordered fifteen copies! They are to send me ten copies. Wish I could sell 'em all at once! It would help out nicely. . . .

. . . Cold Spring Harbor—
9.23. A.M. Fri. July 8 1898. . . .

It is another beautiful day—fine weather, of the best. And not only here but around the green earth, is beauty and perfume and sunshine and song. And only in our cities is foulness and disease and—things in the wrong place. . . .

. . . 9.25 A.M. Mon. July 11th
Cold Spring Harbor. . . .

[*On Sunday, the day before, Houghton had spent the day in Cold Spring Harbor.*]

Wasn't yesterday a lovely one! And didn't we have a fine time—considering.

I'm such a pig. It's all very well fixing these things for Katharine's pleasure, but I want you *myself*—all to myself. I want to talk and read and play chess and go to walk *just* with you. . . .

Thank you and thank you again for all your thoughtful kindnesses. . . .

. . . 3.30 . . .

Dear—I am almost glad when I do not feel so much passionate longing for you; for then steals in the calm sweet friendliness and loving cousinship that makes me feel so solid and comfortable.

I am not *perfectly* comfortable—I never shall be till I have in some way become convinced that I am doing what is right. If I stay sick—earn no money—pay no debts—I shall not marry you.

And if there is no way of making you get over it but by my being out of the world—why that is not a long step.

If well, I'm good for something and not wholly disagreeable. If there is a prolonged return of this steady eating sense of gloom and weakness—I sincerely doubt if I could bear it very long. . . . but . . . if there were such years before me as are behind—with possibly worse results—I shouldn't stand it. Partly couldn't. Partly wouldn't. I've had quite enough.

Now I can say this for quite a while: "It is my duty to live! Keep cheerful, work if I can and wait and if I can't, even when I cannot see an inch in any direction"; but to do this takes a steady dogged pressure of will power; and when that gives out . . . then you collapse. However—I haven't so far. My weakest spot just now is you—the unlifted feeling that I would benefit you by being gone.

9.05 A.M.
Tues. July 12th. . . .

The more I see of you and realize what a mine of happiness you are to any woman, and the more I realize what a mine of unhappiness I am to any man—the wickeder I feel. And that I at my age should be led on by my own weakheartedness and selfishness to bring you to such an assured misery one way or the other—then I keep feeling worse and worse. . . .

. . . 9.05 A.M.
Cold Spring Harbor
July 13th 1898. . . .

I continue to be low in my mind o' nights and mornings, and any quiet times. As long as I can keep doing something it doesn't matter so much; but when I can't then it presses hard. . . .

This is such a fine large letter of yours! I cannot imagine why you should be reading that book over again. [*Women and Economics?*] I should think you had read it quite enough already. . . .

In spite of my gloom and dismal forebodings I notice a steady residue of contentment in the sense of having you there—the home feeling—the brotherliness—the indispensability of *you*. It is a thin layer so far, but it seems to be solid; and each year will add to it.

Not to have you to live with—not to have you to die with—to speak to last of all—to feel your arms holding me when this long long road is really done at last—why I can't seem to think of it.

You belong—I can't spare you. And I love you more and more. . . .

. . . 10.10. A.M.
Cold Spring Harbor
July 14th 1898.

Worse and worse dear. Head thick and bewildered. Can't think straight. Get some words wrong in talking—only "absentmindedness"—but it troubles me. Don't make me happy even to think of you! Except that I'm glad you're not legally bound to me yet. You shan't have any such wife as this I promise you!

My most grievous meditation is that if this comes on so heavily while I have Katharine with me, you at hand, and a comfortable country life—with no worse money pressure than I may always expect—that it must be a permanent condition. Chronic & mean, liable to come at any time. . . .

I have a vague plan for the winter—which I suppose I shall live to somehow, though now I can't see a foot ahead. If nothing opens I'll go to Ruskin, or that Christian Co-operative Colony in Georgia—I forget its name.[17] There I could easily do things that would keep me; and in the flux and stir of such a place I dare say I may pick up some stimulus and start again.

I know there is but one right thing to do—just to bear it patiently and try to work. There's an end to all things thank goodness. And it's by no means a[s] far off as it was once.

Dear me! What a sniveling goose I am to be sure!

But it's very black and it hurts—just squeezes down.

This morning I can really feel it physically—a full blurry sort of feeling in the top of my head. . . .

. . . **Cold Spring Harbor**
July 19th 1898. . . .
About 4—P.M.

Now Sweetheart your letter has come. . . .

. . . I don't exactly see how you are going to be with me in a "real desolate time" because when you come I cease to be desolate! Comparatively speaking.

But this was a pretty bad one all the same. You know I don't show it much till my strength is *all* gone. . . .

. . . Cold Spring Harbor
9.45 A.M. Mon. July 25 1898. . . .

[This letter follows another of Houghton's Sunday visits.]

I am still happy. Happy because you came to me and made things come right again. Because you loved me and comforted me and brought the sunlight back into my soul. Everything is brighter and more real and I have room to breathe. Katharine shines out anew, and I hug her with a lively sense of joy. *That* is worth while too—to have that genuine feeling of mother happiness, even for a little while. . . .

When I shut my eyes I see soft green bright apple leaves against a warm clear sky—Sweet fresh smells of the moist earth and grass, the tender shade and protection of young trees, the warmth, the stillness—and your arms. Those dear arms beneath me—those dear eyes over me—you have healed and helped and made me very happy dear.

And the little quiet talk we had has made things look more steady and rational again, more hopeful of possible good. . . .

. . . Cold Spring Harbor
July 29th 1898.

No such sick old lady as this do you get for Keeps, young man! Don't imagine it. No sir. I shall devote my borrowed funds to gathering strength enough to get away from you, and shall hope to have strength enough to stay away. And if you can't get over it while I'm alive—it is easy to be dead. I can't stand this, simply can't.

My phosphates build up my physical strength a little, thank God, but the misery swings back—the same old smothering sense of something wrong. It blinds and strangles and sets me wild. I must get out—get away—get into new conditions somehow.

Since May '97 I have not felt really well—at my best. And that was the first glimpse for many years.

It is [no] use dodging facts—this is a genuine mental disease of some sort, and nothing touches it—not Love even. This summer has shaken me to the very foundation. . . .

. . . The first partial peace of mind I have known this summer comes from calmly recognizing this fact.

What remains is to seek such conditions as will maintain my strength a little longer, and work humbly and faithfully to get my debts paid before I am unable to work. That's the honest thing to do, and also the shortest way out of the whole business—for of course the harder I work the sooner I give out finally. . . .

. . . c/o Mrs. P. P. Jarvis
Cold Spring Harbor
August. 7th. 1898. . . .
[Houghton's birthday]

This is a sorry attempt at a birthday letter for you; and extends congratulations on your entering the thirties with me! May they treat you better! . . .

Yesterday I felt really very jolly, swept my room nimbly . . . and sewed some; with much sport with Kate. . . . I have to keep up somewhat on account of Kate's instant sympathy. If I cry—she cries. That won't do at all.

I spoke lightly of her losing me one day, saying that she had abundance of other parents; and she said promptly that none of them were as nice as I was! Last night, cuddling me closely, she inquired why it was that one's mother was better than anything else in the world; and I solemnly explained the physiological growth of this feeling. She does seem very fond of me. And a more delightful companion than she is I never saw. I am thankful to say that there have been several days when I have really felt the joy of her—quite some occasions. That is a good feeling to remember.

When I get those little glimpses of what a mother's happiness should be—and think how miserably little I have had of it—it doesn't make me rebellious any more—I've passed the power of even that reaction but it just adds a few more layers to the gloom.

But Katharine is a comfort in spite of all. She is so beautiful to look at, and so continuously pleasing in demeanor, and so loving. And I cannot blame myself for having her—she seems so to enjoy being, and to be so worthy of life. . . .

12.45. . . .

. . . I was trying this morning in the dreary half hour or so that is between waking and rising to plan some way in which I could dare marry you on the good old housekeeping terms—earn my bread as a capable home-maid & cook—and have the joy of serving you. . . .

But I daren't undertake even that. This thing has overthrown me before now in the midst of housework; and then the essential duties of the day drag and grind like juggernaut wheels. Your health and happiness would suffer at once. No—the machine won't work and I dare undertake no partnership with such a wreck. . . .

. . . **Cold Spring Harbor**
Aug. 13th 1898. . . .
5. P.M.

. . . I have never felt that it was *right* to marry you; and with such illness as this settling upon me I am quite sure it would be wrong. I am weak enough, as you have seen, in turning from such a heavenly hope of love and comfort; but I am strong enough, as you have also seen, to refuse to do a thing I felt sure was wrong. So that if my sickness holds I trust I shall be able to refuse even your love.

It is so strong a likelihood that I think you will be wisest to face the facts and use your love in forgiving me for having gone with you so far. That was wrong too—but not so clear as this—there was the big hope always.

Now I don't see any hope at all—except that I may be given strength to live out what remains as bravely and usefully as I may. . . .

You dear dear tender loving soul! Never have I known such wide soft all embracing joy as you have given me. And it will keep too—just to have had it is a great deal.

I grieve so dreadfully to have brought you to this hurt that I simply do not think of it—dare not—as long as I can help it. . . . And any way you have had some good, surely, and are at worst but widowed of a very poor wife before you have learned much dependence on the creature. You are young enough to outgrow the pain and *do far better* in time. . . .

. . . Cold Spring Harbor
Aug. 30th 1898. 9. a.m. . . .

I felt very weak Monday morning, and low, but not miserable. After some games with Katharine I had to give up and go to sleep—about 11 o'clock perhaps. Slept soundly for two hours, and woke feeling well and happy. Such a sudden change—like the passing of a black cloud. Before I *thought* one thing I *felt* the difference. It is no wonder I am cheerful when I'm not sick. "There is no joy so keen as pain's release." It is simple bliss to feel the sunlight in my brain after the long dark. All day I felt better, and though I tired towards night it was not the black tiredness. . . .

. . . You are so *mine* that I can't lose you it seems to me—I feel you close and warm and tender with your arms around me still.

O my lover!—my Husband! I can't think straight about going or staying. I can't tell what it is right to do—I am simply *in* you and can't get out . . . It did me so much good to tell you about it dear. . . . And to just let go and cry—and all the time to be happy because I was with you and—O my darling— that blessed time when you were asleep—really sound asleep— and all the time we were so truly one! . . .

. . . Cold Spring Harbor
Sept. 7th. 1898. . . .

[*Katharine had recently left Cold Spring Harbor to join Grace and Walter Stetson.*]

I'm the goodest little girl you ever saw! About 7.30 I arose— . . . and went out into the lovely water. O it was so fine! Warm yet, soft as silk, glittering and clear. I swam on my back, looking up at the tall locusts and the clean blue sky. . . .

. . . and now a word or two with you. Not many—I mustn't overdo. But I love you, Sweet, in a most piggish and reprehensible manner—I can't get along without you. I don't know how you are going to stand it, but I fear your fate is sealed. It's well posted, anyhow. . . .

. . . Cold Spring Harbor
6.40 P.M.
Sept. 8th. 1898. . . .

Everything here looks lovely to me. I enjoy my days. . . . The whole place seems sort of new, seeing it now alone! . . . Wrote a bit for the Fabian on *The Modern Heart*—not very good stuff; and several notes and cards as well. Rowed a bit before dinner, nap afterwards—fine one; then wrote a bit more, bathed, rowed, played ball against the house, and read for a while also.

Good straight days without any breakdown in them. Sat on the porch and watched the great pink sky with keen pleasure—waiting for your blessed letter. . . . Dear—I love *you*. Not only your dear body. That is a prominent fact and will get in my way, so that I am forced to pay some attention to it; but you, the whole of you, the things you say and do and are, the delight of being with you, the joy of loving you, the undeserved sweetness of your love. . . .

. . . You have aroused all the long-buried home instincts from my very childhood—kindled hopes and wishes I thought mere ashes—and added a lot of healthy new ones.

I never imagined I could so depend on anyone. And there's a terror in it—for I may lose you. No one was ever so necessary to me that I could not face the thought of losing them. I cannot face it *now*. . . .

. . . Cold Spring Harbor
9.15 A.M.
. . . Sept. 9th. 1898. . . .

I see before me that sweet home we have planned, more possible and real and near than ever. Life looks clear and bright again, and the ground feels solid under foot. It is a most delicious air today, cool, clear and full of sunlight. And it's Friday. Tomorrow I see you again. . . .

. . . Cold Spring Harbor.
Sept. 12th.
10.15 A.M. Mon. 1898. . . .

. . . I seem to have been floating along in the world, apparently solid and strong: being thought a brave cold indifferent woman; and now—the minute anybody cares to come near and take hold of me—it is just a mass of ruins—all goes to pieces when you touch it. Now with this weak head that can't stand any sort of pain or strain; and a thousand new susceptibilities to pain and strain that I never had before— you have a fine prospect before you!

Dear heart—I tell you plainly and with a clear mind that I am honestly afraid I shall not live to marry you; will not, I mean. You've no idea how horribly it weighs on my mind—the growing sense of these miserable infirmities. And as I no longer have the power to leave you—I believe I should hang on to you even if I knew I was a leper—there's only the quick sharp step possible to me.

Now I know this is all wrong—that it is weak and wicked, ungrateful and foolish; but my head is gone to pieces this year worse than ever before; not so severely at any one time, but in a more final and general way—and I am as I say very honestly afraid that that last weakness of weak minds may overwhelm me. . . .

. . . Dearest—if—that should happen to me—you will know if no one else does why I did it. . . . This poor heart of mine is unfit to hold the passion of love that is flooding it. I am so happy—and so miserable—and in the immensity of it all the poor patched places give way and burst open again. Sweet—do you suppose that out of this awful tearing open and breaking down there will come some sort of peaceful new life? I am perfectly willing to try. . . . But I know I cannot bear some things—being kind of worn out. Sweet—Sweet—whatever happens to me—I love you as I never dreamed of loving. And don't you ever be sorry—because it wasn't your fault anyway, but all mine—every bit. And to have you—to know your love—to feel your arms about me—your kisses through my tears—is worth dying for—even worth having lived. . . .

. . . Cold Spring Harbor
Wed. Sept. 14th. 11.10 A.M. 1898. . . .

Got a nice short letter from Walter last night—from Humbolt, Nevada. . . . Says he has been thinking much of my poem on Nevada—that it is a fine description. Says furthermore that he finds Katharine much improved by her stay with me!!! That pleases me, I confess. . . .

near 7. P.M.

Most dear Husband—such a lovely letter as I got from you tonight, such a dear dear letter! It is tucked in over my heart now—I couldn't do that when sharp-eyed Kate was here! Presently it will be supper time, but I must begin right away to say how much I thank you for writing so fully—so wisely—so tenderly and strongly. I will keep this letter with me; and if any very black times come it will hold me I know. Your motto is "deeds not words" but I assure you that words mean very much to me. I suppose it is the artist's love for his chosen medium—partly; and partly this outrageously sensitive brain. A kiss touches my lips and is gone (some stay a good while!) but what you say to me I can remember, and what you write to me I have to keep. . . .

One reason it does me so much good to have you write like this is because I am so apt to forget your side of the affair. I am so used to plan[-ning] my life—what I ought to do—can do—must do; and I'm not used to thinking of anybody on earth as having anything to do with it. But you are right. I belong to you, such as I am. You have a right to the article, damaged or not, and I have no right to injure or mislay it! . . . but there is an awful sense of insecurity in having half my life lodged in some one else['s] body— and some one that I love so vastly better than myself. . . . What happens to you I feel more than what happens to me—far more. And there it is, my other self— outside of me. I can't guide or protect it—and it is . . . a terror to which all my life has been a stranger. . . . It really is a new and severe experience. I had a[d]justed myself to life as one person quite triumphantly . . .; but this being two persons! . . . Why if *I* had a graveyard cough 'twouldn't worry me a mite. *I'd* just as lieve die as not—any time. But *you!*— that[']s different.

It is the weakness of wanting something, you see. I haven't wanted any-thing, and so I didn't care. I was willing to give up, even my child if it was right. But you—I *want* you. And it so hurts and frightens. . . . It is a weak-ness, a dreadful one, and hurts my pride . . .

. . . I suppose it comes harder for my being so tough. No, I don't flatter myself I love you more than other women love their husbands—nor as much. I never did think much of my capacity that way. The magnificent self immolation of the truly loving woman is not in my line of business. I have other things which I must do. And as you see I fairly begrudge the amount I do love you!—feeling that it weakens me for my other business. . . .

That is an exquisite argument wherein you wind up by saying I should precipitate my death by denying myself a thing that I want—namely *you!* That is fine. I admit it, absolutely; and shall undertake to prolong my life by giving myself a thing that I want—namely *You.* . . .

9.30 A.M. Friday. 16 [September, 1898]. . . .

I looked over my itinerary for next winter. . . . As I am planning now it looks like—from here—New York, Prov[idence], Boston; then Mich. towns, Chicago & Ill[inois] towns, Milwaukee & Wis[consin] towns (*Perhaps* Des Moines, Omaha, even Denver!)—St. Louis, a try at Kentucky, *Ruskin,* Tennessee, *Commonwealth,* Georgia; Atlanta, Savannah, Goldsboro, Washington, Philadelphia and Penn[sylvania] towns, and so back to New York next May. How's that? It has heartened me up just to plan it. . . . Might as well try for big things as little ones. I have even thought of New Zealand and Australia. . . .

How'd you like to have me in Australia? I'd like to get into the lift and swing of my world feeling again. I am never really at peace without it. A sense of easy room and fluent usefulness—that I am here where I belong—in the world and not cramped for space; and an utter absence of time feeling too—no age, no distance, no personality, simply being an active conscious factor in Life—in the great ceaseless stream immortal, eternal, that is working out God's will on the glad earth. Then I breathe easily, and feel as one does swimming easily on ocean swells.

Now if I was not also possessed of a particularly lively woman's body, and a woman's heart that seems to be rapidly developing all the proverbial amount of devotion—why it would be plain sailing. It is that big range of thought and feeling that has kept me alive, eager, young, with the vivid power that has impressed people so. And it is this other feeling, sweeping over me in vast rising waves, that has resuscitated the little dead heart I carried about with me and made it an insidious tyrant to bring me slowly home and hold me there. I shall have to write a tragedy and call it The World and The Woman! I wonder which will win? And if the combination of elements which holds the things called "me" alive will stand the racket?

We'll see. But I don't exactly see why the present victory of the heart should so age and weaken me. It is one thing to feel like an incarnate Zeitgeist—invincible—superior to pain—patient, full of smooth power, strong to wait or ready to roll out in grand waves; and quite another thing to feel like a crushed wreck of a woman, old, sick, hopelessly crippled, and tingling with fresh shame as each new flood of love shows me what might have been—what should have been—what can never be. To take with passionate gratitude your pure and noble love—and feel always how pitifully beneath it is my real desert—my best return; to have my own personality so long buried and forgotten, rise up between me and life, and confront me pitilessly with its wretched limitations—dear this comes nearer to the way I've been feeling this year than I've had power to put it before.

Well—. All points one way now. I have a year and a half to fill in; and I'm going to swing off as wide as I can and see how it works. . . .

It's a grey day, but warmish. I . . . spent three hours on the dark glassy lake, paddling slowly without a sound; and resting under the motionless bright-leaved trees. And all day I was dodging away from the heavy pressure in my head. . . .

Now it may yet appear that I shall develop a new power—a man's power; and learn to detach my personal from my professional life; learn to be the strong free helpful spirit in my work—giving due time to it, and yet come home to you, a happy wife for the rest of the time.

Come now! This is what women have got to learn to do, if my new world is to come true! It may be part of my work to accomplish just this thing! To do world's work and live large and glad in it; to love and wed and be great mothers too—this is before the women of the world; and I must at least try at it. The most hampering circumstance is the mechanical detail of household life.

Houghton—as you value my life, my sanity, my love; use your clear mind and strong will to work out such plan of living as shall leave me free to move as move I must. You will have to give up a certain ideal of home; I shall have to give up even more—for I have had it, I know it, I love it, and every tingling nerve of endless hereditary use just jumps to be at work in it again! Help me to stand against my own sex instinct and life habits. *I must not* focus on "home duties"; and entangle myself in them. Remember it is not an external problem with me—a mere matter of material labor and time. However vague and absurd my talk may seem to you; it is practical enough to be a question of life or death with me.

The thing that matters to me is the aim and direction of my conscious life; and the kind of forces which lift and fill me if I am aiming right. Since I began to live I have tried whenever I had strength to work for what I considered to be the good of the world. Doing that I have always been strong and happy—in spite of awful loss and pain. Whenever I stopped doing it and tried to point toward some personal goal—all the light has gone out— the power has failed—and no human love or personal happiness can save a smothered soul.

My Chicago doctor warned me solemnly against any further love affairs! [He] could see the physical effects, but he did not know the governing causes. I begin to think I do. . . .

. . . Such a tidal wave of grovelling abnegation I never dreamed myself capable of feeling. I told you what my mother was—saving the very hair she cut from her husband's head—(he wore it curling a little in his neck you know, and she used to cut it), yes, and even the parings of his nails! She loved him, absolutely. It appears that I am her daughter.

But—also—I am my father's child and his nature, however perverted, was facing toward the larger right. He failed and failed, but he meant the biggest best things.

If I had found you young enough I might have been content—though I doubt it; but now—having lived so much—so bitterly long and hard, my choice has no power—I am constrained to live my life. . . .

Help me to feel that our love and our life together is but a part of the real human life, which is for the good of all. It is not that you and I are to have a pleasant home—good times together—that is but a means toward larger service. I must feel and see that our life together is a helpful factor in working for the whole world. It must be to me a means to an end—not an end in itself. . . .

. . . Cold Spring Harbor
Sept. 17th. 1898. . . .

I have defaulted in my weekly sweeping, so that I may devote my energies to that Woman's Journal article, long promised and lately sent for. Shan't waste any time writing to you either! . . .

Sunday Morning. 9.30 Sept 18th. . . .

A note from Miss [Lillian] Wald last night, most cordial, says "Dear Mrs. Stetson, Come! and glad indeed am I to welcome you to our house." . . . And so on. Now that's nice. Miss Wald is a very noble genuine woman and used to the best people. She wouldn't be so cordial without meaning it. And she's no "tufthunter" especially for such skimpy little tufts as mine. So if you want to add this to your list of proofs that I do have some good points I shan't dispute you. I'm really very much pleased. And it will do me lots of good to dip into their earnest brave lives—people who are living for others in frankest reality. So I feel real easy about the first step of my journey.

I've thought of a further extension of my itinerary. Returning to New York next May, with a couple of hundred dollars in hand, I'll forthwith start to England again, and add to my career of lecturing successes by a brief season there. Also visit and make literary and social alliances as it were. . . .

Talk about the Eagle and the Hen—what a preposterously bloated Hen I should be by that time! And I suppose nobody would believe that the creature would turn to the downiest of small chickens and run peeping into your pocket on the first opportunity.

O you dear dear boy! You don't mind these airy brags if they keep my spirits up, do you? And I have every reason for longing to do a great deal in this year and a half before me. To think that a quarter, nearly, is clean lost! However that's done and can't be helped. . . .

I would risk a great deal, my husband, for the chance of leaving you a piece of my heart—and body—to love you when I am gone. You see you're likely to be left anyhow; and perhaps early; and then I'd be *so* much happier to leave a representative to keep on loving you. . . .

As to my two weeks of quiet—I can't say I'm enjoying them. . . . Yesterday I really wrote that article—2000 words. Not bad either. . . . Still I didn't feel any worse for it later, and spent some pleasant hours on the pond in the afternoon. . . .

. . . Cold Spring Harbor
. . . Sept. 19th 1898. . . .
. . . Quarter of eight. . . .

. . . Dearest—under all the murky confusion of my mind, it does seem to me that you are offering to me the best hope for what remains of my life and strength. If I am to break and fail this will surely not hasten such catastrophe; and if there is enough left to build up and go on, the peace and comfort you give me will be its best safeguard. . . .

And like a much transplanted tree it is very slow work for me to take root. But I begin to feel the rootlets grow. . . .

Cold Spring Harbor. Long Island N.Y.
about 11. A.M.
Sept 21st. '98. . . .

I've had a good night sleep, lots of breakfast, a row on the smooth sunny pond. . . .

And then I thought as clearly as I could, "what is this work of mine which has governed my life so far—what have I really done or am I likely to do that will be affected by marriage?" And it seemed to me that at bottom I was really a *thinker;* a kind of social philosopher; and that my best expression was and would always be in writing, and in an essentially amateurish and inspirational sort of speaking. Then—trying to hold on to reality—it seemed to me that there was nothing to prevent this work, and much to help it in our being together; that it would probably grow saner, rounder, sounder, more effective. Against this is always the thought that what I have done that counts most—the best of the poems and lectures, and the thoughts of the book—has come to me in wild untraceable ways, sort of mid-sea currents. While I was afloat and hoped for no harbor. I have the feeling that I am choosing comfort and respectability as against the hard but fruitful path that was truly mine. . . .

You know another thing that has kept me from taking root in this new happiness is the ingrained terror that assails me as soon as I feel fast to anything. The moment my mind really settles with a sense of true permanent possession, shudders of dread run through me—I pull and pull and cannot rest till I have torn loose again and am stammering—"no—I'm not tied—I can get away—I *can* get along without him—I *can!*" But I'm settling more and more all the same—I can't seem to tear loose—it grows *faster than I can pull* off!

9.45 A.M. Thurs. Sept. 22. 1898. . . .

. . . I wish I could make you feel—just for a short half moment—only enough to *know*—what a fearful weariness it all is. The sensation of bad dreams are nearest it—that clinging weight—the sensations that have no sense, the prodigious efforts put forth with infinitesimal results, the over-mastering dread through it all! Well—there is a waking after bad dreams. They pass with the night and one forgets.

Perhaps this will pass.

But I fear me it will not be till life passes; and then I don't expect to wake up! . . .

. . . the strongest most lasting and safe bonds that you can hold me with are in what mental life we have in common.

To think together——! When I feel *that,* the real understanding, the common vision, the same perception in the two brains—then the sense of union goes down down to the very roots of life, and at last I rest.

It is not to be expected that our two brains shall match at all points. . . . But there are many many places where I catch again and again that delicious sense of nearness—likeness—oneness; which I am thirsty for with all my heart. . . .

You know my scheme of life pretty well I hope. First, in youth, "Here am I. How shall I best develop myself so as to do best work?" Field of study and action easy to follow.

Second. "Here is the world. What ails it that it cries so? Hm! Dirty. Hm! Sick. Hm! Hungry" etc. etc. Then "How came it so?" Then—and this [is] the main issue of life—"How can we best apply our personal energy to conditions natural and social so as to soonest and easiest produce better results?"

You know what minor points I have worked out, gradually focussing my study, till I am pretty clear now as to the lines of action best for the individual and for society—the progressive changes in personal relation set forth in my book, and the progressive changes in social relation which are vaguely covered by the word "Socialism."

What needs most to be done now by those who can, is to point out the connections so as to establish solidly what ought to be done; and then— this is the "practical issue"—what actual steps should be taken first.—I see a whole book spreading itself out before me. The book I meant to write this summer!—Well Sweetheart. I believe I'll gather my poor brains together— sweep 'em up in a dustpan! and begin a great long slow book *on you!* Poor "dog"! I'll make you my public and try to convince you first. And such is my opinion of your well stocked conservatism that I think if I convinced you I should have carried all New England!

If I can only have the patience! And the strength!

Do help me Sweetheart! I know you will. I know how heavenly good you were over the other book, our book—that you handled every page of and worked over so patiently. O dearest Heart! To think and work together! If we can do *that* all else will take care of itself. If my mind is occupied on these lines I swing clear of all the weakness and confusion. Literally and physiologically—all my pain and consequent disease and morbid action is in that field of the brain used in personal relation; and the injured tissue there, in its waste or lesion or atrophy, or whatever ails it, weakens the whole mass. All the rest is clear and sound though weak. Now it seem[s] to me plain and practical medicine to gently stimulate action in the uninjured part and so strengthen the organ as a whole while leaving the injured part to heal in the blessed anesthesia of local disuse and unconsciousness. My life alone did this, largely; but left the ill spot all unfed. Now you are bringing me food and drink and blessed blessed comfort where all has been waste so long—and yet the very activity so set up revives the old pain and morbid action. . . .

Truly Houghton I think I am nearer the truth of what ails me than any doctor ever got. .... .

So——I have written myself into a larger hope than I have felt for long; a hope of permanent recovery. . . .

7

"Hope and Power": 4 October–15 November 1898

Charlotte Gilman's next place of residence after the Cold Spring Harbor "holiday" was at the home of Alice Stone Blackwell, in Dorchester, Massachusetts, just outside of Boston.[1] This "is a fine place to be," she wrote to Houghton. "A green garden slopes down before this big yellow and white home; with easy rich old flower beds, and heavy hanging fruit trees." "A big comfortable house" "meant for other people as well as 'the family'." "Good air. Good food. . . . Perfect quiet and freedom. And pleasant people to be with at meals." "[I feel] as if my brain was all open and pulsing pleasantly, . . . a rich sense of fulfilled function." Even Alice Stone Blackwell "says I am good to be with—that . . . it is 'enlarging to the mind' to have me about." She offered "to supply me cash if I needed it," and "on the ground that I was of too much value to the world to be allowed to need anything. Now that is a proper spirit. Why don't I have a shrine and people bring me offerings—it seems no more than proper!" Moreover, "I get these folks into gales of laughter. . . . The tales I tell to get 'em in a good humor— the way I rile 'em with one hand and smooth 'em with the other." But it "wasn't hard, for they probably laugh and 'carry on'" that way every day; "they seemed to be that kind."[2]

For Gilman, the Blackwells had a model family, the kind she wished others would aspire to and the kind she wished she had herself. "Here the people live in the thought of world helpfulness. . . . They care about people at large, 'movements,' and 'questions,' and give their steady lives to helping on what they think right." Long-term activist in the National American Woman Suffrage Association, an 1881 Phi Beta Kappa graduate of Boston University (one of two women in her class), Alice Stone Blackwell was currently "gathering copy, reading proof, preparing book reviews, and writing . . . crisp, hard-headed arguments"[3] for the Boston *Woman's Journal.* And her parents had a rich history of political involvement also—in the abolitionist and woman's suffrage movements and in fighting for women's educational and professional advancement. Lucy Stone, Alice's mother, had been a "genuine pioneer," as Gilman later put it, "one of the first—and sweetest—of our suffrage leaders, in days when speaking for that cause meant real danger as well as abuse." Henry Blackwell, Alice Stone Blackwell's father, was active in the women's movement also. He grew up in a family of professionally active women; his sisters, Emily and Elizabeth Blackwell, were the first two women physicians in America, and his sister-in-law, Antoinette Brown Blackwell, was one of the first women to be ordained and to become a minister. Henry Blackwell was himself a co-founder of the American Woman Suffrage Association and an editor of the Boston *Woman's Journal.* These are "brave progressive people," Gilman later wrote, and "among my most honored friends."[4]

Increasingly Gilman felt confident and happy in the Boston setting. She was talking with suffragists and social activists at the *Woman's Journal* office. She was writing more effectively—"ten short clear pages saying just what I wanted to; and no end of triumphant chuckling as I did it. O it was fine!" And she was delighted also in the enthusiastic response to her talks and lectures. The Boston *Advertiser,* for instance, after a lecture at the Massachusetts Woman's Suffrage Association, described Gilman not only as "very pretty" but also as a speaker with a delightfully engaging wit:

> Her good nature is such that nearly every period in her discourse is filled in with an infectious ripple of a laugh that invariably sets her audience smiling, and so everybody is good natured, and of course they always agree with her. Who could help it?[5]

Moreover, Gilman also was getting enthusiastic press attention for her publications, particularly for her recently revised and enlarged *In This Our World* poetry anthology. "[I went] around to my worthy publishers," she wrote Houghton, and "found their scrapbook of reviews. . . . I do not see how a 'young author' could possibly hope for better reception." "They are seeing what I have tried to do—tried to show."[6]

In *Harper's Weekly,* for instance, William Dean Howells called her poetry the best "civic satire" that America had produced since *The Biglow Papers.* Another reviewer admired the "indignant passion," the note of "revolt at the conditions" of life as we find it. Or as the *American Fabian* put it, "She has a mission—to show a somewhat Philistine world the absurdities and paradoxes of its customs, speeches and thoughts." Of course a number of reviewers expressed some reservations about her occasional stylistic incongruities, about her "excessive" use of didactic arguments, and about her "excessive" focus on the women's issue also.[7] But, for the most part, Gilman was pleased both with the "volume of commen" as well as with the "general high average of judgement." Moreover, she continued, her publishers (Small and Maynard) said they wouldn't "be in the least surprised if they sold 10 or 20 thousand copies of my books this fall." And not just copies of the *In This Our World* anthology. They also "calmly" said that *Women and Economics* "is the book of the time, that it is being called for from all over the country," that "it would be their best seller."—"Am I crazy?" Twelve cents for each book of poems; fifteen for each *Women and Economics* copy. That means a "couple of thousand dollars coming to me in January or February? . . . I say—if that is so—or half of it—it means a lot, don't it? Debts clearing off in fine shape, . . . and *such* a boost to my health and spirits." "Of course this may not happen, half of it, but doesn't it sound *fine!*" "Why—why—I begin to feel prosperous!!!"[8]

Although Gilman acknowledged a note of "high horse" bragging in her letters, she seemed to need to quote other people's affirmations as a backdrop to her strong and cheerful public stance. At other times, she struggled, as women so often do, with the unfamiliar prospect that she could be author/authority herself. "Then comes the 'can I?' Other people do—why not I?" In fact, as she described it, it came as something of a shock when people responded so enthusiastically. When she spoke at Wellesley College, for example, she was delighted that two "eminent and learned ladies" on the faculty had given her a "warm friendly *equal* welcome." And "if women like that think my head is good it must be worth something—don't you think so?" "You see I always give that impression of being learned. Funny!" Or again, following a speech at a small gathering of Boston women: "The talk went well—very well." And afterward, one "dear old lady drew me aside . . ., and poured out a big black sorrow in family life—with tears—and—— O Houghton, . . . even to you I cannot speak of these things. It is as if the very hand of God touched me, when a soul comes to me like that. Don't you see how it proves that this is my work? I can never give it up." "I am praying to keep steady . . . to go slow—not to get excited and puffed up—to take it all easily and naturally" and "to believe that great joy is as easy to God as great pain—success as failure. . . . So I set my face gently toward success—ready to turn instantly to failure with calm acceptance—if it comes." For you "know I never am disappointed when my big rainbow bubbles become mere bits of bread or stone."

To accept the possibility of failure, to prepare herself for its "great pain," clearly this was one of Gilman's struggles, and rather standard, I assume, for many writers. And yet another struggle she was facing was far more typical for women: the struggle to accept success.[9] Like so many women, she needed constantly to test it, to confirm, and then to reconfirm, as though she did not quite believe it. And even more importantly, she had to talk herself around the notion that ambition was not "selfish," "exclusive," and therefore wrong. "I was praying one night," she wrote Houghton, "and it occurred to me that even my one wish for light and strength—the things I have always prayed for—to be able to see what was right and . . . do it— that even this was selfishly exclusive. Why me? Why was it so much more important to give me these things than others?" And "[t]hen I thought of the little [word] 'us' in the Lord's Prayer." It teaches us to emphasize the "oneness of the human race." Instead of thinking of our prayers as "selfish" yearning, we should see them as strivings of the "collective heart." Thus,

"I have been translating the Lord's Prayer to my own language," she wrote Houghton, "and seeing what it means as I never did before": that to "experience" God is to affirm the "Inner creative force of all of us."[10]

As Gilman continued "translating" the Lord's Prayer message, it was almost as though she recognized a problem a number of more contemporary writers also face: that the traditional Christian message *needs* "translating" and revisioning, because otherwise it too often undermines a woman's sense of self-respect.[11] Consider, for instance, most women's response to the Christian emphasis on "selfishness" and "sin." Well trained in turn-the-other-cheek humility, in self-sacrificing concern for family members' needs, many women assume their own creative efforts, their ambitions, their non-domestic interests "selfishly" conflict with "duties" in the home.[12] Thus Gilman searched for a more empowering religious message, not one that would intensify women's "sense of shame" or humility or meekness, but rather one that would affirm their own creative strength and worth.[13] Of course we need to accept our limitations, she wrote Houghton. We need to recognize "the necessary disproportion between what our great human soul can think and feel, and what our small personalities can *do*." That "takes the sting out of life—gives an easy scientific patience with 'poor human nature.'" But if we are to avoid the "morbid conditions in the brain," the "strange haunting sense of discord and disproportion," we need to "let in and accept the sense of power," of "*being* humanity," of believing that "God is a force to give way to—God is *a thing you have to do!*" Or as she put it in a current *Woman's Journal* article, "Living is doing." For "what really lies before us is the improvement of living conditions for the whole world."[14]

Energized by her own living/doing spiritual and political commitment, Gilman could not help but note the striking change from the "unutterable depression and black darkness" of her recent Cold Spring Harbor "holiday." "[M]y astonishing revival in health and spirits upon leaving," she wrote Houghton, "shows but too clearly that a wandering life is . . . more conducive to my welfare than one home." Or, as she put it in a recent article, women cannot afford to stay "motionless" and "sheltered" in our "pre-historic" private homes. Instead of allowing this "immense anachronism" at the "heavy, hidden centre of our lives," we need to resist our "subjugation," demand our "freedom," and learn to use our hands and heads and hearts in larger social service.[15] The result will be the greatest "social earthquake . . . the world has ever seen," she continued, "the great sex revolution which surpasses in importance any trivial change of religions and forms of government." In an article entitled "The Causes and Uses of the Subjection of Women," she thus forcefully explained the spiritual grounding of her commitment to the woman's movement cause.

> . . . The religion of human love and social service demands that we work for each other, and the greatest obstacle to that religion is the subjection of woman . . .: we stand at the beginning of a new age, a new society. Free womanhood is

the essential condition of that new life; that she may lift her head at last, and see that the human being should love and work for more than mate and young. She will not lose the sweet, close love of those old ages, but she will add to it the larger, deeper, wiser love, the open eyes and open hands and open heart from which shall grow the civilization of a new era.[16]

To move back and forth between Gilman's published articles and private letters is to see the same spiritual emphasis developing in both, the same need for a "religion of human love and service." "This morning I had a faint little touch of the power feeling," she wrote to Houghton, "the uniting power I mean . . . the sense of constructive power." It is "almost ghastly to see how the veil [is] lifted from our . . . domestic myths;" and how "eagerly [women] owned to a wild desire" for change. And "as I hear and see and talk I begin to get more and more the sense of what needs saying next and how I can best say it. How about a book flatly on 'The Home'; or 'The Home as a Social Factor'; with deeper and wider analysis of the whole thing and its effects? . . . hurling every idol from its shrine."[17] It "certainly is my business to speak to people—there's no mistake . . . folks flock up and shake hands and say how it did them good to hear me. And it did. I could see it—feel it. I spoke on Hope and Power—and made them *felt*." In fact, she continued, "as I go about visiting and revisiting these places; and as I write letters to 'em afterward, I feel like St. Paul! It's very funny really. They count on my coming—they bring people for me to help—they listen to my words as if they were something wonderful. It is queer and exceedingly pleasant." It is a sense of the "oneness of the human race," the happiness in working together for the "eternal good," and also an inspiring reconnection with the lessons that the Lord's Prayer has to teach. "I am only just beginning to let in and accept the sense of power," she continued. "I have suffered [so] long from being—to my own consciousness—a poor little sick lone woman" that "I can't meet some things yet." But that's "what ails us about God. We have 'believed' in him, intellectually; but we have not acted as that great fact would naturally compel our acting."[18] "I've only begun." But it "is what people feel when they turn to me for help and encouragement, what gives the sense of bigness. It is big. It is a growing feeling of *being* humanity. Not just being C.P.S."

Letters: October 4 through November 15, 1898

9.40 A.M. Tues. Oct. 4th. '98
Boston, Mass. . . .

Behold me ensconced in a corner of the Woman's Journal Office—cool, shady, open window at my left, whole desk to myself, nice screw chair, clean blotter, fresh ink, new pen, and vase of nasturtiums!

All these things arranged for me here by loving ladies who are glad to see me come. It tastes good. . . .

Saw Maynard [of Small & Maynard publishers]. Says my books have sold better than any they have, though the summer has been dead. . . .

. . . *And* a letter from my husband—God bless him! What a day you had of it to be sure! A large and flourishing practice!

Meanwhile Fortune is evidently looking your way. Another offer within a week! Talk about not being able to make a living! Why you are proudly choosing among many. And choosing well. . . .

. . . c/o [Miss] A. S. Blackwell
Boutwell Ave.
Dorchester
9.45 A.M.
Wed. Oct. 5th 1898. . . .

. . . [I]s it as sweet to you as it is to me to feel all those thready little ties knitting our lives together? The common memories, common quotations, common phrases of our own. As I notice them growing I feel little thrills of quiet pleasure, and a further source of safety with each one. . . .

I have unpacked my trunk—all I need to; and hung up my rich and gorgeous garments. My extensive travelling library is arranged on a convenient piece of furniture, with a workbasket or two. I feel as settled and comfortable as I did in Cold Spring, or New York—as I ever shall until I settle for life—with you.

Mr. Maynard showed me a letter from [Maurice] Maeterlinck. He is reading Women & Economics; and cries "Behold a woman extraordinary!" One who sees clear and far—I don't remember it all; but it was very gratifying. To reach recognized leaders of thought in foreign countries pleases me, and Maaterlinck is a leader in his line.[19]

Also Mr. M[aynard] told me of an extravagant admirer in Philadelphia— Mr. Thomas B. Harned . . . —rich man—Whitmanite. He thinks I am the greatest woman in the world or words to that effect. "The Conservator" has my [poem] "Heroism" on the front page in a recent issue. All of which— and as much more as I can greedily gather, goes to make me—not worthy of you, dear love, but a little less sensitive to other people's condemnation of my letting you give your life to me. . . .

. . . Look here! Am I crazy? Mr. Small said he should not be in the least surprised if they sold 10 or 20 thousand copies of my books this fall. I'm not good at arithmetic, but . . . that looks to me like. . . . A couple of thousand dollars coming to me in January or February? I must be crazy.

But I say—if that is so—or half of it—it means a lot, don't it? Debts clearing off in fine shape . . . and *such* a boost to my health and spirits. . . .

Why—why—I begin to feel prosperous!!! . . .

. . . Think of it! I may be out of debt by next May!!! Of course this may not happen, half of it, but doesn't it sound *fine!* . . .

. . . c/o [Miss] A. S. Blackwell
Boutwell Ave.
Dorchester Mass.
Oct. 5th 1898.[20]

This morning I had a little faint touch of the power feeling—the uniting power I mean. . . . The sense of constructive power. . . .

. . . c/o Mr. H. B. Blackwell
Boutwell Ave.
Dorchester. Mass.
Oct. 7th. 1898. . . .

In spite of my magnanimously writing you not to feel that you must write to me so often, I find a day without a letter exceedingly empty and tasteless. . . . But I mean what I say all the same. . . .

Mr. Thomas Wentworth Higginson, good soul, goes for me in the Harper's Bazaar . . . in a most sentimental manner.

Mr. Blackwell suggested that I answer it and I thought of doing so, but I doubt if I can, it is so *thin.* A more irrelevant set of quotations I have seldom seen. . . .[21]

. . . Such an interesting conversation as I heard yesterday. . . . I learned these pleasing facts and opinions: There was seven years difference between Mr. & Mrs. Blackwell—she being 36 and he 29. Alice was born when her mother was 39. Another child came several years later but did not live. Mr. & Mrs. B[lackwell] were exceptionally happy. She lived to be 75—so they had thirty five or six years together. . . .

"People about that age" . . . are nearer together than they are ten years earlier or later. It wasn't as if he was a boy falling in love with an older woman. He was about thirty—quite old enough to know his own mind. In England there are many such marriages. All this pleased me very much. . . .

I wait with eager expectation for February and my publisher's account.

Those books are very genuine, written and published without hope of payment; and if they do pay I shall feel that the money is clean. Well—I must not count on it, but work and wait; and above all keep well. . . .

. . . about 4 o'clock. . . .

Shan't write you any more now! But I love you considerable. It seems ever so much more reasonable than it did. Margaret Fuller married a man younger than she. . . . Come now—why didn't you look up some precedents to comfort me with—that's right in your line, "looking up cases"—I think this was really neglecting an opportunity. . . .

5.5 P.M. Sat. Oct. 8th. 1898
c/o Mr. H. B. Blackwell. Boutwell Ave.
Dorchester Mass. . . .

O *wouldn't* I love to earn as much money as you did! . . . As to the providing—I guess you'll do your share soon enough. I should not have been willing to marry you right away even if you had been rich. . . .

Why I like to sit on the floor at your feet and put my head in your lap because it makes me feel like a happy petted child. . . . Don't you like to be with your head on my shoulder and my arms about you—as if you were a little boy again and I a big sweet mother? Or doesn't it appeal to you that way. . . .

You see this is a fine place to be. Good air. Good food. A big comfortable house. Perfect quiet and freedom. And pleasant people to be with at meals. . . .

9.35 A.M. Sunday Oct. 9th. 1898.

Sweet—I am so much better! I can feel no end of little stirs and beginnings of mental activity. I look better—younger—handsomer. The thought of you and of our life together is a steady force of beneficence, a peaceful healing power. A basis, a standing ground, something to live *from*. . . .

But I find I'm thinking of you too much. I must not focus on it—it is sure to react unfavorably. I must keep wide open in the full current of my work—with the bright sweet background always there. . . .

And as to my work—I am seeing in all the bits of social phenomenon I now touch, more clearly every day, the immediate need of a larger life for women. . . . You can not sit hour after hour and contemplate the fact that you are married—however pleasing that fact may be. . . . Don't you see that it is not *life*? And that we must come to where women can be smooth running active wheels in the great machinery, and that that involves of absolute necessity a change in the household work? I know you see it, but do you see how vitally important and how imminent it is. . . .

. . . **Mon. Oct. 10th. '98**
Dorchester. Mass. . . .
3.25. P.M.

. . . I am going to send you a copy of my morning's work . . . because I love you! Which is to say that [I] can't bear not to have you see what I'm so much interested in. . . . By 12.30 I had it done—ten short clear pages saying just what I wanted to; and no end of triumphant chuckling as I did it. O it was fine! The same power of clarity and condensation, and the same joy in presentation—just as it used to be. . . .

W[oman's] J[ournal] Office.
11.15 A.M. Wed. Oct. 12. 1898. . . .

. . . [Went] around to my worthy publishers. There I found their scrap book of reviews waiting for me; and after some perusal I have bodily carried it off—ostensibly to show Martha [Luther Lane], secretly and additionally to grab out all the stuff—it's loose yet, and send it flying to my husband to amuse him withal. . . . I am impressed with the volume of comment, and with the general high average of judgement. I do not see how a "young author" could possibly hope for better reception. . . .[22]

9.10 or so. A.M. Friday. Oct. 14th. '98
Hingham Mass. . . .

Do you know dear, I have been translating the Lord's Prayer to my own language, and seeing what it means as I never did before. So that I am praying it again with real truth when I go to bed. . . . I was praying one night and it occurred to me that even my one wish for light and strength— the things I have always prayed for—to be able to see what was right and able to do it—that even this was selfishly exclusive. Why me? Why was it so much more important to give me these things than others. Why not pray for "our" light and strength—everybody's. Then I thought of that little "us" in the Lord's Prayer, and realized anew what a great man Christ was. And began to put those old phrases into my modern thought and was amazed to find how much they covered. . . .

First I considered the "our" and "us"—that whole prayer is from the human race to God; not *for* the race in bland benevolence, but from its collective heart.

"Our Father who art in Heaven"—Inner creative force of all of us . . . exists in happiness . . . intense happiness proves God.

"Hallowed be thy name."—may we all recognize and revere this fact.

"Thy Kingdom come. Thy will be done." May the evolution of happiness go on and be worked out in our lives.

"On earth as it is in Heaven—" (See the intense indwelling presence of the thought, over and over, of God's coming out in life. . . .)

"Give us each day our daily bread"—(That's too easy)—the natural desire to have what we need—no further request.

"And forgive us our trespasses, as we forgive those who trespass against us."—(This I thought over a lot, and it works out this way to me—not a sort of conditional request—our forgiveness to be measured by our forgivingness—but—) the conquering absorbing power of love which we feel as fast as we use it, may it flow into us more and more, removing our sense of discouragement and shame over failure—showing all of us always that there is nothing to be discouraged over—that love is able to heal and overcome everything—as is proved by our own exercise of this power and knowledge toward children and other weaker ones who offend us and are discovered.

"Lead us not into temptation but deliver us from evil"—may this measureless current of love so steadily pouring in all the time not press us too far—intoxicate us with the glory of it till we lose touch with common life and forget that seeing is one thing, doing, another; and may we realize in its light and power *that there is no evil*—it is all one long upward way.

"For thine is the Kingdom, the Power and the Glory—" (that's too easy, too) Because all life consists of this same spirit of eternal good—living is simply *experiencing God*—He *is* the whole thing.

Amen.

Now I wonder if you will care at all about that. It means a lot to me. Perhaps these words don't show it. But the sense of the oneness of the human race and the practical facts of what a divine business living is come very fresh to me as I see that great soul two thousand years since, seeing so clear—feeling so deep and true—saying so wisely to the ears that heard.

Now I'll try to answer today's letter—and not be unreasonable about it. Because you are *you*—not me; and your deep steady lasting love expresses itself in years of action— not in hours of talking. . . .

Guess you needn't be worried about losing me. Indeed I begin to think that I really must dissemble—that I am making my mother's mistake, and shall sicken you with over much affection. I've always understood that men did not like too much demonstration of affection—were soon cooled and alienated by it. Never let a man know how much you love him, say the sage matrons. . . .

. . . And perhaps I'd better say already that my astonishing revival in health and spirits upon leaving you and taking to the road again shows but too clearly that a wandering life is my best safeguard, and that many friends are apparently more conducive to my welfare than one home. . . .

10 A.M. Dorchester. Mass.
Oct. 16th. 1898. . . .

It is very good to be back here [with the Blackwells]. I always get blue
at Martha's. Hers is a close range life. . . . It smothers me. I guess I won't
go there again till I have to. Here the people live in the thought of world
helpfulness; and though we disagree on many points the *range* is more alike.
They care about people at large, "movements," and "questions," and give
their steady lives to helping on what they think right.

The big house—a house meant for other people as well as the family;
the care of personal life—each following his own interest smoothly; the
plentiful table and big bedrooms—I can breathe here. . . .

And [your] dear loving letters are such a comfort. It's only that our
gauge in verbal delivery is different, and I must get used to it. . . .

Dorchester Mass
9.05 A.M. Mon. Oct. 17th. 1898. . . .

[*She has been visiting friends in Brookline, Massachusetts.*]

If these folks are anything like fair samples of my "gentle readers" I have
done just what I wanted to. . . .

The[y] were deeply stirred and roused, but not frightened. I was delighted. . . . Also when they got to talking, two young mothers and an old
one— . . . it was almost ghastly to see how the veil lifted from our commonly
consented to domestic myths; and how they eagerly owned to a wild desire
for somebody to take care of the children!

I do believe Houghton that I've done something of what I hoped to
do. . . . I do not believe I could have written this with such restraint and
moderation, such wise reserve and sense of repressed power and half with-
held suggestions, but for those years in California when I said so much so
unwisely and was so mercilessly snubbed therefore. And as I hear and see
and talk I begin to get more and more the sense of what needs saying next
and how I can best say it. How about a book flatly on "The Home"; or "The
Home as a Social Factor"; with deeper and wider analysis of the whole
thing and its effects?

And how beautifully I can do it hurling every idol from its shrine. When
it is discovered that I myself am living in blissful content in a small flat with
the dearest boy in the world! Won't that be lovely. If only I can have a good
healthy baby to brag of besides. . . .

4.40 P.M. . . .

. . . And today's mail brings a letter from . . . H[arry] T[hurston] Peck's friend—asking for "material" about my life for Dr. Peck, who is writing an article about me for the December Cosmopolitan!!! O. O. O. Says it will contain nothing to which I could object. O what *fun!* . . . .[23]

Dorchester Mass.
Oct. 18th. 1898. 9.30 A.M. . . .

I can see in my mind just how you are going on building up your own place in your chosen profession; a quiet steady reliable source of continually accumulating information; with your quick and accurate intellect doing things of unexpected brilliancy at unexpected moments—and you not seeming to be doing anything! Also your human qualities, the big virtues, will count for you all the time. They always do. . . .

I'm *ever* so pleased at your interest in my sudden impression of the Lord's Prayer. It is such a pleasure to talk with you when you care about it. You see I am immensely interested in finding sound sociology as I see it in the teachings of Christ; because I have long felt that our next advance must come through [the] development of existing religious feeling and not in contradiction to it. . . .

Dorchester Mass.
Oct. 19th. 1898. . . .

Yes, you did speak of the clippings I sent—I didn't mean to accuse you of ignoring them; but I didn't gather from those first remarks that you cared particularly to see them and felt kind of sorry I took the risk. But this time you do seem to be glad I sent them, so that's all right. You see I was a little afraid I was doing wrong and that you would think so. But I thought you would be quite eager to see what so many people said about your wife—as I should be to read reports of your great speeches dear. . . .

. . . How beautifully busy you are these days! It argues well for your economic independence at least! As for me, for all my soaring "figures," I shrewdly mistrust that you will be the mainstay of the family. And since I know how extremely that will please you I shall not grumble much. . . .

I took a little walk with Miss Blackwell yesterday afternoon; and she suddenly demanded to know if I had proper clothes for the season—cordially offering to supply me cash if I needed it, on the ground that I was of too much value to the world to be allowed to need anything. Now that is a proper spirit. Why don't I have a shrine and people bring me offerings—it seems no more than proper! So I *cheerfully* agreed to ask her for some money if none came in presently. . . .

. . . I had a fine talk with Alice B[lackwell] yesterday. She says I am good to be with—that . . . it is "enlarging to the mind" to have me about. I like that—way through . . .

Dorchester Mass.
Oct. 20th. 1898. . . .

. . . I met Horace Traubel of "The Conservator." Said Horace Traubel fell at my feet forthwith, and presented me with a bit of his reviewing of *In This Our World.* . . . I am deeply gratified and elated. They are seeing what I have tried to do—tried to show— and even beginning to see that tis not so artless an art after all—that it has its defenses even in literature. . . . You see this [is] more than being a poet. . . . It is being a help to people— and *that's* what I want to be. . . .[24]

. . . Quite a long letter from Walter. . . . Kate—dear soul— has been keeping my letters to herself—and they thought I told her to. *That's* what ailed Grace, but she was too proud to mention it. Walter, being of a different disposition, says "Katharine no longer shows your letters, probably from instructions from you." I think he has an absolute talent for saying things hatefully. But I rejoice to find that I am minding it less and less. . . .

[*The letters continue to discuss encouraging letters of praise that she has recently received, including one from George D. Herron, Professor of Applied Christianity and Grinnell College.*]

. . . Isn't that *fine!* . . . The tide is rising, sure. [William Dean] Howells saw first—or spoke first—God bless him. He didn't wait for the others anywhere or for more books, he reached out a strong kind hand at the first word. I'll never forget it. . . .

. . . I went to the Press Women's High Tea, and was set in high places at once. Spoke fairly enough, provoking earnest discussion, and was pleasantly greeted by many. . . .

I don't think you need reproach yourself for neglected opportunities in kissing. A more persevering and progressive kisser I never saw. Let your mind be easy—you have done good work. . . .

12.15 P.M.—

. . . I feel hypocritical to preach contentment while they do not know my new dear joy. But I did honestly preach just so before I had it—and comforted people too. . . .

7.20–25 Fri. A.M. Oct. 21st.
. . . c/o The Woman's Journal. 3 Park St. Boston Mass. . . .

For you to see so clearly how I feel when we differ sometimes means great things for the not differing, I am sure. If I can only keep on presenting my point of view without undue depression of spirit, I am sure you will see it some time. And once you *see what I am seeing* I am not so anxious for perfect agreement—it isn't identical opinion I'm after, but similar range of vision. . . .

9.30 or so. A.M. Sun. Oct. 23rd. '98
c/o Mr. H.B. Blackwell
Dorchester Mass. . . .

Here's a fine fair breezy morning, warm, clear, bright; here are two letters of yours to answer. . . .

Whether you know the difference or not you have learned the touch that is so dear to me—the impression of genuine contact and converse. . . .

. . . More and more I feel you within range—where I can talk to you. . . . No words can express the blinding loneliness of an isolated thinker . . . nor the comfort of companionship when one finds it. You may think my swans all geese if you like, my paradise a potato patch—but if only you *see them*. . . .

I'm not afraid of your growing absolutely solidified in your mind for some years yet. Agree or disagree no man lets my mind touch his and stays there, and then petrifies. No, sir. I shall keep your conservative tendencies well "oiled" for a long time to come. . . .

Your audacious jests as to your private Press Association and "honor" and "off her" are beyond remark. I giggled deliciously thereat—with some faint consciousness of blushing! What a "sad dog" you are to be sure! And it is always so totally unexpected from a man of your modest appearance and demeanor. It's like Kate's "Hell" remark. Did I tell you how I called her my "little dear darling" and then "little d.d." To which she clucking in the bed responded, "do you mean little damn devil?" A weird child. . . .

I want you to get at dumbbell and chest-weight work. I want another inch to lay my head on—my steadily enlarging head! I want more "expansion"—when you draw big breaths of happiness. I want a little more Romanness in your neck, if you please—dear husband! And I wouldn't want one of 'em if these were not all easily yours. It is partly my own personal taste in "manly beauty"—or womanly either for that matter. Partly for your physical health and strength. And at bottom—under both—for the *effect on character*. There is a direct reactive effect between body and spirit—both ways. . . .

c/o Mr. H. B. Blackwell. Dorchester. Mass.
Oct. 25th. '98
7.45—P.M. . . .

[*She has just spoken in the afternoon at the Massachusetts Women's Suffrage Association.*]

After a fine free flowing speech like that of this afternoon I do feel so good! Feel as if my brain was all open and pulsing pleasantly—in full and easy operation. That i[t] has been, and is now enjoying a rich sense of fulfilled function.

It certainly is my business to speak to people—there's no mistake. And it would have done you good to see those folks flock up and shake hands and say how it did them good to hear me. And it did. I could see it—feel it. I spoke on Hope and Power—and made them *felt*. . . .

. . . c/o Mr. H. B. Blackwell.
Dorchester. Mass.
9.10 A.M. Thurs. Oct. 27th. 1898. . . .

How much did I tell you of my talk with Mr. Small yesterday? . . . He says calmly that he expects to see 25000 of W[omen] & E[conomics], that it is the book of the time, that it is being called for from all over the country, that it will sell steadily for five years or so—and then he wants a bigger one along the same lines, but further. . . .

Then comes the "can I?" Other people do—why not I? If I am going to be a big somebody why not start in and write as such—make remarks about people and places and politics, morals and manners, dresses, diseases, progress in general. Do it *my own way*—as if I was "Master of the Subject-in-Chief"—why not. . . .

Uncle Henry [Ward Beecher] or Aunt Harriet [Beecher Stowe] could have done it, nobly. . . . I'm known variously—you see—I *ought* to be able to do it. I mean to try! I shall think far and deep all round the work—looking at it as a piece of social service— a piece of history. . . .

. . . And I'm not C. P. Stetson aged thirty eight if I cannot, with my present wisdom, please each place a little—please the home readers—and leave many a rankling shaft—no, not that, but many an irritating seed of new thought and life! . . .

. . . I'm much obliged to you for listening so patiently to my rhapsodies. I see it far more clearly, feel far better able to undertake it. . . . Speak plainly if you think I'm wrong. You know I never am disappointed when my big rainbow bubbles become mere bits of bread or stone—I can use even them to advantage.

. . . Now I will descend from my high horse, and answer your letter.

There are words on the last page, dear my love, that I kissed and kissed longing humbly to be worthy of them. . . .

. . . c/o H.B. Blackwell.
Dorchester. Mass.
9.10. A.M. Mon. Oct. 31st. 1898. . . .

[*She had talked at a women's group the day before.*]
. . . Just a small roomful of nice Boston women. It was a most beautiful success. The talk went well—very well. I could feel the artistic success of it even while most sincerely uttering the truth. (That is the fulfillment of my theory of technique—ignore it and seek an exquisite sensitive sincerity—and it shall finally come clothed in perfect form.) One dear old lady drew me aside after, and poured out a big black sorrow in family life—with tears—and——O Houghton, my husband, even to you I cannot speak of these things. It is as if the very hand of God touched me, when a soul comes to me like that. Don't you see how it proves that this is my work? I can never give it up. I could never live with any close companion who was out of sympathy with it. . . .

. . . c/o Mr. H. B. Blackwell—
Dorchester. Mass.
9.50 A.M. Tues. Nov. 1st. 1898. . . .

I am pleased to hear of the offer of partial partnership you have received—but do not incline to it. It shows—coming as it did—that you are making a reputation—becoming known in your chosen line. But I think it would not be of much benefit. You are alone and out for yourself now—arranging for life—not for immediate wages. . . .

If you were a good deal younger I should think it would be an excellent learning place. But he wants a man with a first class head and good experience to play second fiddle. . . .

Don't ever let my views decide you too much in business affairs—it's not my strong point. Especially as I am apt to leave entirely out of sight the "main factor"—pay! Again, with your kind of conscientiousness, you would be more apt to overwork with an employer than for yourself. That's a point especially in such an arrangement as this, where you still have your own shuffling to do. But if he is a good and great man—high principled and able—only cross; and would presently make you full partner if you were able to put up with him—why there's something in that. . . .

. . . Now let me see—what have I done this long time? . . . Went to the Mechanics' Fair and spoke, among others—Mrs. Livermore—Julia Ward

Howe—Rev. Ada C. Bowles—me. Short speech—but they liked it a lot. . . .
Also many cordial greetings. Also Prof. Hayes (Miss I believe) of Wellesley
wants me to come there if it can possibly be arranged and "say just those
things to the Wellesley girls!" Said I would in a minute if she could fix it.
She said she must work carefully as suffrage was not in favor there. . . .

. . . 9.40 or so.
. . . Nov. 2nd. 1898. . . .

[*Houghton has recently received an offer to go into a law partnership
with a Mr. Denning.*]
. . . As to Denning . . . do not let me turn you against him. My judgement
is not good in business matters, especially a business of which I know so
little as the law . . .

The only thing I fear for you (and me) is that in your desire to "provide"
you will get entangled in some business that will pay well, and that seems,
to my sociological conscience, compromising. I wouldn't interfere with *your*
doing what you thought right, but I should hate to profit by it. . . . My safest
plan is to be *sure* that I pay all for myself. I've no faintest wish to hamper
your activities or dictate to your conscience; but feeling as I do toward most
of our business methods and principles today, I feel like a Quaker marrying
a soldier as it were. . . .

. . . c/o The Woman's Journal.
3 Park St.
Boston Mass.
About 9. A.M. Thurs. Nov. 3rd. 1898. . . .

Well,—behold the change wrought in about two months. . . . Two
months ago I roused myself from unutterable depression and black darkness
to plan feebly for some hole to hide in for the winter. . . . Now I am conte-
mplating an 18 months tour of the world. a. Lecturing on an impressive
scale; b. Newspaper letters with deep inner purpose; c. a book of stories to
carry on my work from its plane of mere argument into the popular imagination; and d. a play for the first young actress in America. Um! If I'm not a
genius I'm very near a fool I guess.[25]

But let me put this last wild vision into plain terms. . . . It will mean a
months' pause . . . while peacefully and comfortably housed in Chicago.
Second, it will be, as a season of dramatic thought and work, a magnificent
preliminary to the Stories; and not at all wasted on the Letters:—even if
the play fails. Mind, by my brilliant sudden thought of roping Hervey White
into it, it will not tire me as work alone would. I love collaborative work—

it cheers and stimulates me—and I fancy with a man it will be even better than with a woman. . . .

I am praying to keep steady—calm—quiet—to go slow—not to get excited and puffed up—to take it all easily and naturally but to believe that great joy is as easy to God as great pain—success as failure. Other people have done big brilliant things—why not I. *Perhaps* I can. So I set my face gently toward success—ready to turn instantly to failure with calm acceptance—if it comes. . . .

. . . Wellesley to Boston
Sun. Nov. 6th. 1898. . . .
2.50 P.M. . . .

[*She spoke at Wellesley College on "Women and Government" and on the education of children.*]

Here I am again, dear love, trotting from place to place and trying to talk to you as I trot! cause I like to. . . .

. . . I had a perfectly splendid time [at Wellesley]! I stayed with Prof. Ellen Hayes—mathematics & logic. . . . Dr. Helen Webster—comparative Philology. Both these eminent and learned ladies treated me with marked respect and a very genuine eager interest in what I had to say. I spoke to the girls—the Agora Club—on Women and Government. They had a lovely time—giggled and talked back and were very jolly—after the first awed moments. . . . Prof. Hay[e]s says, "Tell *me* you haven't studied logic!" And says she is going to use quotations from my book in her class work—as syllogisms or something. So—It was lovely. Real warm friendly *equal* welcome from genuinely learned women. . . .

. . . c/o Mr. H.B. Blackwell
Dorchester Mass.
5.45 P.M. Sun. Nov. 6th. 1898. . . .

. . . I was flattered to my heart[']s content by the eager genuine respectful interest of those two Wellesley Professors in my talk on the education of children. My principles and formulae and the illustrative instances appealed to them compellingly. They said I must write it all out—we needed it. Dear—if women like that think my head is good it must be worth something—don't you think so? . . .

My life looks very big and promising just now—but I often think of what the real base of all my contentment is—and how little people know it! It amuses me very much—my lovely secret. . . .

I can "do" most any kind of story just to play at it. . . . And I hereby prophesy that lots of people are going to like my work—just such as it is. We'll see.

I also prophesy that my husband never will think much of it as "literature," however much he thinks of me, and I don't feel a bit badly. Because I'm [n]o self conscious artist. If you care little for my style why I care less—so there's no quarrel. But if I write them easily and people read them widely—that's an end to be desired. . . .

Don't be discouraged dearest heart, or even a little blue. You are in the work you like and gradually making your way. People know you and like you, and you grow stronger every year. . . .

. . . O darling—there's a little touch of anxiety in this letter that makes your wife long to be with you. . . . That's what wives are for—to comfort their husbands when they're blue. And I want so to do it. . . . You *mustn't* feel that way dear! I suppose all this flamboyance of mine makes it seem as if you weren't getting on so fast by contrast? But Bless you! Mine is all talk—a mountain in labor. You have seen the mice I bring forth. Don't let the glamor of my big talk confuse your level head. . . .

You will observe that though I have written you such grand things from here I have not had one paying engagement!

No, my son. I talk big, but don't be too much impressed by that. I want one friend who understands it all and will say—"Yes yes, I know all that, but you are nothing but a dear foolish tired little girl—come into my arms and rest!" . . .

about 3.45 P.M. Fri. Nov. 11th. 1898.
on train for Detroit

Behold me, Sweetheart, well started on my journey, and very comfortable indeed. . . .

It is a beautiful sky now, a clear soft blue where it shows, and lots of nice purplish clouds with gold & white edges. And there is water to reflect it, and brown meadows and grey trees—all the so lovely face of mother earth. . . .

You see they don't know I've got you. That makes me feel kind of hypocritical. . . .

. . . c/o The Woman's Journal. . . .
Detroit. Mich.
11 A.M. Sun. Nov. 13th. 1898. . . .

. . . I am quietly ensconced in a nice little bed room at Mrs. Corbett[']s. . . .

Mrs. C. says my face has changed since she saw me last (spring of '97). Says I used to have a spiritual look—and I've lost it! Hm. Guess it[']s 'cause I'm fat and happy. I'm getting too prosperous. Bring on some more misfortunes! I can't afford to lose that spiritual look. She'd have seen it plenty last summer I guess. . . .

Where my Social Organism concept applies to personal life most help-fully, is in this. Considering my mental consciousness to be that of society, and recognizing the limitations of personal expression—the necessary dis-proportion between what our great human soul can think and feel, and what our small personalities can *do*—that understanding and acceptance takes the sting out of life—gives an easy scientific patience with "poor hu-man nature." . . . The "riddle," the "mystery," the "enigma" of life, the strange haunting sense of discord and disproportion which has distressed us for so long—to which the only relief so far has been in the hypothesis of an other and better world—all this passes when one *begins to understand this one.*

I've only begun. I can't meet some things yet . . .; but that is the basis of my peace and power. It is what people feel when they turn to me for help and encouragement; what gives the sense of bigness. It is big. It is a growing feeling of *being* humanity. Not just being C.P.S. . . .

The facts are all there, clear and undeniable. It only remains to let the feeling grow—to strengthen one's soul by a conscious dwelling on its real power and place. . . .

The practical point is to keep the thing in mind—to live, to act as so great and strong a thing—*which we are*—not as a mere single person, which we are also, inclusively, but which is not our limit. I'm really talking to myself. For I am only just beginning to let in and accept the sense of power— I have suffered long from being—to my own consciousness—a poor little sick lone woman. Of course I knew all this other stuff—but it is a very gradual work to turn an intellectual perception into a "state of mind."

That's what ails us about God. We have "believed" in him, intellectually; but we have not acted as that great fact would naturally compel our acting.

There's a heap of sense in that "God is a force to give way to—God is *a thing you have to do!*" . . .

Life is action. Human action is partly modified by mental concepts. A concept is only normally placed in the brain when it is acted on. If not acted on it causes morbid conditions in the brain—false processes [—] a sort of irritation of contiguous cells, giving rise to other and false concepts, and other and false actions. Yes sir—you can see that everywhere. . . .

. . . Well, there's quite a sermon for Sunday. And it's like putting a drawer in order in my mind—I feel neater and more satisfied. . . .

And it comforts me way down deep to feel this stirring of my natural processes again--dormant for nearly a year! . . .

. . . 10.47 A.M. on train for Dowagiac Mich.
Tues. Nov. 15th. 1898. . . .

. . . Do you know, as I go about visiting and revisiting these places; and as I write letters to 'em afterward, I feel like St. Paul! Its very funny really. They count on my coming—they bring people for me to help—they listen to my words as if they were something wonderful. It is queer and exceedingly pleasant. . . .

8

"My Business First Last and Always Is to Serve": 16 November 1898–25 January 1899

In mid-November Charlotte headed west by train: from Boston to Detroit, and then to Chicago where Marietta Dow served as her hostess "mother" for an almost two-month stay. Gilman planned to be working on a play with Hervey White, a young novelist and poet. She would also take some short lecture trips from time to time. But for the most part, she would turn to Jane Addams's Hull House as the central focus for her work.[1]

A settlement house located in West Side Chicago, Hull House was the "vortex of nations," Charlotte wrote to Houghton, and teeming with activity. It was at one and the same time an unemployment agency, a battered-wives shelter, a day care center, a public kitchen, and a cooperative boarding club for factory girls. In fact, by 1898 it was sponsoring almost forty different kinds of programs for the neighboring immigrant community: college extension courses and summer-school programs; boys' clubs and girls' clubs; kindergarten training classes; workshops for arts, crafts, music, and theater. Social work had not been established as a profession when Jane Addams and her friends began the project in 1889. They were shaping the needed precedents themselves, gaining experience the hard way, and then teaching by discussion and example. The stated Hull House goals were to "investigate and improve the conditions in the industrial districts of Chicago." But, as contemporaries viewed it, this "City of Refuge" was also a nationally respected reformers' training ground. Ex-governor John Peter Altgeld, W. D. P. Bliss, English Fabian Keir Hardie, "Golden Rule Jones"—these were just some of the "vast numbers" currently attending Hull House lectures, workshops, and discussions, in addition, of course, to the women's movement leaders who were the central core of Hull House work.[2]

Writer, organizer, and principal executive director, Jane Addams was the best known of the Hull House workers. As Gilman later put it, she was "a truly great woman. Her mind had more 'floor space' in it than any other I have known. She could set a subject down, unprejudiced, and walk all around it, allowing for every one's point of view." And there were other brilliant Hull House women also: Ellen Gates Starr, organizer of wage-earning women and activist in the Women's Trade Union League; Alice Hamilton, doctor and scientist, later to become professor of pathology at the Women's Medical College of Northwestern, and then professor of industrial medicine at Harvard; Julia Lathrop, pioneer sociology researcher and major inspiration behind *Hull House Maps and Papers* and later the head of the United States Children's Bureau; Florence Kelley, first English translator of Friedrich Engels's *The Condition of the Working Class in England,* a lawyer, a chief factory inspector for the state of Illinois, and an organizer for the National Consumer's League for over thirty years. As one writer put it, these women "did more than any other group of women in American History to improve the position of women in general, and social legislation and administration in particular."[3] Or, as Gilman put it in a somewhat lighter vein, "Lots of sense talked especially by the women; who were practical and pointed if a bit prosy; but the men wandered off the subject and grew figurative of speech—an emotional sex, visibly unfit for the ballot!"

In the energetic Hull House context, Gilman was experiencing directly the kind of empowering social conscience effort she was advocating at the time in articles and lectures: the need to learn "to work and care for each other in the largest sense." We've "got to have the wide long reaching Social Organism idea to get a fair look at human life," she wrote to Houghton, and also help to promote the "vast smooth ocean of good will and power lifting and carrying the world." Here was the "religion of human love and service" put directly into practice. It is the sense of real "connection," of "interdependence," of "common consciousness" that makes us feel so *"rested."* "I think that is what gives the peace of God that passeth understanding."

As Gilman preached her "social conscience" message, she was sharing in the optimistic faith of many of her Utopian and Christian Socialist contemporaries.[4] They believed strongly in the principles of cooperation and joint ownership of the means of production. They worked for government ownership of railroads, factory inspection, the eight-hour day, the abolishment of child labor, and for countless other important pragmatic legislative goals as well. But their overriding political conviction was that human nature was essentially good, cooperative, and reasonable, and that socialism was in accordance with the law of God. According to Chrisitan Socialist minister George Herron, for example, God was not an "unapproachable Being before whom man worshipped in awe and reverence." Rather, He was "an active agent in the social order," a prime force at "work in the world redeeming an organic society destined to become progressively the kingdom of heaven on earth." "The object of sociology is to teach us how to love our neighbor," as economist John R. Commons phrased it.[5] Or, as Gilman put it, "I am immensely interested in finding sound sociology as I see it in the teachings of Christ; because I have long felt that our next advance must come through

[the] development of existing religious feeling and not in contradiction to it."[6]

Although Gilman respected and admired the Christian Socialist perspective, her current articles and lectures also focus on some woman-centered issues that contemporaries too rarely understood or shared. As the St. Louis *Post Dispatch* would put it, she was a "convincing" radical of radicals, but her "views of the status and relations of woman to society are too far in advance of the thought of the time to be accepted. She contends for the absolute economic independence of woman." In her lecture on child labor, for example, Gilman not only offered the standard protest arguments about the suffering of children, or about the long hours and deplorable factory conditions but also insisted that a root cause of these and other social problems lay in women's isolation in the private home. Women were confined to domestic service, denied opportunities to develop their potential, or to understand larger social needs, yet the "welfare of the child has been left to maternity." We need to expose and alleviate the "pitiful backwardness" of the economically dependent woman, Gilman argued, and the resulting "ignorance and cruelty of blood parenthood." Or, as she put it in a *Woman's Journal* article, we need to recognize that "the vast majority of children are very ill cared for and ill trained by their most loving mothers; that they die in vast proportion; that they are most unnecessarily sick; that they are not conspicuously happy; that they grow up—such of them as survive—to be the kind of tired, timid, selfish, unprogressive people of whom the world is all too full."[7] "[U]ntil the heart of the mother is moved by the love for humanity," she continued, until the mother learns to love "all children" and "not her children alone," there can be no solution to the problem of child labor.[8]

Gilman's intention, of course, was to integrate her feminist convictions with the Christian Socialist perspective, in ways that were affirming and positive for women. Like Carol Gilligan and many other later feminists, she sometimes argued that because of women's experience with nurturing their families, women had developed important positive and caring ethical perspectives. Compared to men, women tended to be less individualist, aggressive, and competitive, more cooperative and socially progressive; thus their public contributions were essential to the socialist reform campaign.

Clearly Gilman was attempting to affirm women's public efforts, to urge women to expand their social understanding, and to demand the right to work. She argued that most gender-based dichotomies resulted from differences in experience and opportunity and that women thus were not to blame for the limitations that their isolation and dependence caused. "We might as well hold women responsible for harems, or prisoners for jails," she later quipped. And yet in spite of Gilman's positive intentions, her emphasis on woman's subjugation had its familiar and predictable negative effects. It prompted her to celebrate masculine achievements, to condemn women's "selfish," "prehistoric" loyalties to private needs, and thus to undermine her own and other women's self-respect. There "are heavy charges to be brought against women," she told her listeners and readers, for we pursue a "concentrated unenlightened worship of our own immediate relations." Instead of "the huge, blind, sluggish mass of primitive prejudice embodied in the economically dependent woman," we need "people with larger hearts and larger minds, knowing and caring for other interests than their own."[9]

Not surprisingly, such public statements on the love versus work dichotomy had their counterparts in private letters. We need to "overcome" our excessive loyalty to the "lower plane" of private personal relationships, she wrote to Houghton, and share instead the Christian socialists' "higher" emphasis on service to the world. Almost as though condemning her own time-consuming correspondence, she continued in another letter: when "any personal desire ·. . . holds us—becomes a main issue—a governing factor—we thwart the growth of the subtle co-consciousness . . . and keep society back to its self-centered original basis of growth." "Personally considered," life "is a queer mess enough and its motion slow and contradictory. But once you get that thought of organic development well in place, then you understand" that private yearnings interfere with social needs. "You see the important thing is for us—conscious human beings—to cultivate the common consciousness and hold our individual relations subordinate." For as long as "you want any earthly thing—think you must have it—depend upon it— long for it—you are weak and helpless. My business on earth is first last and always to serve. . . . And I must not, even for this new heaven, forget what I am here for."

Although theoretically Gilman argued that public work need not interfere with private love relationships, she still was clearly troubled by the common accusation that loving women necessarily were "weak and helpless." Men were more rational and socially productive; women were more emotional and private. Men focused on the "higher" plane of social service, and women attended to the "lower plane" of personal relations. Fearing her own "feminine" and thus "backward" inclinations, no wonder Gilman sometimes felt compelled to emphasize her own professional commitments. "All my swaying tendencies are coming into line," she wrote to Houghton; "if ever there was a clear case of a 'call' I think I've got it." In fact sometimes "[I] want to cry with happiness—to know that the light and the power does show through." How about a "world encircling journey," she continued. After all, with her expanding Hull House contacts, lecture invitations were coming at a steady pace. N. O. Nelson, for example, "the great cooperative manufacturer," asked her to lecture at his model town cooperative in LeClair, Illinois. The charismatic minister and teacher, George Herron, invited her to Grinnell, Iowa, to give a chapel talk on the "Social Organism" and to teach some classes in "Political Economy." And after lunching at Hull House with "Golden Rule Jones," the "Christian Mayor of Toledo," she wrote enthusiastically to Houghton: He "talked to me as if I was a prophetess. He swears by my poetry and so on. Upshot, that I am to go to St. Louis *via* Toledo(!)" "These years of separation are doing lovely work—just as I hoped they would," she continued in another letter. "I am certainly becoming a proficient in my business." Or as the St. Louis *Post Dispatch* would put it:

> It is not the least exaggeration to say that there has never been a public speaker in St. Louis, male or female, who cast as complete a spell over an audience as did Mrs. Stetson. . . . Her conversation is vivid and brilliant. She charms everybody with whom she comes in contact by her wit and vivacity. . . . One of the wonderful things about her is . . . the combination of strong mind, radical views and marked sprightliness of manner.[10]

Understandably Gilman was pleased with this public confirmation of her "higher" social service efforts. Simultaneously, of course, and with lengthy almost daily letters, she was attending also to the "lower plane" of love. Associating masculinity with public service and femininity and love with "weak and helpless" private needs, how then could she continue to acknowledge the importance of her social service efforts and still pursue her relationship with Houghton? The answer, too often, was to present herself in two diametrically opposing ways.[11] On the one hand, she was the successful social servant; on the other, as though to assure herself and Houghton she was "just like other women" after all, she described herself as the diminutive little woman, the "rapturously" purring kitten needing Houghton's care. "You talk of being 'overshadowed' by your wife," she wrote him.[12] "I suppose there will be some people who think so—but if they only could know how I *feel!* Why when I think of you I feel like a thin forlorn hungry cold little kitten—a very squalid shivery little kitten that you had taken in and done for, and now it was purring rapturously in your lap. . . . But they won't know. I always look so blazingly vigorous and dominant."[13]

Gilman's letters illustrate, I think, not only the destructive power of standard gender-based dichotomies—reason versus emotion, logos versus eros, work versus love—but also the toughness of the challenge she and many other women of her class and generation faced. What is striking is not only that she and other women struggled with prevailing masculine and feminine dichotomies, but also that they fought so forcefully to heal the rift between them and insisted on the need and right and to have them both. Like so many other women, Gilman was not, of course, consistent in her efforts. Nor was she willing to acknowledge openly her relationship with Houghton: "It amuses me very much—my lovely secret."[14] But by no means was she writing meekly or demurely. "I want to see you—touch you—taste you— handle you—hug you close—closer—closest! I want you deeper and deeper all the time." In fact, it's "very funny," she continued, "a sort of practical joke" on friends as well as on the public. "My public will think I have married a quiet inconspicuous young man and wonder why I should do it." And "[y]our public will think that you have married a cold queer rebellious unnatural sex-failure—old at that—and marvel at your foolishness; you knowing the while that this unnatural monster is—well, is not bad to take!" "I should be more ashamed of myself if I wasn't all the time secretly pleased that I am after all just like other women—not a monolith!"

Not a "monolith" indeed—she was the "stern cold thinker" on the outside, the passionate and sensuous "heathen goddess" within. It "is rather a good joke in some ways," she liked to tease him, yet it was painful also—to take "the man's part" in loving, and to experience the resulting vulnerability and "shame." In partial compensation, she reinstated her "weak and helpless" woman's style. "I'm perfectly unreasonable about you," she told him; "somehow you are everything that I have had and lost—that I have always wanted—that I have never had or known but would have wanted if I'd seen it." And in spite of "all my serenity and busy-ness," "[I] miss you . . . and worry," just "like any other foolish woman, with and without cause." "It's a kind of a blind pain" that "feels insatiate—endless," she continued. "I feel as if . . . when I have you again I should just drop down and cry and sort of rave softly. . . . I shall just want to eat and drink, touch taste and smell you for hours and hours and hours." "How ever *can* you love me Houghton! Such a mess as I am! Such a portentous mixture. I should think you'd be afraid it would explode somehow."

Assertive but also vulnerable, passionate but also frightened of her own "blind ravenous desire," Charlotte was sending twenty- to thirty-page letters off to Houghton on an almost daily basis, and understandably was eagerly awaiting his replies. Even "three days without a letter weakens me very much," she told him; "all my other fine feelings fail to comfort me when I don't hear from you! Of course I keep up and go on—but there is a big hole inside."

Unfortunately, what followed was an unexpected change in Houghton's letters. From her point of view, they showed no "spark of interest," she suddenly decided, or even "tender-ness." She "had been giving and giving;" finally she "*let go* and gave wholly"; and then when she "did not receive," "just fell through space." When "I write you my inmost and utmost you don't notice it," she told him. "My letters do not reach any live consciousness in you—they don't connect—I've been writing in the dark." Besides, she continued, "It is a woman's business to wait, not a man's. It is for a woman to be patient and still—not a man." Perhaps "I took the man's part" in loving, and "said too much," gave "more than was wanted—*from the first.*" "And when I think of what manner of letters I have written to you—of course I want to call them all back and burn them—scatter the miserable ashes—sink them in the sea." "A heavier blow in an emotional way I never remember." "I have worked hard this week—lived and loved and given strength to many—they have not known that I was dead," that "in my heart I'm" struggling with a long black "tidal wave of shame."

Letters: November 16, 1898 through January 25, 1899

. . . About 9. A.M. Wed. Nov. 16th. 1898
Dowagiac. Mich.

Why Sweetheart——
Are you sick? Or have you "ceased to love me"? Here it is Wed., and I have had no letter since last Friday! . . . First I thought I'd be patient and sweet and not complain, but now I'm worried.—You wouldn't let me go hungry for three days unless you were ill. And dearest, you've no idea how all my other fine feelings fail to comfort me when I don't hear from you! Of course I keep up and go on—but there is a big hole inside. . . .

. . . Thurs. Nov. 17th. 1898. . . .
11. A.M. . . .

I'm trying very hard not to worry about you not writing. But if I don't find letters tonight at Chicago I shall be badly frightened. . . .
. . . If I am ever to lose you I hope it will come quick—a sudden blow. Then I could make a prodigious effort to meet it. No wonder women have broken hearts and die—who have only love to depend on and then lose it.
I have so much to live for, to do—to hope; and yet three days without a letter weakens me very much. . . .

. . . Chicago
9.45 A.M. Fri. Nov. 18th. 1898. . . .

. . . I *miss* your letters—more than I would have imagined. . . . You see I never have let myself go so much in loving anybody since the time of Martha Luther—17 to 21—that's 17 years ago. And by your persuasive flattery and external charms you have ensnared my susceptible heart—to such an extent that it is extremely difficult for me to live without you even for a little while.
I'm rather ashamed to have made such a fuss over a little thing. . . .
But that blessed little word that came yesterday just as I was starting made it all right again. . . . And here are two nice ones waiting for me, and I s'pose likely there'll be another by and by! And I'm all right and happy again. . . .

11.30! . . .

[Gilman has been discussing the idea of co-authoring a play with Hervey White.]

Mr. White approves the plot . . . and is willing to undertake the thing. . . .

Best of all, Mr. White's work is now such that he can give me his *mornings*—mostly instead of evenings—and that makes all the difference in the world to my working power. I'm *very* glad of that.

We got to this house about 9. Mrs. Dow very glad to see me. She was one of my first friends in the city, and had sent for my poems from California long before I appeared. Her kindness is very genuine, but besides that I have a pleasant consciousness that my growing fame is not distasteful to her. . . .

. . . **473 Orchard St. Chicago Ill.**
5.25 P.M. Sat. Nov. 19th. '98. . . .

After peacefully writing to you all yesterday morning that was uninterrupted, and after a good lunch and a nap, I hied me to Hull House and saw Miss Addams the Great for a few moments. She is to work some lectures for me after Thanksgiving. Then went down town with her, and home again. . . .

6.40. . . .

Now I have absented myself from the family circle to finish these necessary letters. I get so many that I have a visible excuse; and I write so fast that I can do a lot of little ones besides yours and no one imagines that yours is so much the biggest! . . .

. . . This morning Mr. White at 9 o'clock. And I am happy to say that we work well together. I *thought* he'd do, and he does. We put in over two hours' work—good work—the people defining themselves beautifully. He has written two novels and a lot of stories, & poems too, and I've written some plays, so we go on finely. . . . Collaboration is so much easier than working alone—to me. . . .

. . . **473 Orchard Ave. Chicago**
c/o Mrs. Wm. Dow
6.50 P.M. Mon. Nov. 21st. 1898. . . .

. . . Play this morning with Mr. White, that goes finely. Then I went down to hear Prof. Herron—12 to 1. Don't miss the chance to hear him if you ever get one. He is great. Hung around to see him . . . [and] to go back to Hull House with him and have some talk; but after much waiting he went with some other friend.

I by that was well nigh forced to go to Hull House, with Miss Addams, Mrs. Herron, and others. Lunch (good one) and talk. I don't like to talk after lunch—like to sleep! I rose and fled after a while. . . .

. . . 473 Orchard St. Chicago Ill.
. . . Tues. Nov. 22nd. 1898 . . .
7.10. . . .

Miss [Annie] Russell does not want my girl [in the play] to be a doctor—which is a blow. But as I tell Mr. White I can make her a doctor when I write the novel. Already I feel the story-making capacity kindle up as we work. People stand out in my mind, not the types and classes I analyze and study, but thoroughly marked personalities—the thousand and one persons I have met and known so intimately—they will serve their turn yet. . . .

. . . 473 Orchard St. Chicago Ill.
. . . Wed. Nov. 23rd. '98 . . .
7.37. . . .

. . . I went down with Mrs. Dow and Miss Dow, to a "study class" at the Woman's Club; and heard Jane Addams, Miss Amanda Johnson, and Mrs. Emmagene Paul discourse on street cleaning. They are all in the business, Misses A. & J. Inspector and Deputy Inspector in the 19th Ward. . . . Lots of sense talked especially by the women; who were practical and pointed if a bit prosy; but the men wandered off the subject and grew figurative of speech—an emotional sex, visibly unfit for the ballot! . . .

Afterward I sought Dr. McCracken [a medical doctor whom she had been seeing periodically for several years]. . . . I gave him an account of the last year and a half, since I had visited him before (with a few trifling omissions such as your natural delicacy will suggest), and dwelt upon the summer's collapse. He is a quiet man. Don't say much. But he gave me to understand that I was doing well—very well. That I should probably always have down times more or less—but that it was not sickness—it was temperament. That I must get used to it, and expect to do big work by spirts—and then give out. I told him all the symptoms I could think of—and all the circumstances—including my gloomy forebodings; but he insisted that I was looking well and doing well, nothing to be worried about.

As to immediate "brain tire" he gave me some little tablets—phosphorous mainly I think—for the special nourishment of that organ.

I have a good deal of respect for his opinion. He's been reading the book, with much interest, and says it shows a clean and healthy mind. So I really do feel much reassured as to my future career, and not quite so mean in marrying you. . . .

Miss Addams has besought me to come to tea tomorrow—and read poems to the assembled multitude. I will with pleasure. . . .

Now it's near eight—getting quite late. . . .

O you dear thing. I want to see you—touch you—taste you—handle you—hug you close—closer—closest! I want you deeper and deeper all the time. I miss you more ways than I can find words for. It's a kind of a blind pain—buried and hid, but *there* all the time. I am your own little girl—and I love you so! . . .

. . . 473 Orchard St. Chicago Ill
10 A.M. Fri. Nov. 25th. 1898. . . .

. . . You know I like to sit down right after breakfast and lay out two hours of the cream of the day on you!

I'm afraid it is flatly wrong. For that is the only time my brain is lively, and I *must* do my work then. It takes honest heroism to put you aside for the work's sake, but I've got it to do right along. . . . The best of me belongs to you, and I want you to have it, but I shall come to you the sooner and the stronger by doing good work now, so I must set my face as a flint. . . .

Last night at Hull House were assembled Hamlin Garland, Rev. George E. Herron, Rev. W. D. P. Bliss, & C. P. Stetson—all glad to see each other and talk shop. Also vast numbers of other people. I had next [to] me at supper a young Englishman . . . named Lawrence, was with Percy Alden [of New Zealand]. . . .

I asked him things about my proposed trip, and, as usual it opens before me. He is eager to see me in London—Mansfield House . . . Settlement Work, and show me about. He's a Trinity man—and the University settlement movement in England means the nicest kind of people. That will mean introductions, visits, lectures, and just what I want for Canada and Australia. Then, as they are all interconnected, they'll give me addresses in these colonies, and I shall be handed about from friend to friend, as I generally am. . . .

. . . 473 Orchard St. Chicago Ill.
. . . Sat. Nov. 26th. 1898. . . .
4.25 P.M. . . .

[*The letter notes her calls on various friends, and her continuing work with Hervey White and then continues.*]

O my boy! My boy! I can't help it—I've just had to break right down and cry and sob—it's awful to have you sick and so far away!

I'm not any stronger than any other woman—You're my own own love and I can't bear to be away from you. . . .

. . . 473 Orchard St. Chicago Ill.
5.10 P.M. Sun. Nov. 27th '98

. . . I was so glad of that special delivery letter! It came just as we [were] finishing the climax to the last act this morning. . . . It tastes good.

I suppose I was a goose to be so scared—but I kept right on doing the work and *not* thinking about you. Only the mere chance of your being in pain—in danger—is such a horrible hole inside of me. . . .

. . . I think you are taking a great risk. . . . That thing is always there—in the back of my mind—that I am letting the man I love do an unwise thing in marrying me. I feel base and traitorous and as if I were not being true to your best interests. . . .

I feel as if (I'm not thinking now—I'm feeling—) as if when I have you again I should just drop down and cry and sort of rave softly—gibber as it were—and hold on to you in spots and squeeze hard! It's a sort of blind ravenous desire that is all kinds of hunger at once and that feels insatiate—endless. I shall just want to eat and drink, touch taste and smell you for hours and hours and hours.

I want to now———.

Yes, dear heart, if I am always to have those "down times" it would be heavenly to have you to help me through them. For me, that is—but no fun for you I should think. . . .

Well. The first act is done—fairly good too. Tomorrow we begin the second. . . .

. . . 473 Orchard St. Chicago
Mon. Nov. 28th. 1898. . . .

Mr. White this morning, and a hard stiff pull on the second act. Talk only—but we've got it plowed out I guess. . . . But it's left me thick headed. I find I can't do much. I've had no real "lift" since I came here. However we'll live in hopes. . . .

I'm very lonesome for you. I want a letter with lots of *you* in it. Talk to me—*me;* blame me, scold me, make fun of me, make love to me—I want to *feel* you—*hard.* . . .

. . . 473 Orchard St. Chicago Ill.
8.35 A.M. Tues. Nov. 29th. 1898. . . .

This worrying business is all new to me. I have never worried over any one—hardly over Kate. But you——! To miss and to worry are two new symptoms for me to manifest. But miss you I do, under all my serenity and busy-ness; and worry I do, like any other foolish woman, with and without cause.

. . . And this *dear* letter brings you right close up again—close close to my heart—tight in my arms—all squeezed up and smothered with long kisses.

I'm perfectly unreasonable about you . . . somehow you are everything that I have had and lost—that I have always wanted—that I have never had or known but would have wanted if I'd seen it—you are just *everything* to me! . . ˙.

The work is taking it out of me rather more than I expected, but not badly—it is pleasant. I find that I forget everything else—that my mind works briskly in the work hours, and then is dull and oblivious all the rest of the day. . . .

3.18 P.M.

A fine morning's work. Second act all written in. . . . This was the weakest part of the play—and now it's strong—very strong and dramatic. Mr. White has "caught on" admirably. This is the first day I have really felt as if it would truly go. . . .

[*She has just received a letter from a Mr. F.M. Crunden, a friend of N. O. Nelson, offering to arrange for her to give a series of talks and lectures in St. Louis.*]

. . . I don't need a manager, I don't! nor yet an advance agent. . . . Here's this good man whom I never saw . . . turning the town over for my benefit. And was ever anything more charming than his knowing Mr. Nelson! He is the great cooperative manufacturer I have told you of—who admires my work. . . . And the Wednesday Club! And the progressive ministers! Verily my southern trip opens well. So I must presently send him off circulars. . . .

A good send off in St. Louis will set the papers wagging and make the next tours easy. . . . Now I must make up my mind carefully as to what I am to lecture on—and now. This is no haphazard work—I am playing a steady game now for a long time—with big stakes. It is all cumulative and purposeful and I must go carefully. . . .

. . . Now I'll come back to you dear. . . .

You shall announce the marriage all you want to, as soon as we are finally settled upon it. You don't want to now—do you? I don't exactly know why I don't feel like mentioning it, but I don't, not yet awhile. It's the secretest secret I ever had. . . .

. . . 473 Orchard St. Chicago Ill.
8.40 A.M. Wed. Nov. 30th. '98. . . .

Everything's all straight again. You are well and I am well and you're not too much displeased at my being worried over your illness. . . .
    . . . I should be more ashamed of myself if I wasn't all the time secretly pleased that I am after all just like other women—not a monolith! . . .

. . . 473 Orchard St. Chicago Ill.
. . . Thurs. Dec. 1st. 1898. . . .
5.37 P.M.. . . .

Fine morning with the play. It goes. Fine afternoon sewing on the green gown. A bit of a walk before lunch, and another little one now; but no nap. Too busy in my mind. But I feel stronger and stronger. Am beginning to "think easy" again, and to feel happy all the time. . . .

. . . 473 Orchard St. Chicago. Ill
8.45 A.M. Fri. Dec. 2nd. '98. . . .

Didn't know I had written you any "mournful" letters—must have been a lonesome one I guess. Well, I've written more cheerfully since then. . . .
    When I want you so desperately it is not just—that, which I want. It is *you*—to look at and hold on to and feel and lean against. I'm not pretending to be above those other specific sensations at times; but that's not what I have in mind when I write you so tempestuously. It is my arms that ache for you—my heart—the whole of me. To lay my head on your breast and hold you tight—tight—for ever and ever so long, would be like sweet rain after long drouth. I am thirsty for you—all the way through. . . .

6.30 P.M. . . .

[*She had gone to a lunch party where she "swept up a collection of three" women "to come to Hull House and hear me speak Sunday evening."*]
    . . . That heartened me up for I was dreading that dreary settlement

audience. If I have some thinking people there, people I know, I can talk better and enjoy it. . . .

Mrs. Dow is going to have a Whitman evening or afternoon for me. I shall be delighted to do that much for her and it will be a starter for the Whitman talks I propose giving in future. . . .

. . . 473 Orchard St. Chicago Ill.
4 P.M. Sun. Dec. 4th. 1898. . . .

Tonight I speak at Hull House on "Our Social Progress." I want to tell them how the world is truly moving on, in all the best ways; in spite of visible disabilities. People get so blue—the best people—and don't "see her move" at all. I tell you my brother you've got to have the wide longreaching Social Organism idea to get a fair look at human life. Personally considered it is a queer mess enough and its motion slow and contradictory. But once you get that thought of organic development well in place, then you understand. . . . Miss Addams I am sorry to say will not be there, but I have specially asked various people and want to make the thing clear to them. . . .

America in especial I want to speak of—touching on the public phenomenon we groan over, and show how *healthy* we are after all.

Take the immigrant question—look at it from the wider standpoint of progress in history—show that the thing to be noted is not the incidental disturbance caused by hasty assimilation of varied racial elements—but the wonderful fact that here is a land where all the nations of the earth can live together, compelled by the same free and enlightening popular spirit. . . . Show that these "lower classes" we so condemn as immigrants are healthier grafts upon our body politic than more highly specialized branches would be; and give facts to prove their rapid assumption of citizenship. Show how literature is spreading fast and far to reach all the people; and how our fiction is moving daily toward a more vivid realization of what the world's heart would be speaking—of the social and psychic issues of the times. . . .[15]

. . . 473 Orchard St. Chicago, Ill.
2.49 P.M. Mon. Dec. 5th. 1898. . . .

. . . You talk of being "overshadowed" by your wife—I suppose there will be some people who think so—but if they only could know how I *feel!* Why when I think of you I feel like a thin forlorn hungry cold little kitten— a very squalid shivery little kitten that you had taken in and done for, and now it was purring rapturously in your lap. . . . But they won't know. I always look so blazingly vigorous and dominant. . . .

. . . 473 Orchard St. Chicago Ill.
2.30 P.M. Wed. Dec. 7th. 1898

. . . I set me down this morning with stern determination and wrote an article for the Woman's Journal on The Causes and Uses of the Subjection of Woman, as promised. . . .

[*She had recently been to Hull House again, and met Professor Zeublin of Chicago University, formerly of Northwestern University.*]

. . . [He is] founder of one of the settlements here—who teaches Sociology; highly approves of my book and is recommending it to be read by his classes.

That pleased me immensely. He is a man whose work I admire. . . . it is really the first professional opinion I have had. . . .

. . . 473 Orchard St. Chicago Ill.
. . . Thurs. Dec. 8th. '98 . . .
. . . (5.35 P.M. Miss Addams' room—Hull House) . . .

Everyone was glad to see me—including persons who used not to be so cordial. Behold the virtues of the book! . . .

. . . and I sat and talked, pleasantly and profitably, with a fair frail little woman—Dr. [Alice?] Hamilton by name. . . .

5.08 P.M. Friday Dec. 9th 1898 . . .
. . . 473 Orchard St. Chicago Ill.

I had a nice little visit with Miss Addams last night—but I don't feel at all near her. . . .

. . . 473 Orchard St. Chicago Ill.
. . . (Mon. Dec. 12th. 1898 . . .) . . . (quarter of five P.M.). . .

I arrived [at Hull House] to find twenty or thirty people at the long table; Miss Addams & Mr. [?.] Nelson at the far end. . . . Mr. Nelson viewed me with approval from afar, and after supper he sought me out repeatedly. St. Louis is all right; and he has a dear friend in New Orleans—Dean of Tulane University—and thinks he can get me down there.

So my southern trip is solider than ever, and I gain impetus for the world encircling journey to follow. . . .

A frail youth named Thompson English, lecturing in Physics at Chicago

University, gave the Sunday evening address on Edward Carpenter. It was interesting but I fled early. . . .

. . . 473 Orchard St. Chicago Ill.
. . . Wed. Dec. 14th 1898 . . .
Near 5. P.M. . . .

This month of daily work, broken twice a week by a day off, has done just what I hoped—started the mental processes and I hope for an assured style ultimately, to get over this too humble attitude of mind that often prevents my doing things. Work is what counts. . . .

. . . 473 Orchard St. Chicago Ill.
3.10 Fri. Dec. 16th. 1898. . . .

[*She has taken an overnight trip to Grinnell College, and visiting with President Gates and his family.*]

Well—now in general this is a perfectly splendid visit. I am having more happiness than I've had since leaving Boston.

These Gates are *fine*. He is a big agile merry man . . . sort of Beechery in [his] constant flow of humor and big good will. . . . Mrs. Gates is a pretty, quiet, correct woman; a "lovely mother" and liberal and advanced withal—likes my book! . . .

. . . The home is homey and comfortable; food and bed good, lots of books; and the talk just what I like best. I guess the minister is deepest in me after all. A liberal minister and I are brothers in arms at once. . . .

. . . I was taken to [the] chapel by the good man, and then promptly introduced to Prof. Macy's class in Political Economy—where I held forth unchecked for nearly an hour, on the Social Organism—the Professor sitting meekly by. [In the evening] I was taken to chapel by the whole family and addressed the multitude on "Living." It was not as impressive a discourse as the morning one, but seemed to strike responsive chords in the numerous young hearts before me. . . .

This morning I took Prof. Herron's class . . . and had a good time with them. . . .

. . . 473 Orchard St. Chicago Ill.
9.18 A.M. Sun. Dec. 18th. 1898. . . .

[*She has recently delivered a lecture on "Women and Economics" in Geneva, Illinois, a town just outside of Chicago.*]

. . . I am certainly becoming a proficient in my business. I told those conservative country residents no end of horrors, and didn't make them angry! On the contrary they laughed aloud continually, some wept a little, and they swarmed about me with cordial thanks afterward. I think there's a kind of—friendliness about me, that women like. . . .

[*She offers the following reflections on the family who hosted her.*]

[The husband] is a sort of gentleman farmer—greenhouse gardener, and so on. I never can make their life seem *real*—it is like a Greenaway picture.

They have the sweetest little house in a field by a river—a little diamond paned, rafter-ceiled, sash-curtained home, which they play in and live in all over. . . .

It is a selfish primitive life—this withdrawal into isolation and following the cult of Papa Mama and The Baby. Its effects are seen in the children. The house, place and parents are meant simply for the children's advantage, and they, inevitably and blamelessly, suppose that all the world is. . . .

How you do work! I have a sort of awe of you—a head that can do brain work *all day*—it is astonishing. Three hours of this, and two of that, and four of the other! How can you do it and not get mixed up and make mistakes. . . . Book keeping is an Eleusinian mystery to me. . . .

I have tried sometimes—having a daring brain—and seeking escape from the growing need of you. I have said to myself—he is in many ways not what seems to go with my kind of life—he is not "reformatory" or "advanced"—in no way a "come-outer;" he is quiet, steady, conventional, pledged as lawyer and soldier to the support of the existing order—which my whole life is a working protest against—might there not be another with whom I could work to better advantage?

And then as I think what love is . . .—well, I don't want 'em. . . .

In the haunting dread lest it be wrong for you; in the stern fear-hope that after all you may find what is better. And my self-preserving instinct to buttress my life beforehand against such chance; even when I face the thought of you, more happily and wisely married to some one else—it is by no means all pain. For the knowledge of your happiness would be meat and drink—and I [question] after all, see what I *have had!* Queer unfeminine girl that I was, there was first the long devoted love of him who called himself my husband; then, when I thought myself a morbid strange cold sort of monster—no real woman at all—came the convincing proof that I was more woman than most—the strong lasting love of more than one man and the knowledge of—of—well, sometimes I feel like "a heathen goddess come again"—a wonderful struggling mixed feeling, half shame, half pride, of being—to most people's knowledge a stern cold thinker, a calm pleasant friend of men, dearly loved by women, the favorite of children—a widow— a celibate, a solitary—and inside—Ashteroth!

It's very funny. How ever *can* you love me Houghton! Such a mess as I am! Such a portentous mixture. I should think you'd be afraid it would explode somehow. And then I sometimes think that maybe you are quite a mixture too. That behind those soft pure eyes and that snowy shirt front there is that which is not at all afraid of Ashteroth, but rather glad to have her in his arms! I believe it rather appeals to your sense of humor. A sort of practical joke on all your friends and acquaintances and the world as far as it know me. My public will think I have married a quiet inconspicuous young man and wonder why I should do it— . . . Your public will think that you have married a cold queer rebellious unnatural sex-failure—old at that—and marvel at your foolishness; you knowing the while that this un-natural monster is—well, is not bad to take! Guess I'll let you put in what you think of that side of it! But it is rather a good joke in some ways. . . .

. . . **473 Orchard St. Chicago Ill.**
6.55 P.M. Monday. Dec. 19th '9[8]. . . .

I wish I could put your mind utterly at rest about your getting money. . . .

Mr. Gilman—if you had only your present large income of $600.00 dol-lars; and what you could scrape up outside that for "personal expenses," I would still ravenously marry you. I should like above all things to have you simply pay for your board and your own things; to feel that I didn't draw on you for a cent. . . . Nothing but my regard for your feelings makes me at all reconciled to your paying for the biggest half of things, as I know you will. . . .

No young man. Lack of means shall prove no loophole of escape. . . .

It seems to me that your position as a lawyer in New York is unique—your undoubted ability and your temperamental inability to do as other men do who get rich.

Unless you find a partner of just your sort, I should think it would always have elements of uncertainty in it when consciences disagreed. Whereas, alone, you have a long slow upward road before you; in which you do small things faithfully, give cautious and solid opinions, get more and more known and liked, and, gradually, win a high place as an absolutely dependable man. . . .

I don't think you'll ever be a "notorious"—"prominent"—"successful"—lawyer, but I am sure you will be a well-established one, honored, respected, and liked by no end of people. . . .

. . . **473 Orchard St. Chicago Ill.**
7.45 or so A.M. Tues. Dec. 20th. 1898. . . .

Yes, dear heart, you ought to make calls and see people and keep up with your friends . . .—not to make money out of them—you're looking at business wrong end to; but to serve them—which is what business is for!

Your place in life is not to scrabble up some money for me; but to administer the law as it were—to facilitate the orderly distribution of property. . . .

The pay part is incidental and not the point of attack. If loving me is going to make you mercenary and anxious I shall be deeply grieved. . . .

Please dear—do feel lighthearted and easy about it. You will do good work as long as you live. You will be inexorably honest. You will lose through kindness to others many times. And I shall love you and honor you always— if you never have any more than you do now. . . .

This money part of it isn't anything. Lots of great men—real geniuses— haven't been able to get money. I'm a perfect fool at it myself. If you were the kind of man that was pushing and successful and making money hand over fist—I should not love you—nor would you love me.

Dear—to speak more seriously still—if you really are my husband and to be with me through life—you must be prepared to face heavy consequences.

I am a marked personality with goodness knows what work to do. . . . I might say things—write things—do things that would sharply interfere with your position and prosperity.

Of course I have planned for quiet years in New York with you—. . . but I know perfectly well that if there came any great social call I should rise to meet it *at any cost.* (And—if I didn't—it would cost more, ruin my life.) . . .

Of course we *may* live nice quiet respectable lives and I do nothing bad except on paper; but *I am an uncertain quantity.* . . .

. . . 473 Orchard St. Chicago
8.54 A.M. Wed. Dec. 21st. '98. . . .

Seems to me that I've been writing rather . . . [forbidding] letters lately . . . and hinting of danger. . . .

In truth I do look forward to the loveliest happiest days with you. Only— this is what I pray.— To serve God—to serve the world—to do my work in any case. . . .

You see "fulfillment of function" is my master passion. I live up to my own conception of ethics at least.

Do I seem to you a gloomy old person? Do I take the shine out of things for you? Do I seem to rattle stern ideals before you in unreasonable severity? . . .

6.50. . . .

Again you dwell on my desirability as proven by the cordiality of transient acquaintances. I never said I wasn't agreeable temporarily—I am. I'm quite fascinating sometimes—for a little while. . . . But what I maintain is that I am "trying" and "wearing" to live with permanently. . . . You see I am very busy "being me"—it is engrossing, and I expect other people to be as interested in the process as I am, and they are not! However—you can't say I didn't warn you! . . .

. . . 473 Orchard St. Chicago.
8.50 A.M. Fri. Dec. 23rd. '98. . . .

You see it all comes back to the same thing! While you *want* any earthly thing—think you must have it—depend upon it—long for it—you are weak and helpless. My business on earth is first last and always to serve; as long as I have strength and understanding there is plenty for me to do. And I must not, even for this new heaven, forget what I am here for. . . .

You see *the* important thing is for us—conscious human beings—to cultivate the common consciousness and hold our individual relations subordinate. . . .

Translated to our machinery of individual sensation this knowing social sense is called "a sense of duty;" and, to my own interpretation of social economics, duty to function is the highest social sense. . . . When any personal desire—which must be on a lower plane of life . . .—when any such desire *holds us*—becomes a main issue—a governing factor—we thwart the growth of the subtle co-consciousness . . . and keep society back to its self-centered original basis of growth—a legitimate but primitive plane. (See a certain great work on the sexuo-economic relation!)

Now then; I am a critter with a very highly developed social sense. . . . Well. The minute I begin to centralize—to localize—to "point" to some personal gain—however great—all this vast social feeling of which I carry a past consciousness— begins to plunge and tug; and the localized spot—where a world-feeling is being focussed on an individual desire—grows morbid. There. *There!* Now I know what ails me.

First last and always I must be true to the race-duty which has dragged and forced me on so far. If you are in it—O thank God! Thank God! If you are not———God is still there and I can work. . . .

. . . 473 Orchard St. Chicago Ill.
5.25 P.M. Tues. Dec. 27th. '98. . . .

. . . [I] betook myself to Hull House to lunch. Mayor Sam Jones, of Toledo, was there, and very anxious to see me. So I lunched by his side and he talked to me as if I was a prophetess. He swears by my poetry and so on. Upshot, that I am to go to St. Louis *via* Toledo(!) and speak there next week.

Ex-Gov. Altgeld was there also—very interesting. . . .

Between all these men I spent some exciting hours (—Hull House is the vortex of nations!—) . . .

. . . 473 Orchard St. Chicago Ill.
Wed. Dec. 28th. '98. . . .

I'm going to begin with a few words to you if I *am* busy   . . I quite envy those good women who really feel that the husband is their whole range of duty—it must be so sweet to have no call away from that dear love.

Your letter this morning makes me feel ashamed of myself. Dear—you mustn't mind my swings and changes of feeling. Don't you know I told you before I went that I was likely to have such. I always shall, probably. . . .

. . . I have known men who were in just the position toward life that I am—and who loved me too—and I did not love them! That ought to serve. Moreover, if it were meant that I should be so mated such an one would have won me. Again, it['s] probably wiser for me to have a husband who is more in touch with life as it [is], precisely because I sail around in the future so much. . . .

6.55 P.M. . . .

. . . As to the thing I miss—the initiative along the same lines, the suggestions and stimulus and sudden wide appreciation—that is a help and pleasure I must take where I find it—from whomsoever it may come. . . . And I've no manner of doubt that if I had married one of such mind as mine we should have worn one another out. . . . I'm greedy. I want you to be everything on earth. Whereas the man don't live who could content this voracious comet. As for you I expect to eat you up entirely, and ask for more—just like it, please!

. . . 473 Orchard St. Chicago Ill.
near 10 A.M.. Sunday. ts
January 1st. 1899

The first written word of the New Year to you, my husband. May you be well and strong and happy! . . .

The relation between two human beings is a wonderful thing. The same soul quivering into recognition of itself through each in the other. Delicious flashing co-consciousness, the delight of which is in feeling "we are one!" And . . . then, the vivid live delight of feeling that this one soul has two bodies; two sensitive living creatures to dwell in, through which comes all this joy of *consciousness*. Conscious of . . . ourselves—a living machine that enjoys its own working. Conscious of each other———O the blessed blessed other people! A new consciousness—a new delight—in every one we reach. And the measure of that happiness unlimited, for here they are by the million, and more coming—fresh ones, all the time. . . .

You have brought me such peace and happiness as I never knew. You have made my life far more balanced and natural and useful. . . .

I want you to be glad and grateful too; and feel this vast smooth ocean of good will and power lifting and carrying the world. Religion gave us the feeling of it and called it God. Science is giving us the knowledge of it, and calls it Law. It is a real thing—and we are in it, and it is Good. The name of my optimistic lecture—sermon—article—book—poem—is "Things as They Are." That's all I want to show folks. The living truth. And I so want it to come into your conscious recognition—want it as my Calvinistic ancestors wanted people to "come to Jesus."

I'm not worried about you if you don't; you are living all right; but I want you to *feel God*. It is like getting the sense of the earth's motion. I did that once, as I think I've told you, measuring by a big California moon rising around the shoulder of a mountain—so huge and slow *it* seemed to stand still, and I saw the fir topped edge *swing by it*——! . . .

Well it's like that. To get a conscious sense of the sweep of moving Law inside you . . . and as you vaguely grasp the range of that smooth power— well, it makes you feel *rested*. I think that is what gives the peace of God that passeth understanding. . . .

4. P.M.. . . .

[*She has just seen a copy of the* Times Herald *that included a biographical sketch of her.*]

It was queer stuff and not half as kind or wise as the last little woman did. But it was a prominent article in a prominent paper on a very prominent day and will swell my fame no doubt. . . .

And my resolution for the year is to Live. To be happy. To Work. And to seek still more earnestly toward the self-consciousness of my professions. . . .

. . . 473 Orchard St. Chicago Ill.
Jan 2nd. '99. . . .

. . . By the way—have you seen the January Cosmopolitan? The last page thereof? Mr. H. T. Peck has done himself proud. Note the respectful tone regarding the poems. Well well————is this fame, peradventure? "Even in England," says he; and I write "like a man." There's a difference in men. But the Book has bowled him over and no mistake. It's out and going, isn't it? Can't stop it now—too late to recant. I am a force to be reckoned with, I am. And there's a certain mild-mannered youth in Wall St. that is going to do the reckoning. . . .

[*She mentions having talked with Florence Kelly but says nothing of the content of the conversation.*]

. . . These years of separation are doing lovely work—just as I hoped they would. . . . All my swaying tendencies are coming into line; I am growing steadier, more definite and sure. . . .

. . . 473 Orchard St. Chicago
Jan. 3rd. 1899 . . .
6.45. . . .

I'm not sure about your church going, but my impression is that duty to "God" and one's own soul; intellectual honesty and good example; point to going to the church that suits you—if you go at all. But I'm not sure as I say. It is certainly a kindness to go with your father. Spread it out and apply it to all people and I think you would see the world wag backward pretty fast if we all went to the church of our fathers continually! . . .

[Toledo, Ohio]
. . . 8.52 A.M. Jan. 9th. 1899. . . .

[*She is staying with Mayor Jones and his family.*]
I wish it were possible for you to see me at work. . . .

Now here are these people—entire strangers, both man and wife sitting around and listening to my words as if I were a real old fashioned prophet.

Not only that but the good man calmly offers to give me money. . . . No, I tell him—I'm doing very well now. . . . You see I've no notion of being personally indebted to the good man! But I agreed to come here for my expenses; and it adds tremendous weight to every word I say—people's knowing that I don't do it for money. You should have seen the crowd I had last night! His "Golden Rule Hall" was filled to overflowing. . . .

Mrs. Jones says I have done her so much good! It makes me just cry with happiness—to know that the light and the power does show through. . . .

I don't make much in cash this trip you will observe; but I have made a big impression and more friends.

With the best of intentions in the money making line I can't seem to keep to it. The real things to do open up so much more temptingly.

I can't for the life of me refuse my real work you know. And if ever there was a clear case of a "call" I think I've got it!

Mr. Jones is desperately anxious to have me come back the latter part of March and help in his municipal campaign. Not as a personal matter but in the interest of socialism and all it means. I don't promise. It doesn't "appeal" to me particularly. He is a big genial childish man—oil well business—inventor . . . rich, but not a millionaire, and lifted into his position by a political accident—a "dark horse" sort of man—put in as Republican candidiate by the respectable element. Then he astonished them all by his outcrop of Socialist tendencies; and is now approaching a very exciting campaign. The four newpapers of the place are said to be forming a combine against him, agreeing to down him by the simple process of completely ignoring—not to mention his name between this and election day.

He very honestly feels that it is not a personal campaign but one on great social issues; and so do I; but all the same I feel no call to be in it! . . .

9.22 A.M. Wed. Jan. *11 '99.* . . .

I wonder, when we have a house and "entertain" how it will go—how you will like my methods—and the queer half baked people that always flock around me. I'm afraid you won't. . . .

It['s] a splendid day. The lake is all blue & white blazes of ice and water—mostly ice. . . .

. . . Village LeClaire Ill.
9.35 A.M. Sat. Jan. 14th. 1899. . . .

I guess you'd better send me back my letter of a week ago—Sat. Jan. 7th.[16] It means more to me than it does to you.

Also I don't feel that way now, and it doesn't seem honest to have the thing around.

I have your letters of the week past—have not had time or strength to answer them. Haven't felt like it either for the last few days. . . .

It has been rather too much work, the last ten days, and I've overdone, but shall pick up soon. . . .

. . . St. Louis. Mo.
Jan. 18th. 1899. . . .

In the evening the lecture on *Child Labor* for the Pedagogical Society. I rather shook in my shoes over my large ignorance on the subject; as compared with the learned body under whose auspices I appeared; but I held forth cheerfully on my view of the case; and was received most warmly.

The Beecher reputation weighs heavily in my favor so far—which I had not expected. A big old man got up last night and declared that he felt himself "in the grip of the master mind of Henry Ward Beecher!"—and that "now he was in favor of woman on the rostrum—though he never had been before!" . . .[17]

. . . St. Louis. Mo. . .
6.10 P.M. Fri. Jan. 20th. '99. . . .

I am really interested to hear from you—hoping that you can somehow catch and bring me back to life. I don't know in the least what ails me; but there is a queer dead spot which *I have no desire to talk about.* . . . But as near as I can remember what hit me, it was a great sweeping recognition that I had gone too far—said too much—given more than was wanted— *from the first.*

And then there was a tidal wave of shame—my! how long and black it was!—and I guess I was drowned or something, for I haven't *felt* anything since. . . .

Things go on swimmingly here. Last night the Crundens had a party and I spoke to the unhappy crowd on "Social Progress." . . .[18]

But it's over a week now that I haven't heard a word from my heart— not a peep! . . .

. . . St. Louis, Mo.
3.10 P.M. Sat. Jan 21st. 1899. . . .

Your letter of the 19th . . . has just come. . . .

As this letter makes no remark on the subject it may be that you have not noticed anything between us. But I won't admit that thought till I see your other letters. Because the suggestion is so patent—if he does not notice when I do not speak any more than he does when I do speak—why speak at all—Nobody's listening. . . .

. . . This is the one [of your letters] which I haven't yet recovered from. Says "your letter with its voluminous enclosures came this morning." I was waiting—so eagerly—for that letter. But you overlooked one of the enclosures—my heart. . . .

This has been a very full week, but very pleasant; and whatever ails my heart it hasn't *hurt*—has been just unconscious. So long as I'm able to do my work I don't mind losing happiness. Besides I have all the big outside happiness—loving friends and successful labor. The dear sweet inside comfort is not so long known as to kill me by its absence. I'm keeping up nicely, . . . and have been cheerful and smiling right along. I never was more warmly met than here, and am speaking well each time. . . .

With the same dead blank feeling—
Charlotte

. . . St. Louis. Mo.
Jan. 22nd. 1899. . . .

[*She has just received several of his letters.*]
. . . It puzzles me very much that you are so utterly impervious to a change so sudden and deep as that in my letters. . . .

How can I ever write again—really write to you, from my heart.

When I write you my inmost and utmost you don't notice it, and when I write you more coldly and briefly than I would to any friend you don't notice that either. What have I been writing to all this time—and what for. That day in May '97 when I got a letter from you which I had been eagerly expecting after I had written you all the heart I had then—that was the day when I suddenly lost all the good spirits which had held so steadily during that happy spring.

There was another one in Kansas I remember—I fairly squeezed the poor paper thing to get something out of it that wasn't there. But that wasn't the faint shadow of the feeling I have had for you this winter—a feeling that has grown and strengthened even in absence, until now. But now I feel that I was doing it all—making love to myself in the glass—and am very weary.

I know what you would say—that you don't write freely as I do—that you do love—that your life will prove it. You love something, I know. Something you think is me no doubt; but how can you love *me* and hurt me so and not know it?

I've had many kinds of shocks and pains in my life, as you know, but this was a new kind altogether.

You know I've developed a new heart to love you with—a very tender baby thing—not old and worn and tough like the rest of me. And now it's been in this numb and dumb condition. . . . But you don't notice that I've stopped loving you. My letters do not reach any live consciousness in you— they don't connect—I've been writing in the dark and you've been shaping your replies to what you thought I wanted—with all the good will on earth it is true—but all the time we didn't connect at all it seems. And when I think of what manner of letters I have written to you—of course I want to call them all back and burn them—scatter the miserable ashes—sink them in the sea—and never think of love again lest I die of shame. . . . I don't suppose it is permanent. You are my cousin and my friend. I am attached to you by many many ties. But now I cannot *think* of expressing any love for you without that scarlet dumb reaction. In the past or future—it is the same. I don't feel angry at all. I don't blame you at all. You are not responsible in the least that I can see. I have been making—ah!—I can[']t write it. I am ashamed two years deep and as wide as my heart can reach. . . .

I don't see anything to say or do. My kind of love doesn't reach your kind of heart that's all. I thought something was holding me—and it isn't! it isn't! It doesn't know when I am close, close, and pouring out my whole live loving heart; and it doesn't know when I am gone absolutely.

My health is all right, though a bit tired yet. All goes well here. . . .

. . . St. Louis. Mo.
Jan 24th. 1899. . . .

This is not a happy time, and it is not a safe or healthy experience. I could not explain it to you at first—I was simply dumb. And, knowing my love for free expression I should think that in itself would have alarmed you. . . .

Of course I have no intention of plaintively beseeching you to take any different attitude. You are you and have a perfect right to your own judgment. The worst of it is you see that the wires are down—I cannot tell you how I feel—I cannot suggest or recommend, and your policy seems to be to let the patient serenely alone till she recovers. . . .

Without any pretense of being justified by the facts, this fact remains: I have sustained a severe shock in what we call "the heart." A heavier blow in an emotional way I never remember. Because you see I had been giving and giving to you, till as that letter stated, I had come for the first time in my life to where I just *let go* and gave wholly. I let myself *want*. Very well. I did not receive. And being well off my feet, when the shock came I had no resistance whatever—I just fell through space. I have not got any clear grip on it since. My head is all right—I've done fine work here in St. Louis and lots of it; and am gaining strength; but in my heart I'm blind and dumb and crazy. And I have feared to investigate the thing as one fears to draw out a deep sunk weapon from a wound—feared the pain and the bleeding.

Now it seems to me a sort of opportunity. I feel, blindly, that you can some way take hold of me and make me feel that it is all a mistake and you are really *there*. So as soon as I could speak of it at all I tried to show you my condition, though the strongest impulse was absolute silence. Now you say you will just wait and do nothing. Perhaps you are right. Perhaps I shall be starved into such helpless longing that I shall come back and beg for some word of love. But I don't feel that way. I feel as if every instinct of self-defense and all my lifelong habits of hardening over and shutting out would come to my rescue.

It is going on already—the myriad-handed effort to lay hold on every outside thought and deed and build a wall—a high thick solid wall right over the hurt place. It[']s a fearful risk I know—because so much of me is there to bury; but there is more left yet—I have worked hard this week—lived and loved and given strength to many—they have not known that I was dead.

O HOUGHTON MY HEART WILL BREAK!

Not just now, though. A lady has called—she says I helped her—I must go down and help her some more. I'm not dead. . . .

. . . St. Louis. Mo. . . .
Jan. 25th. 1899. . . .

Your yesterday's letter assures me at least that you have received mine all right. But it does not give me a word of what I am suffering for. . . .

You preserve an attitude of masterly inactivity. You will wait, you say, till I come back. *Don't you see that this simply corroborates my worst fears?* You are only what I call for, it appears. If I am only a friend you are a friend. If I am but a cousin you are but a cousin. If I ardently love you will then come forward and ardently love also. Sort of an echo. That is exactly what ails me you see. I have been suddenly overwhelmed by fearing this very thing. And, by way of treatment, you proceed to prove it.

Well now in one sense I am not in a position to dictate. . . . I ought to be thankful for any kind of love, and if I have to evoke it, why let me labor so to do, and be grateful for the results.

But in another sense I truly believe that I am too valuable a servant to the world just now to take any such chances as this. This present suffering has cost me months of strength. I cannot afford it.

As I have told you before it is easier for me to go without than to suffer. I would rather lose you and live on alone. . . .

. . . I believe I could live on and work without you even now. If I could not—if it means death—I would rather die now, and quickly, than meet this blinding agony at unforeseen intervals.

If you don't love me more than to make dutiful responses to my advances it won't do to marry on. . . . I admit all the blame for this state of things belongs to me. I took the man's part on myself and wooed you first. But as I learned what love was I became a woman and now that woman's heart is closing desperately upon itself—and waiting for you to open it. If you care to.

> It is a woman's business to wait, not a man's.
> It is for a woman to be patient and still—not a man.
> If you are truly lover and husband—show it.
> If not—God bless you and Good bye. . . .

9

"An Endless Love for Women":
1 February–26 April 1899

As we confront the "tempestuous" cycles in Charlotte's Gilman's correspondence—her bold assertive self-exposure, her resulting sense of vulnerability and shame—we know almost nothing of Houghton Gilman's struggles and reactions, of the reflections that inspired his never-ending patience, his tactful and skillful response. We only know that in early February, 1899, Charlotte wrote him, "As to forgiving—I am amused! Here you go on being equally affectionate and true and tender and faithful all the time," even "under torture as it were—and here I . . . proceed suddenly to harass and perplex and grieve you beyond measure, and then you expect me to forgive you! . . . I sternly and utterly refuse. You've got to do the forgiving!" "How are you going to get on with a tempestuous critter like this?" she queried. "I don't hold." It "seems that the whole stuff is shivered through and through—disintegrated—crumbles in your hand like rotten rock. . . . My main purposes hold all right—faiths—beliefs—intentions." But try to "[c]atch it . . . and the whole mass begins to plunge and thrash about." "You are as true and steady as a magnet," and "I have done nothing but wobble. The assurance I feel at one time weighs . . . nothing the next time I lose hold of it."[1]

With Houghton as her steady background, and with work as the central focus of her faith, Gilman continued with her lecture tour, her next stop at the experimental "brotherly" community of Ruskin, Tennessee. Named for the socialist writer John Ruskin and founded in 1894 by "one-hoss editor" Joseph Wayland, the Ruskin cooperative was motivated by the "belief that a successful settlement would by example prove the correctness of socialistic co-operation." As Joseph Wayland put it, "One practical success, widely advertised, showing that men can live and love and have peace and plenty, will do more toward bringing the Brotherhood of Man than a thousand speakers." The object of the Ruskin Association, according to its by-laws,[2]

shall be to own and operate manufactories, to acquire land, to build homes for its members, to insure members against want or the fear of want, to provide educational and recreative facilities of the highest order, and to promote and maintain harmonious social relations on the basis of co-operation.[3]

Most of Gilman's reform colleagues were enthusiastic supporters of the Ruskin goals. Through their articles and essays in the *Coming Nation,* the *American Fabian*, and the *Arena*, they acclaimed Ruskin's sound financial programs, its steadily growing membership, and its socialist ideals of "brotherly" justice, equality, and love. With no police, no church or minister, no institutional religious pressures, the *American Fabian* editors declared that the Ruskin community has "no free love, no immorality, no thieving, no drunkenness" of any kind.[4]

From Gilman's point of view, however, Ruskin had some glaring disappointments. As she put it in her autobiography, Ruskin was "another of those sublimely planned, devotedly joined, and invariably deserted Socialist colonies." "Spend my strength in putting up with the difficulties of the place," she wrote, with the "awful" roads, the inadequate heating, the small and shabby buildings, the "more than friendly rats."[5] Even more importantly, the "brave" and "earnest" Ruskin citizens seemed so "singularly unenthusiastic," so "inferior and queer." Herbert Casson, for example, an editor of the Ruskin *Coming Nation,* was "too violent" in rhetoric, too "wide of the mark." "No wonder they think me merely a 'kid glove Socialist.'" They are "cranks with pronounced views of their own; all tired; and all in that stage of reform work where the boiling enthusiasm for what should be is all poured out in the difficult maintenance" of daily life, in "interminable wranglings," and in rather "pitiful" dissenting wails about "anything that isn't the whole thing."

After the Ruskin visit, however, the next stops on Gilman's southern lecture tour were increasingly successful. In Nashville and Memphis, Tennessee, in Montgomery and Birmingham, Alabama, and also in Atlanta, Georgia, she met a particularly warm and welcoming response. "I guess I'm all right in the South—if I keep on carefully and am not unduly elated." Moreover, "I'm amazed to see these southern women take" to *Women and Economics* so enthusiastically. "I wouldn't have dreamed it." Mrs. Rebecca Lowe, president of the General Federation of Women's Clubs, says she "wants to build me a church and have me come here and settle." "O I tell you I've 'reached' Atlanta!" "The town is at my feet. They want me to live here—stay with 'em always." One woman said "my visit" had advanced "the city twenty five years!" And crowds? "They couldn't get near the door. . . . Ladies stood—it was simply jammed." And they "recognize, as no people have before, the lovingness of my work." "I'm afraid you'll think me a very bragging sort of a person to be always writing you so. But this is the way things happen and I do like to tell you all about it."

According to the Atlanta *Constitution,* Gilman's lectures were, in fact, remarkably well received. She was "one of the modern woman's foremost defenders," one reporter wrote, and had lectured "to the largest and most enthusiastic audience ever assembled" at the Atlanta Woman's Club. "There is no doubt that in her radical views of the status and relations of woman to society, she presents the most 'advanced' of the 'advanced type' of woman, contending as she does for the absolute economic independence of woman." She "does not mitigate the force of her subject . . . by seeking to conciliate those whom she realizes are opposed to her," nor are there any who "could doubt that . . . her very being was absorbed by the force of her convictions." The report continues:

> Gradually she gains possession of [her audience] by her simple expression of powerful thoughts until finally her audience is spell bound. Inspired by their rapt attention she appears to grow more enthused in her subject, and to impart it to her hearers with that suppressed vigor, that impresses one . . . that . . . she brings a message that is being revealed to her at the very moment as a sacred trust that must be guarded by her as the medium of its covenant.[6]

Following the Atlanta visit, Gilman planned to go to Goldsboro, North Carolina, for a longer stay with Clara Royall, her hostess of the year before. "All goes well here," she wrote to Houghton; "violets and jonquils plenty, fruit trees beginning to bloom, all the trees growing misty with new leaves." Moreover, "Mrs. Royall really loves me." She "says I have changed her whole life," that she "has taken hold of . . . this sluggish town and *lifted* it—is stirring and combining and inspiring—and she says I did it!" In fact, "Mrs. Royall fell to telling me things . . . about my work here, that started me crying." She says "that it would be impossible to measure the good I had done Goldsboro, . . . that my power of giving a feeling was simply wonderful. And that she could hardly understand such a life—that it seemed to be all *giving*—with no personal desires at all. Well. It simply brought the tears. . . . To sit there feeling so poor and mean," and to "have people feel and talk so about me!" If only Mrs. Royall knew the "weary sense of hopeless deficiency," the "reproach and agony," the "good for nothing" private side. People always say "[I seem] so clever," or, as one friend recently had put it, so "coldly brilliant—like a diamond." But, if "these diamond theorists could read our last three weeks [of] correspondence," they might change their minds.

Although Gilman was familiar with such "mean" and "weary" doubts and worries, she continued, except for letters, to try to keep them to herself. In recent years, she was even keeping the relationship with Houghton secret. It was almost as though in order to sustain the public's trust in her feminist convictions, she had to project uncompromising cheerfulness and confidence and to obscure some disconcerting problems, which, inspite of the forcefulness of theory, she always knew were there. She did not often publicly acknowledge the strains that erupted in her own experiences of mothering, for instance, or her roller-coaster vacillations as she tried reconciling work with love, or even more important in this context, her fears about her past relationships with women and about the potential public disapproval should she openly acknowledge their importance in her life. For good reason, Gilman often felt reluctant to share such private issues with many of her friends and colleagues, sometimes even boasting that she managed secrecy so well. She was becoming "rich in the tricks and shifts of an old campaigner," she recently had written Houghton, and she was developing "a well-earned skill" in handling her "weapons." How about a book or article "on the various psychic tricks and methods I'm always preaching—*and* practising. A kind of seriocomic treatment—sort of Holmesy—'But why irritate the good man by this tactless opposition to his wishes? Do not oppose him—merely *do* that which you wish to do when the time is ripe— and he has naught to condemn but the irredeemable past. A steady sweetness of demeanor, accompanied by the deft achievement of one[']s purposes, is better than domestic discord.'" In fact, she continued, one of the "reasons for my many and instant friendships is just this swift and subtle adaptability of mine." "I can fit to the shape of a thousand people,"—at least "temporarily"—but then again "it isn't really my shape—(if I have any!) and I let go and swing off—to rest and recuperate."[7]

What Charlotte hoped, of course, was that the relationship with Houghton would provide the needed rest and comfort. At least with Houghton, she honestly hoped to be herself. Unfortunately, however, troubling issues kept emerging, this time resulting from memories of Adeline Knapp, a close and loving female friend. Ironically, the precipitating factor in the current context was the growing warmth and love of Clara Royall. "Mrs. Royall is very fond of me," Charlotte wrote to Houghton; "this morning . . . I took her into bed for a good hug." But then suddenly and quite abruptly her letter reads: "A thought occurs to me," and not a "pleasing" one. "Adeline Knapp has . . . letters of mine most fully owning the really passionate love I had for her." "You ought to know that there is a possibility of such letters being dragged out some day . . . goodness knows what careless thing she might do or has done with them." "I sometimes feel as if you refused to fully realize" that malicious people could make things quite "unpleasant," she continued. "Fancy the San Francisco papers": "Revelations of a Peculiar Past!" or "Mrs. Stetson's Love Affair with a Woman." "*Am* I a woman you ought to marry?" Charlotte queried. "Are you sure you have understood when I told you 'All'"?[8]

For years, Charlotte had known close and loving relationships with women, the empowering sense of mutuality and sharing, the "female world of love and ritual," as Carroll Smith-Rosenberg has called it.[9] "I have an intense and endless love for women," Charlotte recently had written Houghton, "partly in reverence for their high estate, partly in pity for their blind feebleness, their long ages of suffering." Or, more positively, as she had written Martha Luther years before, "The freedom of it! The deliciousness! The utter absence of 'how will he take it?'" "[W]hy in the name of heaven have we so confounded love with passion that it sounds to our century-tutored ears either wicked or absurd to name it between women?"[10]

Even at the age of twenty-one, Charlotte had recognized, of course, the potential scandal of such passionate attachments. "Incidental thought," she teasingly wrote Martha. "What horrid stuff these letters would be for the Philistines! Lock 'em up, and sometime we'll have a grand cremation."[11] For with Martha, and more importantly in her later years, Charlotte had affirmed rather than denigrated or denied her love relationships. She had had a particularly satisfying bond with Walter's Stetson's second wife, Grace Channing, for instance,[12] and later with Adeline Knapp, a co-worker at the California Woman's Press Association. "Delle," she called her in her autobiographical reflections, this "friend with whom I had sincerely hoped to live continually." "I loved her," and she "certainly did love me."[13] Or as she described the relationship to Houghton, "I loved her, trusted her, wrote her as freely as I write to you." "I told you that I loved her that way."[14]

Ideally, of course, Gilman would have more openly stressed the positive value of women's loving friendships, the sense of "integrity and dignity that grew out of women's shared experiences and mutual affection."[15] But understandably, she could only do so indirectly: privately by living according to her "sanction" theory, and publicly by challenging the prevailing view of love, the assumption, as *Women and Economics* put it, that "marriage is the woman's proper sphere, her divinely ordered place, her natural end."[16] In fact, as Charlotte tried explaining it to Houghton, unloving *marriages* were often "wrong," not female friendships. Regarding her own marriage to Walter Stetson, for example: "I married *without* that knowledge of right doing. I did not have my own sanction. I did not reason it out and accept it." And so "I make a wide distinction between such wrongs as I then thought right—and those I was not sure about." According to conventional morality, some of the "wrongest things in my life I have been quite satisfied about, both at the time and after—counting consequences." "Not for nothing have I held my own against mother and teacher and critic and friend. . . . Emerson—Carlyle—MacDonald—I owe them much. I'll try and pay the debt to those who follow me." For "[p]ersonally I am not sorry for nor ashamed of my life. I always had my own sanction at the time; and that is all the guide I ever followed."

One might wish, of course, that Gilman had more openly denounced the homophobic attitudes that condemned women's love for one another, or the prevailing social bigotry that imposed a self-destructive sense of shame and secrecy and silence. Openly expressed anger and resistance might have helped relieve her own and other women's tendency to condemn themselves for loving women. But then again, to promote the positive value of lesbian relationships in articles and lectures was not, realistically, a nineteenth-century option. The resulting scandal almost certainly would have discredited her life and work. Without models, without a strong community of women who could politically and personally affirm the value of loving female friendships, Gilman understandably felt compelled to take a more defensive stance.[17] She had had courage enough to rebel against conventional morality, against "compulsory heterosexuality," as one writer calls it; she had had confidence enough to acknowledge her past relationships to Houghton, but not always strength enough to resist a sense of "evilness" from entering her dreams. "Couldn't sleep much," she wrote Houghton, "much misery— culminating in a touching death bed scene in which you were duly sent for and I frankly admitted that I never was good enough to have you love me and that I was glad to release you in this final way."

At times Gilman clearly had to face internal fears about her unconventional behavior. But clearly also, the relationship with Houghton served to deepen them. "My morals are different from yours," she wrote him, "and yet I can't seem to bear having them different. I value your judgement very much and hate to act counter to it." "[H]ow about our standards? Will they fit?" With his "conservative temperament," his respect for "authority" and "precedent," might he be "newly impressed" with her "evilness"? Or regard her as "a questionable wreck of a character—that has to be 'stood by'— perhaps lied about?" Even worse, might he conclude that in fundamental ways her life had not been "honest. That I am not telling the truth to the world. That I ought to announce 'I have done this and that—I am such and such a woman' and take the consequences." In her own view, she was "honester" the way she was, she told him, and not a "bad woman in any sense of the word." In fact, she even recognized a role reversal in their friendship as they faced this issue. After all, men did not seem to have a problem in relationships with women "whose judgement they do not accept." They can "marry girls they know to be 'purer' and 'better' than they are—and not so wise . . . and it does not seem to trouble them." And yet "to be permanently with a person of widely differing ideals and standards is a heavy tax on me," she apologetically continued, as though to blame herself for wanting his approval or as though her "longing for utter union and acceptance" was just a weak-willed woman's wish to please. "I insensibly fit myself to the measure of the person I am with—can't help it."

There is a certain irony, of course, in Gilman's need for Houghton's understanding and approval. The more she focused on *his* potential disapproval, or on the ways she might compromise *his* interests, the more intense the turmoil that a female friendship might have helped to heal:[18] "the pitiful wish to be picked up and carried and consoled," for instance, the fear that it was "treason and dishonor" not to devote herself entirely to his needs, the assumption that he should be her Lord and Master, and that she should be the "little bitzer witzer girl." "I could wish with all my woman's heart that there was no other place in life to call me," she told him. "I want to crouch down at your feet and say O my Lord and King! I am not worthy!" "You ought to have a *whole* wife to give herself all to you."

With the public, and also with most friends and colleagues, Gilman had found effective ways of dealing with differences of lifestyle and conviction.

In fact, she often had delighted in her "psychic tricks and methods," in her skillful use of irony and wit to promote her feminist cónvictions while deflecting confrontation and reproach. "A steady sweetness of demeanor, accompanied by the deft achievement of one[']s purposes" seemed more effective than "tactless opposition" or direct "discord." "And when I have thought at times of practical difficulties such as some untoward uprising of past events, some personal accusation; I have said to myself—'I will never answer a word.'" In her relationship with Houghton, however, Charlotte wanted far more openness and understanding, resulting in a startling confrontation that her public theory could not heal. "I'm looming up like friend Frankenstein's critter," she wrote him, demanding so much "and then flying off so far—a very big kite in a very high wind!" With all these "tempestuous changeful" moods, this "hopeless irreconcilability on so many lines," "You can't count on me. Can't rest on me. Can't ever be sure how I'm going to feel next day. . . . Nothing'll stop it." "I believe they said the same of George Eliot—that she demanded a great deal."

The familiar themes thus reemerge in Gilman's letters, an eloquent if painful illustration of the complexity of issues she was still determined to explore. "I suppose it is only the essential pain of the woman nature forced out into world service," she more confidently continued. "Loving, the woman longs to have that love thrill through, infill, entirely meet and cover every part of her life. . . . The man is accustomed to having love a department only. To the woman the formation of that department—during these transition years—is essential pain." Now here "is ground for a novel—a real novel—one that would meet glad wondering recognition in a million women's hearts today! O what *a lot* of work I've got to do!"

Letters: February 1 through April 26, 1899

Ruskin Tenn.
7.50 A.M. Wed. Feb. 1st. 1899.

Next to having you with me, Heart's Dearest, is the pleasure of sitting down each morning and talking to you in the first freshness of the day.

I got your letter of the 27th yesterday. . . . It does feel so good! That sense of the strong hand *holding* me—it makes me feel so safe and sure and rested. . . .

Yes, I was overworked and tired the last few weeks in Chicago—things piled up and had to be done. And I dare say that was why I collapsed over this thing so horribly. . . .

For two nights Miss Commander has been sleeping with me. . . . She seems very fond of me. But—woman though she be—I don't like to feel her in my bed. Don't seem nice somehow. Want you there.[19]

She is a plump and cuddlesome lady, like a big affectionate child; and moved to admiration by my airy gymnastics. . . .

All kinds of people are here, but mostly inferior and queer. I am more convinced than ever of the hopelessness of colony life—of any attempt to establish little separate organisms within one great inescapable social organism. . . .

Yes dear. The ground is growing solid under my feet at last. The mists—mists always there—are slowly lifting. . . .

[*She has just received word of the death of her father, Frederick Perkins, but did not know of it in time to attend his funeral.*][20]

. . . It is doubtless all over. I'm so glad you were there to be a comfort to poor little mother. . . .[21] I will write to Mother and to Uncle Charles I think—thanking him as it were for all he has done. Otherwise there isn't anything to say or do that I know of. I was expecting to hear at any time—the sooner the better, really.

Well. That's one of the shut doors of my life that never can be opened. I am grateful for the little chinks of those last few months. If I could have been with [him] during the first years of that illness we could have had much in common I am sure. I am glad mother died first. She loved him so. What a sad dark life the poor man led. And my brother seems [to be] going much the same way. I'm not—thanks to loving the world and you. . . .

. . . **Ruskin Tenn.**
11 A.M. Thurs. Feb. 2nd. . . .

. . . As to forgiving—I am amused! Here you go on being equally affectionate and true and tender and faithful all the time; and heroically keeping it up under torture as it were—and here I, out of whole cloth, proceed suddenly to harass and perplex and grieve you beyond measure, and then you expect me to forgive you! I refuse, I sternly and utterly refuse. You've got to do the forgiving! . . .

. . . **Ruskin Tenn.**
Thurs. Feb. 2nd. 1899. . . .

Miss C[ommander] wants me to write a letter to her coming lord, giving him something of the advice I've been giving her. . . . Talk about destroying families! Here I am laboring day and night to get this one going on a proper basis. . . .

[*Miss Commander told her that one of the Ruskin women had said she was . . .*]

Clever—O so clever—but rather coldly brilliant—like a diamond. . . . If these diamond theorists could read our last three weeks [of] correspondence—it might amuse them. . . .[22]

7.45 A.M. Fri. Feb. 3rd. . . .

I've got hold of what I believe is a principle, in talking with Mr. Nelson yesterday. Production is naturally collective—co-operative—in an increasing degree. But consumption is naturally individual and must remain so. *That* is why co-operative housekeeping doesn't work. . . .

. . . Ruskin Tenn.
7.25 A.M. Sat. Feb. 4th. 1899. . . .

. . . This place is wearing. And I do not like large rats in my bedroom at night—nor large ladies in my bed! . . .
Last night I lectured. . . .
The audience was a peculiarly difficult one. Mostly cranks with pronounced views of their own; all tired; and all in that stage of reform work where the boiling enthusiasm for what should be is all poured out in the difficult maintenance of what is. . . .

. . . Nashville Tenn.
Feb. 8th. 1899. . . .

. . . the water in the pitcher froze! O this is the sunny South, this is! There is sunshine today, but it don't seem to help the thermometer any. . . .

. . . Nashville Tenn.
Feb. 9th. 1899. . . .

. . . though my heart still beats feebly in your behalf I am otherwise frozen stiff. Last night my *ink froze*—inside the black bag! . . .
This afternoon I speak for the Peabody Normal Institute—girls—my best audience always. No pay—but I hated to leave the city and not hold forth at all—seems such a waste. . . .
. . . Thanks for [the] obituary notice. How pitifully it reads! So able a man—and so little to show for it. Poor father! . . .

... **Memphis Tenn**
Fri. Feb. 10th. 1899. . . .

   . . . The . . . Chancellor of [the Peabody Institute] . . . was present [at her lecture]; and a minister. Well sir—I captured the whole outfit! Never spoke easier . . . talked and read poetry and made diagrams on the blackboard. . . . And you should have heard the minister chuckle when I said that the only fault I had to find with "the virtuous woman"—was that she never went to bed: "Her candle goeth not out by night"—"she rouseth her maiden before it is day"; but that except for that habit of insomnia she was a fine person! It tickled 'em all. . . .

... **Memphis. Tenn.**
9.30 A.M. Sat. Feb. 11th. 1899. . . .

   I mail you today—or pretty soon—another *Coming Nation,* a *Social Democrat,* and Mr. Casson's little book. I like you to look at them, and see how wide of the mark, yet how earnest and brave these working Socialists are. No wonder they think me merely a "kid glove Socialist." See how wrong the S[ocial] D[emocrat] is about Lloyd's book, and Quincy's "Municipal Ownership."[23]
   They kick so at anything that isn't the whole thing—it is pitiful to see.
   I didn't read all Casson's book—but it seems to me too violent. . . .
   . . . Miss Commander . . . is simply a fine plump lass—such as men like. *She's* not a spindle-legged little nanny-goat like me! (Nor she can't frisk and skip like me either!). . .

... **Memphis Tenn.**
10.06 A.M. Wed. Feb. 15th. '99. . . .

   Under stress of these improved conditions I begin to feel the stir of work, and am setting my face as a flint against your daily seductions. . . .
   I do not at all believe in the hour for hour theory of payment. . . .
   The essential change in idea is to consider it not as *payment*—not as working *for something one is going to have;* but that the supplies of life come first. . . .
   Then you can see that a wise and liberal education would naturally supply to each child all that he needed to develop his best powers. . . . Our notion of working for payment, and just how to measure what each shall have is a transient misconception of the processes of economic exchange. Under that misconception we fail to get the utmost productivity from the race. The "tendency to vary" and the influence of conditions produces vary-

ing degrees of productivity among us—a natural law. But we[,] with this wrong notion of ours about just paymen[t], are always trying to measure each one[']s value and *return him what he gives*—a thing primarily impossible and secondarily ridiculous.

Fancy paying Shakespeare! or the man who invented matches! No sir! Fix your world so as to raise as many Shakespeares and "matchmakers" (!) as possible—to *produce* them—not pay them! . . .

——O I can not tell you what a delight it is to me! That is what I have been hungering for for so long. . . . To have your mind work the way mine does—to see you thinking about the same things—caring about them—asking—studying—O my dear! . . . it is to my mind something of the same ineffable accord there is in full bodily union. And my mind is bigger than my body. . . .

. . . (I always smile to think of the anguish of my Socialist admirers when I marry a man from Wall St.! You know it is Sodom and Gomorrah to them.) . . .

. . . **Memphis Tenn.**
Thurs. Feb. 16th. 1899. . . .

[*She gave a lecture at the Century Club on "Home, Past, Present and Future."*]

I gave a sort of dress reform lecture to an excited group. . . . I made it rather mild—only came out strong on the care of children etc. . . .

So you see I am gorged with good treatment as usual. I believe there's only ten dollars—perhaps less—in this; but it's worth while.

. . . **Memphis Tenn.**
Feb. 17th. 1899.
6.15 P.M. Friday. . . .

Parlor talk over! Sweeping and unlimited success. I mustn't go—they cannot spare me—they need me—"now that we know you and love you"—said one sweet woman. . . .

[One enthusiast] told a damsel present I was the greatest woman since Jesus Christ—thinks I'm a reincarnation of him! (So are we all that are trying to help.) . . . But he's known for "a crank." . . .
I guess I'm all right in the South—if I keep on carefully and am not unduly elated. But I do feel pleased.

O—and they think I'm pretty! "Did I know I looked like Rossetti's women?" Yes, I did. This purple gown and the long white scarf is a stunner. . . .

. . . I do love the work. And the power grows and grows. I feel very sure that loving you—being loved—being happy—is a great gain in it. For I never was so loving in my speaking before—I touch more people more tenderly all the time.

I'm afraid you'll think me a very bragging sort of a person to be always writing you so. But this is the way things happen and I do like to tell you all about it.

And one of the deepest elements of the power is that I do not stickle for the money. They feel sure I believe it—mean it—live it.

This talk was on Social Progress. . . .

Sat. [Feb.] 19th. 10.45. A.M.. . . .

. . . And I know you'd be pleased if you could really see how constantly you are in my mind. All the time I find you there—just a steady background—a nice thing to turn to —put out my hand and touch. It feels so good!

Yes, I think we are going to have good times together. And I shall be away enough, always, to keep up the charm I think. How I shall want to get back to you—Home! . . .

c/o Mrs. R. D. Lowe . . .
On train. Tues. Feb. 21st [1899]
. . . Atlanta.G. . . .

. . . And mine is a self-absorbed and other-people-absorbing nature—I am apt to encroach. . . .

You must not let me swallow you—pour my life and my affairs all over you. I don't *mean* to be selfish and exacting, but I fear I am. . . .

I'm amazed to see these southern women take to W. & E. I wouldn't have dreamed it. . . .

I still have a secret admiration for rawboned lathy domineering big men—I still get kind of mad at you sometimes because you are so unconscionably *un*like anything I ever expected to love and marry—but there you are!

My assault upon your young affections is like that of Brer Rabbit upon the Tar Baby—and you will not "turn me loose." . . .

. . . Atlanta, Ga.
Wed. Feb. 22nd. 1899.
12.35 A.M. . . .

. . . They've adopted me at once. . . . Crowd? They couldn't get near the door. Ladies stood—it was simply jammed. . . . Such an ardent crowd!

Such congratulations—not only to me, but to Mrs. Lowe for bringing me, which naturally pleases her. . . . I am a great star down here. . . . This morning behold the Atlanta Constitution! It's full of errors—to the horror of the author (who has written a wild note of protest and explanation to Mrs. Lowe) but look at the "space" and the "social notes." And now everything is pouring in. . . . I am to preach in the Unitarian Church Sunday—to lecture for the Club again—to lecture for a Presbyterian thing—to raise money for 'em [and] to speak for a Colored Woman's Club. And there's even talk of the big Lecture Bureau having me a $50.00 one. Wouldn't that be fine! Not only that but Mrs. Lowe is ardently arranging to push me in Virginia, North Carolina, etc.—O it's simply fine! . . .

. . . about 11 A.M. Friday Feb. 24th. 1899. . . .

Briefly, here, things are going *gorgeously*. To be taken up in this way by this Grand Panjandrum Lady Lowe is simply *great*. The town is at my feet. They want me to live here—stay with 'em always. . . .

. . . c/o Mrs. Rebecca D. Lowe . . .
Atlanta Ga.
9.47 A.M. Sunday. Feb. 26th. 99. . . .

I just *cannot* get time for you. Preach this morning in the Unitarian Church—on The Great Commandment. Spoke yesterday morning at High School to a lot of teachers. T'was *fine,* the best one yet; and well appreciated. . . .

They seem to *love* me! And they recognize, as no people have before, the lovingness of my work. I'm very happy. . . .

4 P.M. . . .

. . . one dear little soul . . . said she thought it was "too sweet for a niece of Harriet Beecher Stowe to come down here and make us all love you!" Wasn't that nice of her.

Now Mrs. Lowe wants to build me a church and have me come here and settle. O I tell you I've "reached" Atlanta! . . .

I can't seem to get at you to talk to—out of this whirl. . . . But I'm so on the run from speech to speech here— so under pressure all the time, I can't talk naturally. . . .

O no, that isn't an epoch-making book, that isn't! Aren't you glad you appreciated it *some*—and don't you wish you had appreciated it more? And, best of all, aren't you glad its *our* book—that you helped me write it, you dear dear patient loving soul! . . .

. . . Atlanta Ga.
10 A.M. Tues. Feb. 28th. 1899. . . .

. . . I wish you could really see me at work and realize for yourself what it is. You see you have never heard me when I was truly giving my best. Perhaps you may some time. I hate to just brag and talk to you about it; I want you to *feel* it—and see the other people feel it. Then you'd know—know me, know why I have felt as I have about marrying and all that. Why I so seriously fear lest the housekeeping part of it should prove an injury to my health and a hindrance to my work. . . . You see I am so afraid of my own long-descended instincts getting the better of me—and that, in my love for you and natural wish to make you comfortable, I shall "settle" too firmly. We must be very wise and careful. . . .

12.35. . . .

O how nice it will be to have somebody who doesn't think me grand—not all the time at least; but just a small soft woman—good to hug! . . .

But honest and true dear, I am one of the big workers; and it is no easy job you are undertaking! A he-genius is hard enough to take care of—and a she one!—Poor Houghton! Do you think you can stand it dear? Are you sure you want to take care of me? . . .

. . . Atlanta Ga.
March 2nd. 1899
9.15 A.M. . . .

[*She has received a notice about Walter Stetson's pictures.*]
. . . You know I have no bitterness of feeling toward that good man and yet I take a base delight in little digs. . . . I like to grow and grow and have him see it—is that mean? There is a good deal of justice in what you say of his pictures—as far as it goes. . . . I'm no ardent admirer of C.W.S—his works—never was; but I know their power and beauty somewhat. . . .

8.15 P.M. Fri. March 3rd. '99.
On train for Goldsboro. . . .

You perceive that I have escaped from the hospitable city of Atlanta and am en voyage for peaceful Goldsboro. . . . It's high time I left that place and went to another—tisn't wholesome to be made so much of. . . .

. . . c/o Mrs. George Royall. Goldsboro, N.C.
11 A.M. Sun. March 5th. 1899

The same nice rocking chair, the same large clean sunny cream-colored room, the same cordial welcome—only more so. Mrs. Royall really loves me—so does her sister. . . .

Now some men, when they marry, have to tear a young girl from the ties of home, the playmates of youth; and that is a good deal to outweigh. But you, rash man, have entered the lists with a world of adoring friends and would-be relatives. *Won't* you just have to behave though! . . .

Mothers-in-law are nothing to the "friends-in-law" you will be saddled with—each and all glowing at you as having robbed them in especial. . . .

But—dear—I am growing hungry for a home of my own! I feel it more and more—the nesting instinct. And if I can come to it, not simply for myself, but with an honest desire to work out the home problem for us all, I think it will not hinder, but rather help. I wonder if you realize what a "typical" sort of life you are undertaking—to be the husband of the "new woman" and prove her a supportable infliction. To be contented with such lack and change in domestic arrangements as shall be required by my changeful work. O I *hope* you will be happy!

I have neglected you shamefully this Atlanta time. . . . You know, don't you dear, that it is not that I do not care, but that in those crowded times my mind drifts off its moorings. . . . I suppose that is why I can do it so . . . freshly—bringing the same naturalness—spontaneity—enthusiasm— to each new audience. One woman looked at me in surprise after my—seventh, I think—address, and said "you seem to me like a bottomless fountain of energy!" So I won't apologize for being more like sea-weed than trees! I live among big waves and have to wobble! Doesn't this winter and my *very* professional career shake you at all in your desire to marry me? You see my personal life sinks quite out of consciousness while I am so working— I do not, in any active conscious sense, love you, even! When I think of you it is to wonder vaguely how I dare undertake a personal relation—I who am so increasingly demanded by the world. And this will increase rather than decrease. I *cannot* give you all—or even much. It is simply that you will be there to come back to—and O how *glad* I shall be to come back! . . . but you, dear boy—where do you come in? It doesn't seem as if I ought to have all this world work and the growing loving welcome of it, and a husband too. Seems more than any woman can deserve or have a right to. And if you should be disappointed! If you should grieve and feel neglected. If we had a child and you thought I did not do my duty by it—blamed me—! I just couldn't stand it darling. I couldn't before, and I couldn't now. It seems so miserably little—all that I can really promise you— so unfair in proportion to what you give.

Just my heart—when it isn't otherwise occupied! My body—when it is within reach! My service—when not spent on other people! Dear—it isn't fair! You ought to have a *whole* wife to give herself all to you. . . .

. . . Our problem dear is not the marriage, but the housekeeping. If you still want to marry me in 1900 I know I shall be glad to do it; but the danger lies in the household machinery. We must try to live like two friendly bachelors in apartments. We must really give much earnest thought to it, and plan carefully. . . .

. . . Goldsboro N.C.
Mon. March 6th '99. . . .

Down this way grass is deep—violets and jonquils plenty, fruit trees beginning to bloom, all the trees growing misty with new leaves; or most of 'em.—I shall chase the spring all the way up—a lovely thing to do. . . .

Truly dear—aside from the dear delight of loving you, I think that a home and a husband will be a definite advantage *to me*. It is you who are taking large risks. You will not get at all what men most count on in marriage—the housekeeper. I cannot—dare not—undertake it. I have no right to. When I think of any call to human service being denied because at that time I had no cook——it simply can not be.[24]

Why dear—here is this fine woman here says I have changed her whole life. She has hoped and worked and loved this year past—has taken hold of . . . this sluggish town and *lifted* it—is stirring and combining and inspiring—and she says I did it!

You can see—you *do* see, God bless your noble heart! that no personal comfort or happiness could come between me and such service. . . .

But—Life is the great duty. I do not believe in martyrdom and renunciation. Unless women can live and work and still be wives and mothers there's no use trying. . . . We must simply recognize that the danger lies in the household machinery. . . .

Consider it fully and fairly. Suppose we have a child—two. Suppose I am called away a thousand miles. We must be prepared to face this sort of thing—to meet it through other service than mine—and—and—I must be shielded from reproach. . . .

I recognize perfectly that what would be required of you is most difficult.

Nothing will make it right for you to undertake it save such steady and deep love for me, personally, as will make part of me more to you than the whole of any other; and such unaffected reverence for my work and place in life as shall make you willing to sacrifice much to it. . . .

All people belong to me—need me—follow me. Queer people will come to our house—people that you will not care for. You will be forcibly expanded by such a marriage—spread out—whether you like it or not.

You have a quiet contented conservative temperament. I should think this might contain elements of life-long unrest and pain for you. The fact that *I* suit *you* personally counts for nothing. I suit lots of people personally—utterly different people. I remember dimly groping at this years since in wrestling over the question with Walter. I told him I was a polygon—that he met a certain facet or facets—but not others; and that if I tied myself permanently to those— cutting off the others—I could not "function" properly.

You meet me at a score to his one—you "cover" me more satisfactorily than any man I ever saw—but bless you! it isn't a circumstance to the whole of me. I'm a world critter—absolutely *no* personal relation can cover my life—not hundreds of them. Part of me, part of the time—that's all you get darling; though God knows that when I am in your arms I could wish with all my woman's heart that there was no other place in life to call me! Moreover you will occupy a place most trying to a man's pride. Whatever the evenness of stature of our souls inside—and there's no disparity there you splendid strong true man!—outside I make the bigger noise, and you'll be considered of small account beside me. That'll hurt you and hurt me. A woman so loves to have her husband seem her Master and her Lord— that's heredity.

Against that we can set our little private joke on the world. You and I know when we are alone together and I come yielding—asking—giving myself all to you and begging only to be more wholly taken—*we* know how fully you are all a woman's heart could ask. Perhaps that knowledge will go far to make up to you for being discounted by the outside world. . . .

. . . Think another year dear boy. And—much as I love you —do not [let] your final decision be influenced by fear of its effect on me. . . .

So . . . feel *free* to decide. Be sure you do full justice to all sides of the question. Take advice if you will. And *know* that no wrong could be equal to doing this thing unless your whole undivided heart and understanding mind are satisfied. . . .

Dear—it makes me wonderfully happy to have you write like this. To feel that you really do see what I am doing and care for it. . . . I am a teacher—there's no mistake. And to know you know it—to feel you feel it— I shall never be lonesome again! Just because I have had you.

To feel your strong man's hand there—there where I have stood so long alone! To be recognized for what I am by my *own*—not merely by audiences and passing admirers—it is meat and drink.

Dear—it is an Awful strain to be big. . . And to try to keep sweet and gentle and natural and not step on folks! . . .

. . . Goldsboro N.C.
9.34 A.M. March. 7th 1899. . . .

All goes well here. Mrs. Royall is very fond of me. She came in to turn
on my radiator this morning. And I took her into bed for a good hug—
(hurriedly plucking your letter from my bosom and secreting it under my
bolster).

A thought occurs to me—goodness knows why! Adeline Knapp has (I
suppose she has) letters of mine most fully owning the really passionate love
I had for her. I loved her, trusted her, wrote her as freely as I write to you.
I told you that I loved her that way. You ought to know that there is a
possibility of such letters being dragged out some day. *She* couldn't—being
visibly the party of the second part, but goodness knows what careless thing
she might do or has done with them. Or what malicious thing. Of course
she may have wisely burned them up. . . .

This is not a pleasing subject. But I sometimes feel as if you refused to
fully realize—seeing that I really [am] a pretty good sort of person, and now
generally accepted as such—that there is more than one person on earth
who could make things very unpleasant for me if they tried. My feeling
about it has always been to simply go on and be good; so good and, if
possible, so great; that if ever evil statements were made against me I could
quietly ignore them and let them fall. Personally I am not sorry for nor
ashamed of my life. I always had my own sanction at the time; and that is
all the guide I ever followed. I see no reason, looking back, to regret one
step in a path which has led me so surely up and up—out and onward—to
this place.

But you must consider disagreeable practical possibilities like this. Fancy
the San Francisco papers with a Profound Sensation in Literary Circles!
Revelations of a Peculiar Past! Mrs. Stetson's Love Affair with a Woman.
Is this "Friendship"! and so on. Dear Heart. *Am* I a woman you ought to
marry? Are you willing to give such a mother to your Son—or Daughter?
Are you sure you have understood when I told you "All"? . . .

. . . Goldsboro.
9.10. A.M. March 8th. 1899. . . .

The more I think of it the more thankful I am that you see as you do
now what the essential difficulties are. To feel in you the strong tender
comrade helping me do things—that touches the deepest chord. If I could
feel sure that in helping me your own workday—that I was helping you!—
not taking you from what you ought to do, but really part of *your* best life—
that is too beautiful—. . . .

The sense of definite acknowledged place and power and work is doing me worlds of good.—I feel as if I'd struck my gait at last—and that feeling will grow with regular magazine publication—wide criticism and recognition. It is no wild impossibility. I see no reason why I should not write and lecture—other people have! To be free from debt and to steadily earn two or three thousand a year begins to seem an easy probability. . . .

. . . Now to keep steady. To be true and patient and wise and strong. Not to be bought. Not to let my work weaken under prosperity. To be willing to lose all the high place if necessary. To be simple and natural and *good!* . . .

Not for nothing have I held my own against mother and teacher and critic and friend. I can hold it still I guess. Emerson—Carlyle—MacDonald—I owe them much. I'll try and pay the debt to those who follow me. . . .

. . . Goldsboro. N.C.
9.35 March 10th. 1899. . . .

Nothing succeeds like success—get started and it does itself. You must help me darling. I am going to depend on you ever so much—for sympathy, encouragement, stimulus. I am very weak in many ways—and to be closely with a person always forces me into accord with them—I cannot help it. If you did not care about the things I do it would hamper me a thousand times more than my not caring about your work would hamper you. I am a big heavy grasping thing. Don't let my love or your love blind you to that, darling. I believe they said the same of George Eliot—that she demanded a great deal.

These years are doing all I hoped they would. The wild and changeful currents of my life are clarifying, combining, settling into one clear strong stream of definite endeavor.

You have done wonderful things for me, dear, already. And the work is defining itself more and more—the special work for women and children, the socialistic work, and the big ethical philosophical background to it all. A clear simple working theory of life and the power to teach it to others.

. . . I feel—did you ever row on the open ocean? A row boat on the big rollers—the oars dipping or not dipping as the waves may rise—the cockle-shell feeling—and withal the tremendous elation of that very power beneath—the vast rise and swell that carries you—that is the way I feel now, carried on by the life which claims me. It was blind creeping and feeling for so long—so long! There was no proof at all— no assurance—only I *knew* it was so! And now I can *see.* . . .

I don't want to scare you by these big things.

Perhaps you'd be better pleased to hear those little morning and evening murmured talks of mine—that no one hears or answers—but that do relieve my heart so!

Sweetheart! Sweetheart! Won't you *please* to hug me!———"*You* don't think I'm a Dignitary do you? Not the least bit in the world! Noffin but a little girl—your little girl—your little bitzer witzer girl—what wants to be hugged and generally made free with!"

. . . Goldsboro N.C.
about 8.55 A.M. Sat. March 11th. '99. . . .

. . . I'm going to write a Sunday School book on the advantages of being agreeable. . . . I wish to point out the profits of good behavior in houserent and board! . . . One only has to be pleasant and funny and take an interest in people—and lo! their houses are yours! Yes, I must write it down for the young.

I've got a good idea for a book—article—or somewhat, on the various psychic tricks and methods I'm always preaching—*and* practicing. A kind of serio comic treatment—sort of Holmesy—"But why irritate the good man by this tactless opposition to his wishes? Do not oppose him—merely *do* that which you wish to do when the time is ripe—and he has naught to condemn but the irredeemable past. A steady sweetness of demeanor, accompanied by the deft achievement of one['s] purposes, is better than domestic discord." And such like. . . .

The air is lovely here—clear soft spring weather, violets, jonquils, tulips, and swelling birds everywhere. . . .

. . . c/o Mrs. George C. Royall. Goldsboro. N.C.
March. 12th. 1899. . . .

I've been having a bad night of it. Couldn't sleep much—had to cry—was very miserable. That old heavy dull pain that used to be my constant companion. All about this sudden remembrance of past conditions, my letter to you and your letter to me.

After much misery—culminating in a touching death bed scene in which you were duly sent for and I frankly admitted that I never was good enough to have you love me and that I was glad to release you in this final way—I heavily arose and dressed myself. Now feel better. Life is in front, not behind. . . .

If I'm not good enough for you, Withdraw O Youth!—with my full acceptance of your judgement.

But I am wondering, truly, if this last year might not be a year of complete separation—no letters—no anything—give you *full* opportunity with no pressure. I guess I could stand it. And if I can't—why never mind.

You see your letter did come last night. . . . That scrap of a note from my "affectionate cousin" was chilling. Then the letter came later—and I felt as if somehow you were rather newly impressed with my evilness—had not fully understood before.

Well. This is me. I have faithfully endeavored to make you acquainted therewith. I think perhaps I was not clear about the "my own sanction" theory, which you don't see much in.

There were eight years of my life when I did only what I thought was right—fifteen to twenty three. Mistakes no doubt, but as far as the moral quality goes, good deeds. I married *without* that knowledge of right doing. I did not have my own sanction. I did not reason it out and accept it. Of course, as you say, everybody does wrong things. But I make a wide distinction between such wrongs as I then thought right—and those I was not sure about.

Some of the wrongest things in my life I have been quite satisfied about, both at the time and after—counting consequences.

As you know, the weight on my heart these two years past—the thing that has weighed me down and weakened me in spite of all the joy and strength that came with it—has been the fear that it was wrong to marry you. I did not feel concerned about coming wholly to you—that was part of love—was yours anyway—could hurt neither of us. Was a thing to be passed by if necessary. But to finally link your life to mine—lives so totally different in so many ways—has always seemed to me a wrong to you.

And neither the immense gain it meant to me in every way; or the growing love which drove me to you . . . has blinded my eyes to your interest in the matter.

My size and value as a social factor does not touch the case at all.

A man might be as big as Byron—as Napoleon, and unfit to marry a nice girl.

I *think* my judgement is clear about myself. I do not consider myself a bad woman in any sense of the word. I practice all I preach to the full extent of my powers—and often beyond them, to my sorrow.

I'm good enough to be allowed to serve—that is all I ask. But by nature and experience I am unfit for the pure sweet tender joys of personal union—of home life. I knew it when I was a mere girl—recognized the hopeless incongruity of my mother and father in me—and renounced the one to make the other strong. But I have been weak enough, through all these years, to keep me humble always, not matter what people think me. I *know* I can see the truth and joy and power of life, and show it to other people. For that I thank God. And I do not believe that he gives such power to bad people.

It isn't badness that I'm worrying over—it's "cut offness." Well. You are more to me, personally, than all the rest of the world beside. As far as personal happiness goes you are more to me than my child—far more. I don't need to say anything about that. You *know*. But it is only as I have grown to see, to gradually admit, some fair ground for believing our life together would be a rich and useful one to others, would be in truth a helpful one to you, and not a check to me—that I have settled into some contentment with it. That contentment is not deep. A very little upsets it. I always sweep back to my conviction that I am not a fit person for you to marry. Not truly fit for any man, and a thousand fold unfit for a good man like you.

You see I can carry my life, alone, and it does not trouble me. I am not ashamed of it. It is, to my backward view a path very crooked in its ups and downs, but not crooked sideways! . . .

And when I have thought at times of practical difficulties such as some untoward uprising of past events, some personal accusation; I have said to myself—"I will never answer a word. I will simply *live* and let my life talk. Those who chose to believe evil of me may. Many will not, because they know *me*." Now you may think these things are not honest. That I am not telling the truth to the world. That I ought to announce "I have done this and that—I am such and such a woman" and take the consequences.

That is where we should differ. I believe that I am honester as I am, when men women and children trust me and love me and show me their souls. Those things through which I have come to this place are not bad, in my judgement of life.

Now my Dear Love—Man that I reverence from the bottom of my soul, and love with all my heart and body—how about our standards? Will they fit? Are you going to think your wife a questionable wreck of a character— that has to be "stood by"—perhaps lied about?

You see just as a worker in my own lines, my character hurts no one. What I am giving is good, I know that. As your wife it is quite another thing.

3.30 P.M.

Dearest—yours of March 10th has come. I feel better and happier for various reasons. Have discovered a physical reason for having such a bad night—a premature "X." Suspect the prematurity to be due to my more than affectionate state o' mind lately.

Look here young man! If you think I'm going to take the trouble and the risk—and the pain and all the various chances of having a child in the face of a fond parent-that-might-be's explicit declaration that he doesn't want any— you have an exalted idea of the maternal instinct in yours truly. . . .

This letter is a dear. It brings me that quiet feeling that I love so well— the sense of being yours anyhow—no use talking! O it does feel so restful and nice. . . .

. . . I feel like a flouncing kite—with a strong hand on the string—winding me in! . . .

I'm not so worried as I used to be about our private family as a subject of criticism. As I wax more widely known it matters less and less, especially in literary work. The second marriage will effectually lay the ghost of the first, and an occasionally observed daughter, of admirable behavior will settle all that. . . .

. . . c/o Mrs. George C. Royall. Goldsboro. N.C.
9.20 A.M. Mon. March 13th. 1899. . . .

Yours of Sat. just brought in by Mrs. Royall. . . .

O it *is* so good to have you to help me in all these things—your clear steady head and knowledge and conscience to supplement my weaknesses. I don't half realize how *big* you are—how good to depend on—my Comfort and Strength! . . .

You are of great benefit to me dear, in character I mean. You help make me stronger and better because you are so strong and good. I feel very humble toward you—and very very grateful—always with the sense of utter undeserving! . . .

. . . c/o Mrs. George C. Royall. Goldsboro N.C.
March 14th. 1899. . . .

I am glad to be able to report another [lecture] success. . . .

You know what I was vaguely hinting to you once—a big half-thought— about the thing we feel—and call God—being, in a sense, Humanity—the Great Social Spirit. Here's a point that bears out the idea a little. No sinner is too bad to come to God—to be forgiven—cleansed and set to work anew. No sinner is too bad to serve humanity—if he will. . . . It is never too late— no one is ever too far gone—to turn again and come to—Humanity. Look at the saving grace and comfort of the thing! If we will b[ut] see that great Heart waiting for us—that great Need waiting for us—we can forever and forever turn from our sinful *selves* and be remade in our Humanity. I'll be starting a religious movement next!

'Twas a very quiet resting time you found me in, Houghton. Had I been in full swing I doubt if you would ever have cared. Is it not true that your heart went out most to me as one alone and very unhappy—one needing care and love— one to whom you could be a rest and comfort and reliance?

Does my power and success appeal to you at all? Or do you simply bear with it for my sake? Is it Charlotte sick and weak and sad, that you most love? or Charlotte well and strong and happy? Well do you know that as far as my heart goes—my personal life—I am the little tired lonely woman— hopeless—homeless—with no one to care for her. To that woman you are————O my dear dear love!—you are just Heaven! But how does the rest of her strike you? The rapidly increasing rest of her?

Are you going to be contented with me? . . .

When I try to think of you really *gone,* out of my life—dead or any-thing—given to another woman—it feels like a sort of awful landslide—way down to the bones—a mere rock peak left standing. It seems as if it would take all the flesh and blood off me. You have certainly woven yourself into my life inextricably. And yet I cannot fully harmonize you with the rest of it. I suppose it is only the essential pain of the woman nature forced out into world service.

Loving, the woman longs to have that love thrill through, infill, entirely meet and cover, every part of her life. That is what it has been in the past to her. The man is accustomed to having love a department only. To the woman the formation of that department—during these transition years—is essential pain.

Now there, my dear, is ground for a novel—a real novel— one that would meet glad wondering recognition in a million women's hearts today! O what *a lot* of work I've got to do! Shall I tell you clearly one side of my feeling toward you— just the opposite of what I speak of above.

It comes from this pushing, heaving growing sense of power and purpose and enormous duty. And it is almost cruel— it shocks and frightens me. I hate to face it and say it out. It is————This man is of immense good to me—he rests me—comforts me—makes me happy. What matter about him and his life? I will take him to fill out mine. For my delight and for the good 'twill do my work—.

And then—then I want to crouch down at your feet and say O my Lord and King! I am not worthy! Not worthy [of] any place in that pure noble heart! But if I can serve you—wait on you—make you comfortable in any way!————

How's that for "conflicting emotions"?

Now you are steady and true as a magnet. How are you going to get on with a tempestuous critter like this? One time I shall selfishly use your time and strength and patience—again I shall selfishly ignore it—and again I shall be displeasing you by groveling, and remorses and a pitiful longing to be what I'm not for your sake.

Dear—I am not fit to marry any man—much less you. I'm writing it all out to you—every wobble that comes up. You should fully know. And with it all is the deep deep passionate desire just to feel your hand again and—nothing else matters.

Nice box you're in G.H.G.! . . .

. . . c/o Mrs. George C. Royall. Goldsboro N.C.
March 15th. 1899. . . .

Do you know dear I am having a very low spell—all along now. I feel very selfish, sordid, mean, weak, and generally undesirable. As a consequence, of course, I get no comfort from the thought of you—only distress of mind that I have so far involved you, and a futile half-hearted determination to let you go.

Here's six months passed. You are as true and steady as a magnet. I have done nothing but wobble. The assurance I feel at one time weighs also lately nothing the next time I lose hold of it.

You don't want a wobbling wife. You don't want a person forever raking up the reasons why she isn't the person you should have married. . . . Or else going about gloomily with those dour misgivings buried in her heart and sticking out in spots! It[']s this constitutional flaw in the material that is so horrid. You can't count on me. Can't rest on me. Can't ever be sure how I'm going to feel next day. Being legally married won't stop it. Nothing'll stop it. It's the nature of the beast. . . .

My charms are essentially transient—I'm awfully nice for a while. But you hold me and I spoil on your hands! As I look back on this winter; on your love and patience and endless goodness, and then on my day to day uncertainty—it seems to me that I cannot stand having such a man wasted on such a woman.

. . . But it seems that the whole stuff is shivered through and through— disintegrated—crumbles in your hand like rotten rock. . . . I don't hold. My main purposes hold all right—faiths—beliefs—intentions. A big loose straggling body, advancing by many an irregular wavering line, always in the same direction.

Catch it and try to focus it—to concentrate it—to make a local attach- ment—and the whole mass begins to plunge and thrash about, now heaping itself about the point of attachment with morbid energy, now flowing away in every direction and hanging only by a tight drawn string.

Now it seems to me, the more I know you, that you have as good a chance of being miserable as any man ever had. You have a great respect for sanction—precedent—authority. If you marry me it is not only without that support, but against it. In the face of all reason and common sense; against the earnest wish and judgement of your best friends and advisers you take this step. . . .

My love for you is a poor thing. It was not great enough in the first place to protect you from my own selfish longing for somebody to love me and care for me. . . .

I have weakly and selfishly done you an awful wrong—that's the long and short of it; and I am letting it go on and culminate in a final irreparable wrong—for lack of courage strength and *love* enough to do right by you. But that's not done yet, Thank God. There's another year between us, and I am more and more minded to let that year be a clean cut, begging you to put both faithfulness and obstinacy aside and call it off—clean off at least for that time. . . .

. . . then if I come back, without "pulling" on you at all, ever—and you

can come to me still wishing to marry me—and I still wish to marry you—
seems to me that would be fair as anything could be. . . .

The more I love you the more clearly I see your interests and my abominable selfishness. And, for my own part of it—this hopeless irreconcilability
on so many lines, constitutes a source of distress which I see no reasonable
hope of removing. It isn't a sound rational right relation. A marriage that
dreads children is *WRONG*. A marriage that has no common purpose—
even in the maintaining a household—where one party reserves the right to
go away and stay away whenever she sees fit—it isn't a real marriage at all
Houghton. As to the lovely woman in your arms—it's very sweet—but not
enough to build on.

This woman wasn't born right for that happiness—hasn't lived right for
that happiness—cannot come naturally and sweetly to it now.

It is not for me.

It can never be for me—I'm not fit.

Now Houghton dear—dearest of all in the world—think it out again. . . .

. . . We may have loads of faith that all would go well with us; but what
facts we have are all solidly against it.

Is this the last time? No. I shall continue to shift and vacillate as usual.
My love for you drags me, tears me, pulls me toward you. My reason stands
up like a rock, when the waves drop back—and always says the same
thing—

You are not fit to marry him. . . .

. . . c/o Mrs. George C. Royall. Goldsboro. N.C.
9.20 A.M. March 16th. 1899. . . .

It's a fine bright day and my heart is big and light. You are alive and I
can love you always whatever happens—that's so good to think of. . . .
Yesterday it was pretty black 'cause the personal side was uppermost; but
today I'm bigger. Have been cheering myself up—taking my own medicine.
It's *never* too late to serve! To love! To help! One is never too weak, too
bad. I am some good—perhaps lots of good—and "God's in his heaven, all's
right with the world." . . .

And as to my changeableness—I'm not going to quarrel with it any more.
It's me—part of the character which makes me able to reach so many people
in so many ways. And of course it brings me with exquisite intensity to the
person I love most—and equally of course it swings me away again. I'm not
going to blame myself anymore or grieve because I'm not like you. Why
should I expect to manifest every virtue?. . . .

Mrs. Royall holds me tight. "What will it be when you are gone!" she
says. "You make everything easier. This has been such a different year! I

have lived—I have done so much more and you did it all!—" And they are only two. "Stay here and live" they have said to me in city after city. "We need you." . . .

. . . In the light of your character—as part of your life—I see myself weak and bad and old. Alone and part of the life of the world I am strong—young—good at least to others. No matter if I'm not good to myself. *I don't have to think of myself.* Darling—I have always failed in personal relation, always. Why should I expect anything different? . . .

Whatever of happiness the two years with you have brought, they have not brought any lasting peace. I've had it, by spells—a perfect sense of rest and joy—and then it goes again.

Now I do not think you half appreciate the pain it will be to you to have these variations "in our midst," or the pain your pain will be to me. . . .

And I cannot seem to learn any better way of loving. I'm just as irrational and hysteric over this as I was twenty years ago—. If I could only fix and settle you someway in my mind—but I can't! You are the whole horizon—and then I just want you and can't do any work! You vanish from sight almost, and then I do my work—save for a furious pain in the conscience—a sense of treason and dishonor. Marry me! Why Houghton dear—how *can* you! Marry an inspired jelly fish!

Meanwhile I love you just the same if not more so. Nice person I am! . . .

. . . Note this—my extra-matrimonial character is peaceful and steady enough—*it is the relation that makes me vary so* . Not all the pressure and change of my life has ever moved me from my lines of work—no criticism—neglect—adverse opinion—unwise praise—personal influence.

I'm a contented happy useful public character.

But O me! I'm such a poor dolorous unreliable shaky goodfornothing private character! . . .

9.05 A.M. Friday March 17th. . . .

I've done so many horrid things lately—and then that queer uprising of old things—and this last rush of convictions that I oughtn't to have you—well I'm down to the tear level. Had to hug dear big Mrs. Royall and sob on her shoulder and cry "I want some folks of my *own!*" . . .

Mrs. Royall fell to telling me things (before I thus pathetically embraced her) about my work here, that started me crying . . . that it would be impossible to measure the good I had done Goldsboro . . . that my power of giving a feeling was simply wonderful. And that she could hardly understand such a life—that it seemed to be all *giving*—with no personal desires at all. Well. It simply brought the tears. I *had* to cry. To sit there feeling so poor and mean—suffering keenly from a weary sense of hopeless deficiency, and have people feel and talk so about me! . . . If this good lady had but known—if she could only see that it was no possible credit to anyone to live impersonally when one's personal life was so full of reproach and agony. I *can't* live in my own company—it's too unpleasant. I *have* to live for others—and am eagerly grateful that they take me in so kindly. . . .

Knowing your character to be what it is—just an endless run of quiet heroism—a genius for immolation— specially attracted to specially unattractive people and causes—always ready to bolster up and stalwartly defend— tenderly protect—why I presented a more glittering temptation than any Venus. . . .

But now look, dear. I am growing distinguisheder and distinguisher; and in just such ways as puts any sort of husband at a disadvantage. *I always count for more than I am worth*—always have—always put others beside me at a disadvantage. I can't help it. If I meekly keep quiet they think it's noble modesty. If I wildly brag—just to discredit myself—they think it's "just my way." If I go on steadily and do things—why I loom big and brilliant—I can't help it. You are just the other way. You never count for a quarter of your worth. *I* know you for what you are— and reverence you. But publicly—the more I did that the more it would rebound to my credit— and if I treated you irreverently—they'd make allowance. No man would like it. You are a very proud man—prouder than I—far more sensitive and honorable. You've *got* to consider these things.

When you couple all that with the other facts—that in reality you have the steady weight of knowing me as I am—of ignoring and forgiving—of refusing to admit plain truths about me— *of comforting me against myself*— the situation becomes painfully absurd. . . .

Don't let even my weakness mislead you—with it all I *have* lived through and surmounted what would have hopelessly ruined most women—or men either. . . .

. . . I'm having an awful time; honestly. The desire for you is very great and steady—the pitiful wish to be picked up and carried and consoled is very strong—I never felt weaker and more in need of help (that's not true I'm afraid—I guess I've been just as bad or worse before) and my frank delight in your kindness and usefulness is growing all the time.

But—I feel the *your* side of it more strongly than ever. Just as I can rise out of all personal trouble and go out to talk to other people and help them— so that same big force seems to drive me to talk to you—to talk you out of this—to save you from yourself—from me. It is bigger than I am— stronger. . . .

. . . c/o Mrs. Geo. C. Royall. Goldsboro. N.C.
10.40 March. 18th. 1899. . . .

Things are queer here. I mustn't tell you about it, but there is a very great "psychic strain." I am much needed—and a good deal drawn upon. . . . There are two small boys, both of the whining and one of the bawling sort; and our meals are little vortexes (vortices?) of nervous tension. I jest and make merry and carry the family.

But I 'spect it[']s one reason I've fallen down a bit. . . .

11.06 A.M. Sun. March 19th '99. . .

. . . Guess I'm kind of breaking down a little. The whining of the children grows unbearable. . . . [The little child] in the next room . . . has been crying continuously for ever so long—"mother—! mother—! mother—! mother—!" . . . and prolonged indefinitely. The distress in my mind I wake up with every day now—the steady thinking about you—the dreadful fear and doubt and sense of wrong—and then—if I do what I think right and leave you— the horrible pain and loss.

I don't see any way out of it and it presses on my mind till I can almost feel it physically—almost a headache in that one spot.

The weather is the kind I don't like—an uneasy wind—things flapping and slamming—no peace.

If this goes on I'll be sick soon—that won't do. I'm too busy to be sick— got far too much to do.

12.15.

Mary in, and some Whitman. It is such a pleasure to introduce anybody to Whitman—like taking 'em up a mountain and showing off your favorite view. . . .

. . . The white sandy soil is packed firm and there [are] rippling pools of water all along the roads. Solid white clouds streaming across over head—level parallel banks from horizon to horizon. Pale flame of peach trees, and all dusky greenness and crimsonness and purple brown of bursting buds above and the furry grass awakening beneath. And the whole far stretch of it flushing and darkening and changing color endlessly as the clouds fly. . . .

. . . c/o Mrs. George C. Royall. Goldsboro N.C.
9.40 A.M. March 20th 1899

This is the first morning in a week or more than I have waked without that dull mental pain and pressure. It felt very good. . . .

. . . I got a big letter from [the] Nat[ional] Council of Women, marked *Important* . . . , which contained an invitation to address the International

Council of Women meeting in London June 29th. . . . I have cabled "yes"; and feel very proud to be cabling thus. Twenty minute paper on "Equal Pay for Equal Work." . . .

. . . And I've written a verse of a most consolatory poem—[entitled *"Eternal Me"]*[25]

> "What an exceeding rest 'twill be
> When I can leave off being Me!
> To think of it! At last be rid
> Of all the things I ever did!"

Isn't that pleasing to contemplate? . . .

near 10. A.M.

. . . Your letter of the 18th has just come, and it is *such* a good one! . . .

As an Individual and as a Man you naturally object to being regarded by beholders as a sort of obliging adjunct—a temporary stopping place—a way station instead of a terminus. As an Individual and as a Woman I naturally object to being married *for my benefit*—taken as an interesting patient— . . . a beneficiary. That does not please the feminine side of creation at all. . . .

No sir. I'd rather break down in spots all over the world and weep on any alien bosom that was nearest at the time, than to have the pleasing consciousness that a good man at home had cheerfully laid aside all better prospects that he might minister to my needs. Benevolence is one thing. Love—the love that makes marriage—is quite another. I'm very weak—none knows it better, and very very needy—but I haven't come to quite that place.

When my bad times come I'll go board somewhere—perhaps in a quiet Sanitarium—and just wait till it[']s over. They pass. They don't kill. . . .

You say, "If you need me I think I shall find happiness enough in being your husband in spite of your forebodings. If you were always well, self-poised, & contented I see no earthly reason why you should marry me. It is only because I can help you that the thing is to be justified at all."

Now behold. If I do get well—as I hope gradually to do; if I do become self-poised and contented—as I always am when I am well—most markedly so—then our marriage lacks all justification! So I must stay sick in order to justify our marriage.

No, dear. I am going to be a strong clearheaded useful woman, doing things more and more till I am too old to work. In which case you see no justification for our marriage.

Or say I remain weak, erratic, broken; only doing half work at best; and in that case you find justification for our marriage in you[r] unquestioned usefulness to your invalid wife. That does not at all suit the acute conscious-ness of aforesaid invalid wife.

Now we will take our year's grace. And I think it will be well in that time to let go of each other entirely. . . . I'll take off the drag you have been feeling these two years past. You shall stand clear and untrammeled. . . .

You shall decide from your own honest heart—not from any wish to help or save. . . .

My position is this.

First last and always I must so live as to do my work.

If I have you I have love and joy and peace and help and home. If I do not have you I have a more undivided service to the world, an absolute consecration. I shall have rooms of my own—live some how, and do much. . . .

I am very thankful to have come to this calm place before I see you. Before we part for our last year[']s trial. Drop all the illness and misery and need out of your thought. I refuse the love based merely on that. Think of me this year as a strong free busy woman full of work and hope.

Then if your sympathy with my purposes and methods is truly such that you will *enjoy* helping me do things; and your delight in my society is truly such that you'll enjoy passing twenty or thirty years with me—with every disadvantage in view—then tell me so. . . .

In Heaven's name do not misunderstand. . . . I do not deny my need of you—it is as great as ever. But I refuse to be married on account of my necessity. . . .

. . . c/o Mrs. George C. Royall. Goldsboro N.C.
. . . Tues. March. 21st. '99. . . .
5.15

It has been a good day. A little article for the Ruskin paper—"A Discrimi-nation." . . . A page of rather Whitmanish personal poetry—I don't think you'd care at all for it.

And letters various. None from you so far today. I miss them keenly. What a long year it will be. . . .

But I guess it will be a rest to you in many ways, not to have the tempes-tuous changeful things pouring in across your quiet steady life—drawing heavily on your tact and patience—demanding much—and then flying off so far—a very big kite in a very high wind! . . .

. . . c/o Mrs. George C. Royall Goldsboro N.C.
10.30 A.M. Wed. March 22nd. 1899. . . .

Mr. Royall was in a black rage—underneath—yesterday, but today is more approachable. . . . I wish I could tell you all about things here—but I can't. So much of my life *has* to be carried alone! And I do so love to babble and confide. Not to everybody, but to my own.

If I am ultimately reduced to not having anybody, I shall have to write things down elaborately and then burn 'em—to get them off my mind! But I guess the combined freedom of writing and speaking will relieve the pressure sufficiently. And I *must* get to novels—that will be a splendid safety valve. . . .

near half past three.

A good morning's work. Nearly fifteen pages on the Work article—fairly good too.· . . .

The power is "on"—the prospect good—and I make all sail while I can.

I will make to myself some haven of refuge and flee to it—in coming years—when it darkens.

I wonder if Katharine will ever fully love and care for me? I think not, truly. Why should she. . . .

. . . c/o Mrs. George C. Royall Goldsboro N.C.
10.20 P.M. March 22nd 1899. . . .

My lecture last night was vastly appreciated it appears—they want another. . . .

So its a good visit, and is going to leave a Woman's Club well started behind. . . .

near 10. A.M. Thurs. March. 23rd '99. . . .

. . . You wouldn't believe—being a steady person—how completely widowed I have been feeling of late—what a deep and utter surrender I have gone through; and now the feeling of your being there after all is flowing softly back. It is not fully in yet—I'm still afloat and afar; but I can see the possibility again. . . .

You seem to continue firm in the desire to cast in your lot with mine—and take the consequences. . . .

But I do not see how your having worked harder in the last six years, or accomplishing something extra in this year to come would alter the situation. . . .

The more prosperous you are the more I should feel that you were renouncing better chances for a poor and very *un*certain certainty! No, your main attraction in this way is that you are *not* doing so wonderfully well!

So there we are: most ridiculously at loggerheads! If I get well and strong you see no reason for our marriage, if you get rich and successful *I* see no reason for it!—Was ever anything so funny! . . .

My theory of marriage is that while love is absolutely essential it is not in itself sufficient to base the relation on. There should be a suitability visible to the "naked eye" without love. I cannot establish our suitability to my satisfaction. Can you to yours? We are not wild younglings to cast all aside for an emotion. . . . I think you have let yourself be carried away by your feelings (and mine) and there would follow the slow and painful recognition of a mistake—afterward—and that it would *kill* me.

I'm not so unselfish as you think. *I* daren't face that pain. And the chances are all that way Houghton. The calm devotion with which you admit all these deterring facts and say you are willing to try it, does not reassure me at all! I don't consider it an attractive attitude—from a womanly point of view.

I do not exactly see what it is that is going to satisfy me on this point either. Nothing has yet. When you deny the disadvantages—as you nobly undertook to at first—in a measure; I simply feel that you are unreasonable. When you admit them but brace yourself to endure—I am not pleased. I don't want a sort of consecrated husband—piously devoted to my service.

You see I'm looming up like friend Frankenstein's critter. You found me a weak apologetic thing, and fell to loving me. Solaced and stimulated by this affection I have now become a strong proud person, and demand, forsooth, something more than pitying helpfulness!

If I'm not sure that I am *to you* the greatest good, I shall use my new strength to turn from you! Kind of aggravating, isn't it? Perhaps another year of triumph in my field of action will convince me that I am young, beautiful, healthy, pure, constant, and otherwise fit to marry a good man. I don't see exactly *how* any amount of professional triumph will do it, but we'll see.

Neither do I see how your success—enabling you to command a wider choice among the damselry, and to "support a wife" more suitably, will convince me that you are therefore more fit to give up all real home and wife happiness for the nondescript and intermittent companionship which is all I have to offer.

I'll wait the year all right—but for the life of me I do not see what light it will bring.

Of course I know that a full human companionship—common interests and sympathies—cover great gaps. But it does not seem to me we have enough of that even. The main lines of my work you have no natural affinity for—nor I for yours. You sympathize with my work *because you love me*— but that is quite another matter. Now from my purely selfish point of view—

if I could hold it—you would add materially to the happiness and usefulness of my life.

I should have a more stable home, the support of your love and care, the varied personal services you so tenderly bestow, the better balance and health of married life; a better living by our combined funds—a thousand advantages. But I *can't* hold that point of view—not if I wanted to. My life irresistibly flows into other people[']s. My consciousness of what I was *not* giving you would react upon me worse than a personal lack—far worse. . . .

. . . c/o Mrs. George C. Royall. Goldsboro. N.C.
March. 24th. 1899. . . .

. . . Big work yesterday. . . . Formed the Goldsboro Woman's Club—fifty strong! Meeting in the Opera House—free—public—lots of women. . . . Local lights assisted us. Great enthusiasm. . . .

Long epistle from Small & Maynard . . . [and from the] Phil[adelphia] Sat. Post . . . [requesting a series of articles giving] "advice to young writers." . . .

You see I'm looming up. . . . I shall tell them to consult no authority, study nothing, and scornfully refuse to listen to anything anybody says—in due time they will come out on top of the heap! . . .

. . . I'm glad you've heard Debs. He's greatly worshipped by many, in the West especially. I do not think very highly of him. . . .[26]

. . . c/o Mrs. Geo. C. Royall. Goldsboro. N.C.
March. 25th. 1899. . . .

I am quite capable of doing things that will mortify you keenly. You never mortify me. You are consistent and dependable. In some ways I do feel that my judgement is broader than yours—my insight deeper. There are people I can talk *further* with than I easily can with you, but you are—homogeneous; and I can fully respect you. Now I don't see how you can me—and I shrink from admitting to close and lasting association [with] a conscience of a different grade from mine. Men seem to do it easily enough. They marry girls they know to be "purer" and "better" than they are—and not so wise; whose judgement they do not accept; and it does not seem to trouble them.

It troubles me very much. The woman's longing for utter union and acceptance is checked and pained by the big spaces of difference in opinion—however calmly they are tolerated by the man. Suppose for instance you believed in the sacredness of the Sabbath, knew that I didn't, admitted my freedom to do as I pleased, and yet, to your judgement I was "A Sabbath breaker"—a sinner. This sense of inner difference in values is a grief to me. In my work as teacher, in my years on years of reverent tender study of the human soul—how to reach it, touch it, help it, not hurt it, respond to its faintest aspiration, withdraw from its little wearinesses and repulsions; I have become intensely sensitive to how another person feels. . . .

If I have to speak to an audience of children, I can; or grown ups, I can; but when I have a double set— . . . it is exceedingly tiring. I can feel when they are not following—when I am saying too much for the girls—too little for the other people, or when, striking an average, both miss something.

I insensibly fit myself to the measure of the person I am with—can't help it. Therefore to be permanently with a person of widely differing ideals and standards is a heavy tax on me.

You do not feel this difference as keenly as I do for several reasons—partly because owing to this very quality, I have invariably tended to show you only the side where we harmonize; and shrink from any exposition of our differences.

Perhaps I am wrong in being influenced by this feeling. . . . Perhaps I may as well recognize that the man don't live who can meet me in all my eccentricities, and that I should be thankful indeed for as wide a field of union as we have. . . .

I'm very glad you like the John Smith poem ["Eternal Me"]. I do. There it is—the fact that you like one kind better than another would tend to set me toward producing them; or else, if professional integrity held firm, to being very lonesome in producing the other kind! I can't seem to not care! When I'm alone I don't worry over what anybody on earth thinks or feels. When I'm *with* 'em I do!

One of the reasons for my many and instant friendships is just this swift and subtle adaptability of mine. They feel the smooth gentle full appreciative and intelligent contact—and it delights them. "This person is like me!" they cry inwardly—and I become a valued friend at once.

It could not hold out long. I can fit to the shape of a thousand people, temporarily, but it isn't really my shape—(if I have any!) and I let go and swing off—to rest and recuperate. . . .

I don't mean not to write you at all, dear heart. I mean not to write you love letters. I want to see—as I started to once before—what remains of your feeling when not called out by mine. So far I have pulled—all the way.

I have modified your letter writing to a considerable degree, and occasionally wrung a real tremendous love letter from you. I've a shrewd notion that they won't keep up if I stop asking. I wish to *finally convince myself* as to the individual freedom of your feeling for me. . . .

Neither shall I be by any means content to find you manfully sticking to your agreement—ready to be "led to the Altar." You've got to do the leading! . . .

. . . c/o Mrs. George C. Royall. Goldsboro. N.C.
10.20 A.M.. Sun. March 26th. '99. . . .

. . . I have some hopes of Kate—but no surety. She is a strong character. Perhaps when she has lived and loved and suffered she may come to understand. But if she stays happy and prosperous maybe she never will. . . .

. . . c/o Mrs. Geo. C. Royall. Goldsboro. N.C.
9.10 A.M. Wed.
March. 29th. 1899.

Got very much pulled down yesterday. . . .

You see my pleasures have always been in my mind, in thinking about things, and when that plane of consciousness is— ailing; why I can't *think* of anything comfortable!

I attribute this to the conditions here, and my sensitiveness to them. It is like living in a hospital—the soul-wretchedness, agony, disease, are most distressing. . . . There is not only pain involved but a monstrous spirit of malevolence—and yet that is combined with such fine qualities!

I assure you my business is very perplexing.

And the more deeply I enter into it and see my life, full of such work, opening before me, the more utterly incongruous *you* seem. Beloved!

You are not one to meddle in people's most intimate concerns. It must strike you as a perilous and questionable process. But I'm always doing it and always shall be.

Don't you think you have counted mainly on the literary and professional-lecturing side of my life; and discounted the "reforming" department? I have shown you less of it, of course. Do you not see how close association— identification, with a life so alien to your own is going to jar upon you?

I cannot alter any of it—would not if I could. The headlong martyrish devotion is upon me for life.

You seem like a glittering temptation as it were—delightful but unwise.

I suppose many a woman, marrying a tempestuous fanatic, has been dragged through what lies before you. But she wasn't supposed to have any other life. You have; a life and business or your own. I should think it easily possible for my known character to react injuriously on your business prosperity. . . .

I'm certainly very low this morning—can't work at all. . . .

. . . I'm not writing sense today. I'll just stop. I want to curl up in a little heap and cry.

. . . c/o Mrs. Geo. H. Royall. Goldsboro. N.C.
8.55 A.M. Thurs. March. 30th 1899. . . .

Don't I wish you were with me to rejoice in reading Mr. Peck's article—
(it is atrocious!) and discuss plans of vengeance. Mine enemy is delivered
with mine hand—and I'm to have a hundred dollars for slaying him!

. . . Goldsboro. N.C. March. 30th. 1899
8.20 [P.M.]. . . .

As the name of Stetson looms up under my hand I feel more and more
amused—a most sinful feeling—about the late C.W.S. That Times clipping
you sent me was very funny—"perhaps the artist is some relation of Charlotte Perkins Stetson?" That is the irony of fate.

About this agreement, dear. It isn't just in our work that I mind it—mere
business. It *is* in religious belief. . . .

My morals are different from yours—and yet I can't seem to bear having
them different. I value your judgement very much and hate to act counter
to it. . . .

Yes, I have told you faithfully of my doings, even the bad things. I guess
I'm pretty honest about it. . . .

. . . c/o Mrs. Geo. C. Royall. Goldsboro. N.C.
9.10 A.M. Sun. April 2nd. '99. . . .

Your letters lately have been particularly full and agreeable, mine particularly skimpy, owing to Prof. Peck. I am by no means done with him yet;
and am going to send on the whole business to you presently for strict
criticism.

The man is *such* an ass—and this particular paper so good an example
of his asininity, that I want to be very very careful about mine.

And as your self-elected mission is to assist me in my wild career, here's
a piece of work for you. . . .

10.40. . . .

As to you—I'm in the state of mind at present that you do actually and
permanently belong to me—always did, always will, and what am I thinking
of!? The daily comfort and dependence of you is gaining ground all the
time. . . .

You are quite right in your diagnosis—especially as to my having conducted a fight between my head and heart. That did use me up, awfully. You see as far as mental willingness goes I gave you up—and it takes all my strength and hope and joy and courage—for the time. Seems perfectly futile too. I slip right back into wanting you, and every time the wrench comes it comes harder. . . .

Your recognition of the time when work is over and play hours come will be *very* useful to me. Men get that from the home-&-office combination. Women their unresting waste of energy from the night-&-day life service of the home. You do me lots of good. I think I shall do wiser work and live longer for your practical advice and influence. To work till I drop and rest in intervals of exhaustion does not seem to me a judicious procedure, and that's what I don't seem able to help doing. You'll help me—dear dear heart!

. . . Executive Mansion
Raleigh N.C.
9.40 A.M. Tues. April 4th. '99. . . .

[*She is staying with the Governor and Mrs. Russell at a "vast rambling" mansion, "something between a palace and a barn."*]
The lecture was in a hotel dining room, good audience. . . . My talk was on Kipling—seems to be considered the most harmless subject—and went very well, to my surprise. . . .

I slept from 11 till 7. . . . O it was good! Not to be waked *at all*—by the bawling of babes or the sound of the spanking thereof; and especially not to have a final rousing at about six by the same lively agents! . . . It does feel good to be out of that unhappy household. . . .

. . . *The Oaks*
Georgetown Heights. D.C.
10.35 A.M. Thurs. April 6th. '99

[*She is staying at the home of Mrs. Lucia Blount.*]
Behold me, as usual, fallen on my feet; the honored guest of very nice people in a very nice house. A great spreading house, in a big treey lawn—way up high, with fine air and views.

They are friends of Uncle Edward and Lester Ward and such—rich, travelled, liberal, and so on. Have read my book and are impressed therewith. Mr. B[lount] says it is the most philosophical book ever written by a woman. I do despise that kind of complement. To praise the individual by disparaging the class! . . .

. . . **Washington D.C.**
10 A.M. Fri. April 7th. 99. . . .

. . . How noble is that profession which opens to one[']s use the nicest homes in America. "Talk's cheap" but I find it pays board bills and transportation at the least. . . .

on train to Boston
Wed. April 26th. '99. . . .

. . . [D]ear boy! Can you really be happy with me do you think?

I want to grow so good for your sake, so gentle and reasonable and sweet. . . .

10

London: 16 May–19 August 1899

In early May 1899, Gilman set out for England to attend the Quinquennial Congress of the International Council of Women, 26 June through 5 July 1899. For the first few days in England she stayed at the Nurses' Settlement House in Hammersmith, just outside of London. An association established to provide home care nursing for people in the district, in many ways it was like Lillian Wald's New York Nurses' Settlement, serving also as a boarding/meeting house for reform-oriented friends. "It is ever so pleasant here," Charlotte wrote, the "square old manor house,"[1] the "big fine old garden," the "winding lanes and river roads and queer little brick-walled alleys"; "the sky is beautiful, the wind soft and warm, and the young-leaved woodbine hangs all about the sash."[2]

For Gilman, this was not to be a restful, quiet trip. Not only did she have her lecturing and writing responsibilities but also the "profusely offered" invitations for official and unofficial receptions, teas and entertainments associated with the conference.[3] She would spend time with socialist activist and writer May Morris, daughter of William Morris. She would renew contacts with Edward A. Ross and Earl Barnes, her economist friends in California, with J. Ramsay MacDonald, Mrs. Muriel Norman, and Harriot Stanton Blatch, and a variety of other activists and writers who had also gathered for the London Conference.[4]

In fact, a central purpose of the conference was to encourage and facilitate such contacts, or, as its founders originally had phrased it, to "rouse women to new thought," to "intensify their love of liberty," and to form a "confederation of workers committed" to "an interchange of opinion on the great questions now agitating the world." As one enthusiastic group of writers later put it, the International Council of Women marked a "vital moment in the history of ideas." "Never before had the representatives of organized bodies of women banded themselves together" so effectively, demonstrating an ongoing dedication to the "abolition of discrimination not only on grounds of sex, but also on grounds of race, class and creed."[5] With some five thousand women representatives from thirty-five countries, and with some three hundred scheduled speakers from law, trade, business, medicine, and the arts, the council organizers had planned an impressive variety of sessions.

For example, there were panel discussions on prison reform, child labor, old age pensions, profit-sharing techniques, press reform, and women's representation in local and national governments. Lavinia Dock spoke on "The Professional Training and Status of Nurses," Maria Montessori on Italian Educational Reform, and Susan B. Anthony on suffrage. Other sessions were devoted exclusively to working-class women's issues, to "trade unionism," for instance, the "Technical and Industrial Training for Women and Girls," "The Legal Regulation of Wages," and "Housing for Wage-Earning Women." Meetings on the social settlement movement were particularly well attended, as were those on "'Civil Disabilities of Women' in regard to the marriage and divorce laws, the custody and guardianship of children, and the married women's property laws." Most importantly, as the organizers phrased it, the conference was designed to seek ways to confront the appalling conditions of "overworked and underpaid women in industrial employment," and to focus their energies on the following demands:[6]

- Equal pay for equal work.
- Access to all professions according to aptitude and not to sex.
- Radical improvement of conditions in the nursing profession.
- State-paid maternity maintenance.
- Appointment of female factory inspectors.
- Participation of women in trade unions in order to defend their rights.
- Protection of women and men workers (with the proviso that protective legislation in favor of women must never go so far as to exclude them from work).
- Development of modern household machinery to relieve women from household drudgery.
- Training of housewives and of domestic workers; better working conditions for the latter.[7]

As a freelance speaker for the council, and as an enthusiastic reporter as well, Gilman participated in a variety of sessions.[8] She spoke on "Women in Poetry," on "Parental Responsibility," and most importantly on, as Mrs. J. Hoeson phrased it, the problem of the "unpaid services of the housewife." One speaker on Gilman's panel argued that the state itself should "directly pay" the home-based wife and mother, acknowledging the "social value" of her domestic labor by financially rewarding her. Another panelist, Mrs. Rutgers-Hoitsema of Holland, disagreed. She argued that "the puzzling question at present was not how to get the housewife's services paid, but how to relieve her from the burden of always having to do unproductive work." Likewise Gilman's paper, "Equal Pay for Equal Work," focused on the domestic labor issue, suggesting that women's basic need not only was for economic independence but also for the opportunity to pursue the kind of work that would effectively respond to social needs. As the London *Times* paraphrased her message:

> Cooking and cleaning were no more essential parts of matrimony than the making of soap or spinning and other trades that used to belong to matrimony when women had to do all the work. The working woman of the world needed to recognize the ethical basis that work was not a means of getting a living, but a social function by which the human race was maintained and developed.[9]

Although for the most part Gilman was pleased with the response to her own and other council women's lectures, there were some writers who took firm exception to their views.[10] According to Frances Low, Gilman's talk was "wholly meaningless," and the conference itself was a "lamentable waste of energy and a painful exhibition of ignorance and folly." When you strip Gilman's

> statements of their phraseology and get down to the naked gospel, it comes to this—that unless you are performing "work" in this world for which you receive an adequate market wage, you are a disgrace to mankind and ought to be in a lunatic asylum.[11]

In Frances Low's opinion, and in the view of some other critics as well, the "radical defect" of the conference was its "feminist" bias. As Low described it, "theories of a most startling nature, practically overthrowing present social conditions, were propounded from a purely feminine standpoint." Or as another commentator put it, a striking "mediocrity" was apparent at the conference, a "want of foresight," a "collective fanaticism," a "morbid vanity called feminism." There was "something young and amateurish and beside the mark" about the entire effort, wrote Kassandra Vivaria, "the automatic succession of lifeless speeches," the "air of personal advertisement," the "narrowness of mind." Not only were these "advanced" women "illogical towards nature," but also "intensely feminine in the calm ignoring of facts that have governed the world."[12] Vivaria continued:

> Can woman's originality invent nothing better than the aping of man, whom she pretends to despise in his moral code and his little weaknesses? Can her ambition see no further than the grand ideal of doing "just" what men do, "nearly" as well as they do it? For it is useless to strive and fret, to stand up on platforms and argue that which nature, cruelly, perhaps, but definitely, has seen fit to settle long ago. Even when we shall have worn ourselves out with trying, there are some things which men do which we shall never do more than "nearly" as well.[13]

Although many of the press reports about the conference were respectful and affirming, such negative descriptions occasionally provoked the council delegates to take a quite defensive stance about their work. In her articles for the *Arena* and *Ainslee's,* for instance, Gilman sometimes tried to reassure her readers that the "good dressing, good breeding and good looks" of the council delegates would provide "comfort to those who like to amass fresh proofs against the wry-minded persons who fear that growths and freedom will 'unsex' women." Also by stressing the "beauty and grace of the Duchess of Sutherland," or the "kindness and amiability of the Countess of Aberdeen,"[14] it was almost as though Gilman felt compelled to remind her readers that "femininity" was not, in fact, incompatible with leadership ability, or beauty with creativity and strength. Frau Marie Stritt, of Dresden, for example, "is a most pretty and attractive woman—quietly and becomingly dressed, gentle of manner—one would scarce think she was a leader among the most advanced women in Germany, president of the Woman's Legal Defense Union, vice-president of the German National Council, and an ardent suffragist." Or again, "Dr. Aletta H. Jacobs is another plump and pretty little woman. One would not imagine her to be the first woman to take her M.D. at Groningen University, and the first woman in Holland to ask to be inscribed as a voter." Besides, Gilman continued, "if the light-minded 'society women' of America who scorn women's clubs and reform organizations, will but notice, it is through organization and efforts at reform" that the delegates could enjoy the sheer grandeur of the conference setting, the "soaring halls," the "velvet carpets," the "luxurious entertainment," and as "crowning glory," the reception given by the queen.[15] As Alice Stone Blackwell put it, Queen Victoria's reception "proves conclusively that 'the cause of women' has reached a point where its advocates are the object of attention and social consideration in the highest quarters. It marks a long step in advance from the days when Miss Anthony was pelted, and Lucretia Mott was hooted by mobs, and Lucy Stone was played upon with cold water through a hose in the middle of her lecture." Or as Susan B. Anthony would put it, "I . . . could not but feel a thrill when . . . I saw her . . . welcoming the women's movement." Her reception at the palace was "a recognition of the great womanhood of our country."[16]

Although there were, in fact, some striking incongruities of the conference—the debates on poverty in the context of such elegance and luxury, the aristocratic flavor contrasting with glaring social needs—at the time, Gilman, like many of her colleagues, was reluctant publicly to say so. "Very gaudy, bright and splendid," was her diary entry after one particularly lavish party.[17] Or, as she had written earlier to Houghton, "rich kind of people have an atmopshere which I don't like." Likewise, Anna Howard Shaw mentioned discomfort with all "the hand-shaking and hob-nobbing with duchesses and countesses." And yet whatever the ambivalence she and other delegates may have felt about the aristocratic nature of the setting, most publicly expressed a profound appreciation for the positive support the council had provided for their work. As Anna Howard Shaw would put it, this was "the greatest assemblage of women from all parts of the world that ever had taken place."[18] In Gilman's words, this was "a great week," "a week of stir and bustle and weariness, a week of accumulated impressions to last a lifetime." "Of congresses of women, the more the better—of internationalism the more the better." And while a "meeting like this does not result in a series of legal enactments," Gilman readily acknowledged, at least it "teaches—teaches in a thousand ways" and its "effects filter slowly through the lives of the people" in ways "impossible to follow and define." Besides, she wrote, just consider "the amount and quality of executive ability" it took to bring about the conference: arranging for lodging, securing convention halls and scheduling the lectures, and printing an impressive "Who's Who at The Congress" pamphlet. Consider, too, the "community of interest and feeling" among different nationalities, the "splendid spirit" of the conference, the "stirring papers," the "great and enthusiastic crowds." The "mother of the world is bestirring herself at last," Gilman continued, for not only is she rejecting the "sacred selfishness" of her home-based isolation, she is also demanding first-class status as an agent of reform.[19]

> Back to Finland and Holland and Sweden and Denmark, to New Zealand and Queensland and New South Wales and Tasmania, to India and Persia and Africa and China, to Russia and Austria and Italy and Palestine and the Argentine Republic—back to the ends of the earth these women will go, richer, wider, deeper, wiser, for their coming together.[20]

*   *   *   *   *

During the several weeks following the conference, Gilman traveled.[21] She spent a week with Hubert and Edith Nesbit Bland, in Well Wall, Eltham, Kent. She visited her "adopted" mother, Annie Dowie, in Edinburgh. And she had a "memorable" visit also at the "cream-walled castle" of the countess of Warwick; it had "white peacocks on the velvet lawns," "harebells on the battlements," and a "baronial hall" large enough for "three distinct parties," she later wrote.[22] Understandably Gilman sometimes was exhausted from her travels, but for the most part she had good reason to be proud. She was often writing effectively and easily.[23] She was pleased that *Women and Economics* was being positively reviewed.[24] And for the most part, her lecture audiences also were encouraging. It "did me good," the "*real* feeling of those women," their "anxiety to hear more," she wrote to Houghton after one particularly satisfying lecture. Or again, "I [have] made a ten strike just as I hoped . . . am greatly liked as a speaker." "I'm *having* to respect my work more now that so many [others] do," and "it is beautiful the way people keep on liking me." "I have stood it wonderfully—but am pretty tired now as you may imagine." "Only poor you will have to put up with all my disagreeablenesses and infirmities and get no credit for it!"

Unfortunately, Gilman's letters in these weeks of lecturing, traveling and writing suggest that she was still struggling to withstand and comprehend a sense of "heavy darkness." In her view, the central conflict this time was between her "clamoring long-starved" need for his affection and attention, and her "imperative need of freedom and work." "*Now* I know what they

mean when they tell about the fool things people do when they're 'in love,'"
she wrote him.

During the last few weeks of Gilman's stay in England, Houghton had
in fact been with her on a number of occasions. Perhaps anticipating some
of the strains she would experience, he had booked Atlantic passage for a
mid-July arrival, and while traveling with his Aunt Louisa, he had arranged
to meet her for some brief though secret rendezvous. Not always happily,
however. "This glimpse-of-you-on-suffrance is maddening," she wrote him.
"I went away from you with my heart in my boots—where there was naturally no room for it."

> Ow! Ow-ow-ooo-w! This is awful! I never was so be-panged in my life. That I
> should live to come to this stage of whimpering besottedness! It is "too ridicu-
> lous." . . . I *was* so forlorn. Couldn't muster up courage enough to go anywhere—
> just stood about.

According to her letters, Gilman currently was facing a variety of fears.
First that she was selfish for wanting him to write more fervently and frequently: "Your present letters—to my hungry heart, are as peanuts to the
elephant!" "Great greedy thing—swallowing you alive!" Second, that she
was a weak "vacillating wretch" for needing him: "I wish I had more stiffening in my character. . . . How on earth I ever have succeeded in impressing
upon people at large the idea that I was a fierce and violent person—is a
puzzle. If ever there *was* a *soft*-shelled egg I'm it!" And a third fear was that
she was "foolish" for becoming so depressed: "And here I drivel on as usual.
Evidently not well—the usual excuse. My brain won't work and my body
won't work—and my heart just sits and bawls!" Worst of all, she concluded,
"I have failed in keeping up to my own perception of right. This is to me a
hideous confession. . . . I have no reliability." "I can't seem to come close
to a person and behave myself at all." All this was "Pure selfishness. Mere
passion," she decided, however aggressively and sensuously expressed.

> . . . Apparently this diamond-blooded lady is becoming an exacting insatiable
> passionate lover. Woe is me. As if I hadn't had enough kinds of affliction with-
> out this!
> The affection and admiration of a vast and increasing multitude does not satisfy
> me in the least. . . .
> . . . I want a man's love, big and deep and strong and—fierce if you like. I
> dare say you don't like to have me talk so. But I feel so. And if you don't like it
> you'd better learn about it now. . . .

"Insatiable" and "passionate" in her need for Houghton, at times Gilman
could boldly and confidently insist upon her right to love despite her work
commitments. "Once in a while," she wrote him, it "sort of dawns on me
anew. That you are. That I belong to you. That it's no wonder—and no
wrong—I couldn't live without your letters and your love. I'm caught and

held at last—in spite of my screams." But then again, the "plunging," "shift-ing" feelings, the "below-zero" fears—these would reemerge to plague her so intensely that "renunciation" seemed to be the only cure. It was like "living in a hole in the ground in a beautiful landscape—and knowing that efforts to crawl up and see the sunlight only cause one to drop back ex-hausted to the very bottom," she wrote him. "That is why it is better for me to drift about alone, having no responsibility save to the world in general, making friends by my casual virtues and not exposing these pitiful weak-nesses." All this "restless doubt" and "fear" were simply a sign of her own weakness and infirmity, she decided, as though the conflicts she was facing were not experienced by many other women also, and as though they had no connection to the insights of her public writings. But then again, she continued:

> . . . Perhaps——If I *can*——If what I have to do is to carry this strain too—
> . . . To prove that a woman can love and work too. . . .
> To give up neither. To be both, to do both, to prove that it can be done. It seems lighter as I write it dear. I guess that's right. And if you love me well enough I think it can be done.

Letters: May 16 through August 19, 1899

Mrs. Norman's again[25]
27 Grosvenor Road
Westminster.
About 9. Tues. A.M. May 16th '99. . . .

[In this letter, Gilman mentions having met a number of prominent En-glish and American writers, but since her comments are brief and for the most part uninformative, I simply list them here: Beatrice Webb, May Mor-ris (daughter of Henry Morris), Earl Barnes, Mrs. J. R. McDonald, Edward Ross, a professor at Stanford and a nephew of Lester Ward.]

The Sesame Club lecture is over—and a pronounced success. . . . I got a note from Mrs. Norman requesting to interview me for the Chronicle . . .
The place [*where Gilman intends to stay*] is a Nurses' Settlement, the room very comfortable! Meals plain and as I like—rather scanty though; and a big fine old garden out behind. . . .
Then came in to The Sesame [Club] and . . . [met] Earl Barnes. Concern-ing whom I hasten to remark that he makes no faintest impression on my erstwhile susceptible heart—that useful organ seems to be otherwise occupied.
I was so pleased to find it so. And I thought you'd be pleased too!
The lecture—"The Club Conscience"—went well—very well. They

laughed heartily, and were duly impressed also. Another Stanford man was there—Prof. Ross—sociology— nephew of Lester Ward. He is profoundly impressed with the book—Barnes too, though they had but looked over it; and Ross agreed heartily with the lecture. . . .

. . . Carnforth Lodge. Hammersmith.
10.48 A.M. Tues. May 16th. 1899

O dear Heart! Dear Heart! I just can't stand it. I must write to you as what you are—my dear dear husband, my closest truest friend; my tenderest lover. You['re] all there is—and I'm so lonesome for you! . . .

The Rosses are most cordial—are to invite me there soon. I am to lunch with Brother Barnes today—he says he wants to talk. I've no objection to his talking. But I'd rather hear you talk. . . .

. . . It is ever so pleasant here . . .—the sky is beautiful, the wind soft and warm, and the young-leafed woodbine hangs all about the sash. . . .

It is hard not to write you every day—I want to turn to you with every little thing. But it's much wiser not—if I expect to do anything else. . . . I know I'm a vacillating wretch to rush back at you this way after all my fine resolve to let you go for a year—but I'm not very well—and I'm way off here alone—and—and you are my husband! . . .

. . 3.40 P.M. May 17th. '99
My room—Carnforth Lodge Hammersmith. . . .

. . . I went in town to the Sesame—(this being Honorary Member of a nice club is mighty pleasant. To think of all the good things we women have not had!) and met Brother Barnes for lunch. . . . I was five minute late, not wishing to appear too eager! . . .

We talked, Mr. Barnes and I, quite cheerily and impersonally—the same misfit as to mental processes that always was there; but much general friendliness. He said my talk to the Club was emiminently successful,—said he knew them well—had been there as a member for about a year and a half, and spoken for them often; and that he knew how exactly I suited them. That pleased me much. Said Prof. Ross was working much as I was—and that he disagreed with him precisely as he did with me. We had a little more talk in the smoking room (men and women serenely smoking together—it is very funny) and he went off. . . .

Thurs. May 25th. 1899. 9.08 or so. A.M. . . .

I'm getting to feel easier about not hearing from you. I don't believe you are sick—for ten days—too sick to send me a word. I think you are just taking me at *my* word and not writing, quite unaware the while that I have been writing to you so steadily.

Also it is possible that you are perhaps seeing someone else—and . . . finding it hard to write to me under the circumstances.

Dear—if that comes, never doubt for an instant my ability to bear it. All my foolish weakness turns to strength the moment I think of it. . . .

And I have showed you so much vacillation, such irresolute helplessness along the lines of taking the happiness you have offered me, that I confess to a certain satisfaction in the thought of showing you a better stronger side.

It is truly there dear. Please trust in it.

But then I think again that this is idle doubt and fear, that you are *there,* just as you were, only letting go of me as I myself was trying to let go of you—and couldn't. And I smile to think of how close and dear you are— and how the days are going—only six weeks and four days till you come— and of the blessed future that comes steadily nearer.

And most of all I put the thought of it out of my mind—because not hearing from you in ten days does hurt—and try to be steady and good and get on with the work. . . .

It does seem so queer—to *lack* anybody so! I resent it still—this *needing* feeling—battered, old wreck that I am, with nothing left worth conquering— I hate to give up. What! To admit that I can't get on without some other person! Well, it yet remains to be seen. Perhaps already you have seen the error of your ways and I'll have to! . . .

I think it's good for me—not hearing from you. It hurts awfully, but it pulls me very close. . . .[26]

. . . London. England
Carnforth Lodge. Hammersmith W.
10 A.M. or so. Sun. June. 4th. 1899.

A soft warm summer Sunday—sunshine and sweet air and bird songs— a beautiful day. . . .

. . . I do want you with me so, in all I see and do. Just a mere selfish personal love, and it grows and grows.

And I'm so afraid that yours is mostly pity and self-sacrifice. But I don't care so much what it is. I'm getting back toward the place where I was last January—wanting you whether you like it or not! . . .

I feel very grand about my return passage. It never would do in the world to be on the same boat. But won't it be funny to be crossing at the same time on different [ocean] lines! . . .

9.30–35 A.M. Mon. June 5th. 1899. . . .

. . . It has been fair sweet weather for over a week.

The laburnum tree outside my window has come out in dropping showers of pale gold; and the woodbine is fairly prancing with new shoots. . . .

Our river trip was rather a failure. It was hot—very hot; Mr. Ghent did not row very well, and did not like it. Also, he blistered his hands in what small effort he made. Whereas I proudly rowed all the way back—(a small matter enough) without affecting my horny hands in the least.

I wonder if your Aunt would not like one day on the river. It is really a lovely sight, and thick with houseboats, rowboats, punts, canoes, all manner of craft. The banks lovely beyond words, and dotted with beautiful country houses.

I am anxious not to push or intrude, but I do want to be with you all I can while you are here. . . .

I have scored another victory—to my surprise. Mrs. Curtis—our cold and stiff "superintendent" confides to Miss Foote her extreme approval of me—that I am so witty—that I am so beautiful—that I have (listen to this!) *such exquisite manners!* Isn't that funny! To make an impression like that on a reserved little English woman! . . .

8.30 or so. A.M.
Tues. June 6th.

Found your letter yesterday. . . . I have eaten it all up and am hoping for Wednesday[']s already! . . . Your present letters—to my hungry heart, are as peanuts to the elephant!

They're good,—but O so little. But you are a proud person and of a most determined character. You have been persuaded by me that it is wise to let go of me this summer, even as I ruthlessly determined to let go of you; and the incidental fact that my determination went to the winds (or the waves!) on first trial, and that now I not only have my arms around your neck but my feet off the ground . . . does not alter your position in the least. . . .

I wish I had more stiffening in my character. When I was ten I used to wish it—so that I might "stay mad" with Thomas. But I never could. How on earth I ever have succeeded in impressing upon people at large the idea that I was a fierce and violent person—is a puzzle. If ever there *was* a *soft-shelled* egg I'm it! . . .

Mr. Barnes I am now distinctly angry with. Because that first miserable fortnight I should have been so glad of any society and kindness, and I *think* he did not do any of the things he spoke of [invitations to her for dinner and for sightseeing tours] for fear of my reviving things! Which rankles. Wait till I see him again, that's all. A change of climate will take place. I'm afraid the worthy man has a very small mind in some ways. Which is quite enough space on him. . . .

. . . 9.10 A.M. Thurs. June 8th. 1899.
Carnforth Lodge. Hammersmith. W.C.
London. England.

Bad again. Can't think what I ought to do—and very anxious and guilty about it. . . .

Fetched out the little packet of your letters which I—fortunately—did not rigorously leave behind; and hunted through them for the words I love. Found 'em too, and went to bed with the whole bunch! It's all mixed up and black, but I'm hanging on to you like a sick octopus! Poor Houghton.

4.20 or so. P.M.

A letter after all! A dear dear letter that I am crying over because I'm so glad to get it! . . .

I'm gradually reading the [William] Morris book, so haven't sent it. It didn't occur to me at first that I ought to read it! It's very nice too—a most interesting man. . . .

The tender words at the end of your letter are an unspeakable comfort to me. Why should you be ashamed to say you love me over and over?
. . . Love is not a mere historic fact to be stated, proved, and left at that. If one feels it all the time one wants to show it all the time. At least I do. Our difference is that words are not your natural expression as they are mine. You do not like to play and sing in them as I do. But thank Heaven you do like caresses, both to give and take—I will be grateful for that. The trouble is you see that I so rapidly sink under the sense of my unfitness for you—an aching conviction that never has been removed— that I particularly need continued encouragement. . . .

And here I drivel on as usual. Evidently not well—the usual excuse. My brain won't work and my body won't work—and my heart just sits and bawls! A nice lady! . . .

. . . 9.35 A.M. The Mount. Basingstoke. Hants. England. [no date]

My dear. My dear. The deep sweet beauty of the life you offer me is gleaming through the fog of my mind again, more and more clearly. I wish only that some power could give me a full insight into your share in that happiness—that I could see *plainly if it were really* to your benefit.

This is the home of Mrs. Stanton-Blatch, you remember Katharine stayed here while in England. . . .

Dear Mrs. Blatch comes in continually to talk. . . .

. . . It is terribly discouraging—this long long weakness. To want to do so much. To be able to do so little. And the awful *confusion* of it—not to be sure of anything. It is, as I told you, very like the reeling misery of seasickness. . . .

6.50 P.M. Monday June 12th. 1899. . . .

How can you be so good to me. I don't deserve it a bit—haven't ever. No matter how foolish I am, how weak and vacillating and trying, you are always just so noble and gentle and kind. . . .

Mrs. S[tanton] B[latch] is very friendly. She has around her bedroom for a frieze the names of the world's great women—from Deborah up; and verily she has "Stetson" among them!! That's one on Walter, isn't it! . . .[27]

Mrs. S.B. took me for a drive and a walk through a most beautiful park, with grand old beeches, deer, cattle, and so on—all the loveliness one reads about. . . .

Back to town to a meeting on "The Bureau for the Employment of Women.". . .

. . . 10 A.M. Tues. June. 13th. . . .

Your dear letter is still uppermost in my mind; and the sweet and steady hope of our life together is undermost—a lovely background. You see as soon as I can settle into that view of it it is an endless reservoir of peace and health to me. And the stationary literary life appeals to me more & more.

Do all you can—if it be truly so—to keep me convinced that it is for your happiness too. . . .

There's such a constant tendency to think it isn't that I need continual reassurance. I shall always be afraid it isn't. You will have the obligation upon you of being visibly happy with me!

I'll wake you up in the night and say "Houghton! Are you truly happy?" And you'll say, I *was*—a minute ago!" . . .

. . . Carnforth Lodge. Hammersmith W.
London. England.
8.45 A.M. June 14th. 1899 . . .

. . . I do get so impatient with my "lot," sometimes. To know intellectually that one has cause for so much pleasure and yet to feel so much pain. It is very wearing. Like living in a hole in the ground in a beautiful landscape—and knowing that efforts to crawl up and see the sunlight only cause one to drop back exhausted to the very bottom. . . .

Last night to dinner at Mr. & Mrs. J. R. MacDonald's. Interesting set of people there. Miss Toynbee among them. She was very cordial. But it was tiring—a room full of jarring talk. . . .

Things are all right really, dear. And I'll get out of this fog in time. Now I'll try and do some work. . . .

8.45 A.M. Thurs. June. 15th '99. . . .

Yesterday I made two copies, partly rewritten, of my Congress paper. Not bad either. . . . and to the Rosses to tea. They are very kind and friendly. I like 'em. . . .

I have a fine compliment from May Morris. Mrs. Cobden-Sanderson told her she must not live alone there—it was quite wrong. To which she replied that she did not know a soul she would be willing to live with—unless it was Mrs. Stetson!!! This is hearsay by two voices, but it pleased me. For she is a sad and unhappy woman, and many people don't like her. I would much like to befriend her. Now I'll try to get at something of a day[']s work. . . .

[undated letter]

. . . I have failed in keeping up to my own perception of right. This is to me a hideous confession. . . . I have no reliability. That is why it is better for me to drift about alone, having no responsibility save to the world in general, making friends by my casual virtues and not exposing these pitiful weaknesses. . . .

. . . 8.45 A.M. Sat. June. 17th '99.
Carnforth Lodge. London . . .

. . . Once in a while that sort of dawns on me anew. That you are. That I belong to you. That it's no wonder—and no wrong—I couldn't live without your letters and your love. I'm caught and held at last—in spite of my screams. You quiet patient gentle thing—how did you do it. I suspect you occasionally of having worked out a deep-laid scheme of conquest, ruthlessly carried out regardless of my vain throes. Well—there's nothing I like better. . . . May I do good work enough to justify your faith and love. . . .

Yesterday . . . [I met] Hamlin Garland, who was presently to speak to the Woman's Institute on the younger writers in American Literature. This he did, after his kind. I think it would have been a piece of excusable courtesy if he had gracefully put me in his list—the audience would have considered it as justified by my presence, but the good man didn't. . . . I was asked to discuss, and made a few remarks. They liked 'em too. . . .

8.30 A.M. Tues. [June 20. 1899] . . .

. . . [*She is disappointed that her publishers have not sent copies of* Women and Economics *to the convention.*] It has spoiled all my fine plans for making an impression in England. I have neither lectured nor written as I should have if they had been here, out, reviewed and discussed. . . .

. . . But it prejudices me strongly against Small and Maynard. Maynard is smart but I don't like him. Small I like but he isn't smart. A greater blunder in a business sense they could hardly have made—you see "The Season" is practically over and it's too late to do anything now; no booksales, no lectures, no nothing. But it isn't troubling me an atom. . . .

. . . They sent me two reviews, one a brief notice from *The Boston Evening Herald,* mentioning Howell's "The New Poetry" in the May *North American,* in which he speaks of my work in complimentary terms; and the other an astonishingly long and good review from the New York *Nation.* That did surprise me, and please me too. I hope you saw it. So my work makes its own way though publishers lag. . . .

8.45 A.M. Fri. June 23rd '99. . . .[28]

Yesterday brought me yours of the 13th—with cutting from Post. Isn't it grand! . . . I am very much surprised, and pleased of course—because those papers count for much with *some* people! It's a good moderate discriminating criticism too. . . .

. . . Midland Temperance Hotel
76 Guilford St. Russell Sq.
4.25 or so P.M. Wed. July 5th. '99. . . .

The Congress is all over. I made a ten strike just as I hoped; book or no book—am greatly liked as a speaker. And I have stood it wonderfully—but am pretty tired now as you may imagine. . . .

. . . **76 Guilford St.**
Near 9. P.M. Thurs.
July 13th. 1899. . . .

[*Houghton has arrived in London, but they have seen each other rarely.*]
When I found I wasn't to see you again today I went all to pieces—felt so miserable and lost. And you won't be here much longer anyhow—and then there[']s six weeks without you and then, thank goodness, three weeks of you in New York. Or most of it. . . .

And to know that you are right here—within reach—and I can't have you! . . .

9.30 Fri. eve. [July 14, 1899]
My room.

Ow! Ow-ow-ooo-w! This is awful! I never was so be-panged in my life. That I should live to come to this stage of whimpering besottedness! It is "too ridiculous." I went away from you with my heart in my boots—where there was naturally no room for it. I *was* so forlorn. Couldn't muster up courage enough to go anywhere—just stood about. . . .

. . . Houghton Gilman—I don't know what your feelings may be—you keep very quiet about 'em—but mine are too numerous to mention! This glimpse-of-you-on-sufferance is maddening.

I am plunged at once into a state of semi-idiocy. *Now* I know what they mean when they tell about the fool things people do when they're "in love."

Why I don't know where to go nor what to do.

When I found I couldn't go to you yesterday there didn't seem to be any other place *to* go—the sky shut. This never'll do. The sooner I can scrabble through the next nine months and have done with 'em the better. . . .

. . . **9.25 A.M. Sat. July 15th. '99.** . . .

I'm awfully upset by your coming—that's a fact. Not that I object! But I can't seem to think at all—everything is a daze—except you. . . . This is only an aggravation. We can't even *talk* and that isn't much! . . .

noon—

Have written letters and cards. Read and corrected ms. of yesterday and sent it off. . . . The Arena don't pay much, but it's a better magazine than this paltry Ainslee's [sp?] that S & M let me in for! And if it isn't but 25 or 30 dollars—what that's not bad for three hours. If I keep well—when we have our home together—I can surely do lots of work. And it is beautiful the way people keep on liking me. Only poor you will have to put up with all my disagreeablenesses and infirmities and get no credit for it! . . .

. . . 10. A.M. Tuesday. July 25th. 1899.
76 Guilford St. Russell Sq.
London.

How I ever shall leave you in New York I do not know! You are part of me now—it *tears* to leave you—to have you go away. . . .

Nevertheless I have to say that my spirits and appetite are good this morning—. I feel better than for many days. That, perhaps, is because you are off my mind for the present. I can't be looking out of the window for you and wishing you would come.

Will you be "off my mind" I wonder when I marry you? Shall I be able to assimilate and carry your life with mine, or shall I cling to you, unable to go away and unable to work with you—pulled to you by all this hungry clamoring long-starved humanness; and driven from you by the imperative need of freedom and work.

I should tear off finally, if that were so—and die of the wound I fancy. . . .

. . . Great success yesterday . . . went to the Girls' High School in Dulwich. Spoke to a small but earnest group, and so impressed them that they wouldn't go home—just sat and sat and hung on for more. . . .

A letter from Hervey White last night. He says Maynard has been in to see him—and that he said anything I might choose to write now "would sell well enough to justify publishing." So there. Surely if I keep decently well I can do a lot of good work now. . . .

I'm *having* to respect my work more now that so many do.

I should write many letters this morning—but my head has clouded up again—can't think. O it is so *long*—this heavy darkness. So many years.

I wish you were somehow Bigger. Could take me right off the ground and say—"Little Girl! Little Girl! Stop thinking. It is all right. You are mine and I've got you and I'll never let go—never. You shall rest and sleep and work and play—I won't let anything hurt you or bother you. Rest on me." That[']s what I want. And I lean farther and farther toward you—and you kind of *give*—it don't seem as if it would *bear*, really.

And I've nearly lost my balance—it's a horribly trying position.

Dearest—dearest—if you can carry me for Heavens sake *make me feel it.* If you can't ——— I must know before it is too late. I'm heavy. I always told you I was heavy and hard to carry. And I'm *so* tired. Please help me dear. . . .

4.40 P.M. . . .

My lecture yesterday did me good. The *real* feeling of those women. Their anxiety to hear more. It was good. Also the little two guineas was a practical solace to my feelings. . . .

Wed. 10.25 or so A.M.
July 26th. 1899. . . .

Say—the man Peck, in his article on Balzac in the July Cosm[opolitan], quotes that worthy as saying "It is only the last love of a woman that can satisfy the first love of a man." Now how about the other way? Apparently this diamond-blooded lady is becoming an exacting insatiable passionate lover. Woe is me. As if I hadn't had enough kinds of affliction without this!

The affection and admiration of a vast and increasing multitude does not satisfy me in the least. I want to be *loved*—by you, more and more and more.

Pure selfishness. Mere passion. Call it anything you please. All that beautiful "family affection" that I talked so much about fails to meet this want. I want a man's love, big and deep and strong and—fierce if you like. I dare say you don't like to have me talk so. But I feel so. And if you don't like it you'd better learn about it now.

Perhaps this is only a physical condition too.

Dear Houghton—do you begin to see why I told you I'd rather have loneliness and *peace* than begin to be tossed about again. It is these changes of feeling, this plunging and shifting, that keeps me so weak. And here is where I always have the instinct to cut off—to kill out—to escape somehow from the tearing thing inside.

I don't know. I'm not built right. I can't seem to come close to a person and behave myself at all. Calmness and power, for me, seem to involve complete renunciation. Away off and going without everything I stand steady and am loving and cheerful and serene. Drawn close to another heart—O Houghton—I am so *tired* of all this restless doubt and hope and fear and flickering joy. Is there no way you can hold me *still?*

I'm likely to be always like this for aught I know. Well. Here it is, and I can't see. Can't see an inch.

I've got to the place I wanted. I can write what I please and say what I please and the world is ready to listen. And here I am floundering helplessly among my own affairs—doing no work at all. It is shameful—shameful. . . .

Look. I'm forty—nearly. They said I should be stronger then. I'm not stronger, that I can see, at all. I've worked as I could—waited—suffered— kept my heart open and my courage up—now; as far as opportunity goes I've *got there*—and here I am so weak and clouded in mind that I cannot do any work at all.

And the pressure—the awful pressure of the world's need for just what I can do—driving and grinding me on. These mothers waiting for me to explain things to them—asking for it—the children by the million that words of mine might really help to a fairer juster homelife—the men who see things clearer and feel a new hope for the world when I talk to them—this tremendous Call—everywhere—and here I sit moaning for my husband.

Nice kind of wife you have! Perhaps ——. If I *can*—If what I have to do is to carry this strain too—. To prove that a woman can love and work too. To resist this dragging weight of the old swollen woman-heart, and force it into place—the world's Life first—my own life next. Work first—love next.

Perhaps this is simply the burden of our common womanhood which is weighing on me so.

To give up neither. To be both, to do both, to prove that it can be done. It seems lighter as I write it dear. I guess that's right. And if you love me well enough I think it can be done. . . .

. . . c/o Mrs. Hubert Bland.
Well Hall, Eltham Kent.
Thurs. P.M.
July 27th. 1899. . . .

I went to see my new doctor & got his little tablets to take, and some more advice.

I asked him plain questions, and he gave plain answers—said I was all right—should be all over this trouble in a few few more years—that I should make a desirable wife, and that I might conscientiously have a child—that there was nothing hereditary the matter with me.

So I went away feeling quite set up. . . .

Dear—be patient yet a while—I shan't always be so unreasonable and difficult to handle. I *am* yours most fully, such as I am. . . .

. . . c/o Mrs. Hubert Bland. Well Hall
Eltham. Kent
Friday. July 28th. 1899. . . .

More and more I wish for you. Not merely as my lover—though that is there, but as my dear friend, my most enjoyable companion. When my letters come I want you, when I meet new people I want you, when any thing happens I want you. And when nothing happens I want you awfully! . . .

It has been very blind since you went away—I don't know what I've done; nor how.

Except that both the Dulwich lectures were beautifully successful—really reached people—made new friends—and deeply stirred the girls. . . .

[*The doctor's report has "cheered" her.*]

. . . I suppose, when we are together, that every year of improved health and of quiet happiness together will build up my confidence in my value to you—I shall gradually cease to be anxious and grow complacent! But, dear Heart—in all the perplexity and suffering that I have caused you, you must see *why* I so urgently declared I was unfit to marry—you see what I mean by being "shattered"—instead of the sound and beautiful goblet to hold sweet wine for you to drink is this broken thing that everything spills out of—I can't *keep* any feeling—they flow over and through me, and you never can be sure of what you are going to find.

But—under all the changes—you do find love for you, don't you dear. That grows and grows. . . .

. . . I get tired so far below zero that it seems as if I never should see light again, never come to the surface. . . .

So dark and thick and nightmarish. That clogging weight on every movement. Mire, deep mire, and a gloomy twilight, and everything moving vaguely about so that there's no top or bottom or sideways or distance.

I can come out of it for a lecture—spoke really well both times at Dulwich—but when it's done I slide and slide and feel it shutting in again. . . .

. . . These last years of weakness have been more hopeless somehow than all before, and I build more and more on this one hope. That somehow you can save me from the darkness and the heavy pressure. . . .

. . . 10.30 Sat. July. 29th. 1899.
Well Hall. Eltham. Kent. . . .

I do feel better. And you've done most of it with your dear letters. You are so good to me! So strong and patient. And I get a most restful sense of bigness out of it too—which is just what my weariness wanted. I *can* rest on you. I can be cross and nervous and most aggravating—and however I rush about I don't get to the end of you—you are there just the same. . . .

Of course with most people I *have* to behave—can't give way at all. But you are so near and warm—so tempting—that I just want to let go of everything and sit down on you! . . .

All my doctors have told me that I should get over all this at about forty five. So then we may count on more peaceful years ahead. If I can manage to bring you a child first—a dear baby of your own. O I do hope for it Houghton. . . .

. . . You are so modest—you don't half realize how I need you. My notions of not being "supported" are exclusively economic you see—and by no means let you out of far harder tasks.

That's why I've dreaded it so, dearest—for you; knowing what a burden I was bringing you. But—O it does feel so good to be carried! . . .

Mon. 12. 45. July 31st. 1899.

Wrote about 16 pages on the Kitchenless Home article—had to stop. . . .

If I should by any happy chance come to the end of my life I should be so glad.—I'd be glad for you because you'd be vastly better off—an honest widower and able to do as you liked.

And I'd be glad for myself—O so glad—because it is so tiresome to think at all—my brain is so heavy.

Kate wouldn't miss me—it wouldn't hurt anybody but you and hurt you less than my living will I fear. What a bad lady it is to write such dismal letters! I'll try to brace up—read some of my own poetry!—and be good.

I love you—when I'm loving anybody. But this slow heavy halfaliveness doesn't love any one much.

Don't worry dear—I've had several hopeful glimmers lately—I think I'm nearly through this bad place.

And I play Badminton quite reassuringly. . . .

. . . Well Hall. Eltham. Kent.
Fri. Aug. 4th. 1899. . . .

I am gaining, slowly—still fuzzy headed and dull, but not so low-spirited. Everything is so bright and promising now—except my poor brains! . . .

Nothing could be better for me than this quiet place with the nice people to "take up my mind." . . .[29]

. . . Well Hall. Eltham. Kent.
Aug. 5th. 1899. . . .

I'm getting such *good* letters—it ought to make me very happy. And it does. Only I'll be happier when I can put my arms around you. . . .

And I judge from reviews sent me from America that I am a writer of some importance and can not be spared! . . .

19 Warrender Park Crescent.
Edinburgh
about 11 A.M. Aug. 9th. 1899. . . .

It was so good to see you yesterday. Just to sit still and look at you and know you were there. And I'm wickedly glad that you don't find it easy to do without me! For all your philosophy. . . .

. . . 12.15 P.M. Sunday. Aug. 13th 99.
The Cottage. Levenhall.
Musselburgh. . . .

I'm thinking that I might get a Scotch girl for ourselves by and by—one that wanted to come to America. They are good workers, good cooks, and very conscientious. I think I'd like it. And "a pound a week" would move Scotch mountains. . . .

A nice responsible body, who could do purchasing and keep accounts and run things while I was away.

Might follow my favorite plan of getting a girl with a baby—she'd be glad to change her country perhaps. I should be so much happier if I had a servant who valued the position and was glad to be there—who would be fond of me. I think I could make her very comfortable too. . . .

10.05 or so. A.M. Friday. Aug. 18th '99.
On train for Newcastle. . . .

This is a fine country about here. What beautiful things we can do with the earth when we get ready—what endless gardens! What sweet health and upwelling animal happiness for our basis, and the great vibrating waves of human feeling on top of these. Ah! The sea! Blue, white, and yellow—white sands. . . .

About 10 A.M. Sat. Aug. 19th. '99
Ashfield House. Elswick Road.
Newcastle-on-Tyne. . . .

Such good news! A bit late for this year, but promising well for the future. I find here, and further receive this morning, a circular and letter from J. B. Pond. In the circular I shine forth triumphant. . . .

. . . Isn't it good to have the great Pond so ardent. I wonder what has happened to him. . . .

Now if only I can keep *true*, be simple and natural and genuine, not work just for money, nor according to what people say of me—not be altered and inspired by the pressure of praise—. I think I stood the other kind pretty well. I'll have a try at this.

But it does please me to look forward to a comfortable solidly based home; a center of health and strength; a place to work from and go back to.

And as I grasp the idea of being able to hire a competent person to manage it all, it does not weigh on me as it used to.

You see in my bringing up, a home meant much personal labor and care; and I['m] not equal to that.

But as I realize that . . . there are still women to be had who can manage these things, and that I can on the one hand pay them, and on the other make friends with them—the whole things looks more and more feasible.

To make a beautiful comfortable home that Katharine will enjoy and be proud of—to be able to give her the kind of background she should have—it all begins to look possible. And you do fit in so beautifully. . . .

11

"To Eat and Drink So Largely of Human Life": 26 September–6 December 1899

After the summer months in England, and after a brief stay with Houghton in New York, Gilman set out for her fall and winter travels. She would continue with her lecturing and writing, but according to her letters, she felt a growing optimism, an increasing confidence that her goals might be attained: "To prove that a woman can love and work too. . . . To give up neither. To do both. . . . I think it can be done." And as "I look back at my earnest struggling girlhood and think how I longed . . . to reach wide and deep—to see and know; and then think of the splendid freedom and depth of knowledge I have come into—it makes me very grateful." "It's no wonder I love the world so," she continued. "To live so wide and find so many friends—so many open homes. The wildest dreams of socialism are only what I live in—to move freely among the people—to be loved and cared for everywhere—to ask for nothing and get much—that has been my life for near five years."[1]

As usual, the itinerary Gilman planned was an ambitious one. She would stay for several weeks with Alice Stone Blackwell in Boston, with May Wright Sewell, president of the International Congress of Women, in Indianapolis, Indiana; in Chicago she lectured at Northwestern University and renewed her Hull House contacts; and in Toledo, Ohio, she worked briefly with Samuel Jones on his political campaign. "Went forth to speak in Golden Rule Hall," she wrote Houghton. "Big crowd, and much interest." "Toledo" Jones is "doing great work here," and is "ripping up things pretty generally." He is "immensely popular," and it is "a good cause, to my mind—what he stands for." "So consider me as 'on the stump' for [the] next week," engaging in "my favorite pastime—preaching" on women's basic rights and needs. Women "are so bound up, so compressed as it were, . . . that we want no interests beside our little home circle," as she put it in one Toledo lecture. We have not been allowed to vote, nor run for office, nor assert our rights and interests, and yet are "citizens as well as men."[2]

One of the last stops on Gilman's western tour was Salt Lake City; Susa Young Gates, daughter of Brigham Young, served as her hostess. "I am in the center of Mormondom," she wrote Houghton, and "like it thoroughly." "I was introduced to the butcher, the baker, and the candlestick maker. Real primitive American good fellowship . . . so homey and nice." They "are eagerly interested in my various heretical doctrines," she continued, and "last night I addressed my first Mormon audience. Unqualified success. 'Our Brains & What Ails Them.'" Some of the women want "to form a society, build a Baby-School, and fall to at once on the lines I suggested." "And while we should probably differ forever in basic views, yet they seem singularly open to conviction as to improved methods of all sorts."[3]

According to current press reports of Gilman's lectures—in Chicago and St. Louis, for example, in Indianapolis, Denver, Salt Lake City, and Ogden, Utah—such enthusiastic affirmations were widely shared. In city after city, reporters praised her as a "genius-endowed woman," a "brilliant public speaker," a "Woman Radical" with "startlingly advanced" ideas.[4] As the Deseret *Evening News* put it,

> There is probably no woman in America today who commands more attention from the best minds of Europe and America than Mrs. Stetson. Her book, *Women and Economics* is recognized as one of the brightest, most original and readable on women ever written. It is selling all over the United States and England, and is being translated into French, German, Dutch and Swedish.[5]

The key to Gilman's genius as a lecturer, according to some reporters, was her ability to preach radical convictions in "eloquent" but nonthreatening ways. She might be "a radical of radicals," as one reporter put it, but she is a "most fascinating and charming woman." She is "slight and not beautiful." She has a face that "genius" saves "from being plain." And she has that winning "combination of strong mind, radical views and marked sprightliness of manner." Her nature is one of "personified refinement, her voice soft and pleasing, her black eyes a glory of light and beauty and expression." Her "masterly" lectures thus were never "cut and dried" nor "coldly scientific;" instead they were like "a confidential chat with serious-minded people"—"brilliant," "full of common sense" and "simply put."[6] As the Salt Lake City *Herald* put it:

> She may be a "new woman," but she doesn't wear bloomers—nor corsets, and she doesn't ride any hobby horses. In fact, she is a very womanly woman, with more brains than nine hundred and ninety-nine men out of a thousand, and she evinces more alertness, brightness and intelligence in ten minutes' conversation than does the average man during his lifetime. Contrary to the notions bred by critics and reviewers of her book, she doesn't preach doctrines that are obnoxious when her meaning is thoroughly understood.[7]

Or, according to the St. Louis *Post Dispatch:*

> It is not the least exaggeration to say that there has never been a public speaker in St. Louis, male or female, who cast as complete a spell over an audience as did Mrs. Stetson. It was not done by flights of eloquence. Mrs. Stetson is not given to flights. She first won the people with her simplicity and sincerity and the

sunshine of her nature and then held them and moved them by the force and eloquence of tersely stated truths. . . .[8]

"Isn't it all going beautifully," Charlotte wrote to Houghton. *Women and Economics* was receiving national attention.[9] Most lectures were enthusiastically received. "And all of it is simply my own natural dearly loved reforming! Don't have to do a thing but 'relieve my mind!'" Moreover, Small and Maynard were so enthusiastic about her economic prospects, they were "hot" to have another book. "A thousand a year from royalties," Charlotte calculated optimistically. "That's not so bad, is it?" "Why I'll be living on my income soon! Think of it—an income—*ME!*" Her publishers had promised "15% for the first 5000" copies, "18% after that, and $500.00 down." "So if I do [a book] this winter," *Human Work,* she would call it, "there's another little nest egg. . . . Isn't it fine." It "opens and opens. I begin to see how many of my big ideas I can put into it. I won't be stingy—I'll just pour—there will be 'another crop for the next one!'"

Although Gilman was enthusiastic about her economic prospects and also about the popular impact of her work in the winter of 1899, she was still struggling with some discomforting underlying fears. As the St. Louis *Post Dispatch* had phrased it, "She proclaims the truth as she sees the truth without apology." But her "views of the status and relations of woman to society are too far in advance of the thought of the time to be accepted. She contends for the absolute economic independence of woman."[10] Even Houghton seemed to struggle with the economic issue: "I think it is pathetic—and funny," she wrote him, "that the only solace to my poor pride—my growing fame and fortune, should act as a disadvantage to your eyes! . . . And now that these three years have lifted my head a little, . . . why lo and behold you don't like it!" "Do be fair," she continued. "Do not begrudge me . . . the only poor straw of worth that I have to cling to." Here is "my only redeeming feature—almost—that I shall not be an expense to you, and perhaps be a real help—[and] that redounds to your discredit and acute anguish of mind!"

Work was her "only redeeming feature"—the only "straw of worth" she had to cling to—clearly Gilman had to face some troubling implications of her professional success: Houghton would feel threatened by her economic independence, and that it would undermine *his* self-respect. Houghton "is feeling badly about business things,"[11] Charlotte recently had noted in her diary. "I appreciate how trying your position is," she wrote him, "Pegging away there in the big city, and not thinking a thousandth part as much of yourself as you ought to think! You are a man of a clear fair well-balanced mind uncommonly well stocked with information and trained in careful use. You have both general knowledge and special training in your profession—lots of 'em." "You are sure . . . of making a place for yourself in time." Yet, as she attempted to respond supportively to Houghton's insecurities, she felt compelled to ressert worries of her own. Apologizing that her "service and devotion" were not "given wholly" to his interests, and that her "boundless whole souled love" was not directed "absolutely" to himself, she tried at times to minimize her own achievements or to write as though she actually regretted them. After all, she defensively insisted, "For all my brag I haven't much confidence in my moneymaking power." Since any professional achievements were but a paltry compensation for her "feminine" inadequacy, a "solace" for her failures as a woman, she still needed his sympathy and help.

In light of Gilman's theories on women's right and need for economic independence, what is most striking in her current letters is the variety of strategies she used to sustain and justify her own professional success. Like many women of her class and generation, and so unlike the majority of men, she had to approach the economic independence issue cautiously and indirectly. "I have a brilliant idea," she wrote him. "I will confine my contribution to the family to exactly yours," and we will "live so simply and plainly—so within your means—that people can't say you are being supported." And she suggested gently in another letter that maybe he would allow her to "be of some use in these years." Maybe she could help provide him with the time and opportunity to get on his feet financially, and to find the kind of work he wanted.[12] "I'm not above having you keep elaborate accounts and paying it all back when you are an eminent lawyer in the prime of life and I am a feeble old lady past working!. . . I'll let you all right! Count on me as a kind of partner (sleeping partner?) quite willing to bank on your future."

It was a delicate task that Charlotte was attempting, trying on the one hand to protect and nurture Houghton's ego, and on the other to claim what she regarded as a basic right. Still apologetic, still sometimes circuitous and indirect, and always affirming Houghton's competence, gentleness, and kindness, the fall and winter letters nonetheless reveal an important change. In the past Charlotte had focused almost solely on her own insecurities and conflicts and thus supported Houghton's "proper" role as male protector. In her current letters, however, she was ready to acknowledge a greater reciprocity and mutuality in their relationship and to offer some advice. He was "an exceptionally well-endowed young lawyer" with many "splendid qualities," but he also had some "pesky little angel" faults that needed to be changed.

In point of fact, of course, the "faults" that Charlotte found in Houghton were characteristically more troubling to women: his tendency to "habitually depreciate" himself, to be too "modest" and too "bashful." "That is why I love so utterly," she wrote him. He was "so kind to everybody, so considerate—so self-effacing—. . . so *Good*"—but too much so at times, and thus suffered from the same dilemmas that women usually faced. "Be a little badder some ways," she told him. "Claim what belongs to you. Do unto yourself as you do to others!" Stop assuming, as women so often did, that assertiveness was selfish, and that confidence was wrong. "There's no danger of your growing selfish and grasping—you can practice for quite some time before you tip the scales that way. But because your natural mental habit is to underrate yourself, you now want conscientiously to *over-rate* yourself . . . and it takes time—less as you go on!"[13] "I don't mean to torment you by constant exhortation," she told him, because in an equitable, just society, his virtues "would be more widely recognized and more justly valued" as would his gentleness and modesty, his "delicate conscience," "social intuition," and his sensitivity to other people's needs. But since in a highly competitive, materialistic society, such characteristics were often thought to be a sign of weakness and dependence. Therefore he needed calculated strategies to strengthen and protect himself. Develop an "attitude of self-confident power," she wrote him, "of absolute assurance in success," and "straighten up your spine and expand your chest when you think of it." "Make up your mind just what you want to be. Then *feel as if you were.*" And then "*act*" as you have learned to feel. "I'm sure I don't know why I am possessed to preach to you so ardently just now. I guess it means two things. One that my current is on—which always means joy and power to me. And one that you have grown so blessedly near that I *can* speak to you with full freedom—as I could not even a year ago."

Whereas in the past Gilman had focused on her own insecurities and conflicts and blamed herself for tensions in the friendship, in her fall and winter letters, almost as a precondition for their marriage, she was ready to acknowledge that Houghton had some attitudes that needed to be changed. It wasn't that she wanted him to achieve a more prominent professional position or that he enhance his economic prospects either. Clearly his status or income never had seriously concerned her. Instead, the question threatening to undermine their friendship was far more fundamental: whether he could accept her economic independence without losing self-respect. "Don't be so proud—in that way; and be prouder in others," she wrote him. After all, "Lots of men marry poor and build up. Pity if you can't." Or even more directly, "If you do marry me, you want to have it out with yourself once and for all on this money question. It is evident that you haven't yet."

> Can't you get along with the money idea better by seeing that it is what men in general have got to come to soon—unless they carefully adjust their love affairs to ladies of inferior earning capacity! . . .
> Of course it's hard to break down these mountainous old prejudices—but they've got to go someday.

Letters: September 26 through December 6, 1899

Near 5 P.M. Tues. Sept. 26th. '99
Boutwell Ave—
Dorchester Mass. . . .[14]

Mr. Small, being freed from the keen eye of my legal adviser, talks business this morning. Says they'll give me for my next book 15% for the first 5000, 18% after that, and $500.00 down. That's not so bad, is it?

So if I do one this winter there's another little nest egg. . . .

This royalty business pleases me. I'll have an income of a thousand or two soon *even if I'm sick*!!! Isn't it fine. He's hot for the book. . . .

9.25 A.M. Wed. Sept. 27th. 1899.
Boutwell Ave. Dorchester Mass. . . .

I shan't write much today either, for my head is fuzzy and I'm diligently resting after the lecture last night. But I'm glad to say that it was a success. . . .

Money down is a great comfort when you have a book to publish. Royalties are a great comfort when you are not able to work. I am to have both it appears. . . .

Why I'll be living on my income soon! Think of it—an income—*ME*! . . .

3.20 or so. P.M. Fri. Sept. 29th. '99
Dorchester. Mass. . . .

Went in this morning. Read reviews at S & M's—great stuff. You must get you a copy of the "Bookman" of September; *London.* It's a fine article, and a very nice picture. . . .

Met Miss [Amy] Wellington at 11.35 in the W.J. office; and went with her to her room on Mt. Vernon St. The child had provided me with a room in the same home for possible use this week! And I never got around to it at all. She presented me with $87.00—having agreed to give 75.00—and nearly wept when I tried to make her take the odd 12. Her work she has simply given. A damsel to remember. Miss Amy Wellington. . . .[15]

9.30 A.M. Sun. Oct. 1st. 1899.
Dorchester, Mass. . . .

Dear little Miss Wellington came out to see me yesterday afternoon, and we had a fine walk and talk, sat on the high house roof, and "visited" in my room—I preaching and she absorbing. She's a dear. Says she has loved other people better since she loved me!

If only I can turn it all—*all*—your dear love and all the other blessings—into better *WORK!* . . .

About 9.30. A.M. Tues. Oct. 3rd. 1899.
Dorchester. Mass. . . .

Miss Wellington . . . wants me to come back in the spring—in the fall—in the summer to visit her mother. Says she'll get me *more* money next time. It is pure love and discipleship. Too good for this world? That is the way people *are* I tell you—lots of 'em. Just live so as to find 'em, that's all. . . .

Hingham. Mass.
8.15 or so. A.M. Wed. Oct. 4th. 99.

Here I am at Martha's. They are all glad to see me except her mother—she never did like me much (Nor I her.) . . .

I think one reason I like the Blackwell's is because they are serving society with all their hearts—according to their lights; and their home is only a means to an end.

That is what I want ours to be. A place of real beauty, of a high degree of healthful comfort, but always with a sense of open country beyond. Not that heavy-lidded finality which so oppresses me in most of 'em. You see they have no other aim in life—"this life" as they call it.

I wonder if you are going to find it unrestful—the kind of a home I shall make.

I am not afraid of it, for, to my mind, though you have not thought out and consciously accepted the position as I have, your whole life is really on the same basis. You love to serve, and do, every chance you get. I never feel you as any check to noblest living, and I think you are quite convincible by truth and logic. Meanwhile your healthy quiet nature is a great rest to me.

You are heavenly to be so patient with me—about the children. If I have any—and I hope it may be so—at least one—and if I *provide* right care and training; and if I influence and inspire and am loved and followed to good ends—you at any rate will not call me "an unnatural mother!" I may be a new variety— but not necessarily a monster. . . .

But we must be very careful about our home—its running mechanism I mean. At first I think we'd better "meal out"—till I get used to things. Then we'll see. . . .

9.15 or so. Sat. Oct. 7th. 1899.
Dorchester. Mass. . . .

Glad you're reading [Lester] Ward. I should so like to! but I can't. That *dynamic* sense is what we want to get—that humanity is a *process*. . . .

If only I can make *you* happy dear—as a husband ought to be.

I am so hopelessly unfit for the old wife and mother role—and yet I need you so!

It's an awfully hard position for you—no one but myself will ever know the heroism it takes for you to marry me. But I know. You have made life over for me dear. . . .

9.30. A.M. Sun. Oct. 8th. 1899.
Dorchester. Mass. . . .

I've had a new idea—The sense of justice is in ethics, exactly what our muscular balancing power is in physics. We become socially conscious of other persons *as part of us* (not intellectually conscious yet—that subconscious social recognition I so often find at work); and we *feel their might.* The better organized a society, more highly organized, more socialized and therefore more widely individualized, the wider and deeper is our sense of justice.

Maybe that don't mean much to you. Maybe I haven't caught the idea well yet—or clothed it well; but to me it was a distinct new perception—the kind I love to have. . . .

9.10 or so. A.M. Mon. Oct. 9th '99.
Dorchester, Mass. . . .

I dreamed about you last night—hungrily.

Don't forget to make love to me once in a while by letter—you see it[']s all I have. Your philosophic policy of repression is all very well from your point of view; but not fattening to me. . . .

I am trying all the time to keep steady and peaceful—not to fret at my persistent limitations—to be willing to be weak. And I want so much to do everything I can for my body—as the only way to help my poor head. I'm beginning to do a few gymnastics at night— rather perfunctorily, but hoping to make it a habit. . . .

I wonder if learning to be patient with my own limitations is what makes me so patient with the world—not bad practice if so. . . .

. . . 9.30 P.M. nearly; My room.
Oct. 9th. 99—
Dorchester. . . .

It is so good to have you mine even to think about. Because you see if you loved another woman I couldn't even think about you as mine and I should miss it. Thinking is *realler* to me than having I really believe. When I have you in my arms I have to stop and *think* that it is so—try to make myself realize it.

You see I have always tried to live oblivious to what was happening, and comforted by what I had in my mind. Now that nice things happen I find it hard to change. . . .

. . . 9.30 P.M. Oct. 10th. 99.
Dorchester. Mass. . . .

. . . I found such a good letter when I got home tonight—such a lovely letter. Makes me feel nice all over—as if I had been kissed. You dear thing. You are so good. It makes me feel as if I was young and pretty—to have you talk so to me!

I read it before dinner, and then was so friendly and pleasant all the evening! They supposed it was my natural demeanor—but it wasn't. It was just you—you, who makes me nice. . . .

11.35 or so. Wed. Oct. 11th. 1899. . . .

. . . I'm happy because you love me. And because I've got *two* dear new letters to tell me so. You're so good not to be cross with me when I tease for more.

You see my lifelong conviction that I was not lovable nor ever to be loved—deeply and lastingly that is—is not to be overthrown by three years of even your tenderness.

The assumption that people are good to me because they think they ought to be, seems always more reasonable than that [they] do truly want me.

There are times when the vivid recognition that you *do* love me floods my whole consciousness. ——— Ah! That feels good. Then I feel like the rest of the world and hold my head up. I wish I could hold the feeling! But it cools and dives and deadens and slips away. Then—hungering for it—I bother you for further "testimonials." It is not that I question the *fact*—but I want to feel the *feeling*. . . .

You needn't fancy that people will not lay all my progress to your credit—because they will. The world is too seriously convinced of the advantage of being married—especially to a woman—to be easily fooled. They will say—"There now! See this woman! She was an erratic girl—her first marriage sobered and steadied her. Then when she tried to live alone she got into dreadful trouble. Some desultory struggles but no real achievements. Now as soon as she falls properly in love everything begins to come right. She

gets publishers, writes a successful book (with his help) and grows perceptibly sweeter and wiser. After her second marriage—with the background of
a Happy Home and a Kind Husband, she becomes really a decent member
of society. Ah! It takes a man to manage a woman. 'Twas a tremendous
undertaking for this young man—few would have cared to try it—but he
has really made that woman over!"

That's what they'll say; and so will the biographers. And they are quite
right. It is the blessed peace of knowing I am loved that has made me
better. . . .

You'd enjoy seeing my present series of evening gymnastics. Just in my
skin I hop around; doing high kicking, swinging one leg in circles while
balancing firmly on the other—forward backward and sideways; doing the
triceps movement on the floor—touching my fingers to my toes straight-
kneed—singly, and together; standing still to the hips and waving my body
around like a tree in the wind—lots of things. I must be as well and strong
and beautiful as I possibly can—for your sake my husband. Because this
poor little property is yours— all yours. . . .

. . . c/o H. B. Blackwell
9. A.M. Thus. Oct. 12th. 1899.
Boutwell Ave. Dorchester. Mass. . . .

. . . had a visit from my little adorer Miss Wellington. She has sent me
carnations—brought me violets, and this time brought me a rubber ball! So
we played ball gaily, and I did not tell her I had one already. . . .

Say dear—in behind all these things that people are going to think and
say; and our own amusing efforts to prove our several inferiorities and the
other's superiority,—behind all that—we are two grown people who think
we can live happily together. . . .

And, while many will disapprove no one is directly injured by our
marrying that I see. And many will be benefitted if it works well.

So I'm just going to stop considering those other people and their never
so righteous indignation. I love you, dear man, and you love me, and
that's enough. . . .

9.40 about. . . .

. . . I consider your running commentary on the batch of correspondence
I sent you as distinctly good literature—pleasant reading. How much arduous labor, spurred by my reproaches, you have spent in acquiring this art I
do not dare to think but the result is noble. . . .

. . . 9.20 A.M. Friday Oct. 13th. 1899. . . .

. . . [Received a letter] from Mdme. Schmall of Paris, an English born, medically educated, prominent "feministe" of wide reputation. A most rational dignified letter, asking to translate my beloved book, which she says "seems to me so remarkably calculated to do good amongst . . . intelligent men & women that I most earnestly desire to see it become known in France." Oddly enough she refers me to Dr. Elizabeth Blackwell of England, who she says I shall probably know as the sister in law of Lucy Stone. (Alice was naturally pleased at that.) . . .[16]

Isn't it all going beautifully! I am getting a world hearing by my beloved book, and that promptly. I *knew* it was a valuable theory. And the fact that nobody else ever seemed to recognize its importance never altered my views of it appreciably. . . .

And O how wonderfully good it is that now all this is rising around me I am going to have peace and joy and loving care *at home!* My precious love—don't you see how indispensable you are to me. . . .

And if Katharine loves me too! You will help me to woo her—won't you dear. I want her to love me for myself—not just because I am her mother.

If I have you both I shall be proud and glad indeed. And even if she does not greatly love me—I have *You.* And I care most for that. . . .

Do not *worry* nor *over-work* this winter dear. If you owe me any service it is not in money; but in the value of your personal love and care. . . .

Keep your health for me—your patience and courage—we shall have money enough to live together somehow.

Later, when you earn more I'll let you even up all you like. And always remember that I'm likely to have long spells of helplessness. Then you can do for me and I'll gladly depend on you, my own darling. . . .

9.30 A.M. Sat. Oct. 14th [1899]

. . . I look forward with absolute pleasure to playing games with you. There's a thing we are both fond of and both good at—(it means about the same thing!) And I shall have a permanent "partner" right in the house. Katharine is good material too. And I can play games agreeably when I am able to do little else. We will have lots and lots of games—all kinds and sizes. . . .

. . . c/o Mr. H. B. Blackwell.
9 A.M. Sun. Oct. 15th. 1899.
Boutwell Ave. Dorchester Mass. . . .

The work book opens and opens. I begin to see how many of my big ideas I can put into it. I won't be stingy—I'll just pour—there will be another crop for the next one!

That big "Soul & Body" thing goes in—wasn't I telling you this before?—how the Human spirit finds its body in what we make you know; and so the intimate relation between our work in its completed form and our psychic progress. . . .

I expect I shall be dribbling Book on you all winter—that's part of your Cross, young man! But O my *dear*—think how I shall enjoy it when we have a slowly growing little library along these lines, and I have *YOU*—you who can answer a thousand questions "without looking" and know how to look up a million; you, who will give me the aid of your scholarly criticism and cultivated taste—!

My "later works" will show it you may be sure. I shall be inoculated with a college education! You blessed blessed treasure! I just want to run and tuck my head under your arm and hug you *tight*. . . .

Later. . . .

Perhaps they will let me have Kate this winter!!! They may be able to go abroad and not able to take her! Then we'd have a nice winter getting acquainted and doing things—I could teach her some—and then you, poor man, would have to marry your wife's relations! I should be sorry about that—but you could bear it, couldn't you? . . .

I'm rather meanly hoping they can't take her! I begin to want her awfully. . . . If it comes your way to get a little in touch with painting and drawing people, I want it for bait for Katharine!

I am going to woo that damsel with all arts I can compass—really plan for it—my idea of "a good villain" you know. And you will be a magnificent ally! Bless your loving heart and wise head. . . .

Just beyond Dunkirk Ohio
Lake Shore train
9.15 A.M. Friday Oct. 20th [1899]. . . .

O but I do feel fine! You are the biggest part of it, of course—you Blessing! Then I had a letter from Kate to start off with; a book of a letter—written from day to day for a week or more. And as full of starling adventure as Robinson Crusoe. Also some little pictures. Also much joy over the things I sent her, and the money. Also a gratifying expression of affection. You shall have the letter soon—but you must return it again—I can't spare it. Bless the dear child! You see as I "limber up" in learning to love you so well, I also learn to love her better—it comes more natural— I am thawing out all around. You did it. You have made me sweeter and happier and better every way—I told you you would!

So between the thought of you and the thought of Kate I bask in smiles. . . .

Kate says they "may spend the winter in California," and wants to take me to Las Casitas, her beloved mountain resort. I am so glad that her youth is spent in that lovely country—Health, pleasure, and beauty. . . .

Now my dear—don't do anything in your business on my account that you wouldn't do if I wasn't there. On the other hand—if I am so situated that you can *better* afford to wait than you could otherwise, why do it. I want you to gradually acquire just the kind of business you want—it will pay in the end. Your kind gets what it wants—give it time. And if I can be of some use in these years, I'm not above having you keep elaborate accounts and paying it all back when you are an eminent lawyer in the prime of life and I am a feeble old lady past working!

For all my brag I haven't much confidence in my moneymaking power, and what I have may fail anytime and your turn come to do it all. I'll let you all right! Count on me as a kind of partner (sleeping partner?) quite willing to bank on your future. . . .

"A Wide House to Lodge a Friend"
Monroe St. Toledo. Ohio
3.50 P.M. Friday—

Behold me under the roof of the hospitable Joneses once more, serene in my room. . . .[17]

This is a fine new comfortable house. I've just thought that one reason the good Mayor's conscience pricks him because of it, is *Heredity*. He is of working people—and not used to dwell in marble halls.

Two or three generations would ease it I guess. . . .

Dear me! How nice it will be when I have you to show things to and talk 'em over with. Dare say you won't agree half the time, but then I don't mind that as much as I used to. And you continue to be disputatious and say things you shouldn't—why I can make you stop. I know an easy way. Specially if I have on my little grey silk gown! You'll succumb then when you are sat on! I am going to develope a wardrobe of a surprising nature. One ordinary, fashionable street dress; and the rest of 'em silky things, plain and huggable. I'll have long cloaks to wear outside, and be renowned for my "distinction" in dressing. . . .

. . . 2439 Monroe St. Toledo. Ohio
c/o Mr. Samuel M. Jones
12.10 noon. Sat. Oct. 21st. 1899. . . .

Now you habitually depreciate yourself and are inclined to anticipate evil and be discouraged. You hang on all right to the bitter end—all the more bravely because you don't hope for much. But inspite of your fine qualities and splendid preparation you don't get on as fast as much inferior men. And even your friends who know your ability don't seem to be as confident in you as they ought to be. . . .

What I want you to do is to deliberately set to work to alter your habit of mind. . . . It is as easy to do as to alter a habit of body—takes time and perseverance, and a wise care in development. And by the way there is a connection between the two—you will find a high chest makes it easier to feel proud.

It will take you two or three years of course—perhaps more before you make a complete change—but you can see it grow within a year. . . .

Now you are an exceptionally well-endowed young lawyer. You have splendid qualities, and education. Also experience. You are sure in any case of making a place for yourself in time. But you will make it quicker—much quicker—if you make a better "approach."

Now you know the attitude of self-confident power—of absolute assurance in success.

Very well—take that attitude every morning when you wake up—every time when you think of it—just exactly as you straighten up your spine and expand your chest when you think of it. Please don't think I'm silly. You may say, "That won't alter the facts." *But that's exactly what it will do.* Why any rascally promoter—church debt raiser—confidence man—who is successful—unconsciously works on this law.

There is no reason on earth good people should not use it too. It makes things happen. Things are going to happen anyway, but how and where and when depends on a lot of things; and *the way you feel* is one of them. Make up your mind just what you want to be. Then *feel as if you were.* Then . . . *act* as you feel.

I mean all this very seriously dear, and for life.

Take a new kind of grip on it. You'll be glad always if you do—and so shall I.

If you want a reason from my side of the case it is this—it will make more difference to me how you *feel* than how much money we have or anything else. I am pitifully sensitive to other people's depression—the more so in proportion to their nearness. And I am growing so close to you that your feelings will be mine. So you'll simply have to keep your spirits up—for my sake Mr. Pickwick! . . .

2439 Monroe St. Toledo. Ohio.
. . . c/o Mr. Samuel M. Jones
8.45 A.M. Sunday October 22nd. '99. . . .

. . . I speak in Golden Rule Hall this afternoon. So I won't write you much today. . . . Do you see the *Outlook?* Read the last one—those two things on the Boers; and "The Forgotten Woman." It's a good number.

I begin to realize that I can read a good deal more than I used. It does not seem to me so much, and I have more appetite for it. That's good. To feel again some little sense of *horizon* and *range*—not just grope from page to page and feel tired at that. . . .

I think you are a most highly desirable person to marry me. It seems rough on you—very—but from my point of view it is lovely. You see if there have to be some women to do my kind of work, it stands to reason that they can't marry as ordinary women do, and that ordinary men can't marry them. Then the poor things have either got to live single, or some hero and martyr must rise up to meet the occasion. That's you. How you ever brought yourself to do it I don't see—but you seem to have done so. . . .

. . . c/o Mayor Jones.
2439 Monroe St. Toledo. Ohio
9. A.M. Mon. Oct. 23rd. 1899. . . .

. . . [I] went forth to speak in Golden Rule Hall. Big crowd, and much interest.

Mayor Jones returned in the evening, and there are these new developments. He wants me to do some campaign work during the next week. . . .

I really haven't any reason to refuse, and there are some reasons for doing it—so I'm going to try a little I guess. . . .

I feel rather halfhearted about this business, but it seems to be on the books. . . . And the talking I have to do is simply my own lines of preaching. So consider me as "on the stump" for next week! I wiggled out of it last year, but this year it seems practically unavoidable. . . .

8.30 A.M. Tuesday. Oct. 24th. '99. . . .

. . . No wonder I can be loving to other people and they think I am nice—with you close beside me. They think I'm wonderful to be so happy, and I feel like an impostor. When I have you in plain sight—they'll say "Huh! It's no credit to her! Any woman would be happy with such a husband." . . .

about 9 A.M.. Mrs. Sewall's library.
. . . Indianapolis, Indiana.
Wed. Oct. 25th 1899. . . .

Poor Br. Jones is very miserable in his house, and it does not add to their domestic happiness much, for she likes it. I think he's wrong—but I doubt if he'll see it. He is Mayor yet, and is running for Governor with a fair show—alarming to the old party men a good deal. It is not Jones—it is the thing he stands for. He can't do much to alter things, in either office, but in voting for him people show what they want. And he is immensely popular. . . .

. . . Mrs. Sewall's Library
Thurs. near . . . 9. A.M.
Oct. 26th. 1899. . . .

. . . [Katharine] is a splendid creature I think, just the kind I admire. To see her *do* things! Catch pigeons—drive cows—get water—what you please. I particularly like it because it is what I used to be like myself, at that age, and it gives me hope that she will be somewhere within [my] range by and by—something of my own kind after all.

My humanitarianism came later. . . .

. . . I set for to visit Mrs. Sewall's school. It appears . . . that she is a woman after my own heart. As a happy young wife she started a girls' school *because she wanted to*—the real thing; and now is glad of it on other grounds, her husband being dead. He taught a Classical Boys' school—but later sold it and *joined hers*—a fine man that.

First to "let" his wife teach, because she wanted to, then to recognize the growing importance of her work and join it. It's a fine school—from kindergarten to College preparation.[18]

It has a nice gymnasium. When we entered it I perceived my adored travelling rings; and, mounting a chair, proceeded to sally forth upon them. . . .

[In the evening] the lecture What Work Is. It's a large subject but I am getting it more in hand. All good practice for the book. A nice club—men & women. Some discussion, not much of value. The most interesting response was from a black-haired earnest youth whom I had noticed as listening intently. He really saw something of the bigness of the new point of view—of what it is going to mean to the world. I liked his "feel" very much. Come to find out—too late to speak to him again—it was Booth Tarkington. "The Gentleman from Indiana." I am so glad to have seen him. And I can write and tell him how much I think of his book. . . .

It was a pretty solid lecture, and a rather heavy audience—stiff work.

However—just to have made connection with one of our strong young authors was worth while. . . .

You dear boy. Pegging away there in the big city, and not thinking a thousandth part as much of yourself as you ought to think! You are a man of a clear fair well balanced mind uncommonly well stocked with information and trained in careful use. You have both general knowledge and special training in your profession—lots of 'em. . . .

You owe the state good service. You are a good servant. You will do better service by recognizing how good a servant you are. . . .

Now among your weaknesses is a too quick and sensitive reflection of others' feelings about you. (I have it too—an awful nuisance it's been to me!) . . .

Now you fail of your best service, because . . . you sort of "scrooge" under it. You don't *hold yourself* right. That's the thing I'm after with you all the time. And I recognize right now the danger of my advising you. It is dreadful to have a person near one—dear to one—and feel them critical. I love you as you are darling. I take you as you are and am proud of you. You know that. But now that we are a good ways apart—perhaps I can be of some use in this way without hurting you now, or our happiness later. . . .

I'm sure I don't know why I am possessed to preach to you so ardently just now. I guess it means two things. One that my current is on—which always means joy and power to me. And one that you have grown so blessedly near that I *can* speak to you with full freedom—as I could not even a year ago. . . .

. . . c/o Mayor Jones
9.25 A.M. Fri. Oct. 27th. '99
2439 Monroe St. Toledo. Ohio. . . .

. . . I calmly called on Mr. Booth Tarkington to tell him what I thought of him!

. . . [He had] dressed in wild haste (evidently much overcome by my visit;) and we sat down in a convenient park, before a fine sunset, and had a good talk. He is a youth of promise. He seemed greatly pleased with my approval. (James Whitcomb Riley is visiting there—ill with bronchitis, and sent his regards to me by one of Mrs. Sewall's friends the day before. He remembered the day we went to Joaquin Miller's together with my . . . friend Miss Knapp. I was pleased with his remembrance.) And it was a real pleasure to talk to this young novelist. Have you read his book—The Gentleman from Indiana? . . . I love it for its splendid Americanism. It made me feel better than any book I had read for a long time. . . .

. . . c/o Mrs. S.M. Jones—
2439 Monroe St. Toledo. Ohio.
9.15 A.M. Sat. Oct. 28th. 1899. . .

. . . It's no wonder I love the world so. To live so wide and find so many friends—so many open homes. The wildest dreams of socialism are only what I live in—to move freely among the people—to be loved and cared for everywhere—to ask for nothing and get much—that has been my life for near five years.

. . . Yes, Jones is cutting considerable ice. He has a chance of really winning. And in any case he proves the people's wish for something more than they have now.

If he don't win I hope the Democrats will. But my notion of a political speech is not pitching into either of the other parties but showing what good things Jones stands for. . . .

. . . c/o Mrs. S.M. Jones
2439 Monroe St. Toledo. Ohio.
9. A.M. Monday. Oct. 30. '99. . . .

. . . Jones is doing great work here, really. Of course we don't really think he'll get it; but he's ripping up things pretty generally. . . .

. . . About 9.40 P.M. Mon. Oct. 30th '99. . . .

You are an angel to take my preaching in such good part. But then you always were an angel anyway.

I wish *not* to preach to you. It is very dangerous work between lovers. I want you to love me—to have me for your wife, not for your teacher. And I do so worshipfully love you just as you are that it seems absurd to think of any fault in you. But this is a thing which does not affect our relations at all—it is between you and the rest of your life; and for your own dear dear sake I want you to outgrow and work off the limitations—innocent qualities in themselves—only bad in their interaction—which keep you from your own place. You can keep on being proud all right—as proud as you like—the prouder the better. I'm proud—prouder than folks imagine—in some ways.

But the sensitiveness and over-modesty are qualities you can train out of in large measure. Not wholly, ever—but you can *act independently of them.* . . . I am not ambitious for you in any sense of profit and advantage. I've often told you that you are too good to be rich and I'm glad of it. But you will not be happy unless you are working up to your full capacity, and recognized somewhere near it. We all want that.

You can easily formulate to yourself how a man should act in a given case—who was not sensitive and bashful—and then you can act that way in spite of the shrieking protest of those estimable qualities. They stop hollering in time! . . .

. . . 9.35 A.M. Tues. Oct. 31st '99
2439 Monroe St. Toledo. Ohio. . . .

Just a word more about my prescription. You know I've worked out some real practical moral gymnastics—things I'm sure of.

Now what you want to do is not in specific and prominent action, but *in modification of temperament.* . . .

There's no danger of your growing selfish and grasping—you can practice for quite some time before you tip the scales that way. But because your natural mental habit is to underrate yourself, you now want conscientiously to *overrate* yourself. . . .

It is pure brain gymnastics. It grows easy and natural with time; and it takes time—less as you go on! . . .

I hope you truly don't mind—don't think me presuming and officious and dictatorial and all sorts of horrid things. . . .

What I'm working on most now is to offset the intensity—almost ferocity of the Blazing Reformer with an ever-growing calmness and lovingness. I *know* that the largest wisdom is patient with all things, and that, conversely, to be patient with all things leads toward the largest wisdom. I am working daily as I want you to work, dear—always trying to make the machine a little better—that the Power may have more way. . . .

. . . c/o Mrs. Wm. C. Dow
473 Orchard St. Chicago. . .
10 A.M. Fri. Nov. 3rd. 1899. . . .

Do read in Nov. *Cos[mopolitan]* Olive Schreiner's fine paper on the woman question. Her power as a writer is great—but I don't see that after all she is saying more than I do. But she says it splendidly and it "carries" far and wide. Let the good work go on! . . .

Mrs. Dow tells me sad news of Mrs. Campbell. It appears that her reported "accident" is a delusion, that she has been temporarily affected in her mind. Naturally it has stopped her work, and her friends are trying to do something for her. How glad I shall be to help! If she's going to be that way I can't afford to have her with me—my own head is too shaky; but I can do things for her. . . .

. . . c/o Mrs. Wm. C. Dow
about 10 A.M. Sunday. Nov. 5th. 1899.
473 Orchard St. Chicago Ill. . . .

[*A number of letters have complained about a recent delay in receiving
Houghton's letters.*]
I can't write much either—'cause it makes me feel bad. Guess I'm a bit
tired among other things, and that's why I feel blue partly.

That is due to the presence of this unruly infant in the house. His sharp
high voice, his unreasonableness, and the futile behavior of his grandparents
annoy me exceedingly. It is astonishing how little grasp of the first principles
of practical psychology people have.

The contact between this little soul and theirs is ineffably clumsy and
erroneous. It makes me hot to write my book about children. I can see with
vivid clearness just how this bright eager child has been injured, deeply
injured, by his most loving parents and their concentrated care. Well—the
very sensitiveness which makes it so unpleasant is what gives me power to
see and do differently—so I won't complain. . . .[19]

Then I look forward with eager hope to a dear little boy that may be—
and pray to be able to save him from at least some of the pains and errors
of childhood. . . .

Do you see what an international force Olive Schreiner Crownright is
becoming? Isn't it fine! It gives me great hope and high ambition. "O may
I join that choir invisible!" . . .

1.35 or 40 A.M.
Chicago & Northwestern **Station**
Mon. Nov. 6th. 1899. . . .

[*Having not heard from Houghton recently, she worried that he had
been in an accident.*]
. . . It's awful. I'm learning how to be all the kinds of fool that most
women are. . . . Makes me kind of angry too. Seems a weakness. To be so
tangled up in another person. . . .

. . . Under clothes too tight to do gymnastics in seem to me worthy of
taking off on such occasions. Yes, I do mine in my own skin— that's part
of the fun. It is so good to be bare! . . .

Wed. Nov. 8th.
8.22 P.M.. . . .
Going to Sioux City. . . .

[*The letter complains about "yes dear" mamas who fail to check the rude-
ness of young children.*]

. . . Kate was taught to consider other people by the prompt and simple method of getting no consideration herself if she didn't.

If she had spoken to me as rudely as Dow does I should *not* have spoken to her— should have "treated her with studied coldness"— should have promptly made her realize the impossibility of such conduct. . . .

8.23 A.M. Thurs. Nov. 9th. '99. . . .

Do you know, this last week or so, I sort of lost hold of our happy love—lost the sweet certainty of it—had that recurrent horrid feeling that you only held on from a sense of duty. I've suffered from it off and on from the beginning (our beginning) and you don't ever take much pains to remove it apparently. Then I say miserably to myself—"He can't! He knows it's so. He can't lie to me—he just keeps still." And then I *am* miserable. . . .

Well anyhow I feel better now—that little period of doubt is passing. . . .

10.40 A.M. . . . for
Sheldon. Iowa
Friday Nov. 10th. 1899.
Still at Sioux City—delayed. . . .

. . . was escorted to the Unitarian Church. It is Rev. Mary Safford's church, and under her fine influence has been a vitalizing influence in the town. She has given it up for missionary work throughout the state. . . . They tell some good stories in this land of women ministers. A little boy, going as usual one day, perceived Rev. Mr. Somebody in the pulpit. "Where's the preacher?" he said to his mother. "Why that's the preacher," said she. "That! Why that's a man!" Creatures of habit. By and by we'll call it "effeminate" for a man to preach—eh? It does seem peculiarly suited to a woman's nature—the pastoral service.

My lecture was "Mother House & Child" again; and this time it went well—was a smooth easy stream, with effective heights and hollows in delivery. An elaborate lady who teaches "Elocution" expressed herself in terms of exalted admiration as to the modulated music of my voice. . . .

[*After lengthy calculations, Gilman decided that her annual income might be around $4,000 per year.*]

. . . And all of it is simply my own natural dearly loved reforming! Don't have to do a thing but "relieve my mind!"

Now if only you are happy. That is the main thing. I begin to feel safer about Katharine. Guess I can endear myself to her considerably this winter—I shall try. Great plot—the Traitorous and Seductive Mother—secretly wooing her Child! "Alienating her affections." My natural bent of plotting villainy can come out strong. (What a delightful lot of "Good Villain" stories I can write when I get at it! Nice book it would make! Come! Why not! A Stetson story book would sell well I know. More income! Your property is waxing fat and kicking. If I had a big business . . . publishing and so on— would you consider it ignominious to be my manager. . . .

[*The letters continue calculations as to possible sources of income.*]

You are such a dear boy to write to. Do you truly enjoy my everlasting babble? I just sit down and tell you everything. . . .

Such a highly superior and delightful sort of man. I do wonder why he hasn't been et up before!

8.25 or so. A.M. Sat. Nov. 11th. '99
Spencer, Iowa.
Room in Hotel. . . .

. . . And to think that I've been in love with you these three years and haven't told a soul! It's because I had you to talk to you see! Somebody that is interested—that loves me— that really cares! . . .

[*She lectured on "Public Ethics."*]

. . . But somehow it didn't go very well. The night before it was *fine*— and just as easy! But this one was rather labored and felt comparatively ineffective.

Afterward I was told that the town has just been having a severe "revival!" You know my views on ethics. I *was* hitting a stone wall.

I came back here very much depressed in spirits—feeling like "a naughty girl"—had to reason with myself severely to feel that I was good for anything. . . .

. . . You have lifted and cleared away the fogs and clouds and puckers and perplexities which have always been a part of my life. More and more often I see daylight—the clean calm daylight of our sweet home life together. . . .

. . . 10.35 or so. A.M. Sun. Nov. 12th. '99
473 Orchard St. Chicago. Ill. . . .

. . . You are right about the relations. Go ahead and tell 'em all. . . .

As I've said before you'll get the worse of it—they'll pitch into you mercilessly I've no doubt. You are wise in giving them time to get over it. . . .

Anyhow they can't help themselves and they'll get used to it in time. . . .

It's all very well for you to deny that you are throwing yourself away just because I am apparently likely—that's all—to earn more than you. You take the chances of having an elderly invalid on your hand for life—and maybe children too. Marriage is not just money.

A man wants other things in a wife—things I haven't got I'm sorry to say. Now you have the real qualities that I want, and the lack of wealth is no figure at all—doesn't enter my calculations. If I were young and healthy and handsome and fresh and handy with children and everything your wife ought to be, I'd be content to marry you on what you've got—and keep house for you on it! Could, too. My real genius is for living on nothing and making good dinners out of it.

No, the only thing you lack is the thing I don't care for at all. But I lack lots of the best essentials. . . .

I have a brilliant idea. I will confine my contribution to the family to exactly yours—(always providing I have that much). I can find plenty of use for what else I may earn, if any, and people won't know if it is little or much. We can live so simply and plainly—so within your means—that people can't say you are being supported. Then as you earn more, which you're sure to, I'll let you do the most. Especially if we have children.

Nobody will wonder that I take care of my previous one. I should think we might "save your face" that way. I am sorry about it. I appreciate how trying your position is. That's the worst of it. In the first place you are heroically marrying a woman that most men wouldn't touch—middleaged, not strong, divorced, with a grown child, and—so on! All of this of course you protest against and won't have mentioned. Then my only redeeming feature—almost—that I shall not be an expense to you, and perhaps be a real help—that redounds to your discredit and acute anguish of mind!

It is a shame. I shan't blame you *one bit* if you want to drop it dear— not an atom. . . .

If you feel that it is too serious an undertaking—that the pain is greater than the pleasure—there is still time to drop it. . . .

Remember that you can do me no greater wrong than to marry me with anything less than your full heart. . . .

You see, if you do marry me, you want to have it out with yourself once and for all on this money question. It is evident that you haven't yet.

It mustn't make trouble between us afterward. . . .

I won't even be loving in this letter—just leave it for you to think out. . . .

. . . c/o Mrs. Wm. C. Dow
473 Orchard St. Chicago. Ill.
9.30 A.M. Mon. Nov. [13th]. 99

Dear Heart—

What is the matter? You are unhappy about something and are not telling me. Is it big or little? Can't you tell me about it? Can't I help you? . . .

Are you getting perplexed and uncertain about our relation? Do you feel mixed up and sort of guilty and angry—tangled as it were? Fond of me all the time, and yet full of misgivings, and *angry at the perplexity.* . . .

Do not dare to marry me unless you are satisfied in your own mind. It is never too late to change—it could be done even afterward but we should grieve at that. It can be done now, and no one beside ourselves need ever know.

If you feel a weight on your conscience about it—bear it as other men have. You are not the first man who has loved unwisely. . . .

I know how far we have gone—but it doesn't count compared with the tremendous sanction and weight of marriage. And no sense of obligation is equal to the obligation of perfect truth between us—truth in act as in word.

For my own part, knowing from the first the full discrepancy between us, suffering and struggling over it these three years, I have slowly and painfully grown into the full acceptance of you as my husband. I know you— know your noble strength, know your weakness—love you all over and through faults and all. I expect nothing of you that you cannot give—and take from you with grateful joy what you can give—which is all the world to me.

I feel more solid and square about it than I ever thought it possible to feel again—than I ever did even in my first youth.

Then I entered a relation in doubt and confusion—because I had said I would—and meaning to do my duty—thinking I could. Do not commit that Sin—and bring back on my devoted head all the sorrow I brought to the unhappy man I married first! That would be too dreadful—it cannot be. . . .

Do not marry me unless you are sure. . . .

. . . c/o Mrs. Wm. C. Dow.
473 Orchard St. Chicago Ill.
9.45 A.M. Tues. Nov. 14th. '99 . . .

Some way your letter of this morning sounds a little more contented— more reconciled to your hard lot in marrying a woman with a prospective income. I think it is pathetic—and funny—that the only solace to my poor pride—my growing fame and fortune, should act as a disadvantage to your eyes! How could I hold my head up at all if I came to you as a broken down old thing, distrusted and ill paid. My personal deficiencies are enough to keep me humble without that. And now that these three years have lifted my head a little, . . . why lo and behold you don't like it! I think it's kinder hard. Don't you see dear how much at a disadvantage I am beside you? Try and feel like a woman for a moment—put yourself in their place. You know what a woman wants to bring a man—a boundless wholesouled love, absolutely and primarily his own—all his own.

I haven't that.

A beautiful fresh body to be to him a garden of delight—his first and always and only.

I haven't that.

A long life of beautiful service and devotion, given wholly to his interests.

I haven't that.

A rich motherhood which shall surround him with happy children.

I have a slim poor chance only.

I can only give you a share of what's left of a life—not the whole of a new one.

I can only give you a divided love—I love God—the world—my work as well as I love you.

I have so little to offer—so pathetically little.

And because I am so poor it is granted me at least to hold a place in popular esteem, and to be able not to drag on your growing career with heavy expenses—to save my face.

And then you don't like it! Do be fair, dear.

You *know* that as man to woman you have all the advantage—that I have never been able to put on any flirtatious airs and feel as if I were granting a favor.

You feel a man's natural desire to give me things as men do—and I—O my dear—do you not see what poignant grief and shame it is to a woman to have no woman's gifts to give!

. . . Do not begrudge me the one thing that has reconciled me to it—the only poor straw of worth that I have to cling to—to say I'm not much good personally—but—but other people love me and I can help pay bills. Dear—it is *so little*—for a woman! . . .

Now for your letters.

Jones is now a back runner. Well, "all good work counts." It was a useful campaign. And New York as usual is bound by the majority, which is right. We can not expect a city with so immense a low class European population now to show it in the government. . . .

I can clear up all that child case to your satisfaction I'm sure. The only main difference is that I substitute the *real cause* of the action for mere parental authority—they have to behave just the same! And I substitute a simple and easily appreciated system of retaliation for the solemn and arbitrary "punishment" of the old way.

It is to surround the child with a flexible but constant pressure in terms that he understands, instead of the rigid and often varying pressure of arbitrary authority.

I've made a good phrase for it lately—"The child should act from perception rather than from instruction."

And it's our business to furnish him with "perceptible" causes. Even this little unruly Dow is getting quite rational with me—because I'm rational with him. Kind, but firm and *fair*. Fair to his own admission. . . .

(This is the letter that says I'm your darling little girl. Which remark I have kissed many times.) . . .

I had a fine time yesterday at the Englewood Woman's Club. Lectured on *W&E*. Went well—audience pleased. Got $45.50. . . .

. . . c/o Mrs. Wm. C.Dow—
473 Orchard St.
About 9 A.M. Chicago.
On C & N.W. train for Fond du Lac. Wis.
Wed. Nov. 15th 1899. . . .

I can give some money to Margaret for Basil, too. And some to dear Mrs. Campbell, if she needs it. Did I tell you her friends had been trying to raise some money for her? And that her numerous "adopted" sons had proved "unavailable" for the purpose. But I never shall forget that she fed me all winter in S[an] F[ranciso]—her work brought in our only steady income—she paid for our food *and cooked it*—in real illness and awful discouragement and intense personal suffering which I did not dream of then. She is the bravest creature—and the lovingest and forgivingest I ever knew. Bless her.

When you are able to take care of me I'll let you (maybe!)—cause "every true woman wishes to be supported by the man she loves;"—and I'll spend my money on other folks. They'll be plenty to do for. . . .

Can't you get along with the money idea better by seeing that it is what men in general have got to come to soon—unless they carefully adjust their love affairs to ladies of inferior earning capacity! And that in neither woman nor man is that the measure of merit in marriage. Some of the best men in the world earn but little (for instance You!) and yet they are far better to marry than lots of "successful" men.

Of course it's hard to break down these mountainous old prejudices— but they've got to go someday. It seems particularly easy in your case because you have all the other advantages—which fact weights heavily on me. . . .

5.10 P.M. Thurs. Nov. 16th. 99.
Mrs. Dow's— . . . .

. . . A stack of letters. Your two blessed ones—makes me feel quite "married" again—I was preparing my mind for the single life!!! And think of this—a Russian gent, Mr. Andrew Kamensky M.E. writes to inform me that he has translated my "epoch making book"—to be published in Dec.— and will I kindly send on some autobiographical data for the preface!! I'll set S & M on his track. Maybe we have no copyright with Russia. But it goes to show the power of the book, doesn't it. . . .

. . . Chicago Ill.
Noon. Fri. Nov. 17th. 1899. . . .

. . . I want to suggest something as to "appreciation of property" from my point of view. . . .

I am going up like a rocket at present—but my powers will presently wane, and yours will steadily rise for some thirty years yet—as long as I shall live probably. Your business is a permanent one—you a[re] steadily building a reputation—and your strength—professionally—grows all the time. As I go down you go up. . . .

Honestly—as a mere investment—I marry the kind of man who will take care of me by and by when I need it, though he can't now when I *don't* need it.

Your income will increase and increase—from year to year. If I have to pay the most now you may please yourself by keeping all our accounts and evening up in good time! I'm willing. I'm willing you should pay full half of *our* expenses and two thirds of the children, if any. And if you can't do it now you can later. You shall make it all square, and when you do have more you shall pile me up with bracelets and anklets and such to your heart's content. . . .

You've got enough to pay your board—that's all that's required of you at present. I admit that it's hard on you—real hard. I'm sorry. But it is only temporary—and not one of the *real* troubles.

It's an affliction like those debts of mine—which I *refused to feel*. . . . Take the sex pride out of it—suppose I was just your friend—and could make life pleasanter for you for a hard place—to no loss in the end— wouldn't you let me? . . .

What has kept you back is not lack of ability, but some of those minor personal characteristics you didn't learn to manage soon enough. Two years work at them would have set you five years ahead in professional advancement, I think.

If you weren't so kind to everybody, so considerate—so self-effacing— so—your "faults" are a lot of pesky little angels that get in the way of the machinery! O my dear dear love—you are so *Good!* That is why I love so utterly. You blessed man. Be a little badder some ways. Claim what belongs to you. Do unto yourself as you do to others! The only *real* trouble in all this is that it eats into our happiness. Don't let it dear. Bear it—it is one of the burdens I bring you when I so wish that I might bring only joy! But bear it for my sake. . . .

10.30 A.M. Sat. Nov. 18th '99.
Wisconsin Central R.R. "*Sherry*" Wis.
About 3/5 of the way to Minneapolis. . . .

. . . On arrival at 1st Methodist Church Evanston . . . was impressively greeted and waited upon by elegant Persons clerical and collegiate. Fine big church. Fine house. And, to my surprise, uncommon fine lecture. "Public Ethics" 'twas. I am growing to be quite an orator—I can feel my voice *count* in its handling. It's all as natural as it ever was, . . . but far more impressive. The Theological dignitary who introduced me did it wonderfully well—high praise, but well put. I was quite interested to hear him describe my virtue & ability—didn't know I was so distinguished. And when it was over the *men* flocked up to say how much they liked it—college professors— so impressed they tumbled over their words in trying to tell me how much good it had done them. . . .

. . . **Minneapolis, Minn.**
12.35 Sun. Nov. 19th. 1899. . . .

Lecture in large theatre. Fine audience. Introduced in glowing terms by Mr. Simmons, Unitarian minister. . . . I held forth as best I might; but O! I was tired! Scarce knew what I said or how I said it.

It worked all right though. The papers this morning give fine notices. I'll send 'em tomorrow. And Dr. E's husband—a nice man, says "That woman is all *steel!*" So I guess I didn't *look* tired. . . .

Talk about money! Why you'll *take care of me* lots more than most men have to. They pay the bills, but often their wives keep them going. Now I shall be an awful load on you. I shall expect you to do no end of things for me—things most men don't have to do—and wouldn't.

You get it pretty hard all round. All the discomforts of a home—and no credit for it! Folks thinking you are "living on me"—and I, such a contented little vampire, just living on you! . . .

. . . **10.35 or so. A.M. Mon. Nov. 20th. 1899.**
Chicago & Great Western R.R.
Near Des Moines. Iowa. . . .

. . . I sincerely recommend any one suffering under "a long engagement" to take a lecture trip! Tempers fidget to such an extent that poor Cupid can but run weeping after the train. In these latter days my life revolves itself into a mere blind desire to rest all I can, eat, sleep, and catch trains; all ruled by the Engagement at the end of each day. That must be met, and in as good form as possible. Home and matrimony have become a blur upon the far horizon as it were . . . but Life is a process of going somewhere as fast as I can. I fancy I'm getting a little too tired—but it can't be helped now. I'll "rest up" in Cal.

The enclosed clippings will show you that Minneapolis was pleased even if I was tired; and admiring friends more than corroborate the papers. Guess it was all right. But Evanston was the top notch. I'm particularly glad of that. . . .

But you mustn't speak so disparagingly of yourself dear heart.

Your worth is no more to be measured in money than mine is—and as you know I never had any till I was thirty eight or nine. It's a shame for you to be depressed in spirit by such shallow popular notions. You know I value and honor you for what you *are,* not what you *earn.* And you do *earn*—in the sense of giving value—I shouldn't think so much of you if you couldn't *do the work*—though you had an inherited million. But I feel about you as I used about myself when I gave my work so freely—that I was rich and *could afford to give!* So can you. Calmly and royally giving your labor and knowledge—giving good money's worth—you can afford to wait. And you can count just as surely on getting what belongs to you. It will come—same as mine has. But you mustn't feel poor and as if you couldn't wait till your caravan came. . . . Meanwhile we can be married if you wish, any time next summer that suits our convenience; and, if necessary, we can just board for a while. You can as well board where I am as elsewhere—you've got to live somehow. . . .

. . . Lots of men marry poor and build up. Pity if you can't. Don't be so proud—in that way; and be prouder in others. And all the time remember that I'll call it off if you want to—any minute. . . .

You are "worth" uncounted wealth to me—in real personal value and usefulness. You can pay your own board *anyway.* And your cash value will rise every year. So there. There's only one thing I'm afraid of—that you know. In mercy do not marry me unless it is wholly desirable to you from so much love that you don't mind anything else.

I think dear that one reason it looks dark to you is from your "day to day" theory. You don't measure your life in the large but by what's happening now—which is not wisdom. . . .

. . . On Burlington Route to Denver
Just across the river from Kansas City Mo.
10.50 A.M. Tues. Nov. 21st. 1899. . . .

The "World" clipping mortifies me—to think I shouldn't even yet have learned better than to give myself away like that. I don't blame the reporter—Miss Knobe of the Times Herald—I sent you the clipping.

She is a member of the Chicago Women's Athletic Club and offered to take me over it. We got to talking athletics . . . ; and I hopped through the yard-stick for 'em, and bragged—like a school boy. I'm sorry. I'm very childish and cheap in some ways. . . .[20]

. . . What a lot of nice friends we shall have! I don't believe you'll mind my having dignitaries at the house, for they'll come not as lions, but just because they want to. We'll have a *natural* kind of society—I won't have anything else! "Call" I will not—"socially"—nor go to a lot of foolish parties. But I mean to know people worth knowing, and on my own terms. I feel real big today—calm and widespreading, somehow. . . .

The sense of popular esteem which lets me off from the arduous labor of hold[ing] up my own opinion of myself alone! (I propose to boost hard on *yours* till later years save me the trouble. . . .)

. . . But somehow it is beginning to dawn on me that *I* can be some good to you—not the mere drain and drag I feared I should be. If I keep well—and that looks more and more likely————. . . .

I love you you dear sweet strong soul; better all the time. You are my comfort and helper, and have made life over new for me. Through loving you—and your loving me—all this later richer sweeter growth has come. And my "success" today is largely due to the change in me—that you made! . . .

. . . 9.30–35 A.M. Fri. Nov. 24th. '99. . . .

Here I am in Greeley, Col. . . . Nice town too. Had a packed house last night, and gave a middling good lecture—not my best. . . . I have it in for [Mrs. Pelham] again. She wrote the people here—so they say, that she hoped the club women would do all they could to make it pleasant for me! So they arranged an elaborate reception for the afternoon—preceding the lecture—which I abhor of all things. . . .

Fortunately I missed the letter which told of it, and did not arrive in town till seven o'clock p.m. so I was saved. But what folly in Mrs. Pelham! Commend me to the judicious tyranny of Pond—they say he won't even let his "talent" go out to dinner! . . .

. . . Mon. Nov. 27th. 1899. . . .
12.10 P.M.

Here I am, darling, happy and comfortable as can be, in Provo, with good Mrs. Gates. She is a daughter of Brigham Young you know, so I am in the center of Mormondom. . . .

We have been out marketing, Mrs. Gates and I, and I was introduced to the butcher, the baker, and the candlestick maker. Real primitive American good fellowship. I like it thoroughly. They want me to stay over Thanksgiving, and if nothing calls me away I guess I will. It is so homey and nice. And the town is all ready to listen with awe and enthusiasm to my doctrines. . . .

Found yours of the 22nd here. You have hit it right every time so far. And it *is* such a comfort to me. You see for all my glory and the general friendliness and good will of the people, I am *personally* alone. Your letters, and dear Kate's, are the nearest touches I get—and hers are not any too frequent or too near. . . .

But—well I guess I'm a little lonesome and want to be cuddled. And you are the one—the only one—who *Loves* me. Please to put some of it on paper dear—! . . .

. . . **c/o Mrs. Susa Young Gates**
Provo. Utah
near noon. Tues. Nov. 28th. 1899. . . .

Well—last night I addressed my first Mormon audience. Unqualified success. "Our Brains & What Ails Them." . . . Mrs. Gates took me over the place this morning—into class room after classroom, and there they were holding forth to the effect that Joseph Smith was thus proven to be a True Prophet—that the Book of Mormon was thus and so—and in one room they were filling in a map of South America with some vague prehistoric Mormon cities—all to me interesting, but apparently not to the classes, for they yawned prodigiously.

It is like a Catholic school, you see. No harm. Religion has got to stand on its own legs today. If this one can ———— let it. They are after education, and education—the real thing—will lead them on to more truth.

Meanwhile they are eagerly interested in my various heretical doctrines as to brain culture.

Brigham Young was a very great man—he saw deep and wide, and could handle men (and women!) This daughter of his, my hostess, takes me in most warmly. She has just shown me a big photograph of seven or eight of her father's wives and a vast multitude of daughters. Some she explained were not his true wives—they were widows, and he married them to give them a home!!! . . . As I look back at my earnest struggling girlhood and think how I longed to be *OUT*—to reach wide and deep—to see and know; and then think of the splendid freedom and depth of knowledge I have come into—it makes me very grateful. What a wonderful life it is—to go everywhere—to meet everyone—to eat and drink so largely of human life. . . .

. . . **10.25 A.M. Thurs. Nov. 30th. 1899**
Provo. Utah. . . .

I had a good rest yesterday P.M. And have to report a thorough success in the closing lecture. . . .

It was "The Child" last night. And I really did well, and made a splendid impression. It's worth while talking to a lot of young folks like these students. Some one out of the number may be impressed in a way that will last a lifetime. . . .

It has been a very pleasant part of the trip, this visit in Mormondom. Real ones, too. I have been introduced to "plural wives," and, no doubt, to plural husbands. Every one is "Brother" and "Sister." They are pious to a degree, religious like Mohammedans, openly and without shame. . . .

Anyhow I am glad of the opportunity for close personal touch with this "peculiar people."

And while we should probably differ forever in basic views, yet they seem singularly open to conviction as to improved methods of all sorts.

Tomorrow I go to Salt Lake again, and stay as long as the next engagement demands.

I want to get to California—and my letters. . . .

. . . Fri. Dec. 1st. 1899. . . .

. . . I received from my friend Mrs. Howe the enclosed; which decided me not to go to her house after all. . . .[21] Mrs. Howe has a perfect right to her opinions, and even to express them—if she gets the *chance*. But I don't propose to give her the chance.

My conscience smites me still for trying to "reform" her, too hard—for not seeing that she had inexorable limits, but I at least meant to serve her—strove to serve her. I had forgotten this condemnatory streak in her. And I don't propose to dip up any old unpleasantness in California if I can help it—I can't afford any unnecessary personal friction—I'm too tired. It does seem so funny—after the steadily growing respect and affection of the last five years to step back to this atmosphere. No, I shall confine myself to friends of whose understanding and approval I am sure—and not trespass upon the hospitality of this good lady who seems still oppressed with the responsibility of answering mysterious questions about me. . . .

[from Salt Lake City]
. . . Dec. 2nd. 1899. . . .

Well—Provo's done. I have made a deep impression there. They want to form a society, build a Baby-School, and fall too at once on the lines I suggested. That's the kind of folks I like. Brother Gates plunged into *Women & Economics* at once—and I bequeathed that copy to the family. Seeing as they entertained me five days, and worship at my shrine as it were. . . .[22]

... Ogden. Utah. Dec. 4th. '99
10. A.M. . . .

[*Although Gilman was invited to lecture in Ogden, Utah, the real purpose of the visit was to look up her brother's wife, Margaret Perkins, and their child Basil, age nine.*]

... I chased about till I found her [Margaret] with her mother and Basil in two rooms in a down town block—pretty badly off I guess.

Basil is a darling. Bright, gentle, clever—just a lovely boy. . . . To see that fine child in such surroundings naturally grieves me, and I shall pluck him out as soon as I can. . . .

Now my dear, as Cousin and as Lawyer—as my Business Adviser, you must help me do my duty and prevent me—if you can—from being foolish. To do what I can for my brother's son is an immediate duty. But I mustn't tie myself up with them to my own hurt. There is Katharine too. You will be wise for me, won't you dear. I guess it will take all the money I get to take care my of my "family," and you—if you really conclude to do it—will have plenty of chance to take care of me. Now I want Basil *with me*. He needs home influences of a higher sort than he has ever had, poor child. . . .

O dear! I feel as if my visions of new personal happiness were vanishing into thin air, and a big flock of new duties taking their place. And yet duty and sacrifice have a fascination for me always. If it is the right thing to do I must do it. . . .

... I must write to Thomas and tell him how fine a boy he has. . . .

... There are two redeeming features in his [Thomas'] life—it isn't wicked, and it's healthy. And I know how he loves his son. Suppose this was Kate, and Thomas in my place—he would do anything for her. To think of that sensitive affectionate sweet-souled child living cooped up with a shallow-pated mother and a morbid garrulous sick old grandmother. . . . I've half a mind to take him to California this winter with me! You see how reckless I am! I could board him there—love him and pet him and tell him stories of good things—he and Kate could get acquainted—they'd have great times together on the sunny hills. It wouldn't cost very much. I'll try and earn a little more. This will be a horrible winter for the child—in those two miserable little rooms. . . .

Well— you see I'm in it! . . .

... 11.30 A.M. Tues. Dec. 5th. 1899.
Ogden. Utah. . . .

... The sudden enlargement of my horizon of duties is appalling. But I don't know when I've had anything appeal to me as does this child. He is such a nice boy, such a little gentleman. . . .

I must write to Thomas and talk Basil to him. It pleases me to think how glad he'll be to have his boy better placed. I wish I knew how he felt about Margaret. . . .

. . . **10.30 A.M. Wed. Dec. 6th. 1899**
Ogden Utah. . . .

[*She has had dinner with her brother's wife, Margaret Perkins, and their child, Basil.*]
I never coveted a child so much. And I can have a good share of him I feel sure, and make a home that will give him real advantages. It does feel good.

But I must be careful this winter—keep cool—do my resting and working—I can't do much for anybody till this good book is done and further income assured. . . .

I believe there is a whole lot of bottled up motherliness in me. Wifeliness too, perhaps. . . .

12

The Blessed Joy of Natural Beauty:
10 December 1899–16 April 1900

In December 1899 Gilman returned to her "blessed" California. "The drowsy bliss . . . is flooding over me as I knew it would," she wrote Houghton. "I love" seeing the clouds "as they break and lift and float across these jagged peaks and bulging shoulders," and enjoying the "mountains, the valleys, the brilliant sea, the endless profusion of rich foliage and flowers and fruit, the long, sweeping contours of the topography, the blessed calmness of the air." California is "the only place I ever was 'homesick' for," she continued.[1] It "appeals to the deepest sense of joy in natural beauty." "Every morning I think with delight 'now for my work!'—and the long still hours on the sunny hillside fly softly by."[2]

During the winter and spring of 1900, *Human Work* was Gilman's major project, the southern California hillside serving as her outdoor study. "The book runs well," she wrote to Houghton. Or again, "I got a splendid new grip on the book—splendid." It is a "popular" series of essays, with "easy thinking and clear familiar illustration." It "does not try to be heavily scientific—I can't." But it "is for people in general to read," and "it brings in several of my very deepest—theories?—views—? whatever those special glimpses are whereby I measure and arrange the other things." "Of course I'm in a dozen minds as to whether it is worth a cent or not. The stuff written seems so self-evident and simple."[3]

In some respects, *Human Work* was an eclectic rephrasing of contemporary theoretical perspectives. Like Thorstein Veblen's *Theory of the Leisure Class* (1899), it offered a scathing critique of poverty, of "the sea of human misery," of the wasteful divisions between rich and poor, between leisure class and useful worker, between man and "captive wife." And like most progressive writing, it also offered an optimistic, humanistic view of social change. We tend to blame individuals for their own unhappiness, Gilman argued; in fact we assume unhappiness is the condition of human life. And yet given the "progressive" force of reason, science and technology, human kind could build a society based on cooperation instead of competition, on peace instead of warfare, and on altruistic caring instead of aggressive fending for oneself.[4] "The wealth of the world is enormous, and the power to multiply it is not nearly used, yet a vast proportion of our members are not fully supplied with the necessaries of life." In fact, those "who do the most valuable work for Society are precisely those least paid, sometimes most punished, and . . . the men receiving the largest rewards are often the most ordinary functionaries and sometimes rascals." If only we could direct the "instinct of workmanship" toward the "collective interests of the community" rather than toward selfish private needs, she argued; if only we could be see that "social action" is the natural "expression of social energy for social use," then we could open "the way to such swift advance of civilization as the world has never seen."[5] Or, as she also phrased it,

> With right economic belief and action there would be no division of Producer and Consumer, no Leisure Class, no Working Class, no serried ranks of Capital and Labour. All would produce, all would consume; all would work and all would have leisure; all would share in the social capital and the social labour.[6]

Human Work was a continuation of Gilman's effort to integrate her socialist and feminist perspectives and to offer a critique of contemporary patterns of dominance and power. Whereas *Women and Economics* had focused on women's need for economic independence, *Human Work* focused on a corollary theme: the human need for satisfying, socially productive work. Work is a "primal condition," she argued, a "basic impulse," a "social passion" as "natural as breathing"—but one that had been destroyed by the "madness" of capitalistic greed. Like a "steam engine fired up and superheated . . . must let off steam or burst," so people experience a "quenchless misery" when denied the right to a satisfying work. Drawing on Thorstein Veblen's *Theory of the Leisure Class* (1899), she argued that the "instinct of workmanship" was purposeful, useful, and universal, and that work had originally been valued and respected. But when the workers were "conquered" and "made slaves," the most selfish, least productive members of society were emulated and respected, while the useful were held in stark contempt. As goods and services were directed increasingly toward private profit, people learned to "despise" productive work and to admire instead "the ability not to work," the accumulation of "power to make others work for you."[7]

Although *Human Work* was in some respects an adaptation of contemporary theory, it gave far more attention to the women's issue and to the patriarchal family structure as a root cause of destructive dominance and power. Work was originally "performed by women," Gilman argued. Because of their capacity for nurturing and caring, because of "mother energy, producing for its young," work itself was "primarily an extension of the maternal function." Tragically, however, private ownership had intervened. Women had been the first workers but were then "enslaved" by men, thus ensuring that the "respected" were in fact the preeminent exploiters, while the majority of useful workers were oppressed and scorned. Isolated in the patriarchal family, confined to work that was nonspecialized, kinship-based, and private, the "bountiful producer" had become "a destructive parasite," a selfish and regressive force. "Nothing will conduce so much to the right growth of society in body and spirit," she concluded, "as the progress of women from their position of prehistoric sex-bound egoism and familism, to their rightful share and place in the vital processes of Society."[8]

* * * * *

For the first few months of 1900, Gilman did some traveling—to San Francisco, Stanford, and Santa Barbara—but for the most part she stayed in Las Casitas, in the foothills just outside of Pasadena. "Do you realize that I am spending all day and every day out in this sweet high air and blessed sun?" she wrote Houghton. "I sit and gloat on the wild beauty of it all." "Such trees—such flowers—*such* skies and stars!!!" The "fruit buds swell, almonds are long in flower—the sycamore leaves are coming out. The wood doves are calling to each other all up and down the shadowy wooded canyons." Besides, she continued, "I am contracting a passion for mountain climbing. . . . Such constant temptation to go up higher—'just one more!'— and such innocent but boundless triumph when there!"

It was almost as though Gilman were turning to the natural beauty of the California landscape as the central inspiration for her writing, and as a central source of healing also, as she attempted to resolve some problematic issues of the past. "Get well! Get well! Get well!" she jotted in her diary as her January New Year's resolution. "And do good work." Or, as she put it in an opening "faith and purpose" diary entry for the coming year:

> Because God, manifesting himself in Society, calls for ever fuller and more perfect forms of expression, therefore I, as part of Society and part of God owe my whole service to the Social development.[9]

While Gilman's California visit helped to reinspire her "human work" commitments, it was reviving some painful private memories as well. In fact, in some respects, her California years (1888–95) had been among her toughest ones. Professionally she had been struggling to begin her work in lecturing and writing—with the California Women's Press Association, with the statewide Women's Congress, and with Helen Campbell on the *Impress Magazine.* And personally she had experienced the final break with Walter, while also nursing her mother through death and dying, while mothering and then separating from her daughter, while developing, but then losing, some important female friends. Not only had she had to struggle with other people's lack of "understanding and approval," but also, even now, with her own recurring "retroactive sense of doubt as to whether after all I had done right." Or, as her friend Harriet Howe recently reminded her:[10]

You have some very unrelenting enemies here [in California],—but I should not say *enemies*, for while sternly disapproving of you, they would not lift a finger to harm you. Yet your name is to them as a red flag to a bull.

Many and strange are the questions I am asked, and I could wish sincerely that you had not been so indiscreet.

From Gilman's point of view, Howe's letter all too vividly recalled memories of the "old unpleasantness in California," of often being "harshly judged." After calling on an old neighbor on Christmas day, for instance, Gilman wrote, "I've just made a fool of myself. . . . Went across the way to call on some old neighbors, . . . and got violently slapped in the face. . . . It's the 'unnatural mother' racket—same old thing." "[W]hen it comes to people, never have I been so misliked and misunderstood as in that state," as she later put it.[11] She described the "bitter swollen choky feeling" she was having at this time: "I lie awake nights and suffer about being thought an unnatural mother." "How did I ever live when everybody, most, was down on me!"

For years, Gilman had struggled with a sense of guilt and self-reproach about her repeated separations from her daughter, but in recent months she had finally begun to hope that following her marriage she could provide Katharine with a settled home.[12] Realistically, Gilman still sometimes had her reservations. Katharine is "human, very," and "she does 'take it out of me' still." She "is such a colt yet," so "desperately careless about her personal appearance" and so "provokingly lazy and procrastinating" that it takes a "sort of pushing . . . to get her to do things." But as "people go she's one among ten thousand"—"kind, obliging, dutiful—and a lovely companion." And because she "seems to regard me with increasing favor," "I do not despair of winning her young affections sufficiently to persuade her to give me this year." Moreover, since Grace and Walter were currently visiting relatives in southern California, there would be time to discuss their wishes on the subject, and to think through the implications for herself. For instance, perhaps Katharine might actually prefer to live with Grace and Walter, Charlotte worried. She "does not care much for me" and "expresses herself strongly in favor of going abroad with them." "Well, I shall try all I decently can to have her come." She is such a "splendid creature," such "a darling," and so "affectionate and familiar." But "I can't force it, and wouldn't if I could." "I would not keep her against her will for anything."[13]

As Gilman worked on improving her relationship with Katherine, however, she began to recognize some festering resentments with Walter and Grace. "I gather a deep bitterness of feeling as to my 'free' life for these years—and my selfish unloading of Katharine upon them," Charlotte wrote. "They feel that I have shirked a duty as long as it was inconvenient and now wish to assume a pleasure," and that "because of my personal characteristics I am not now the best companion for her—should probably injure her— therefore she had better go with them!" "I can see how it looks to them. . . .

[B]ecause 'the mother' is necessarily the best companion for the child, therefore nothing excuses my 'giving her up.'" So "I had some black hours"
trying to "reassure myself" that "after all my real personal duty, biggest of
all, was to speak and write. Not at the expense of my child surely—but it
has not been."

Given the complexities of Charlotte's relationship with Grace and Walter—Grace was Katharine's second mother, Walter's second wife, and
among her own closest friends—what is surprising is not that tensions would
occasionally erupt between them, but that after several marathon discussions they would be quite successfully resolved. By mid-March, for instance,
instead of worrying about Grace and Walter's disapproval, Charlotte began
describing their "misfortunes" instead: Grace's "terrible" miscarriage and
the foreclosure pending on her father's home. "Such a terrible pile of troubles as those dear people have had and have yet. I am so sorry for them. It
doesn't seem as if mine were anything in comparison." Immediately Charlotte responded, of course, with emotional as well as practical assistance,
helping with the care of Dr. Channing, with household matters, and with
the financial responsibility for Kate. "I am very much better able to carry
her expenses than they are," Charlotte noted, and "now it is straightened
out a lot." "*O* it is such a load off my mind!" "[I] have now a sense of warm
goodwill to them both which is vastly better than the hurt feeling I had
last summer."

In the context of an improving relationship with Grace and Walter, Charlotte regretted, however, that she had not yet told them of her marriage
plans. It "seems as if they had a right to know," she wrote. After all, if
"Walter, still single, was to take her from me and then whisk in a step mother
I should feel that it was hardly fair." Fortunately, when Charlotte told them
of her relationship with Houghton, their responses for the most part were
supportive. "Walter wrote me a very touching and sweet note of congratulation and good will." Kate "takes it very sweetly," though is "not overpleased
I fancy."[14] ("Why did I wish to marry?" Kate asked. "You have me!") And
Grace Channing was particularly loving and supportive. Her "only question
seemed to be whether I was going to stand 'the relation'—(my great plea
before having been that I couldn't, you know!) Well—circumstances alter
cases, that's all I can say." "[W]e have disproved that [worry] pretty thoroughly I fancy. Anyhow I am willing to risk it." "Folks are different, very."

For years Charlotte had kept her relationship with Houghton secret, in
part to work through ambivalence she felt herself. In fact, it had taken a
three-year, book-length correspondence to establish ground rules for their
marriage and to weed out conventional assumptions. For instance, they must
have "a room apiece," she reminded him. "Everybody ought to." They
would make arrangements at a nearby boardinghouse for meals. And obviously she would continue working. In fact, how about using the manuscript

for *Human Work* as "amusement on our wedding tour," she teased. "The bride's book on 'Work'! No, I guess I won't take it along—it's too heavy."

In these last few months in California, Gilman occasionally feared some negative reactions to her marriage, yet she sometimes also hoped it might become a kind of model, a positive example others could consider. "I hope we shall give out" an "influence of love and trust, mutual respect and freedom," she wrote, "helping to show what man and woman may be to each other on a true basis." "I have a lot to do," she continued. "Big useful work that is worth while." And "if you do truly think I have great work to do for the dear world—far beyond helping me—your love and faith, your strength and knowledge, will help humanity in and through me." In fact, Houghton was her grounding, she told him, her "point of attachment to the universe." "My body simply purrs with satisfaction at your approach. My heart is brimful of present joy and lovely plans for the future—our future." And "my mind—that used to kick so . . .—is so calmly assured." So "You're wrong about my not needing you," she quipped. "I need, what every woman needs, a man to take care of her," to "protect me," and "to try on my books when they're cut and basted!" And if people "make remarks about your wife's wearing the trousers . . . I'm so sorry," but "I'll take 'em right off—when I get home!"

Letters: December 10, 1899 through April 16, 1900

. . . **10.45. or so. A.M. Sun. Dec. 10th. 1899.**
San Francisco. Cal. . . .

[*The letter begins with a description of her arrival in California.*]
    . . . All my love for this country rises in a flood. It is the only place I ever was "homesick" for—it appeals to the deepest sense of joy in natural beauty—I honestly love the place. . . .
    . . . The rest and pleasure of it are balm and strength to me at once. I can feel the poetry coming. . . .
    Yesterday began my financial picnic. I called on my good dentist & paid him his 50. . . .
    . . . O this delicious country! rich, green, warm, full of flowers . . . and there I discovered my erstwhile land lady in the very home I rented of her. . . . She answered the bell herself, and seemed naturally surprised to see me. "Good morning!" said I amiably. "I've come to pay my rent." You should have seen her. She was nearly paralyzed with amazement. 'Twas great fun. . . .
    . . . It comforts me amazingly to see you really planning about our house. Makes it look *real*. Bless you—Mr. [Thomas] Carlyle is *20* years younger

than Mrs. [Helen] Campbell! See George Eliot & Mr. [John Walter] Cross; Mrs. [L.F.] Ward, etc. I think I am really very moderate!

You're wrong about my not needing you. I do, tremendously, and shall more and more; to take care of me. Not to furnish all the money, but to *take the care*—which I am so helpless about. To protect me—from my friends! To see that I do not spend foolishly and undertake responsibilities beyond my strength. . . . I am liable to do foolish things with my money— I see that clearly. I shall be a prey and a spoil if I do not have some one to defend me. And your quiet conservative practical wisdom is just what I need. . . .

. . . I do need you, darling. With my temperament—with my growing responsibilities—ever larger demands on my time and strength—I need, what every woman needs, a man to take care of her.

It is not money dear. Money wouldn't begin to do it. It is *care,* thought, and labor—lots of real work, that I shall cost you. . . .

. . . near 11. A.M. Tuesday
Dec. 12th. 1899.
621 O'Farrell St.
San Francisco. Cal. . . .

You hope I still love you in spite of your faults? You angel! You haven't any faults—only some ill-adjusted virtues. And I love you in spite of and because of—those! . . .

If you take pleasure in knowing how much I miss you and really suffer for lack of you—why I'll send you a large slice of that agreeable emotion for Xmas! . . . I hate to have you suffer—and yet—seems as if you *ought* to—some—when your wife is away so long! But the nice little chunk of solid ground which I have had recently inserted beneath my weary feet sort of gets away from me, and I swing out along again! With the great world and the folks whirling by—and I have to get clear back to God to *rest.* You see you are my ground—my *own* ground—my point of attachment to the universe; and when my grip on you loosens—O dear it is *dreadful!* . . .

. . . But darling—you do misunderstand, even yet. I am *not* asking you [to] sit down and dig into your sensations and make yourself suffer in order to give me the pleasure of hearing about it! I particularly admire you for your rational self-control; and that true chastity which I honor as much as any one.

But I want in your letters—these times when I need reassurance—I want the tone of intimacy and—*possession* which makes letters to a wife differ from those of a cousin. Sometimes there isn't a word in them that I couldn't show to any friend—and I feel chilly and lonesome. You may say "But I wouldn't write every day—anything—if I didn't love you." . . . I know you wouldn't—if you didn't love me *some*. But . . . I want to feel that I *belong* to you, that you have taken me, that I am yours. . . . I don't have to be touched through the senses dear—it is my *brain*—my poor damaged brain that is trying to get a grip on you and can't hold tight—and that wants to *be* held close—close! . . .

O you dear patient tender strongsouled man. How good you are to me. And I'll have to always be under obligations to you——'cause you are so much to me and I can be so little to you—but I don't care! I *like* to be obliged to you!!! "Every true woman wishes to be supported by the man she loves!!!" Supported, yes, by the man's blessed Strength—which the woman so needs. Be patient with my weakness dear. . . .

. . . 11.35 A.M. Wed. Dec. 13th. 1899. . . .

Speaking of money—if you marry me next spring I shall be beautifully poor—because my debts are not paid! You will marry a pauper—with encumbrances! You'd better do it quick while I present these disadvantages. If you wait till Thomas strikes a gold mine and Katharine marries a Duke and I pay all my debts and have fourteen books with large international royalties coming in—where you'll be worse placed by far than you are now! . . .

. . . 10 A.M. Thurs. Dec. 14th. 1899.
621 O'Farrell St. S.F. Cal. . . .

How I want you to talk with! You dear live thing! You reasonable intelligent cultivated polite agreeable man—I want you. Other folks don't know so much, and they aren't my cousin. Besides—when I'm tired of talking we have so many other amusements. . . .

Dearest—can't you see how little your success in business—your prominence as a lawyer—matters in your value to me? Of course I want you to succeed for your own sake, and know you will; but in my heart you have "succeeded" already—as kings do.

You are of measureless value to me—to me as a woman, a sorely tired and overburdened woman so long unhappily alone. Of course it isn't much to say to a man—that he is all in all to a woman—to women it has always been their only pride. But—if you do truly think I have great work to do for the dear world—far beyond helping me—your love and faith, your strength and knowledge, will help humanity in and through me.

I'm not much. . . . But I have a lot to do. Big useful work that is worth while. I do not think you will regret or be ashamed of your share in—your great share, dear.

I'll be your "avocation"—is that what you call it? And an absorbing one. . . .

. . . **4.15 P.M. Tues. Dec. 19th. '99. . . .**

. . . This morning Hattie Howe came over—she is really fond of me; and I have a high opinion of her in many ways. . . . She is a real booklover, is Harriet. . . .

At Prof. Ross's Stanford home.
9.20–25. A.M. Wed. Dec. [20th.] '99

Dearest—
Now I am comfortable. . . . And with people more congenial. . . . I have an enormous capacity for getting on with people—all kinds and sizes. It is only when I slip into easier grooves that I realize the unfitness of the others. That's where you are so good for me, through your young likeness. I don't have to be on the strain. . . . What a deep unfolding joy it will be when at last I can settle down into the peace of your companionship. I do not expect you to be a stimulant, a spur to great deeds, a leader—*I don't need that.* I've got enough "go" in me, and meet stimulus everywhere. But you give me rest. You dear! . . .

[The Rosses] are such nice people. And the good man sits down and pours out to me his new book—makes me feel so nice and professional. How on earth did I get to be a sociologist and the equal of learned men! I never studied it as they have. Some are born learned I guess. It's that kind of brain that gave rise to the Buddha myths I suppose—and similar ones. Two or three thousand years ago I'd have made quite a goddess, wouldn't I!

It is all very helpful to my book, this little visit and talk here. Gives me a fresh grip. . . .

And to grow in power yearly—in influence and weight—to be able to do more and to help others do more—O it is so good to be alive!

The gradual establishment of new standards—the learning of new methods—the delicate patient experimenting that shall establish the best processes—conscious human culture is great fun. And I do think I have got my feet on some really valuable basic facts in this line. . . .

. . . **11. A.M. Dec. 21st. 1899. Thursday.**
Stanford University. . . .

. . . I could wish you with me on a visit like this. Many of my friends you would not enjoy at all. You'd be just as polite, and you'd never say a word against 'em—that's the kind of gentleman you are; but it would be a strain. But this hulking young Professor [Ross]—he is six feet five!—(she five feet one, about) with his scientific enthusiasm, and his vivacious artistic cheery little wife. They are very devoted—and it is good to see their cheerful affection. Makes me goodnaturedly envious. . . .

. . . **7.15 P.M. Friday Dec. 22nd. 99.** . . .

Yesterday afternoon I went to ride with the tall professor, enjoying the rich beauty of the Santa Clara Valley and also a lot of scientific talk. He thinks well of me. Says when . . . he considers my ideas he feels like saying "O King! Live a thousand years!" . . .

. . . **Las Casitas Villa**
Pasadena. Cal.
Dec. 24th. 1899. . . .

The drowsy bliss of this exquisite land is flooding over me as I knew it would. I love it—always loved it—it's the only place I ever was homesick for. Some day I will bring you and then you will love it too. . . .
. . . [In Los Angeles] I was met by my tall daughter, clad in a gold-brown denim suit—(knicker bockers underneath) and wearing a sombrero hat. She is fine. . . .
. . . She insists that I shall come down today and stay over till tomorrow afternoon—and I guess I'll have to. I can't refuse her her first request at Xmas time. Arriving in Pasadena we were met at the train by Walter and Grace going in town—final errands I suppose. Dear me! What a disagreeable looking man he is! Isn't it funny how one can go through things and come out *absolutely*—as if never in! . . .

. . . **Dec. 25th. 1899.**
Katharine's Room. . . .

I came down here yesterday P.M. and helped dress the tree as Kate so wished. Slept in her little bed up here—or tried to! Such a queer bare little room as she has—just as she likes it. . . .
We had a good supper and a merry time in general—all easy and unaffected; and I for one genuinely glad to see them all, and the dear place too.
Such trees—such flowers—*such* skies and stars!!!
And running out to pick my own orange for breakfast! . . .

12.45 or so.

Dear Heart—I turn to you for comfort—for sympathy. I've just made a fool of myself. Went across the way to call on some old neighbors, and—I foolishly supposed—friends, and got violently slapped in the face.

I might have known too, if I had but thought. I went in such open good will—so full of pleasure to be back here—and forgot the way folks think of me in California.

I've been so used of late to friendship—affection—honor; that it was painfully surprising. It's the "unnatural mother" racket—same old thing.

Dear dear! I haven't felt so uncomfortable inside for ever so long. The same kind of bitter swollen choky feeling I had when reproved as a child. And I can see where I was to blame all along—in saying things. But one cannot *always* remember to talk according to the limitations of one's interlocutor. At least I could not in those days.

Well. It will count as ammunition for a story at any rate. I have the advantage of them there—I can talk the farthest! . . .

. . . I slept miserably. . . . Also I was a bit hurt because I had labored to write a verse for every little gift, and they were not noticed or valued at all—they threw them on the floor with the wrappers. So I'm in a very bad state o' mind. . . . I'm very cross—very. I want to be mean to folks. Guess I can do it in a story—I'll try. . . .

How did I ever live when everybody, most, was down on me! . . .

. . . **Las Casitas Villa**
Box 152. Pasadena. Cal.
near 9 A.M. Tues. Dec. 26th. '99. . . .

I feel so lonely and cold—so harshly judged and cruelly—. And all the popular admiration and kindness is necessarily shallow—I want to be *known* and then loved. . . .

You do know me—and you do love me—don't you? I am hanging on to it as if I hadn't another friend on earth. I haven't—like that. . . .

We had a fine Xmas dinner; then . . . set off about four. . . . It seemed very lonesome and miserable—going off from the house—"the Home & Family"—and my child on Xmas day. But I paddled along boldly, looking with warm interest at the little house where I used to live, and other familiar places; and honestly enjoying the rich beauty of the place although my heart was heavy. . . .

The ride up [to Las Casitas] . . . was nice too. . . . *And* the beauty! The great rugged heap of far spread mountains flaming rose color in the sunset light; all the near things delicate brilliant green; the far wide valley behind us one sea of splendid color, and the big liquid stars coming out above. . . .

. . . Las Casitas Villa . . .
10.30 A.M. Wed. Dec. 27th. '99. . . .

. . . I lie awake nights and suffer about being thought an unnatural mother; but that's only because I'm "low" and bound to suffer about something. I have so few things to be unhappy about now that I have to make the most of what afflictions remain! . . .

[*Walter and Grace have apparently suggested that they do not want Katharine to live with Charlotte.*]

. . . But I shall do all I can to get her for a year at least. Give me a year to make love to her in—then she can decide more fairly. I don't want her to grow up European. And O I want a new baby so! I want to begin again and have a fairer chance. . . .

. . . Jan. 1, 1900. . . .

This is a fair day, cool and bright. Down the far valley the fog lies white like a level sea. . . .[15]

But I am at a low ebb now and no mistake.

Today I hope for letters from you—one at least. I do feel so isolated here. Katharine does not care as much for me as she did that summer I think. I feel shut off somehow. But I try to lay that to my "state o' mind," and assure myself that it will be all right later. She has her life to live. I must not complain even if she never cares greatly for me. . . .

. . . Still New Years Day. 1900
about 5.30 P.M. . . .

. . . [Katharine] is a darling.

I take a base delight in my present possession of a little money. She wanted a dime to buy a rabbit—I gave her four. She still wished for an "express wagon" . . . so I presented her with a dollar therefor. . . .

I am absolutely unprincipled just now about her. I'll do anything to please her—I want her so.

I want to get in a year of loving companionship at least. And I am viciously hoping the others won't have money enough to send for her right away either!!! It is rather hard to make you marry the two of us; but if you *want* a laborious method of proving your love for me and winning my deep and lasting gratitude and affection—why here it is! . . .

I feel quite relieved in my mind by your statement as to "emotions" in passing, with regard to other women. I have been feeling so for the last year—not any direct physical sensation, but a general appreciativeness of any nice man I chanced to be with. Sort o' sized 'em up as potential husbands! I was very much ashamed of this and thought it was only another proof of my morbid horridness—best treated by ignoring it altogether. But bless me! If *you* are thus speculative as to adjacent charms, I guess it only proves that—well that I'm in love! A husband, you see, has become a desirable thing in my eyes—not an affliction. Dear me! How you have changed the world for me! You've no idea how I look forward to the housekeeping. And I believe it will do me good too—the little details of occupation. . . .

Katharine says she don't want to live in New York. Wants to go abroad again.

Well—she may later. But I want her *now*. However—if it seems thoroughly best for her to go—I have still the alternative of clear you—and that—under all the mother-ache—is really an attractive thought! . . .

. . . Las Casitas Villa . . .
near 8.30 P.M. Tues. Jan. 2nd. '00. . . .

. . . You would like to see me prancing about these mountains. I'm not past being nimble *yet*—if I am forty! The folks here gaze at me in amazement.

As soon as I begin to feel well—why then I shall feel well! As it is I keep on not sleeping, and am thickheaded and blue. I knew it would be so—it will pass—it is all natural enough; and yet I do hate it so!

When I wake up in the morning I have a dark brown taste in my *mind*. Joy is not joyous, nor hope hopeful—things are flat, low, and dark.

But it is not bad—not a serious time—only what I had every reason to expect. And there is nothing for it but to breathe the good air, eat, sleep, climb around, and wait.

And then I have the happiness of loving you—that is so much! And of feeling you love me ——— ah how good it is! . . .

. . . Las Casitas Villa . . .
9.15 A.M. Thurs. Jan. 4th. '00

My Precious Comfort—

How satisfactory you are! The moment my head clears a little I realize more fully your agreeable attributes, and see how more than fortunate I am. And among all things I like about you your constant courtesy stands out always. . . .

You're so nice looking too. You're "not perfect as we are"—who is? I'm no Venus! But there isn't any bad thing about you—nothing unpleasant or evil in significance. . . .

I shall always, in my "managing" heart, wish I'd had a hand in your athletic training in early youth—just so's to have built you up a bit more in the trunk & chest—but then I should find something to think I could have improved on in any man—or woman alive! That's one of my faults—always wanting to do things to people. But you *are* so nice. . . .

Katharine is coming up today, to stay nearly a week. I shall be so glad to have her. . . .

. . . Las Casitas Villa . . .
10. A.M. or so. Fri. Jan 5th. 1900. . . .

Katharine arrived, later, riding on Jocko, the favorite donkey. . . .

Such a big splendid girl! She expresses herself strongly in favor of going abroad with them. Perhaps it will be as well. I would not keep her against her will for anything. And we shall have a more settled home for her later. It is a peculiar pull. I want her awfully—yet I know full well that it will be better in some ways for us to start in by ourselves for a while. . . .

Of course she does not care much for me; and does for them. And she does not like New York—doesn't want to live in a city. It will be pleasanter for her there when she is a bit older perhaps.

Well, I shall try all I decently can to have her come. But I can't force it, and wouldn't if I could. . . .

She is not dainty and careful in personal matters—is more like a boy of her age. No harm. She'll grow to it.

Such a beautiful strong sweet girl. Everybody loves her. . . .

9.30 A.M. Sat. Jan. 6th. 1900

Dear Love—

I feel better. Lots better. Had a quiet day yesterday with Katharine to look at a good deal. She *is* so lovely. She is merry and affectionate and sweet, but her heart is set on going to Europe. Maybe I can unset it. I shall try. I shall do all I fairly can without forcing her to get her to spend a year with me, now. I do not want her foreignized. The books she is reading at present are about Italy and foreign parts, in general. Aha! Let's you and I see to it that she has a course of good American reading next winter.

Richard Carvel—Janice Meredith—Hugh Wynne. Will you—when you get to it and can easily look up a set of really interesting stories of a strictly American nature. She need not be a "reformer" but she shall at least be an American if I can fix it. . . .[16]

. . . I'm sleeping better now. Today I feel perceptibly better. The horizon in my mind widens, and the things before visible take on brighter colors.

What a queer disease it is! If my work was not so wholly dependent on the brain condition I could perhaps ignore it more. . . .

The blessed early rain has brought out the flowers. Dear familiar things—how I love to see them again. And the whole country flushes and blazes with color in the rich moist warmth. . . .

. . . **Las Casitas Villa** . . .
Sun. Jan. 7th. 1899. . . .

Another day I've skipped you! It is too bad. But things are mixed and hurried while Katharine is here. . . .

This splendid air, the peace and stillness and beauty, are balm and strength to me. And dear Katharine. She *is* so lovely. . . .

. . . **Las Casitas Villa** . . .
Tues. Jan 9th. 1900 . . .
9.10–15 P.M. . . .

. . . Miss Katharine I rejoice to say, seems to regard me with increasing favor. I do not despair of winning her young affections sufficiently to persuade her to give me this year. And if I get the year—we will see! . . .

If the year goes well I shall try to persuade her to stay with me till she's eighteen. With that much America, home, and mother, I'd be willing she should go abroad and study art with her father. . . .

. . . One of my letters is a $10.00 check from the Independent. Didn't know they had any article! . . . Well, that's so much unexpected gain. . . .

. . . Another letter is a charmingly appreciative one from an English lady—I'll send it [to] you when I've answered—and in it she says that Olive Schreiner knows and admires my book—thinks it *the* book. I am proud! I have so long and so deeply reverenced her. . . .

. . . **Santa Barbara. Cal.**
10.10. A.M. Thurs. Jan. 11th. 1900. . . .

I am sitting in the shade of a round white column, on a "loggia" (if that's the way to spell it) of the Radcliffe-Whitehead's beautiful house. Never have I been in a house so beautiful—real *beauty*—not prettiness or splendor or style—beauty. No—I can't stop to draw it. It wouldn't give you the color—the light—the warmth—the ineffable sweetness. Fresh lemon blossoms are in my belt, great scarlet poinsettias and the star white jasmine flame between the white pillars and against the fair blue sea—blue sky—and dull rich green of the live oaks. . . .

The house is Italian—white walls and red tiled roof. I *wish* I could show it all to you. The terraced garden—the scarlet passion flowers—the sweet alyssum run mad in the fresh grass.

Off to the left is the curve of this delicious bay, and back of it the mountains and the soft sweep of the curving valley. . . .

. . . We left Las Casitas about 9, and I . . . returned Katharine to her other mother's arms. Then Mr. White and I called on the Lummises, and they kept us to dinner.

Mr. Lummis only sleeps three hours—he says. Lives mainly on meat—largely pork, and coffee. Builds his house day times & writes nights I suppose. An interesting man, very. We had a charming little visit. . . .

. . . Pasadena Cal.
Jan. 14th. 1900. . . .

I feel a bit lighter and clearer today. And always when I do you seem dearer to me—more satisfying.

Yours is a deep still lasting personality. You wear well. As I meet people of all kinds freely and fully, as I have done in these years past, I gradually learn that while no one person can possibly meet my kaleidescopic nature, what I must tie to is the kind that fits my "average plane"—as you do.

You suit my "mean height" very well. I soar and dive and adjust myself to fluctuating multitudes of people; and then with a sight of restful pleasure come back to *you*. And the people I meet at various extreme points will one and all wonder "what she can see in him"!

These are the most "aesthetic" people I know; and socialistic too—I can touch them at many points; but—well it tires me. It is not where I *live*. It is where I *go*, but not where I *stay*. You, dear "family" are mine own people. I like you, much.

Mr. White is a delightful fellow. I like him hugely—always shall, but he does not draw me in any way—he always remains "Mr. White," and at a distance. Charming comrade, reliable friend—and fixed there. Now you grow closer and closer, more and more tenderly intimate—you wind and wind into my heart as subtly and gently and irresistibly as a growing root. . . . Peace and power and sanity I find in your companionship—a life of settled work and healthy rest and play. . . .

. . . Mr. White, Mr. Whitehead and I walked a bit on the north beach in the glowing sweet color, and Mr. White & I ran and skipped and jumped over stones and were jolly. In the evening he read more of his book. A heavy solemn terrible novel.

They all say I am an excellent critic.

Tomorrow I go back to Los Angeles. I shall be glad when I'm at Las Casitas again—and begin to itch for work. . . .

. . . On S.P.R.R. "Miramar" to Los Angeles
8.50 or so A.M. Mon. Jan. 15th. 1900

Now I am started back again—wishing it were Las Casitas instead of Los Angeles. . . .

Great country this . . . but am glad to leave. Those good people are exotics.

It seems to me very unnatural to go to other countries and other centuries for the inspiration of one's life—and be a homesick stranger in one's own place and time.

Life without duty is a poor thing too. I suppose that is the way mine seems to Grace. She does not know how warm a home feeling I have for America—how closely bound I am to my world—my age—my dear people.

There is negation—denial—criticism—in this artistic attitude.

I prefer my Whitman.

This is the sublime lesson & reception—neither preference nor denial.

It seems—this other life—first epicurean and then dyspeptic. To pick and choose at such a table, to limit one[']s dietary to such a narrow choice— it seems a pity. What they admire they admire intensely, and get more pleasure from perhaps than I; but all the rest is jar and disappointment to them while I find happiness in so many things. . . .

. . . Pasadena. Cal.
Jan. 16th. 1900

My Dearest Love—

Such good news! Thomas has written me from Boise City—he has done as he said—they are there now. O I am so glad! So there is one load off my mind and heart—and future pocket! . . . It makes me so happy. He and Basil are all right together, and Margaret is "not a bad sort"—isn't it good to think of! . . .

I like to be liked. The sense of dis-like and criticism here is heavy upon me. It outweighs almost the dear beauty of the land I love. . . .

. . . Santa Monica—
Thurs. Jan. 18th. 1900. . . .

You are quite right about Kate. I shan't force anything. . . . But I want her to know me better—and feel as if more alienation would postpone understanding very seriously.

I just want her—that's a large part of it.

As to living here—I'd like to have a "country home" here. But I don't care to live here altogether. My main ties are with people—not places; and the people here are poor stuff. I am a general, not a local agent, and can not afford to settle so far out of the common way. Moreover I love cities too, as well as mountains and seas; and belong with my time. . . .

My health is not dependent on climate you know dear, but on happiness. You are my sun and air, dear love—you will keep me well. And I love our dear East Coast as well as this—the earth is good everywhere. . . .

. . . Pasadena. Cal.
10. A.M. Sat. Jan. 20th. 1900. . . .

Grace and I had a quiet long talk yesterday afternoon as to Katharine's immediate future. I gather a deep bitterness of feeling as to my "free" life for these years—and my selfish unloading of Katharine upon them. Being stronger than when I came, it did not hurt me—much—at the time, but I had some black hours between two and five last night. . . .

I can see how it looks to them—how it must look to them—how impossible it is that they should see it otherwise. I can also see almost ludicrous contradictions in the logic of the whole assumption.

For instance—because "the mother" is necessarily the best companion for the child, therefore nothing excuses my "giving her up."

But because of my personal characteristics I am not now the best companion for her—should probably injure her—therefore she had better go with them!

It is very trying—very difficult to handle. I do not know how it will come out. I wish they had been franker about their money affairs. I wish—almost—that I had kept Kate in '98—they (it now appears) wanted me to take her then! They feel that I have shirked a duty as long as it was inconvenient and now wish to assume a pleasure. Well. I want to have her come to me more than ever; for I fear she never will if not now. Also I see that she is "not perfect"—and think I can really do her good. . . .

I must be gaining strength very solidly now—this has been a taxing week, and yesterday a real drain, yet I feel fairly well today. I tried to reassure myself last night in the dark—that after all my real personal duty, biggest of all, was to speak and write. Not at the expense of my child surely—but it has not been. Had I kept her it would have been.

I have been true to my own principles—as far as strength went—after all that is what we must each do. . . .

. . . Las Casitas Villa
about 10.10 A.M. Sun. Jan 21st. '00. . . .

. . . Grace and I had a long talk about things in general—their affairs mostly; Walter came in and we all talked; and the "feeling" grew very much better. We all feel nearer together and understand one another better. Walter gloomily says that they'll never see her again if she comes to me! But that's only talk. . . .

She wisely refused to choose—said her parents must settle it—she wouldn't. And it is provisionally settled. But I felt wrong in not telling them of my approaching marriage. What do you think? Shall I tell them in confidence? It seems fair that they should know. If Walter, still single, was to take her from me and then whisk in a step mother I should feel that it was hardly fair.

However, things are very much pleasanter somehow. I think I have a little altered their ideas of my life—showed them that I'm not such a "reformer" as they feared; and have no intention of making Katharine one.

It is a great load off my mind and heart and conscience. The winter is vastly lightened. That doubt and anxiety, the yearning which I feared I must even yet stifle, the retroactive sense of doubt as to whether after all I had done right—all this was against my resting and working as I ought.

But now it is straightened out a lot. They admit that a quiet winter of schooling—a practical course in certain branches, the restraints of a city life,—and its advantages, such as the theatre and music—will be good for her.

She is such a colt yet, and so desperately careless about her personal appearance.

I must share her support—as much of it as I can—from this time on in any case. They are suffering under a series of misfortunes—a unique and almost improbable collection; and at present I am very much better able to carry her expenses than they are. . . .

But *O* it is such a load off my mind! Walter was really very nice about it when it came to definite talk. I am so glad to feel on better terms with them. Grace I have always loved so dearly. It was as I feared about her illness last summer. That was too much—I know no woman who would feel it more keenly—and after all she has been through it was cruel. . . .[17]

. . . Las Casitas Villa
Jan 22nd. 1900. . . .

[H]ave Veblen's Theory of the Leisure Class here to read—must return it to Prof. Ross. . . .

My poor sweet brave noble Grace! She has suffered so much. That last grief was truly too much—it is not right for one woman to have so many terrible burdens. But she is younger than I. Perhaps—even yet—I pray it may be so. . . .

. . . Las Casitas Villa . . .
Jan. 26th. 1900
10.10 or so. A.M. Friday. . . .

I'm counting my mercies. There's You. There's Katharine, now very probable. There's Home and Quiet, and Regularity and Peace. There's enough to Live On. Just think of that! I never had enough to live on but one year in my life—that I remember. There is the Gradual Paying of Debts—a hopeful process now. There is Thomas & Basil off my mind. There is an Assured Reputation which I hope to add to. There are Friends, various. There is a glimmering possibility that I may be of material service just now to Walter and Grace—that is a great joy. And—such are the vagaries of human nature—I know full well that if I do well by Kate now, and *am* of service to them, that it will redound retroactively to my credit during these past years. Which will take a big load off too. . . .

I feel very free and nice about it. My head is still not clear. I'm not up to my top notch by any means, but things look well in all directions. . . .

You needn't worry about my lecturing. I shan't lecture any more than I can help, and shall call it half a year's work, and rest two or three months after it—rest and play with you!

Guess I'll do it, hereafter, in the late winter & spring, so as to rest in summer. Then I'll write in the autumn.

That's a fine arrangement. A book in the fall, a trip in the spring, and a long vacation in winter & summer! . . .

. . . 10 A.M. Sat. Jan 27th? 1900. . . .

. . . [You should] read some of Veblen's *Theory of the Leisure Class.* There's a lot of truth in that. . . .

. . . I put Kate to bed—undressed her limp—which is no end of fun. She is so sweet and merry. . . .

I have very tender associations with Cold Spring. We'd give Kate your room. And lock the door! . . .

Katharine asked me, "Where do you expect to spend the summer?" I replied guardedly "Somewhere on the sea shore I hope." Then her lovely eyes danced and she said "O do let's go to Cold Spring!" . . .

. . . Box 152 Pasadena Cal.
Thurs. Feb. 1st. 1900 . . .

I made a beginning [on *Human Work*] this morning. Not so much in bulk, but an easy and fairly promising start. Sort of list of chapters and then launched off on the beginnings of one or two of them—not trying to be thorough, but to start the current of thought in easy stages. It opens promisingly I think. . . .

My strength flows slowly in. It is so good to be out doors in this blessed air all day. I think I can make a good useful book about this. "Furnishing Employment" is one head. "Degrading Labor" another. "His own Labor" a third. It does not try to be heavily scientific—I can't. It is for people in general to read, and I think they'll read it. A sort of series of essays on popular fallacies on this subject—based on a serious and deep theory of sociology & ethics. . . .

One good thing about this book is that it brings in several of my very deepest—theories?—views—? whatever those special glimpses are whereby I measure and arrange the other things. . . .

Katharine comes up tomorrow. . . .

. . . Sunday. Feb. 4th. 1900 . . .
6.45 or so. . . .

Your "flat" plan is fine—would we could find such. We want a room apiece if possible. Everybody ought to. . . . Will not our rate of mortality decrease 50% if we have a room apiece? Verily! Besides—it's better in all ways.

But you can come in when you're good, as you say—and that is all the time. . . .

. . . 10.55 A.M. Mon. Feb. [5th.] 1900.

The Reformer of Nations is very late in her workshop this morning—having swept her room thoroughly before starting—It was a very confusing morning too—lots of people going off—. But she finds it hard to begin her work without a word to the man she loves.

Such a dear good man!

So brave and sweet and patient and wholly noble! Whenever I think of how fine you are it distresses me that you are not getting a better wife! . . .

No wonder empty-lived and "over-sexed" women get into such trouble when "crossed in love." It is hard to bear—not having one's lover—even with clear sailing ahead and a fully happy life in all other ways.

Do you feel that way? Do you want me, friendliwise, at the end of the day to talk to? To tell things and kind of "even up" with? . . .

About 3. P.M. . . .

. . . I got a splendid new grip on the book—splendid. . . .

. . . 3.45 P.M. Thurs. Feb. 8th. . . .

Behold me on "the point" of our mesa, sitting in the partial shade. . . .
O there's a lovely songbird—close by—a very sweet one.

Do you realize that I am spending all day and every day out in this sweet
high air and blessed sun? That I am exercising more or less steadily so that
six miles doesn't seem anything extra. That I eat as much for breakfast as
I used to for dinner—and for supper too. That I sleep fairly well now. That
I am beginning to do my mornings work and not feel it. . . .

More than I could believe possible have I swung round to a normal frame
of mind toward home and husband—to a peaceful steady affection. . . .

. . . 10.10 A.M. Fri. Feb. 9th. 1900

Here I am at the Channing-Stetsons. . . .

Grace is very sweet. She asks earnestly about my New York plans—
am I sure I can afford it and so on. I think I must tell her. It seems as if
they had a right to know. . . . She has certainly earned every consideration
from me; bless her great heart. . . .

. . . 9.40 A.M. Tues. Feb. 13th. 1900. . . .

. . . There are clouds today—and as they break and lift and float across
these jagged peaks and bulging shoulders I sit and gloat on the wild beauty
of it all. . . .

2.35. P.M.

Had a fine morning. O it is so good—to sit up there in that big still
beauty—and feel things grow and grow in my brain! The book opens well—
better and better. Pretty soon I can begin to coordinate it all and write
sequentially.

I think there needs first certain "popular" chapters—easy thinking and
clear, familiar illustration—lots of point.

Then my "principles." Then, based on these my philosophy and
application. . . .

Wed. A.M. . . .

O see here—last night I read "Monsieur Beaucaire," another of Booth Tarkington's—short one—ran in two numbers of McClure Nov. & Dec. I *think.*

I was afraid to read it—thought it would be a come down—but though a light little story it has the same charm as his other—the same distilled clarity and delicacy of description, and the same exquisite moral taste. I do like that man's work. . . .

Another letter from one of the Cosmopolitan editors yesterday asking for 2000 wds within two weeks on most anything—I'll send it [to] you. . . .

. . . 10.30 A.M. Thurs. Feb. 15th. 1900. . . .

I feel so much more married somehow, now that some one else knows. And I want to sit and talk about your virtues to [Grace]—all the time. Which suggests to me that I shall probably find a growing comfort and support in the fact of being really married and recognized as so. . . .

. . . Near 4. P.M. Fri. Feb. 16th. 1900. . . .

I had a very nice time with Grace. She is so brave and sweet and strong, so tender and patient—a noble woman and a wise one. I feel more even with her than I used, less at a disadvantage, but I love her dearly. It hurts me so to think of her losing that baby! That was terrible—an unbelievable anguish to her of all women. It's bad enough to any woman, thousand fold bad to her, she cares so much. . . .

My book opens and opens. Such a fine chapter as I laid out this morning—on "Gift Theft and Payment"—subprocesses of Distribution.

I'm getting a fine lot of material, and shall soon be ready to fall upon and arrange the mass. I guess I can put in all my time here on it. And this summer I'll be revising—with help from you, poor dear. . . .

"Our work" I think I'll call it, not to trespass on Miss Alcott. . . .[18]

Speaking of health I think my machinery must be in pretty hearty condition to stand all this climbing and tramping and never peep. I guess I'm all straight. . . .

. . . About 10. A.M. Sun. Feb. 18th. 1900

Another Sunday, Darling.

How fast the "home run" is! I knew it would be, but am astonished as usual at its gathering speed. This book business bridges eight or ten weeks at one jump—it is "on"—and carries me with it. Then the trip home, once started, is another six weeks that run through my fingers. The Milwaukee week will loom large at the end—apparently—and then suddenly slide by into vacancy—and there is just You! . . .

I have told Katharine. She seemed puzzled. Why did I wish to marry? I explained that it was pleasant to have some one to love me. "You have me!" she said. But I easily convinced her of the advantages of the arrangement to her. She made no doubt of that, and considers you her captive already.

We mustn't spoil her, Dear. She is a guilesome persuasive young charmer, sweetly bent on her own way in some matters.

Now my folks are all told—and you can "announce" when you want to. Only let me know, so I can do my further "announcing" simultaneously. . . .

As for me I am contracting a passion for mountain climbing, and expect to spend the rest of my life—(vacations)—in such trips!!! See your approaching fate! We will take the White—the Green—the Adirondacks, to begin with; then as we get richer the Allegheny's—Pennsylvania—North Carolina & Kentucky—Know them all. Then we'll strike out and try the Rockies! And then the Nevada's all up and down. Aha! I see a fine prospect! How do you like it? Are you fond of mountains or not? I find it a growing fascination, really & truly. Such constant temptation to go up higher—"just one more!"—and such innocent but boundless triumph when there! . . .

. . . Feb. 18th. 1900. . . .

The sun is off to my left now—near setting.

The sky such a clear deep brilliant blue!

Small cloudlets wisping across old Brown, and big soft ones rolling up grandly from the ocean.

I love it all. The perfect quiet. The lovely solitude. Only I'd like you in it!

Must go in pretty soon now. There's a bit of a chill at sundown—to sit still on the ground.

But it's spring all right—the fruit buds swell, almonds are long in flower—the sycamore leaves are coming out. The wood doves are calling to each other all up and down the shadowy wooded canyons. I'd like you to hear them with me.

Near 8. P.M. . . .

. . . I can remember that dear mother of yours very distinctly and most tenderly. Such brooding yearning love—such wonderful love. May I love her boy—always—as she would wish me to. . . .

. . . You can send what you think right about the wedding—I can write what few friends I feel like notifying.

Can't we have a mere "notice" card and send that—Married, June 11th, 1900, G. H. Gilman to C. P. Stetson. . . .

My friend Veblen would class the cards under "Conspicuous Waste" I fear. . . .

. . . Mon. Feb. 19th. 1900. . . .
5.35 P.M.

Every morning I think with delight "now for my work!"—and the long still hours on the sunny hillside fly softly by. . . .

I am so happy Sweetheart—so happy in your love. It grows and grows on me—the steady joy of it. . . .

I felt rather mixy this morning, so I wrote a little article for the Woman's Journal—on "Superfluous Women." That pays my subscription.

Then, getting my hand in, I wrote a piece of a chapter—good one. . . .

Feb. 20th. 1900 . . .
Near 3. P.M.

Ah! Mm! Such times as I have loafing and scrambling along finding new places, afternoons. Mornings I always go to the same—it is all desirable, and I want a free mind!

But afternoons I just mosey around. This is a fine spot—not *over* comfortable—but it will do. . . .

I had a lovely morning—wrote only about 1500 words—but got on well in my thinking—saw another good chapter which I had forgotten to work in. It was on "The Social Passion." This morning a good chapter. We call it "Altruism"—a miscellaneous love of "the other" which we are puzzled to account for. But the social passion is as clearly derived as the maternal—as simple and natural. . . .

Near 7. P.M. . . .

I don't think much of S[mall] & M[aynard] from a business standpoint, myself. If this book makes a hit I shall demand greater accuracy and promptness—or leave! And this time I particularly warned them that I should need the money. I'm rather cross about it, being now reduced to $5.50 or so. But I'm paid to date all right, and go to Santa Barbara Thurs. to Monday.

. . . Feb. 21st. 1900 . . .
12.25

There—I can't do any more now. Good morning's work. "The effect of our Payment Theory on Population." 22 or 3 pages. And a clearer grouping of our current misconceptions on the subject. I'll have to write a book on misconceptions yet. It is wonderful to see how the brain, which we thought led us—has invariably held us back; and the far reaching seers have been merely *catching up with the facts*—all along.

. . . 9.45 A.M. Fri. Feb. 23rd. 1900. . . .

Walter wrote me a very touching and sweet note of congratulation and good will—I'd like to show it [to] you but it wouldn't be fair to him. Isn't it funny how completely one outgrows an emotion—I haven't the faintest flutter of consciousness with regard to him, and yet have now a sense of warm goodwill to them both which is vastly better than the hurt feeling I had last summer. He sees the advantages to Katharine—that's one good thing. Makes him feel easier in his mind about her. I'm very glad they know. That much is off my mind anyhow. Katharine is delighted with the beauty of the place here, and they are very nice to her and admire her beauty greatly. . . .

Such a terrible pile of troubles as those dear people have had and have yet. I am so sorry for them. It doesn't seem as if mine were anything in comparison—at least now that I don't have any—only happinesses.

Such a sweet daughter. She seems to grow more fond of me, more affectionate and familiar. She's human, very. A bewitching tease, and provokingly lazy and procrastinating. Needs a prompter coordination of nerve & muscle. But kind, obliging, dutiful—and a lovely companion.

But as people go she's one among ten thousand and we shall be so fond and proud of her.

Such a sweet daughter—and such a perfect husband. You are so good. (Always the inner sense of not being worthy— of accepting a sacrifice.)

Such blessed work to do. Such a good world to live in. So many lovely friends. And half a life yet, to bear fruit in—something to show my happy gratitude. . . .

. . . my room. 9. A.M. Tues. Feb. 27th. 1900. . . .

Kate and I had a very pleasant journey, as chummy and nice as could be, her dear bright head on my shoulder and playing all sorts of baby games with our hands. She is certainly getting acquainted.

But she does "take it out of me" still. I haven't got used enough to having her so close.

We had two little beds, at the Whitehead's, but her merry gambles kept me awake some, and the sort of pushing it takes to get her to do things— I'm quick and exact—she's slow and rather looseedged—that's what I've got to fit to.

You'll be such a help to me. You'll be so wise and steady and hold me up if I get a bit discouraged. I'm so grateful for you. . . .

. . . Tues. . . . Feb. 27th. 1900. . . .
7.35. P.M. . . .

So now you know that Grace knows and is not displeased. . . .

Grace's only question seemed to be whether I was going to stand "the relation"—(my great plea before having been that I couldn't, you know!) Well—circumstances alter cases, that's all I can say. Folks are different, very. Anyhow I'm quite willing to risk it. And you *needn't* be bashful about kissing me dear—I shall not chide nor turn away. . . .

. . . 6.45 P.M. Wed. Feb. 28th, 1900. . . .

. . . Tomorrow is the first day of spring. It is full spring here—the gay young leaves dance green in the canyons and around the houses.

The spring is between us—three beautiful months— and then our summer begins.

I'll take my trip as easily as may be—and rest well in Chicago—make the week in Milwaukee a short one—I want to be well and strong to come to you, my darling. . . .

8.15. . . .

I figure that I had best hurry up and send off a story and some ed's. to my friend the Post! I want a little more money just now than I'm likely to get—when the S[mall] & M[aynard] check comes in! . . .

. . . 9.40 A.M. Sat. March 3rd. 1900.
Channing House. . . .

I'm ashamed to confess what a bad week it has been. Right across all my happiness this old sense of pressure and pain—and no work done. But I won't think about it—it'll be gone soon. The beautiful things are all time— *You* are there—its only that sloppy brain of mine. . . .

. . . 8.50 P.M. Sun. March 4th. 1900. . . .

[*Charlotte is currently staying at the Channing home with Katharine and her cousin, Dorothy Channing.*]

Katharine is being angelic. . . .

Katharine is housekeeper. Dorothy helps. A woman comes in and does the heavy work.

I help wash dishes and such—and today had much satisfaction in scrubbing things. . . .

All my professional instincts stir—I want to clean house, arrange the closets—start in thoroughly.

New England ancestry! I have had to deliberately fight to get beyond these strong impulses. And people think I don't know or care about housework.

I look forward with keen pleasure to our home that is to be. To arrange and plan and buy—all clean and new. Guess— O well, we'll *have* to have some sort of a cookery, if it's only a chafing dish. . . .

. . . Monday. 5.30 P.M. March 5th. 1900. . . .

The book runs well again—have done very nicely with it here considering. Got a *fine* opening this morning, and both other days will stand I think. . . .

My old friend Miss Seuter, she who smote my self-esteem so violently on Xmas day—has just been over to see me. Grace told me that she had spoken most cordially of me—and wanted to come . . . to Las Casitas to see me. So we thought—Grace & I—that she was contrite over that attack. Now she countenances my presence here as it were by calling, and is eager to hear about the book.

This is admirably opportune for me—I was wondering who I could hire to listen to it—so that I can relate the parts more coherently. So she is to come over some more—and I am to read some more.

I'd like—being of a pertinacious disposition—to make her see that she was wrong. And admiring interest in my work will help her somewhat to realize my true position. . . .

. . . 9.15 P.M. Tues. March 6th. 1900. . . .

As to immediate facts—I have one dollar and fifty one cents—and begin to owe for board! I am very wroth with S[mall] & M[aynard], the slow staying kind of anger I am cursed with. They have been very kind—several times. They have been very remiss several times. I think the remissness is getting larger than the kindness.

Even if they had not their account ready, they could have sent me an advance in cash after I told them distinctly and repeatedly that I should need it. . . .

Another good day's work—*fine*. Got after my old friend the Want Theory, and chewed it up. You've got to help me in that chapter—it must be bullet proof.

To me it sounds quite conclusive now. But it'll bear mending no doubt. . . .

I've fixed Katharine's dress nicely, mended some other things, read to the children, helped get dinner—making an excellent stew, veal stew—with dumplings; washed the dinner dishes—and feel very domestic and virtuous.

And I keep thinking of our brand new little kitchen— of all my old-maidish little ways in furnishing—of what nice things I shall make for you.

It'll be such fun, finding out what you like best, and what is good for you—and making 'em. If only you are happy with me—truly happy and glad you did it! . . .

Getting a *very* satisfactory grip on my beloved book. All my previous chapters are falling into shape and relation. I felt rather mixed over it awhile back. Reading it to Miss Seuter is a real help. But I want to read it to *You!* What do I marry you for I'd like to know—if you're not at hand to try on my books when they're cut and basted!

. . . that down spell appears to have passed by—thank goodness. . . .

. . . Wed. March 7th. 1900. . .
9.45 P.M. . . .

I'm afraid they *will* make remarks about your wife's wearing the trousers! I'm so sorry. I'll take 'em right off—when I get home! . . .

I'm afraid we're going to differ on the marriage announcement question.

Anything so absurd as calling on my brother who hasn't seen me since 1885—to announce a marriage he knows nothing about, cannot attend, and may not approve of—no, that won't do. Make all the announcement you want to—*yourself*—but I'm not going to be "given away" in that fashion— it's too funny. Surely I have seen forms to the effect that Jane Doe and Richard Roe were married at such a date—that's enough surely. I can't see why you want to tell so many people—but if you do just go ahead—I'm willing. But this brother idea—O no! Makes me grin to think of it.

If you honestly think it is "great rot" how can you conscientiously do it? I couldn't. Why not tell your family and friends—just tell 'em—it'll spread fast enough— don't be afraid of that!—And then if any one complains of being neglected lay it on me where it belongs—say "Mrs. Gilman rather objects to those formalities." That's fair.

Isn't that a more reasonable and straightforward course—as long as you don't honestly approve of the absurd method? It isn't as if we were having a show and leaving them out—this wedding is not an exhibition. You can't make it a stylish and proper affair by any minor concession like this. . . . Now letters are easy things to misunderstand—and I love you too well to want to hurt or offend you even in a little thing like this. But do think it all out honestly with yourself. You know I am so different—it is going to cost you so much in all these ways. I always feared it would hurt you. . . .

Thurs. near ten A.M.

. . . I feel as if I was cross and inconsiderate in what I wrote last night—but I'll send it—you ought to know . . . how bad I am. . . .

I've been reading over a lot of my stuff to Dr. C[hanning] and am about to begin to work on it now. It certainly is a promising book. And I don't doubt I shall add as much again during the summer. . . .

. . . 9.10 A.M. Fri. March 9th. . . .

I'm still afraid my last letter wasn't quite kind, but count on *you* being kind enough to forgive me. . . .

I've done a lot . . . on the book this week—good work. Dr. Channing speaks most highly of it—says [it is?] full of original thought. . . .

. . . 1.40 P.M. Wed. March 14th. 1900. . . .

So you are about to broach the news to your father— or have already! Well, I'll tell Thomas & Mrs. Dow and Mrs. Campbell. Guess we're pretty fairly committed to our course.[19]

I'm not afraid? Are you?

But I am sorry for your dear people, especially your father. I grieve sincerely to add one straw to his troubles. . . .

As to Grace's misgivings about my health—we have disproved that pretty thoroughly I fancy. Anyhow I am willing to risk it. Even if I don't get any stronger than I am—I shall lay my weakness to previous conditions—not to you. . . .

My place in life is *mine* now, I have made it, all myself. My work is clear before me. A temporary depression will not make me think that marrying you has "spoiled my life." From my personal point of view you come in a beautiful collateral happiness—not as a hindrance, but a great help and joy.

I'm sorry that I can't add my life to yours—woman fashion. I'd like to. But I can't—mine is too thriving and "set" already. But I think we can sustain a very charming home life—a very beautiful married life—quite aside from the usual style of immersion of the wife in the husband. . . .

As to your helping me when I'm "down"—I begin to think it is only a natural hallucination to think anyone can.

If the troubling is a wilting of brain tissue—how can any outside person help it?

No, I think my reproachful attitude toward the innocent bystander is part of the disease. Anyhow I'm not bothering about it *any* more at *all*. . . . We all have something to bear—that's one of my defects, that's all. You have a weak throat—and a precarious digestion. Mine are strong. My brain goes back on me. Yours doesn't. No harm! Trust myself to you! . . .

It will seem funny enough though—to have any one taking care of me! Or trying to; so long—so very long— alone. . . .

. . . near 9. A.M. Sat. March. 17th 1900. . . .

Yesterday I got another chapter arranged and the sixth started. You see I have a mass of material, and am now reading and writing in and occasionally cutting out—to make a connected whole. . . . Of course I'm in a dozen minds as to whether it is worth a cent or not.

The stuff written seems so self-evident and simple. . . .

In the evening I finished . . . "To Have & To Hold"— such a fine story! I began it piecemeal, in the Atlantic. . . .

A beautiful love story used always to leave me with such a piercing hungry pain! Now—when I lay the book down—your face comes up—and I realize that it is all *true*—that the living love is there, is truly mine, is better than all books. . . .

The influence of love and trust, mutual respect and freedom, which I hope we shall give out—helping to show what man and woman may be to each other on a true basis. You give me everything, dear heart—to make me personally as happy as a well-mothered baby, and to sweeten and soften and strengthen my work. . . .

. . . 2.40 or so P.M. Sunday March 18th. 1900 —. . . .

The wide smiling valley lies before me—all velvet after the rain—such colors—such light—such softness and richness and bloom. I do want you to see it so! . . .

Of course I want "to keep house and do cooking." Didn't I tell you I should blossom into rampant domesticity? But we'd better get all meals out until after my fall lecture trip I think—then it wouldn't upset anything to have me gone. (Except your heart may be!) . . .

I start toward you in a month now—four weeks from yesterday! Lecture trips always fly marvelously. Four weeks here—then six on the wing—then Milwaukee week—then You. . . .

. . . 7.45 or so. A.M. Wed. March 21st. 1900. . . .

Last night, at last, in response to a somewhat angry letter of mine of March 9th . . . S[mall] & M[aynard] have sent in their account to Jan. 1st. And what do you think is their "check to balance due"? $100.84! ! ! ![20]

Now I am dished. I shall begin to talk poor at once and say I can't afford to marry! However we are not yet committed to any date—guess we can manage it somehow. . . .

This, as you perceive, upsets many of my fine plans, and is I fear a real injury to my dear Grace,—as my proudly undertaken 25 a month for Kate is not forthcoming.

I felt very badly last night I confess—it was a blow. . . .

I have just been going over my beloved "figuring," on a very modest basis. My minimum, as you know, is to get Katharine east and to earn thereafter a steady $25.00 a week. On that we could live, serenely. . . .

. . . I propose to drop the book and write paying stuff in the three weeks that remain—(I can do a lot, too.) . . .[21]

However—I am now in a hole; not having enough to get to Salt Lake. . . .

Are you rich enough to lend me a hundred dollars for three months? . . .

Then I shall proceed to write all manner of stuff—hand over fist.

I've got a lot of 'em ready & waiting to come out.

Even this small 100, paying board etc.—makes me feel better.

Will you please tell me if the *Criterion* is going on all right? And will you, at your Bar Association or other Library, please send me the addresses of half a dozen of the best Weeklies—yes—and any other thing that strikes you as a possible market. Meanwhile I'll do Post stuff—I'm sure of that. . . .

I hope you will not be alarmed by this sudden drop in my assets. I'm not. It'll all pop up again presently. Time I did some more articles anyway—to keep my name before the "world of letters" while the book grows.

It is a great book all right. . . .

. . . March 22nd. 1900 . . .
at the Channing House—
Just after lunch—

Grace is going down town this P.M. . . .

We have been having a nice talk. It is *such* a pleas[ur]e to be able to speak to anyone about you. And she is so sweet and understanding about it all; and reiterates that I am absurd to feel as if I were injuring you. That if we love and suit each other that is the main thing—the whole thing—nothing else matters. . . . The family troubles here are piling rapidly—the mortgage is foreclosed on the 2nd of April instead of the 20th as they had supposed. It is terribly hard in many ways; and Grace is so brave and sweet— I do love her. . . .

. . . 11.15 A.M. Sunday. March 25th 1900. . . .

Grace and I had two nights talk—sat up late and talked deep, about Katharine and ourselves and beliefs. . . .

Much of the talk would have been deeply painful to me even a year ago. Now it isn't. Why? Because you love me. . . . Being sure of my standing in your heart, what other people think does not count. We can't all see alike. It would be quite impossible for her—being the kind she is, to rightly appreciate the kind I am. No harm. She loves me still. We have come near together again, and I am glad. . . .

. . . Tues. March 27th. 1900 . . .
7.20 P.M. . . .

(Grace, poor dear, is "foreclosed" on the 2nd of April. I doubt if Dr. Channing survives the breakup. He is 80 now). . . .

5.25 . . . March. 28th 1900.

. . . I like to imagine some beautiful witchcraft by which I could [be] . . . so changed—so beautiful! Firm sweet health and perfection in every tissue—clear radiant beauty—not too palpably girlish, but what a woman of my age ought to be if she had lived in all ways perfectly right from birth. I suppose—I hope—it is the effort I have made to live right as far as I knew and could, which keeps me in some ways more active and young than many women of my age are.

But I would like to be an Aphrodite—just for you! If nobody else knew it at all—just so that when you came to your property it should be of a glowing loveliness!

Well—it's no use wishing. I am as I am. At any rate you know it all— and yet love me. The sweet miracle of it is always fresh in wonder. How *you* can love me! . . .

I try to think what it will be like—to have a permanent person who sort of belongs to me—who stays! who has a common intimate knowledge of my affairs to make all impression mutual—to give interest to us together in the little things that happen. I can sort of imagine it, a little, as I can imagine flying. That sort of companionship— I suppose I had it in childhood with Thomas; but my mean way of remembering small injuries and offences sort of blotted out the pleasure. . . .

The book falls into shape nicely. Eight chapters in place—the ninth well on the stocks—only five more as at present listed. . . .

My room. Quarter past eight. . . .

I've been thinking of you today and trying to be more polite, more nobly and deliberately courteous, more like you.

I don't think you realize at all how disagreeable and mean I am sometimes.

And I hope you never will. I will strive to outgrow it before you find me out. . . .

. . . 7.45 or so A.M. Sun. April 1st. 1900.

It being April there intervenes but one more month between us; and in literal count, ten weeks—seventy days. I think perhaps we'd better be married on the 19th—or 12th. Because? Because when I was telling Grace she burst into the merriest laughter and told me it was her wedding day! I'm sure I had no memory of it. But the 11th of June, 1894 is their date. Still I don't know as a day makes much difference—I don't care if you don't—only I thought it only fair to tell you. . . .

9.20 A.M. Tues. April 3rd. 1900. . . .

It is very beautiful to me, and promises well for your happiness, to say nothing of mine, to see how steadily this "home prospect" grows in commonplace reality in my mind. I can hardly make a steady minded person like yourself—or indeed any one—understand how much of my living has been done on a basis of self-made and self-held hypothesis.

By "flights of imagination" I instantaneously construct, destroy and reconstruct a groundwork on which to act—*and act on it*—have done so always. Now at first I misdoubted that the easy bliss I saw with you was also hypothetical—and so liable to change. But for three years past it has been "building in," with a growing sense of reality and permanence. It is as if I had always been pretending—aspiring—trying—and now I just begin to feel what I really *am*—namely your wife "Mrs. Gilman, of New York—one of our literary woman—very pleasant person to know—you ought to make her acquaintance—husband a delightful man."

All the worry, the can I?—ought I? or "I can't" is disappearing.

I just *am*—that's all—

And I do like it.

It feels so *good.*

I suppose it was the misfitness with my mother that gave me the feeling first. I didn't really live there and that way—I only had to for a while.

All my dreams were of getting out—going away.

You remember my "bird-without-feet" illustration? I always had it. Well—now I've lit! . . .

. . . About 2. P.M. Wed. April 4th. 1900.

. . . I nimbly wrote an article—probably a forty or fifty dollar one; and felt well pleased. . . .

8:15 P.M.

. . . A letter from another Oakland party—asking meekly if I'll lecture there. Certainly I will, for fifty dollars. Good—the more the merrier. My trip thickens. Of course all these won't hatch, but they *look* promising. . . .[22]

Some one sends me *The Oakland Inquirer* . . . with big notice—two columns wide—third way down—on The Remarkable Literary Success of Mrs. Charlotte Perkins Stetson. It appears to be the text of my circular with a few additions. Well—no harm. . . .

. . . 9. P.M. Fri. April 6th. 1900. . . .

. . . Came out this morning and spent a pleasant day with Grace. It appears that that 200. I dropped in came in the very nick of time. A sudden overall claim came in—and she threw various sops to various tradesmen—it was really very convenient. . . .

. . . about 2.30 P.M. Sat. April 7th. 1900. . . .

I've been weighing chances carefully as to this year's duty . . . there is a six weeks of greater or less strain. The summer will be pretty full. The book will have to be done in six weeks too, most of it—and I expect to do a good deal of work with Katharine. Then comes the choosing and fitting a home, and starting Katharine on her new life in harness. Then the six weeks lecturing.

I think all things considering, we had better take care to add no complications to these essential duties; or to deplete either my strength—or theirs.

But I shall come home in the middle of December and there is only rest and the sweet home life for the next year—with light incidental work.

So I think it would be wise to avoid contingencies for six months—don't you?

After all I may never have the blessed possibility again—my precautions may be needless; but there is the chance—and I should feel sorry indeed to risk any harm to life together by carelessness. . . .

. . . 9.30 A.M. Mon. April 9th. 1900. . . .

Bless me! Here is an alarming sentence. "When each of us can exercise rights of proprietorship over the other"!!! Now I *am* scared! I prithee give me some notion of *your* notion of these same rights of proprietorship! I may cry out like the young Scotch lassie at the altar—the agreement "to obey" had been reached & the groom muttered grimly "I'll see to that!" "Are we married yet?" quoth she; and being told they were not she promptly fled the field. Now aren't you scared? . . .

. . . Tues. . . . April 10th. 1900 —. . .
9 P.M. . . .

[*In this letter she has asked Houghton to find a minister for their wedding.*]

. . . Mrs. Dow has a worthy preacher up her way, who called on me once, a good man. But he's a Presbyterian by trade—and I'm afraid would want me to obey or something dreadful. . . . But you've got to look into these matters! I'm not going to do it all! Twon't look well to have the bride managing right & left! Dear me! How hard I shall have to try to look meek and be taken care of! . . .

. . . April 11th. 1900. . . .

I'm glad you feel that way about the 11th of June. It was pure coincidence. Grace . . . laughed immensely over it; and Walter, in answer to her, wrote gravely that he saw no reason my happiness should not begin on the same day with theirs! I don't mind—it seems rather poetical somehow. . . .

[*The letter continues with financial calculations about her lecture fees, and about royalties from articles she is writing for the* Atlantic *and the "friendly" Post.*]

. . . I'm not worried a bit. . . .

Yes, you "earn" a lot more than you get—like the housewife. . . .

. . . It is very strange to me—this feeling of pure sensuous pleasure in you—which is growing all the time, same as the deeper feeling does. . . .

Well—I won't bother to analyze. It's all right, and I like it! And I suppose you feel the same way, and that's why you don't care if I am a "crone"— any more than I would if you were a———what is the masculine of crone? Crouje?

My body simply purrs with satisfaction at your approach. My heart is brimful of present joy and lovely plans for the future—our future.

And my mind—that used to kick so, and that you never *would* take the trouble to convince!—is so calmly assured that I at least am getting a very good thing. . . .

. . . Thurs. April 12th. 1900. . . .

I've done nothing today but pack . . . and get some ms. ready to send off. About $100.00 worth to the Post. Hope he takes it. And still one more to go. This little batch is over $200. worth at a 2 ct a word rate—ought to pay my bills all summer.

But then—they may not go!

I haven't sent off the book yet. . . .

I sort of "feel" that I'd better not send it to them—yet.

So I'll mail it to you. I'm not at all anxious to have you read it—in this crude form—would much rather read it to you. How would it serve for amusement on our wedding tour!!! The bride's book on "Work"! No, I guess I won't take it along—it's too heavy. . . .

. . . Mon. April 16th. 1900.
San Francisco Cal. . . .
10–10. A.M. . . .

I'm so glad some of your friends are approving. It is a real grief to me— for your sake—that your family do not, but it's no surprise. Perhaps they'll get reconciled in time. And as you know I am especially sorry, genuinely sorry, to add to your father's troubles. But it can't be helped. I cannot "give you up" on that account. . . .

3.45 P.M. Tues. April 17th. 1900. . . .

I'm beginning to take an interest in spring gowns and bonnets. In the interest of my business it will be expedient for me to have a nice new travelling dress for Milwaukee!

I think it will be grey. Grey with soft white blouse or tie; and with violet, or pink, or yellow to give color. I know you like me in grey. . . .

. . . 4 P.M. Fri. April 20th. 1900.
San Francisco. . . .

Today your telegram.

I'm frightened—but am trying hard not to think about it. Shall watch the papers—nothing in today's about any New York strike.[23]

13

"With Thanks for Life and Love": 26 April–7 June 1900

After the winter months in California, Charlotte headed east by train, lecturing as usual in women's clubs along the way—in Denver, Colorado, for example, in Salt Lake City, Provo, Utah, and Fargo, North Dakota. The "'power' is on," she wrote Houghton, and "I am glad to feel it work." These "western towns always please me—such vigor and spontaneity." And the people "just love me." They care about "*me* as well as my books"—"live people, who dare think, and to whom my thought is a real help and stimulus." And "instead of being exhausted by it I feel fine—nothing is so good for me as to feel this kind of power and light." They "seemed particularly surprised to find I was really a woman, with a heart as well as a head." "It's the real *me*—my own real business; and it is so good to have them like it!"[1]

For the last few weeks before her marriage, Charlotte spent some time at the home of her "Chicago mother," Marietta Dow. Occasionally she did some lecturing and writing; she attended meetings with her Chicago friends at Hull House; but for the most part she occupied herself with sewing, shopping, and making personal arrangements.[2] "I'm really going to 'give my mind' to the dress question," she wrote Houghton, and not only in "the interests of my business." "I'm not a vain person . . . but since loving you I have . . . thought more and cared more about my looks than I ever did in my life. . . . See the corrupting influence of being in love!" So "I've been having an orgy of needlework," she wrote him, and also have "purchased a black (Japanese) silk waist—'special sale' for $8.65." In fact, all "I'm going to do this coming week is to buy things and sew. Also rest—a lot; better less clothes and more health!"

Although for the most part Gilman wrote enthusiastically about her coming marriage, one issue still seriously concerned her: the "honest regret" of Houghton's friends and relatives, their awareness of the "dangers" and "risks" to him. His aunt, Louisa Gilman, for instance, who had raised Houghton since his mother's death (1879), was "sadly" worried that she had not duly warned him about the meaning of a happy marriage: "It is such a sacred thing,—so truly a sacrament, that I could not talk of it." Another relative tried to reassure him: "You need have no apprehension that we shall, having spoken very frankly once for all . . . continue to express disapprobation. . . . I hope you will bring your wife to this Norwich home to be welcomed and loved." Or as another family member wrote:[3]

> This is not what I should have planned for you, but I feel sure that you know what is right for you and what you most want. . . . Charlotte is very clever and very inspiring and has a truly affectionate heart. But this is no ordinary marriage. You will have the eyes of many upon you and if you make a success of it will help many another fellow-being and assist in straightening things out in this much vexed question.

Or as their aunt, Emily Perkins Hale, wrote him:[4]

> We are so sure of your deep love for us underneath all your shy reticence; we so firmly believe that you mean to do the things that are right—that it puts us in a strange position not to be able to rejoice with you and congratulate you in a matter which concerns us deeply. Of course you did not mean to grieve us!
>
> But when some one whom I love proposes to do something which looks to me both unwise and wrong, is it strange that I am inclined to cry out Stop! Consider! . . .
>
> Dear Houghton I have been thinking about you a great deal lately, both waking and sleeping, and praying for you more earnestly than I ever prayed for you before—and this is my great desire that you "may both perceive and know what things you ought to do and also may have grace and power faithfully to fulfill the [?] through Jesus Christ our Lord."
>
> I am very sorry for you—It must be hard to find that your father does not see things as you do—it must have been hard to write to us! It is not altogether easy to answer your letter!!

Predictably, Gilman was tormented by the relatives' negative reaction. "No year or two of sorrow now could be as bad as the years of blank misery if this go wrong," she wrote, as though momentarily spiraling back to the familiar pattern of self-hatred. In fact, it is only "with the utmost difficulty that I refrain from casting myself at the feet of your relatives and beating my breast, with tears—so conscious am I of my demerits." "I am so *thankful* you are not rich," she continued. "They can't think of me as 'interested' in that way at least." But to his family the marriage seemed so "terrible," so "dreadful," and she necessarily so "selfish," that "even yet" she wondered whether she was "fit" to marry, and whether it was her "duty to run away." Perhaps the family would "sort of half get used to it in time," she wrote him if only she could make a "a beautiful and comfortable home" for him, and even more importantly, if only they could "have a lovely child." She could barely hope for one, she told him. "But if we did—and it was good and beautiful and clever—they might be sort of half way reconciled." So she would soon "pitch in and have a child if I can," she wrote him. "A fine one. Yes sir! If I'm well and happy and can give you that," "it won't look so bad for you."

Although Gilman no doubt struggled with a variety of motives—of which the need to please his family was only one—for the most part she had enthusiastically claimed in letters that she wanted to undertake another pregnancy. Like most women of her generation, she simply assumed that children were "essential" to a marriage, that Houghton needed and deserved a larger family, and that it was her clear "duty" to oblige. "O how glad! how proud! how triumphant I should be, if I could announce that coming joy to you," she had repeatedly insisted. Simultaneously, however, and "selfishly," she claimed, she was concerned about the risks and dangers: those resulting from their "cousinness," for instance, or from interruptions of her work commitments, or from possible depressions such as she had experienced with Kate. After all, "the worst of it—for me personally—is the wreckage it would mean to my conscience if the thing went wrong. It is terrible to contemplate."[5]

In these last few weeks before the marriage, Charlotte thus decided to consult two physicians in Chicago. The first, Dr. McCracken, "expressed himself very strongly against it—very strongly: A bare one chance in twenty of having an exceptionally fine child," he said, "and all the rest toward degeneracy of some sort." The second doctor, a woman by the name of Dr. Lowe, was less concerned about the "risk" to Charlotte. She did, however, recommend a "mild treatment to offset a local condition—slight malposition" of the uterus, which assured that the chances of pregnancy were "very slight." Gilman enthusiastically responded, "Happy thought—take no precautions—take no treatment—all runs smoothly and naturally and nothing happens!!! There's an easy way out of the difficulty!"

* * * * *

With plans to marry Houghton in mid-June, Gilman nonetheless set out in early June for the biennial Woman's Rights Convention, Milwaukee, Wisconsin. "These great meetings of women are very inspiring," she wrote Houghton, such "masses of women," and such "wide friendliness." "I do earnestly hope to make a strong good address"—"Women and Work," she would call it. In any case it would be a "splendid opportunity" to "summarize and philosophize as I like best to do." And the "more friendly and helpful I can be in that Convention the more chance for lectures next fall." Besides, "it *is* so good to be useful to folks," and for the most part "I was pleased to find how widely—and apparently favorably known I was." "You've got the Beecher voice," said one enthusiastic colleague. Another "told me with tears in her eyes that I had helped her." So overall she had "the same pleasant sense of acceptance that I always do at these meetings." In fact, "I am a rich and happy woman," she concluded, "thanks to you," and "thanks to the dear Lord for it all—for Life and Love—to be here in the wonderful world, and feel his love flow out and in through the people.

And now I've got a main pipe direct into the reservoir—that's You—you beautiful piece of God!"[6]

* * * * *

For the last several years, Charlotte had used her letters to Houghton Gilman as a major source of healing and as a bridge between her public work and private self. Instead of the "fogs and blizzards" of the past, she saw "blessed meadows" and "sunshine and new flowers." She had poured out all her "sins and errors" into letters and thus had finally found a sense of "peace and rest," of "joy and strength," of "passionate gratitude and love." "I keep finding out what [love] means," she continued, "and what the books mean." It was as "if some system of irrigation were gradually spreading in a desert country, reclaiming more ground daily, and making the wilderness to blossom as the rose." "You've done something to me Houghton dear—I'm not what I used to be at all. The world has wiggled and turned round and has new values." "Perhaps you're getting weary of my vociferous love letters. Bear up a bit—they'll soon cease," and "all this literature can be diverted to the uses of the general public." Besides, there "isn't much to say that I haven't said—over and over. It is to be and to do now. And not to let the happiness blind and mislead me—dull my sensitiveness, check my sympathy, stop my work. It will not, I know; it has not so far and it will not. On the contrary I shall do more work and better—thanks to your dear help."[7]

Letters: April 26 through June 7, 1900

. . . Ogden April 26th. 1900.
Utah. 10.25 A.M. . . .

Feel well this morning, and shall get through the lecture tonight all right I guess. . . .

The Provo people are fixing for me tomorrow, it appears. Then Denver—and more letters! . . .

Provo. Utah.
April 27th. 1900. . . .

The lecture at Salt Lake was a fizzle—$16.00 entire proceeds! . . .

. . . I got on finely with the lecture; and when I stopped the folks rose up in entreaty and wanted more. So I talked some more. It's the first time I've held forth since last fall, and I was pleased—considering the condition

of my body and mind—to say nothing of this gnawing pain in my heart—
that I could do so well. . . .

. . . Sat. April 28th. 1900. . . .

[*She speaks of her lecture in Provo.*]
The folks turned out nobly, and were very glad to see me. I have warm
friends in Provo.

They are very poor there just now—sending an exploring party to South
America to look up their prehistoric cities as described in the book of
Mormon. I didn't expect they could have me at all. But bless me—they
stirred up the town—sold tickets two for a quarter—and made $25.00 for
me, at that!

There was a good crowd you see, and very enthusiastic. . . .

. . . 9.45 A.M. Tues. May 1st. . . .

[*Charlotte is staying with Helen Campbell in Denver, and had just lectured at the Denver Woman's Club.*]
. . . The crowd was not large but was enthusiastic—and I scored a distinct success.

It was really very gratifying. And . . . another lecture is to be given
tonight. . . . Also they sent me a basket of roses. And are coming around
this morning to pay cash.

Lots of them said that now they understood the book better—the lecture
was on that vexed subject.

A reception was held after the lecture—with refreshments and a long
line of grins and introductions—all very cordial. . . .

All this helps toward further lecturing of course—there are many
women's clubs in America! . . .

11.45 A.M. Sat. May 5th. . . .
C. P. Stetson. c/o Mrs. Wm. C. Dow
473 Orchard st. Chicago Ill. . . .

I'm thinking of doing a few newspaper articles—if I can—while here—
just to ease over these little extra incidentals. . . .

I'm afraid you've been having a very hard and painful experience darling—in the honest regret of your own people over this [the marriage].

I know you are too considerate of me to say anything about it, but of
course I know—and am neither surprised nor displeased. Of course, they

feel badly for you. My friends are pleased—they know that I am getting a good true man to love and care for me. Yours see the risks you take, and, loving you, are sorry. I shall do the best, the very best I can, dear husband, to justify your choice. . . .

**. . . Towards seven P.M. Sunday
May 6th. 1900**

You dear Darling—

I do nothing but write to you! It will certainly save money to be married—all this literature can be diverted to the uses of the general public. . . .

Mon. A.M. [May 7, 1900]

Yours of the 4th—and your Aunt Louisa.[8] O Houghton I am so sorry for them. It makes me cry for sympathy—they love you so—and it seems to them so dreadful. I knew it must. It is a terrible thing to bring pain into a family. I've written as humble and sweet a letter as I knew how—there isn't much to say, you know. Of course they'll sort of half get used to it in time—if you are happy. But it must be terribly hard for you. It makes me wish I had been stronger in the beginning—had not come back to New York that winter. And yet—I don't wish it—I can't—I love you so. I do not ever remember doing so selfish a thing before in all my life. Well———.

It remains to make a beautiful and comfortable home for you— they don't know I have talents in that line! To be agreeable and entertaining to your friends and even—perhaps—be of some service in helping your business advance—that they don't imagine I can do.

And if we did have a lovely child—that I scarce dare hope for. But if we did—and it was good and beautiful and clever—they might be sort of half way reconciled. . . .

Just the home and the writing and our nice evenings—nice people there—it will grow more tolerable to them in time I'm sure. . . .

7.30 P.M. Mon. May 7th. 1900. . . .

I am so weary of waiting. So lonely—so sad at [the] thought of my unworthiness.

It makes me afraid. Afraid that I have chosen wrong, and that this happiness was not for me.

I should have left you no matter what it cost—you would have found your own in time. . . .

I've done a heap of crying today. How hard this must be for you, darling—and you've never said a word. Of course I *knew,* but this effort to be sweet and kind and do the right thing and "welcome me into the family circle" when they *can't* in their hearts—O it is too bad. I feel so remorseful to bring a real sorrow to such loving hearts. . . .

And I don't know exactly by what cheerful prancings you can prove to them that you are happy with me. I am so *thankful* you are not rich! They can't think of me as "interested" in that way at least. . . .

Has not this distress of your relatives and friends shown you the danger you are in more plainly than I could? Though I did try—honestly.

No year or two of sorrow now could be as bad as the years of blank misery if this go wrong.

I mean this very honestly dear—I'd face it calmly and go on living as before. And I'd have Katharine. . . .

I feel sort of starved tonight—want to be mothered. It was good to be with dear Mother Campbell. She does love me, really, and is far nearer me than my own dear mother. . . .

9.20 A.M. Tues. May 8th. 1900. . . .

I'm still low. It was a blue day and a poor night. I wish I had you to say reassuring things to me. You see I'm so painfully conscious of not being fit for you to marry—and it all comes across me so clearly sometimes—and I feel as if even yet—perhaps—it was my duty to run away.

Please tell me I'm good for something and that you particularly want me for yourself! . . .

2.35 P.M.

So I wrote a lot more letters crying again over the one to Aunt Emily. Then I read a bit in "The Ethical Review" which some one sent me, and that did me good. Cause I got hold of the big things again—the things that need doing and that I can help in— and it set me up more strongly. . . .

And then . . . your letter. . . .

I *was* so glad of it! And it happened to be a particularly nice one, and comforting to my heart, which is grievously torn of late by renewed "conviction of sin" in feloniously marrying you. . . .

Please don't mind my being sort of tempestuous—it's the way the tiredness works I expect. . . .

. . . Chicago Ill.
May 9th. 1900. . . .

A reviving sense . . . is taking place of my recent abasement. You see I feel other people's feelings so keenly—when they think I'm no good I agree with 'em.

That's why I need so to be loved, and to be continually told so. I forget that I've ever done anything, or am likely to. . . .

. . . got . . . two fat [letters] from Mrs. Campbell.

These I want you to see, but can save them. We must have something to talk about on that fortnight.

I don't want you looking like the man in *Punch*—do you remember? The honeymoon couple on the sands—

She. "Don't you wish some friend would come along?"

He. "Yes. Or even an enemy!"

Don't know but I'll have to take the book. I never heard of brides doing such things as that—but then I'm a queer species of bride anyway. . . .

7.10 P.M. Wed. May 9th. 1900.
473 Orchard St.
Chicago—Ill. . . .

I've come to the conclusion that my main business in life just now is to be well and happy; and further more to pitch in and have a child if I can! A fine one. Yes sir!

If I'm well and happy and can give you that—it won't look so bad for you. Now I'm going to bend my endeavors to just that end—well-th and happiness. 'Tis a fine combination of duty and pleasure, isn't it! . . .

I begin to have hopes again of beguiling dear Mother Campbell to come and help for a while. Dear me what comfort I'd take with her to run things a bit! And to be there with Katharine—so we could be freer evenings, you know.

Mostly I want her to have a sort of home place to come to—she's very unhappy with Mrs. Westendorf now, and not go and marry this man because she has no other hope or home. She is writing freely now—or has been; and ought to be easily able to take care of herself for a good many years yet— if she has some body to love her.[9]

Of course if the man is all right it's the best thing in the world. But if he isn't—if he's just a kind of an enthusiast—I can't see her have any more suffering. She's had quite enough.

And she stood by me in San Francisco when her friends wrote to her that in going to me she risked her whole reputation! Mmm! I'd *love* to make a comfortable background for her old age. Also it is perfectly true that she'd make an inestimable helper to me. . . .

I never knew a nobler woman—unless Grace—and Grace has not had to bear what this one has. I'm rather mixed up between my honest love for her and desire to help her; and the undeniable usefulness of having her near. . . .

10 A.M. Thurs. May 10th. 1900
473 Orchard st. Chicago. Ill. . . .

Life back of me looks so cloudy and mixed and difficult— fogs and blizzards and slow cold—long deserts, and very high mountains. Also holes—ugh!

I'm never going to look back. Never did, much.

Now blessed meadows open out before me—sunshine and new flowers.

I perceive that the proper thing is to put all my pride behind me—to cease longing to be young and beautiful and strong and worthy of you— (which only makes me feel older and less worthy!) and just honestly and humbly recognize the great blessing which has come to me; that you are the Giver—giver of peace and rest—joy and strength—and I must Take— and be grateful. O I am, dear, I am. It wells up and runs over—the deep deep sense of passionate gratitude and love. . . .

So I'll be contented with that. I try to give to other people. From you I'll learn to take—my first lesson. Never as a child—since I outgrew my mother—never as a girl—never in my first attempt to be a wife—never in any strange step— have I leaned on any one and asked of them.

Now I do humbly lean on you. . . .

8.45 P.M. Thursday. May 10th

[*The magazine* Bazar *has changed its name from the* Bazaar, *has become a weekly, and is publishing an article by her.*]

. . . It was about a 2500 word thing—and may be anywhere from 25.00 to $50.00—I hope the latter. What makes me feel good is the thought of a new market—and a weekly. Weeklies can use more stuff than monthlies! And the kind that take the *Bazar* are just the ones I want to reach. I'll try 'em again forsooth.

Then it pleases me to have the check come in so soon— shows that my last fortnight at Las Casitas was not misspent. So I shall buy my grey gown— (for the Biennial!) with a clear conscience. And write more stuff with re-newed spirit. . . .

8.35 A.M. Fri. May 11th. 1900.

. . . I . . . rejoiced greatly in my *Bazar* letter. It betokens a large long steady prospect. My kind of easy chat, casting new light on common home affairs, ought to be wanted right along. . . .

Once my easy minor essay style gets to acceptance in the various weeklies, and our income is comfortably buttressed, I am more and more decided to let the book wait.

Miss Wellington writes that Small is out of the firm—I *think* that's what she means, and he was the brains of it. I've no use for Maynard. If I sit quiet and just say I can't get the book done this year—make no quarrel— let 'em go on with the others—why a season's appearance in good magazines will do me no harm—I may get better offers elsewhere, or as good.

Then next year—with money matters easier, Katharine probably gone to her Papa for a while, just you and I together and *maybe* prospects of more!—then it would be regular quiet unhurried home work to finish it. With your dear help—can't write books without my husband, I can't! O you blessing! And I'm quite sure I can do nearly as well this summer on short things. . . .

3.35 P.M. Friday May 11. 1900. . . .

Darling—it seems to me each day that yesterday I did not love—so much more do I love you as they pass. I keep finding out what it means. I see what other people mean, and what the books mean. I begin to see how people die for loss of love—not all at once, dramatically, but slowly—because they do not have what they need. Sometimes it grows on me slowly; and sometimes it comes in big jumps. That is the way it happened this week—a long step all at once. . . .

. . . 8.30 A.M. Sat. May 12th. 1900. . . .

Good Morning Heart's Dearest!

Fair weather—fair as my hopes—bright as my prospects—warm as my heart. It becometh apparent to my mind that Love with man is an episode— with woman a history. There you sit and attend to business as calm as a door post, and here am I singing daily hymns of praise because I'm going to be married! Perhaps you're getting weary of my vociferous love letters. Bear up a bit— they'll soon cease. . . .

8.30 A.M. Tues. May 15th. 1900—. . .

. . . I . . . met . . . Mrs. Corinne Brown . . . and talked concerning the Convention. She is at the head of the "Industrial Section" as I think I told you. My speech is in the morning, and last,—I am to summarize and philosophize as I like best to do. . . .

Then I came back, lay down & read awhile, and went to Hull House to dine. Hull House always uses me up. Such a flux of disconnected people. Such a noisome neighborhood. And wonderful Miss Addams handling it all so well and meeting the thousand calls upon her so gently and effectively— it is magnificent, but it tires me very much. . . .

Dear I am sorry, on your account, that Katharine comes too—at first; but it did seem the inevitably right thing to do. It would be a bit easier for me—to have only *you*—but it is both joy and duty to take the child now. . . .

. . . 9.50 A.M. Wed. May 16th. 1900. . . .
near 12. noon.

I am now waiting in Dr. Lowe's office. She is a flourishing and capable physician, and, as I believe I told you, a great admirer of my work. I am going to confide to her the open secret of my matrimonial intentions, and ask her to look over my machinery. Then I'll know how I stand to begin with. . . .

. . . I . . . purchased a black (Japanese) silk waist—"special sale" for $8.65. It is cheap, but looks nice—and is exquisitely light and cool. Emboldened by success I plunged into another shop, and another "sale" and got a black silk skirt for $15.00. . . .

I am mightily pleased with the skirt—it will do me yeoman service for ever so long. And it is made something after the fashion of one Annie Russell wore—so I know I'm all right! . . .

I'm really going to "give my mind" to the dress question—I want folks to admire your wife. It didn't matter much how *I* looked, but it does matter how your wife looks—matters much. I can't ever be very "swell"—but I hope to keep within range of the correct thing, and have a distinction of my own too. . . .

. . . 5 P.M. Wed. May 16th. 1900. . . .

I got home about 3.30 I guess—found your dear letter . . . and one from the Chairman of Program Committee—would I do so and so if Mrs. So & So didn't come? Mrs. Lowe said I would. And of course I will—that's exactly what I'm good at, at Conventions—filling holes. I won almost tears of gratitude from a literary program lady at London—would I give them a poem—and *would* I mind that my name was not on the program? As if I cared about having my name on programs!

The more friendly and helpful I can be in that Convention the more chance for lectures next fall. . . .

Now to finish my afternoon medical conversation. . . . Dr. Lowe . . . thought I might risk having a child. Physical condition good—the Cousinness bad—but a good fighting chance. Still she does not know as well as Dr. McCracken. He expressed himself very strongly against it—very strongly: A bare one chance in twenty of having an exceptionally fine child—a genius; and all the rest toward degeneracy of some sort. . . . But it is a big risk—and the worst of it—for me personally—is the wreckage it would mean to my conscience if the thing went wrong. It is terrible to contemplate. . . .

O—Dr. Low[e] recommends some mild treatment to offset a local condition—slight malposition—which makes any such chance at present very slight. So much so that she thought I need use no precautions at first. Happy thought—take no precautions—take no treatment—all runs smoothly and naturally and nothing happens!!! There's an easy way out of the difficulty! . . .

. . . 9.15 A.M. Thurs. May 17th. 1900. . . .

It is not so much "greater intensity" that I feel in loving you more and more. It seems wider and deeper somehow—to cover more ground. As if some system of irrigation were gradually spreading in a desert country, reclaiming more ground daily, and making the wilderness to blossom as the rose. . . .

I too think it would be well for Katharine to stay with us for several years. And I hope she will elect to do so. It seems to me a better start for an American woman than the miscellaneous European life. But Grace and Walter particularly want just that for her, to say nothing of wanting her, and the child—at present—prefers the European idea. I am not sure enough to insist—even if I had the right. But I shall do my best to make this country and our home agreeable to her. She has been reading a lot of foreign novels; good ones enough but adding to the pull that way. I propose to momentarily surround her with American stories this year—of the best. . . .

I would like to keep her till she is eighteen, and then let her go study art and languages and be in that sort of atmosphere. But it depends on how she feels, mostly. I am in great hopes that our home will be agreeable to her, and that she will form pleasant associations with New York and like to stay. . . .

As I wrote you yesterday I am rather shaken on the child question. Don't I vacillate though!

I really need your wisdom and strength dear to help me in this matter. The responsibility is partly yours—and your head is steadier than mine. Also your conscience is good. . . .

According to this good woman [Dr. Lowe] who examined me yesterday there is no present danger. And she is the only one who has the "inside facts." I was going to have Dr. McCracken make the examination—but—since I have learned what love is I have learned some modesty too. I couldn't bear to have him. Come to think of it I never did have a man doctor—at that end! But I shouldn't have minded if I had. And now I do. . . .

. . . Fargo. N.D.
Mon. May 21st. 1900. . . .

These western towns always please me—such vigor and spontaneity. And to [think] of how full the country is of them. . . .

. . . 10.15 A.M. Tues. May 22nd. 1900. . . .
[Fargo, N.D.]

It is a pity I can't write you more—but the days fill up thick; and I forgot even you in the preaching! Only for a little while—but the "power" is on up here, and I am glad to feel it work.

The lecture last night was not a great success from my point of view; but it was to the people. They just love me. They say I am so "womanly"! Good! I am. (Especially in these days.) Pity if a waiting bride can't be womanly! It is really one of the best times and places I've struck—live people, who dare think, and to whom my thought is a real help and stimulus. The family here sit around and I preach, severally & collectively, and even the old mother—grandma—agrees with my doctrine. . . .

These folks are friends now,—they like *me*—as well as my books, and are not shy in saying so.

And instead of being exhausted by it I feel fine—nothing is so good for me as to feel this kind of power and light. . . .

3.45 P.M. . . .

This morning I went to the State University and spoke to some of the students—quite a crowd. . . .

A fine "occasion"—gave 'em a good one.

Then a lunch party—one of the rich women here. All very pleasant and popular—another place to come to from year to year. . . .

But I do feel so happy about it. It's the real *me*—my own real business; and it is so good to have them like it! . . .

. . . 9.25 A.M. Wed. May 23rd. 1900 . . .
[Valley City]

. . . Although early, as you see, I have already been to the Normal Institute and addressed the assembled pupils and professors.

A brief address, but vigorous and impressive. Then I read 'em "Heroism," and they clapped so that I further read "An Obstacle." . . .

People are alive out here. . . .

And the beauty of it is to have 'em so pleased when I do come. They seemed particularly surprised to find I was really a woman, with a heart as well as a head. Mrs. Amidon had lost a baby last fall—a great blow to her, though she has three, and was puzzling much over death and immortality and God. We talked a good deal and she says she has really got a better grip on things. . . . and she, like so many others, wants me to come and visit them—stay and work or rest—"make their house my home" as it were. . . . Of course I'm a bit tired with all this— yesterday was a very full day; but it is good tired—everything has gone well.

There's a young man here, teacher of psychology, who has just taken [a] Columbia scholarship. . . . Perhaps he'd like to come to our house, and I no doubt can make him useful. You know my scheme of laying in an education by means of other people's work, and the conversation of agreeable persons!

Katharine also will be profited by the discourse, though she scoffs at "epochs & eras!"

But if they are nice young men I think she can bring herself to listen; and it will gradually give her a new feeling toward her mother and her work— I hope. . . .

. . . 9.30 or so A.M. Sat. May 26th. 1900. . . .

Glad you approve of my black silk skirt. I think you'll like it. Yes you will learn in time something of the details of expense in women's clothes, but not much. You see I'm no "dresser"—and not a good shopper. I really know very little about it myself, except on the inside margin. I can dress to the height of my ambition on about 200.00 a year; and with contentment on 100.00. . . .

It makes me fairly purr to have you say such pretty things about my good looks—and not needing pretty clothes. I dare say *you'd* be contented if I wavered between that grey silk and a nightgown—but I want to dress well now that your friends may admire and not criticize. I am sensitive for your sake dear. . . .

What fiendish interpretation is this you put upon my innocent words about "the peaceful industry of the summer"! I never saw anything funnier in my life than you are when you are wicked. It is as if lamb should swear! . . .

. . . All I'm going to do this coming week is to buy things and sew. Also rest—a lot; better less clothes and more health! . . .

. . . About 7. P.M. Tues. May 29th, 1900. . . .

. . . I cannot express how the home-hunger grows on me. To have a place to *stay* in! O it *is* so good. And to have You in it—it doesn't seem as if it could be true. But the time draws on. We're inside the last fortnight—the long long years have gone. . . .

I wonder why it is that it is so impossible for me to feel lovable and deserving. I don't see that most women feel this way— they seem to take what's coming to them very calmly. . . .

. . . 9 P.M. Friday. June 1st. . . .

. . . I've been having an orgie of needlework, all day. . . .

I just sit and sew and think of you and smile and smile. And I sing, softly—I'm so happy. . . .

. . . 9. A.M. Sunday. June 3rd. 1900. . . .

You've done something to me Houghton dear—I'm not what I used to be at all. The world has wiggled and turned round and has new values. And it's mostly You—just now. Work and Duty are somewhere—they'll wake up again I don't doubt—but just now life is very simple. . . .

. . . 9. A.M. Tues. June 5th. 1900
Milwaukee. Wis. . . .

Yesterday was gratifying—but exhausting of course. I went to a Press Club reception. . . .

And I was pleased to find how widely—and apparently favorably known I was.—They came up and greeted me—delegates from Des Moines and Omaha, Kansas City, St. Louis & Toledo, Chicago; Atlanta, Denver and

Washington—from everywhere, they had heard me speak, or read the books, or both—and were most kind. . . .

. . . in the evening I . . . had a very nice call on Mrs. L[owe]. She is cordial as ever—greeted me with effusion, says to stay there to meals—to use her carriage—and has given me an order to sit in her box (the meetings are held in a theater). So I'm top o' the heap and feel fine. . . .

I mingled a bit in the crush outside—such masses of women. . . .

There are heaps of "politics" going on in this thing— thank goodness I don't have to participate in that part of it at all.

But I do earnestly hope to make a strong good address. It is my own ground—Women and Work—and a splendid opportunity. . . .

9. A.M. Wed. June 6th. 1900.
Milwaukee. Wis. . . .

I'm glad you had a good long day with the Aunts—sort of a fare well visit. Dear brave old ladies—trying to make the best of it for your sake. And how much of my happiness I owe them, for "bringing you up" so well. . . .

Mrs. Lowe made one of the best addresses I ever heard—remarkably good. I just went up and hugged her when it was all over—said I was proud of her. And she looked up as sweet as could be and said "Well—you made me!" Wasn't that nice of her. . . .

Came home, ate a nice dinner, rested an hour or more, dressed up and went to a reception at *The Atheneum,* a big woman's club house. . . .

There I met a great happiness—a little woman—Mrs. Basset of Pittsburgh P.A. who told me with tears in her eyes that I had helped her. My poems. She just meant it all, too; and held on to my hand tight. It was very sweet and went way down into my heart. O it *is* so good to be useful to folks! . . .

Altogether it was a very very pleasant day—with your letter on top— and the steady sense of you coming underneath— and all this wide friendliness around. I am a rich and happy woman dear—thanks to you for all this new sweet tender personal part of it—which is just now bigger than heaven and earth. And thanks to the dear Lord for it all—for Life and Love—to be here in the wonderful world, and feel his love flow out and in through the people. And now I've got a main pipe direct into the reservoir—that's You— you beautiful piece of God! . . .

. . . 8.50 A.M. Thurs. June 7th. 1900.
Milwaukee.

My Own Dear Love—

This is truly the last last letter from C.P. Stetson. It's a name I never liked and shall be very glad to change. But I fear me it will stick for many a year yet! . . .

. . . I have two more days to look forward to—then Sunday—then that slow crawling train to Detroit. Don't you go and be disappointed in me now if I don't look pretty! You've been idealizing me for nine months by the aid of calm photographs and rose colored memories. Now I'm three years older than when I called at your office to renew our acquaintance; and nearly a year older than when you saw me last. . . .

I mention all these things so as not to see your countenance fall when I emerge from the train! . . .

Yesterday morning I attended the educational session and was very favorably impressed with the assembly. . . .

These great meetings of women are very inspiring. . . .

Very last thing of all I was produced, and read "Heroism." I had the same pleasant sense of acceptance that I always do at these meetings, when my large clear voice sails out into these strained ears and they all *rest*. "You've got the Beecher voice" said a lady in the car to me, coming home.

Afterward a request was sent up from the audience that I read Mother to Child—and I did.

Mrs. Lowe was pleased of course, to have her experiment so warmly received.

And I was pleased over again, by the dear people coming up and saying things afterward. . . .

"You *are* the *sweetest* thing!" was one woman's ardent comment. . . . Another, with tears in her eyes, said she had never seen anyone who was so like her mother! Even the reporters were impressed. So that was a good time too. . . .

There isn't much to say that I haven't said—over and over. It is to be and to do now. And not to let the happiness blind and mislead me—dull my sensitiveness, check my sympathy, stop my work. It will not, I know; it has not so far and it will not. On the contrary I shall do more work and better— thanks to your dear help. . . .

I suppose I shall get used to love and peace and comfort and forget to be grateful every day! But I doubt it. The other life has been too long. It will take many years of happiness to blunt my sense of gratitude.

I notice I'm just as pleased with kind words today as I was ten years ago—just as surprised and touched. At least it seems so. . . .

Dear Lover—you have been most perfect in that place. Never once have you grieved or offended me in any way. Always kind and tender, always patient with my wearying changes of mood—my doubts and questions and straining this way and that. Always sweet and desirable in your own person—always so courteous and nice to other persons. I have *liked* as well as loved you, from the first. So strong and quiet and kind—such a rest to my tired soul and worn body.

And with such unmeasured greatness of soul that I have poured all my sins and errors into those pure depths and lost them there. You seem to have forgotten—and that helps me to.

Dear great sweet soul—you are so much to me! You are everything that I am not, and the good things that I try to be—you help me up—and you are a steady basis to rest on when I can't climb any more.

And I feel so sure—so unutterably safe and sure in your love. It spreads horizonwise about me—I can't see over—and don't want to.

These three years have I known you, known you more and more intimately; and I find you in all ways a Good Man. To your pure and noble manhood I come humbly, gladly, fully, bringing all that I have and am—willing to be taken as I am—learning new great lessons in the new position.

With devout gratitude to God—with infinite content and peace of mind—with an overflowing heart—and a body most gladly and fully yours—All of me, Dear, I am coming to be your happy wife.

Afterword

On 11 June 1900, Charlotte and Houghton were married at the home of Mr. and Mrs. Sidney Corbett, Jr., in Detroit, Michigan. Charlotte's diary entry reads: "Arrive at 6. Houghton in the station. . . . Mr. Reed Steuart, Unitarian Minister, arrives about 7:30, and we are married. Very short and reasonable service. Then a very nice little dinner—far too long, and then we go." Or as she put it in her autobiography, "If this were a novel, now, here's the happy ending."

In this volume of Gilman's letters, and in much of her fiction as well, the conclusions, some might note with disappointment, suggest a disconcerting parallel to traditional nineteenth-century expectations: a woman marries and lives happily thereafter. Yet the purpose of this volume, like much of her fiction, was in fact to expose the destructiveness of nineteenth-century marriage norms, to show courtship battles in which women were fighting for their lives. In both her living and her fiction, Gilman was attempting to redefine the ground rules for marital relations. She tried to shape a "revolutionary marriage" by insisting that love include the opportunity for full autonomy and freedom, for spiritual growth and sexual expression, for creative work and fundamental self-respect.

That is not to say that Gilman thought marriage would eliminate her own or other women's cycles of insecurity and suffering. Because life is process rather than linear progression, spirals inevitably circle back before progressing forward, and well-established self-doubt since one's childhood almost necessarily returns. Unfortunately, however, for the years post–1900, and also for her fictional heroines' postmarried life, she offers very little insight; despite a thirty-four-year marriage, virtually no later letters to Houghton Gilman have as yet been found.[1] What she did make clear, however, is that married women should and could continue working, which in her case meant enthusiastically lecturing and writing. She published *Concerning Children* in 1900; *Human Work* and *The Home, Its Work and Influence* in 1904; *Man-Made World* in 1911; and *His Religion and Hers* in 1924, to name only several of her major works. In addition, she published hundreds of poems, critical essays, book reviews, and fiction pieces in her seven-volume *Fore-runner* series, and in numerous contemporary journals as well, for example, in the *Atlantic Monthly,* the *Independent,* the *Saturday Review of Literature, Cosmopolitan, Harper's Bazaar,* the *New York Times,* the *American Socio-*

logical Review, and the *Woman's Journal.* As an active participant on the national and international lecture circuit, as a socialist, a humanist, and feminist, she attended the International Suffrage Convention in Budapest in 1913, served on the National Advisory Council of the Woman's Party from 1916 to 1920, and spoke and wrote so effectively on a rich variety of subjects that she would become, in the view of many, "the leading intellectual in the women's movement in the United States during the first two decades of the twentieth century."

Because Gilman's life post–1900 is beyond the purview of this study, I will only briefly summarize her important contributions and achievements. As a public leader, her goal would be to reflect upon the world in order to improve it; to create a humane social order; and to provide a complex, unified social and historical perspective that would help inspire social change. Drawing from contemporary work in the fields of anthropology, history, ethics, sociology, philosophy, and religion, she would provide an historical and evolutionary analysis of widespread human inequality, and she would also sketch an impressive variety of pragmatic steps for societal improvements. Like many of her reform-oriented contemporaries, her view of human potential consistently was optimistic. Because she believed that evolutionary forces were essentially progressive, that human beings were basically cooperative and altruistic, she would envision a collectivist alternative to the contemporary reality of poverty, inequality, and suffering. Using the analogy of the human body to reflect her political perspectives, she argued that society is a living organism, hands and feet and brains working naturally together, just as in a socialist society individuals will work cooperatively and smoothly for the common good. In her view, a just future depends upon the growth of the collective spirit, the ability to move beyond individualist, personalist perspectives, beyond private property and selfish greed, to a society committed to the well-being of the whole.

Although many of Gilman's political perspectives reflect the thinking of her socialist and Reform Darwinist contemporaries, her writings on the gender issue show both originality and brilliance. With her powerful indictment of the patriarchal family structure, and with her radical critique of contemporary gender norms, she managed not merely to legitimize the women's issue in the contemporary intellectual arena but far more importantly to challenge and expose the sexist base of most contemporary thought. In her view, most contemporary writing was masculinist and androcentric. It either ignored women, or blamed them, or justified women's longterm subjugation as a means of legitimizing patriarchal dominance and power. Gilman, by contrast, viewed gender as critical to any meaningful theoretical discussion, and women's freedom and equality as a central social goal. She would use the "scientific" insights of her era. But she would then alter and subvert them, circling back to offer a radical indictment of the means by which dominance and inequality had been maintained. She argued that the central source of women's subjugation lay in the private patriarchal family, in the "sexuo-economic" relation, in wife and mother expectations, in the most intimate personal relations in the private home. Yet, even as she challenged the "primitive" or privitized domestic institutions, she also sketched pragmatic possibilities for change. She insisted on the need for day care centers, for example, for public kitchens and community dining rooms, for well-planned archetectural designs for homes. Because women had been isolated from the major institutions of society—from politics, law, religion, business, crafts, and trade—not only had they been thwarted in their own development, but they had also become a major obstacle to progress. In Gilman's view, therefore, the emancipation of women was a precondition for human liberation, and the restructuring of the family a precondition for needed social change.[2]

*   *   *   *   *

Although Gilman left us with a rich legacy of arguments and insights in her published writings, the assumption of this volume is that she left us with another important legacy as well, and one which in her lifetime she was unwilling publicly to share. She often was apologetic about her letters, to be sure. She sometimes was afraid that their vivacious spontaneity was simply "babblesome" and "childish," that her assertive sensuality was "dangerous" and "wicked," that her "feminine" emotionality was proof of her neurosis, or, at very best, of an excessive absorption in herself. And yet in spite of her persistent and often debilitating fears, Gilman's private letters demonstrate both fortitude and insight. Attempting to bridge as well as challenge traditional gender norms, she explored the "catacombs" of "feminine" self-hatred and depression, but she became "richer," "wiser," "stronger" in the process. Having learned to trust her intuitive as well as rational perceptions, to affirm her spritual and sensuous needs, she experienced a "miracle" of healing, she told Houghton, a "mended strengthened re-born feeling" which suggests the importance of her private as well as of her public work.[3] The differences, she knew, were often striking: the "voracious comet" versus the cool and distant public theorist, the "poor wild floating soul" versus the rationalist woman's movement pioneer. She was both the "fanatic and the great discoverer," as she put it in one letter, the "prophetess" challenging "acceptable" homophobic boundaries, the "heathen goddess" subverting traditional heterosexual norms, the woman warrior sustaining a powerful campaign. Understandably Gilman was secretive about her corresponaence.[4] Silences, she knew, were sometimes needed. Warriors need not publicly reveal their battle wounds and preparations, nor need they unnecesarily expose themselves to brutal charges and attacks. But since Gilman nonetheless retained the faith that her own and other women's happiness would depend upon continuing the struggle, she had approached her letters as a private battleground, the private explorations that would serve as catalyst and inspiration for her later work. She used her confrontations with disturbing family issues—with sexual identity, with child-rearing and motherhood, with conflicts between love and work—not simply to enhance her personal growth and understanding but also to respond more effectively to collective needs. In this sense, Gilman's letters document a journey from within, an effort to use her suffering as an opportunity for understanding other women's burdens, and her happiness for envisioning progressive social change.

In her published work Gilman had shaped a cool and distant public image. She had been happily married, her autobiography acknowledged occasionally and very briefly. But to work successfully with in a male-dominated intellectual community, to battle most effectively against the stereotype of women's emotionality and weakness, she had assumed that women's most prudent and effective public strategy was to emphasize the rational and intellectual dimensions of their social justice efforts.[5] Publicly Gilman thus had emphasized her work commitments more than her private struggles, her theoretical sophistication more than the vital understandings she had gained within the women's world.

This volume presents a very different Charlotte Gilman. Compelling, disquieting, and very human, her letters had not originally been meant for publication. They had not been intended to impress, to persuade, to express artistic needs. Instead, for several years they had served as her survival tools, as an essential resource for her living, and also as an early confrontation with almost every woman's issue that she later publicly discussed. At the time, she urged Houghton to destroy her letters as potentially too damaging, too far from what audiences respectfully could hear. But because in later years she decided purposefully to save them, I can only hope this volume pays sufficient tribute to her private efforts, her willingness to have her story known, her compelling wish to inspire other women on their journeys.[6]

Notes

Introduction

1. Born Charlotte Anna Perkins in 1860, she became Charlotte Perkins Stetson after her marriage to Walter Stetson in 1884, and Charlotte Perkins Gilman at the time of her second marriage to Houghton Gilman in June 1900. I thus note the strange anomaly of discussing a portion of the life of Charlotte Perkins Gilman when she was not Charlotte Perkins Gilman at all.

2. Charlotte Perkins Gilman, *Women and Economics* (New York: Harper Torchbooks, 1966), 331.

3. CPS to GHG, 26 July 1899, AESL.

4. Mary Armfield Hill, ed., *Endure: The Diaries of Charles Walter Stetson* (Philadelphia, Pa.: Temple University Press, 1985), 58, 140, 107, 75, 129.

5. CPS, Diary, 30 August 1885. AESL; Hill, *Endure*, 246, 279.

6. *The Nation* 68 (8 June 1899), 443; *North American Review* 175 (July 1902), 71–90; London *Daily Chronicle* (25 June 1899).

7. Alice Rossi, ed., *The Feminist Papers: From Adams to de Beauvoir* (New York: Bantam, 1978), 568; Mary Gray Peck, *Carrie Chapman Catt: A Biography* (New York: The H. W. Wilson Company, 1944), 454.

8. Gilman, *Women and Economics,* 14–15, 21, 97, 63.

9. Although there were a few women of Gilman's generation who had relatively satisfying middle-class positions, for the vast majority the work options were few. Some women were factory workers, secretaries, and salespersons, for example, but the largest single group of women in the paid labor force—2 million of the 5 million in 1900—worked as paid domestic servants in other people's homes. See, for example, Alice Kessler-Harris, *Out to Work: A History of Wage-Earning Women in the United States* (New York: Oxford University Press, 1982).

10. Gilman, *Man-Made World: Our Androcentric Culture* (New York: Charlton, 1911), 35–36, 117, 246, 225.

11. Gilman, *His Religion and Hers* (Westport, Conn.: Hyperion Press, 1976) 134, 331.

12. Ibid., 156, 83, 268.

13. Ibid., 17, 26–27, 87–95, 300–303.

14. See Mary Field Belenky, et al., *Women's Ways of Knowing: The Development of Self, Voice, and Mind* (New York: Basic Books, Inc., 1986).

15. CAP to GHG, 25 May 1897, AESL.

16. CAP to GHG, 23 November, 4 December, and 17 December 1879; 19 July 1880, AESL.

17. CAP to GHG, 5 January 1880, AESL.

18. CAP to GHG, 19 May 1897, AESL

19. Delia VanDeusen, "Gardening for Harmony: More than Mere Flowers and Vegetables Grace the Garden of Mrs. Charlotte Perkins Gilman." Claverack, N.Y.,

AESL; Charlotte Perkins Gilman, *The Living of Charlotte Perkins Gilman: An Auto-biography.* Forward by Zona Gale. New York: D. Appleton-Century, 1935, 326.

20. CPS to GHG, 19 January 1880, AESL.

21. Gilman, *Mag-Marjorie,* serialized in *Forerunner,* no. 1 (Jan. 1912), 10.

22. Delia VanDeusen, "Gardening for Harmony," AESL.

23. CPS to GHG, Diary, 8 March 1897, AESL.

24. Gilman, *Living,* 219.

25. My impressionistic description is based on early photographs and on indirect comments in Gilman's letters.

26. CPS to GHG, undated letter, April 1897; 4 June 1897; 2 September 1897, 5 September 1897, AESL.

27. CPS to GHG, 5 June 1897, 28 November 1899, AESL.

28. CPS to GHG, 14 November 1899, AESL.

29. CPS to GHG, 14 March 1900, 16 September 1898, AESL.

30. CPS to GHG, 25 January 1899, AESL.

31. Gilman, *Herland,* serialized in *Forerunner* VI (1915), 321.

32. CPS to GHG, 6 November 1898, 5 December 1898, AESL.

33. CPS to GHG, 3 November 1897, AESL.

34. See Carter Heyward, *Touching Our Strength: The Erotic as Power and the Love of God* (San Francisco: Harper & Row, 1989).

35. CPS to GHG, 20 January 1899, 5 May 1898, 15 March 1899, 14 March 1899, AESL.

36. CPS to GHG, 7 November 1897, AESL.

37. CPS to GHG, 16 May 1899, 6 November 1899, 28 July 1899, 26 July 1899, AESL.

38. CPS to GHG, 5 December 1898, 16 June 1897, AESL.

39. According to conventional narratives, white middle-class women were expected to experience the "erotic impulse." But if they also experienced the "impulse to power," almost always they "suffered individual guilt, each supposing herself a monster when she did not fit the acceptable narrative of a female life." Carolyn Heilbrun, *Writing a Woman's Life* (New York: W. W. Norton, 1988), 45.

40. CPS to GHG, 1 October 1897, AESL. The use of violent metaphors is not unusual in women's writings. Consider Kate Chopin's *The Awakening,* for instance, or George Eliot's *The Mill on the Floss.* See also, the work of Sandra Gilbert and Susan Gubar, *Madwoman in the Attic,* for example. Moreover, it was not only fictional women who lost their lives in battle. Virginia Woolf, Anne Sexton, and Sylvia Plath are but a few more contemporary examples of tough, courageous women who ended their own lives. As Carolyn Heilbrun puts it, "Suicide became a part of life, so violent was the action necessary for rebirth and truth" (Heilbrun, *Writing a Woman's Life,* 70).

41. CPS to GHG, 8 November 1897, AESL. Although the traditional myth suggests that Persephone was raped by Hades, and then was taken forcefully to the underworld, the more feminist version of the story envisions her as traveling voluntarily, purposefully, and autonomously. See, for example, Charlene Spretnak, "The Myth of Demeter and Persephone," in *Weaving the Visions: New Patterns in Feminist Spirituality,* eds. Judith Plaskow and Carol Christ (San Francisco: Harper & Row, 1989), 72–74.

42. CPS to GHG, 10 March 1899, 3 November 1897, 14 March 1899, 7 June 1897, AESL.

43. See, for example, Helen Cixous, "The Laugh of the Medusa," in *Women's Voices: Visions and Perspectives,* eds. Pat C. Hoy II, Esther H. Schor, and Robert DiYanni. (New York: McGraw-Hill Publishing Company, 1990), 481–96.

44. CPS to GHG, 22 April 1898, 21 April 1898, 10 March 1899, 17 May 1900, 20 February 1898, AESL.
45. CPS to GHG, 5 October 1898, 8 May 1898, 21 May 1898, 20 February 1898, AESL.
46. CPS to GHG, 20 February 1898, AESL.
47. CPS to GHG, 6 May 1898, AESL.
48. CPS to GHG, 29 November 1898, 4 May 1897, 28 December 1898, 2 April 1898, 12 March 1899, 18 December 1898, AESL.
49. CPS to GHG, 18 December 1898, AESL. In Greek mythology, Astoreth was a ruler of the universe, a charioteer trying to live her life with authority, with self-mastery, trying to keep her balance while moving at high speeds.
50. CPS to GHG, 8 November 1897, 10 February 1898, 22 April 1898, AESL.
51. CPS to GHG, 16 September 1898, AESL.
52. CPS to GHG, 11 September 1897, AESL.
53. While male journeys have been studied, charted, and celebrated for centuries, women's journeys are still too often dismissed as trivial or self-indulgent. See, for example, Nelle Morton, *The Journey Is Home* (Boston: Beacon Press, 1985).
54. CPS to GHG, 29 August 1897, 5 September 1897, 29 August 1897, 25 May 1897, 5 September 1897, AESL. Although Houghton saved Charlotte's letters, it seems likely that most of Houghton's letters were in fact destroyed.
55. See, for example, Bonnie Thornton Dill, "Race, Class, and Gender: Prospects for an All-Inclusive Sisterhood," *Feminist Studies* 9, no. 1 (Spring 1983), 131–50. For more discussion of the issue of Gilman's racism and classism, see the work of Ann J. Lane, *To Herland and Beyond: The Life and Work of Charlotte Perkins Gilman* (New York: Pantheon Books, 1990); Gary Scharnhorst, *Charlotte Perkins Gilman* (Boston: Twayne Publishers, 1985);
56. CPS to GHG, 11 November 1897, AESL. Although I would not deny that Gilman suffered from serious psychological disturbances that dated back to childhood, the focus of this study is on the social/political restraints that almost certainly stand as a fundamental underlying cause and/or exacerbation.
57. A number of contemporary writers have pointed out that women writers face an almost impossible dilemma as they attempt to use male language. As Mary Jacobus puts it, "Women's access to discourse involves submission to phallocentricity, to the masculine and the symbolic: refusal, on the other hand, risks reinscribing the feminine as a yet more marginal madness or nonsense" (Mary Jacobus, "The Difference of View," in *Women Writing and Writing about Women,* ed. Mary Jacobus [New York: Barnes and Noble, 1979], 10–21).
While *Women and Economics* at least in part emphasizes woman's victim status, her weaknesses and disadvantages compared to men, Gilman's later books would be far more affirming of femininity and womanhood. In her utopian novel *Herland* for instance, Gilman portrayed a society of women who had successfully organized and sustained a clean, efficient, cooperative utopian community and thus were shocked to learn of the atrocities and violence in "Ourland." See *Herland,* serialized in *Forerunner* VI (1915). Reprint, with introduction by Ann J. Lane. New York: Pantheon, 1979. and *With Her in Ourland,* serialized in *Forerunner* VII (1916).
58. See Virginia Woolf, *A Room of One's Own* (New York: Harcourt, Brace, Jovanovich; Harvest ed., 1981), 4, 25.
59. Although this volume focuses on Charlotte's push for an equal relationship with Houghton Gilman, it seems likely that in fact she preferred relationships with women. "I love women most," she wrote him, and feel a "reverence for their high estate, pity for their blind feebleness." Yet in my view she never had full freedom to explore her needs and preferences. Because she was struggling with what some

writers have called "compulsory heterosexuality," we will never know how much of her recurring unhappiness resulted from conventional patterns of heterosexual relationships and how much resulted from "compulsory heterosexuality" itself, the violent wrenching of women's emotional and erotic energies away from themselves and other women and a violent enforcing of women's loyalties to men. For further discussion of Gilman's relationships with women, see Mary A. Hill, *Charlotte Perkins Gilman: Making of a Radical Feminist, 1860–1896* (Philadelphia, Pa.: Temple University Press, 1980), chapters IV and IX.

60. Alicia Suskin Ostriker, *Stealing the Language: The Emergence of Women's Poetry in America* (Boston: Beacon Press, 1986), 176.

61. "No one speaks," as Toni Morrison has put it. "They don't want to talk, they don't want to remember, they don't want to say it, because they're afraid of it—which is human. But when they do say it, and hear it, and look at it, and share it, they are not only one, they're two, and three, and four, you know? The collective sharing of that information heals the individual and the collective" ("In the Realm of Responsibility: A Conversation with Toni Morrison," *Women's Review of Books* V, no. 6 [March 1988], 5).

62. Heilbrun, *Writing a Woman's Life,* 48.

63. Hannah Arendt, quoted in Heilbrun, 71.

64. Leslie Marmon Silko, *Ceremony* (New York: Penguin, 1988), 2.

Chapter 1. "Open the Doors of Your Heart"

1. CPS, Diary, 10 March 1897, AESL.

2. The Gilman letters quoted in this introductory essay were written between 18 March and 25 May 1897, although they may not necessarily be included in the section that follows.

3. CPS, Diary, 28, 31 March 1897, AESL.

4. Gilman, *Women and Economics,* 51–52.

5. As Shere Hite points out, men often benefit from women's emotional nurturing and then blame them for being overly emotional. Charlotte Gilman, by contrast, demanded reciprocity in her relationship with Houghton. At least in letters, she prodded him to respond in kind. See Shere Hite, *The Hite Report: Women and Love: A Cultural Revolution in Progress* (New York: Knopf, 1987).

6. Edward Bellamy, *Looking Backward: 2000–1887* and Ignatius Donnelly, *Caesar's Column: A Story of the Twentieth Century,* 1890. Reprint, Cambridge: Belnap Press of Harvard University Press, 1960. Edward Bellamy, *Looking Backward: 2000–1887,* 1887, Reprint, Boston: Houghton Mifflin, 1917.

Chapter 2. "The Fanatic and the Great Discoverer"

1. CPS, Diary, 1 July 1897, AESL.

2. As Rebecca Harding Davis put it, "And then, fanatics must make history for conservative men to learn from, I suppose" (Davis quoted in Tillie Olson, "A Biographical Interpretation," in *Life in the Iron Mills,* Rebecca Harding Davis, [Old Westbury, N.Y.: Feminist Press, 1972], 93).

3. Webster's seventh Collegiate Dictionary (1967) notes that the word "fanatic" derives from the Latin fanaticus, which means "inspired by a deity, frenzied."

4. Gilman, *Women and Economics,* 59, 101.

5. *Ibid.,* 110–13; CPS to GHG, 10 July 1897, AESL.

6. Gilman, *Women and Economics,* 260.

7. On 10 June Gilman's diary mentions writing a poem entitled "Loneliness," presumably the poem later entitled "Our Loneliness," which was included in the 1898 edition of *In This Our World.* Gilman, *In This Our World,* 1893 reprint, (Boston: Small, Maynard & Company, 1913), 60. The poem reads in part:

> . . . Our agony of heart
> When love has gone from us is loneliness. . . .
> Slow death of woman on a Kansas farm;
> The ache of those who think beyond their time;
> Pain unassuaged of isolated lives,—
> All this is loneliness.

8. There is an interesting parallel here to Virginia Woolf's comments in *A Room of One's Own.* In self-derogatory terms she contrasts her own haphazard techniques of doing research about women to those of a neighboring male scholar who is busy "shepherding his question past all distractions till it runs into its answer as a sheep runs into its pen." On the surface Woolf seems to envy male capacity for learning, but in point of fact she prefers the more "essential" female "oil of truth" instead, or writing that is "attached to life at all four corners" (Virginia Woolf, *A Room of One's Own,* 25, 28, 43). Moreover, as Phyllis Rose argues in *Virginia Woolf: A Woman of Letters,* women's apologetic tendencies might be viewed as a more democratic form of writing than is usually typical of men. Instead of asserting their own authority and insisting that readers should accept it, women tend to approach readers more respectfully, and to remind them that no writer has a monopoly on truth. Phyllis Rose, *Woman of Letters: A Life of Virginia Woolf* (New York: Oxford University Press, 1978).

9. For a fuller discussion of Ward's influence, see Hill, *Making of a Radical Feminist,* 263–271.

10. Gilman, *Living,* 230.

11. On 23 August 1897, Gilman's diary entry reads: "Mrs. Campbell stays with me overnight" (CPS to GHG, 23 August 1897, AESL).

12. Gilman, *Living,* 232. Several days later Gilman offered another explanation: "I have heard later, with regard to the animadversions upon me, that exception was taken to my *title.* The New Motherhood was held to mean the producing of new children, and this was held unseemly for to contemplate—in my position" (CPS to GHG, 29 August 1897, AESL).

13. Gilman, *Living,* 231–32.

14. Diary entries as quoted in *Living,* 231–32.

Chapter 3. "When the Wheel Turns Round"

1. The Gilman letters quoted in this introductory essay were written between 1 September and 12 October 1897, although they may not necessarily be included in the section that follows.

2. In *Silences: Why Women Writers Don't Write,* Tillie Olsen describes the kind of setting writers need to be creative and productive. They need quiet peaceful surroundings, the flow of life made easy, she insists, which is precisely the kind of setting women writers rarely have. See Tillie Olsen, *Silences: Why Women Writers Don't Write* (New York: Delacorte Press, 1978), 12–13.

3. Gilman, Diary, 31 August 1897; 1 September 1897, AESL.

4. Gilman, *Living*, 235.

5. Gilman, *Women and Economics*, Preface.

6. Patrick Geddes, and J. Arthur Thomas, *The Evolution of Sex*, rev. ed. (London: W. Scott, 1914), 26, 312.

7. Gilman, *Women and Economics*, 135; Gilman, *Living*, 187.

8. Lester Ward, *Pure Sociology: A Treatise on the Origin and Spontaneous Development of Society* (1903 reprint; New York: Augustus M. Kelley, 1970), 275. An early critic of Herbert Spencer's Social Darwinist laissez-faire economic policies, Lester Ward argued that competition was extremely wasteful, and prevented the most fit from surviving. Note also that his assumption that the first forms of life are female now has considerable scientific support. See, for example, Alice Rossi, *The Feminist Papers: From Adams to de Beauvoir*; John Money and Anke A. Ehrhardt, *Man & Woman, Boy & Girl* (Baltimore: Johns Hopkins University Press, 1972). For a more complete discussion of Gilman's indebtedness to Lester Ward, see Hill, *Making of a Radical Feminist*, 264–70.

9. Lester Ward, *Pure Sociology*, 275.

10. Gilman, *Women and Economics*, 1–5, 38.

11. See Samuel Chugerman, *Lester Ward, The American Aristotle: A Summary and Interpretation of His Sociology* (1939; reprint, New York: Octagon Books, 1965), 392. Despite his Gynaecocentric acclamations—"the grandest fact in nature is woman"—Lester Ward often depicted women in stereotypically hostile ways, for example, loving, kind, and gentle, women nonetheless "care very little for truth for its own sake, take very little interest in the abstract, and even concrete facts fail to win their attention unless connected more or less directly with persons and with some personal advantage, not necessarily to self, but to self or others. In short, they lack the power to see things objectively, and require that they be presented subjectively. Innate interests are ever present to their minds, and anything that does not appeal in any way to their interests is beyond their grasp" (Lester Ward, *Pure Sociology*, 296).

12. Geddes and Thomas, *The Evolution of Sex*, 18.

13. Gilman, *Women and Economics*, 164, 8, 74, 119. Gilman also argued that women should feel no "bitterness" about the past, "no resentment . . ., no shame, no sense of wrong." For whatever the sacrifice, whatever the "unspeakable injustice and cruelty" in women's lives, their subjugation had served the evolutionary progress well: It had been "for such enormous racial gain, such beautiful and noble uses," that women would have borne "not only this, but more,—borne it smilingly, ungrudgingly, gladly, for [man's] sake and the world's" (Gilman, *Women and Economics*, 128–29, 135). Gilman's later writings, however, were not so apologetic about the "bitterness of feeling": "some natural animus may occasionally be visible; but if any man be offended by such error in fact or feeling, let him examine the many books that have been written about women" (Charlotte Perkins Gilman, Preface to *Man-Made World*).

14. Gilman, *Women and Economics*, 280, 168, 65–68.

15. CPS to GHG, 11 September 1897, AESL. Hubert Bland, in a review of *Women and Economics*, rather cleverly paraphrased Gilman's critique of woman's economic and psychological dependence to buttress his own antiwoman views. After all, Bland wrote, "Equality is for equals," and Mrs. Stetson "admits—nay, not admits, but rather asserts" that woman "is a rather dismal human failure, endowed with the promise and potency of better things, but afflicted with . . . inefficiency." "Briefly put, Mrs. Stetson's appeal to men . . . amounts to this:—You men, she says, largely unconsciously, . . . have created a creature to be your mate who is no fit mate for you at all. So far from having got a help-mate you have acquired only a

most potent hindrance, a being who appeals and ministers to but one side of your nature, and that the side of which in your finer moods you are least proud. Look at her with the veils of prejudice, of affection, of tradition from off your eyes, and you will see her for what she really is. The sight will not greatly please you" (Hubert Bland, "A Sane Word in a Mad Controversy," Manchester *Chronicle*, AESL).

16. My analysis here is informed by the work of Carol Gilligan, who has suggested that because of social conditioning women's ethical perspectives tend to be based on contextual considerations more than on logical ones. See Carol Gilligan, *In a Different Voice: Psychological Theory and Women's Development* (Cambridge, Mass.: Harvard University Press, 1982). For an analysis of women's self-demeaning tendencies to view authors and authorities as male, see also Sandra Gilbert and Susan Gubar, *Madwoman in the Attic: The Woman Writer and the Nineteenth-Century Literary Imagination* (New Haven: Yale University Press, 1979), chapter I.

17. Charlotte's early friendship with Martha Luther is well documented in a series of letters (1881) which, in some ways, are strikingly similar to those she later wrote to Houghton Gilman. Charlotte often referred to the friendship with Martha as the deepest and richest she had known. "Four years of satisfying happiness with Martha, then she married and moved away. . . . It was the keenest, the hardest, the most lasting pain I had yet known" (Gilman, *Living*, 80).

18. It is impossible to determine precisely what material was in the original version of *Women and Economics* since Gilman later revised and rearranged the chapters, but it nonetheless seems likely that the early and most "scientific" chapters (I–V) were first written while she was staying with her Belmont friends. On 8 September she wrote Houghton: "[H]ere I am at the end of Chap[.] V. It runs easy" (CPS to GHG, 8 September 1897, AESL).

19. For more discussion on the Hazard and Hale families, see Hill, *Making of a Radical Feminist*, 55–59.

20. Gilman, *Women and Economics,* 80–81.

21. Nursing her mother during those grim last months of illness, hearing her mother's stories, sharing her mother's grief, Gilman later would describe what she believed to be one of the deepest sources of her anger, that is her father's, Frederick Perkins, insensitivity to Mary Perkins's plight. "Divorced or not she loved him till her death, at sixty three. . . . She longed, she asked, to see him before she died. As long as she was able to be up, she sat always at the window watching for that beloved face. He never came. That's where I get my implacable temper." Mary Perkins died on 6 March 1893. For further discussion of Charlotte's relationship with Mary Perkins, see Hill, *Making of a Radical Feminist*, 25–37, 193–97, 228–37.

22. In her later fiction, in *Benigna Machiavella,* for example, or in the short story entitled "Making a Change," Gilman offered a fictional resolution of destructive mother-daughter conflicts; she emphasized the need for mother-daughter connection and alliance rather than competition and resentment. Rather than stressing the mothers' victim status, or the narrowness women suffered in their family roles, Gilman focused on women's ingenuity, courage, and resistance. *Benigna Machiavella,* serialized in *Forerunner* II (1911); "Making a Change," *Forerunner* II, no. 12 (December 1911), 311–15. See also Gilman's *Herland.*

23. Gilman, *Women and Economics,* 86–90.

24. Gilman, *Women and Economics,* 85–96. Like Nancy Chodorow, Gilman argued that the mothers' oppressive roles were taught and therefore reproduced within their daughters' lives. See Nancy Chodorow, *Reproduction of Mothering* (Berkeley, Calif.: University of California Press, 1978).

25. CPS, Diary, 18 April 1887, AESL. In late September 1897, Charlotte noted in her diary, "Go to R.I. School of Design and Art Club," and "see Walter's pictures

there" (CPS, Diary, 13 September 1897, AESL). Or, as she wrote to Houghton, Walter's pictures "are great." "I was dilating on them to one of my cousins, Sunday night. 'Ah!' said she: 'it makes the old love come back after all, doesn't it!' I was wroth" (CPS to GHG, 15 September 1897, AESL).

26. Gilman, "The Yellow Wall-paper," *New England Magazine* 5 (January 1892), 647–59.

27. Charles Walter Stetson, Diary, 9 October 1882, in *Endure*, 107.

28. Although Gilman to some extent adopted the Reform Darwinists' assumption of the existence of certain innate masculine/feminine behavioral characteristic and although, like most turn-of-the-century evolutionary thinkers, she tended to blur the distinctions between acquired and inherited human characteristics, her emphasis was for the most part not on biological determinism but on the destructive effects of social conditioning. Most "weaknessess" of women, she argued, resulted from their subjugation to men. As many contemporary feminist theorists currently argue, however, an emphasis on woman's subjugation and victim status has its dangers. It too often results, as was the case in some of Gilman's writing, in a focus on women's limitations rather than their strength.

Although Gilman's current letters suggest memories of being "unattractive," some earlier letters suggest a different view: "What joys were mine!" she wrote to Houghton at age nineteen: "I went sleighing, went to the theater, I went to parties, and I received calls. Bye and bye, when you 'are old and hideous, and the hairs of your beard are mostly grey,' as the poet says, you will understand the joys of such an existence" (CAP to GHG, 1 January 1880; 5 January 1880).

29. Emily Baldwin Perkins was sister to Frederick Perkins (Gilman's father) and wife of Edward Everett Hale. There is an interesting letter to Emily Perkins Hale from Gilman, dated 22 January 1934: "My very dear Cousin—Next to Houghton you are far and away the dearest. I wish I hadn't wasted so much time talking nonsense—and abusing other relatives. There was so much to say of my lovely memories of you when I was 15—16—17. You were so *kind!* My mother wasn't. She 'did her duty' with ceaseless devotion, but strove to make me self reliant by 'inhibiting' all tenderness. A Pity. I needed it" (CPG to Emily Perkins Hale, 22 January 1934, Sophia Smith Collection, Hale folder).

30. Dr. E. B. Knight was not only one of Walter's closest confidants during the tumultuous years of marriage, he had also served as Charlotte's physician during her "illness."

31. Bliss Carman was a Canadian born poet and journalist for a variety of literary magazines in the 1890s. His first collection of poems, *Low Tide on Grand Pre* (New York, 1893), is among his best.

32. In her autobiography, Gilman described her decision to publish with Small and Maynard: "These young publishers had been to England and knew my reputation there, I think. Appleton's also offered to take the book, but I chose the new men just starting, partly because they were beginners, partly because they made the proposition entirely without recommendation. In later years when asked how I made my 'market' so to speak, I explained that it was by giving away my work until it made an impression" (Gilman, *Living,* 236). Ripley Hitchcock was the reader at Appleton's. According to the diary she spoke to him about the book in mid-October. See Diary, 11 October 1897, AESL.

33. Later in September, Gilman returned to the Small and Maynard office—"my publishers," she called them (Diary, 22 September 1897, AESL). "They want to do the poems & also to look at the book. Good" (Diary, 25 September 1897, AESL).

34. Edwin Meade was the first publisher of "The Yellow Wall-paper."

35. "The Beds of Fleur-de-Lys" was published in *In This Our World*, 78–79.

36. As she later put it, "My Cousin Houghton was visiting his aunts in Norwich at the time; he called on me and Mrs. Rudd [her Norwich hostess], and took me to see his aunts in the old home. The diary says: 'Nice people, nice house.' Little did I think I should come to live in it!" (Gilman, *Living,* 237).

Gilman spent most of her time in Norwich with her hostess, Mrs. Jean Porter Rudd. "I intended to go on with the book," Gilman wrote, "but found more important business in talking" (CPS to GHG, 1 October 1897, AESL) with the "brave, strong talented" (Gilman, *Living,* 237) widow Mrs. Rudd. She was struggling to raise her children, to write, and to cope with precisely the kinds of issues *Women and Economics* raised. "[Mrs. Rudd] wrote, wrote more than well," Gilman noted, "but life gave her small time for that work" (Gilman, *Living,* 237).

Chapter 4. "Letters Are Like Morning Prayers to Me"

1. CPS, Diary, 23 October, 7 November 1897, AESL.

2. The Gilman letters quoted in this introductory essay were written between 29 October 1897 and 22 April 1898, although they may not necessarily be included in the section that follows.

3. The diary entry continues: "That is finish first draft. Date and arrange the separate chapters as written in different houses and do it up" (CPS, Diary, 10 October 1897, AESL). Or, as she put it in her autobiography, it "was rather less than half the book when published; but it contained the argument, it showed method and style, it was the manuscript the publishers accepted. It was done in seventeen days, in five different houses, on this little string of visits" (Gilman, *Living,* 237). In fact, however, there are some discrepancies as to the actual time Gilman spent working on the manuscript, depending on whether she counted days for revising, preparing typescript, etc. "The entire time spent on that book was fifty-eight days—just inside of two months" (Gilman, *Living,* 240). Or on another occasion, "The book was finished on December 14th. . . . Twenty-three days' work this time, total of forty" (Gilman, *Living,* 239). The diaries also document the progress of revising: 18 November 1897: "Work on book—begin third chapter again." 20 November 1897: "Write—arranged to 4th chapter—now becomes 5th. . . . Read *Evolution of Sex,* or rather look it over." 2 December 1897: "Work on book. IX Chapters done. Houghton stops and brings me many books, borrowed, and Ward's *Dynamic Sociology*—a present." 5 December 1897: "Houghton comes. Read last three chapters—10 done. Splendid time. He is more and more impressed." 12 December 1897: "Houghton as usual. Good day. Read on book as far as I've gone, and talk it over."

Although Gilman was for the most part proud of her fast-paced writing, she occasionally acknowledged some anxieties. For instance, when economist E. A. Ross asked about how long she took to write it, she protested, "If I tell you you will never respect me or the book any more" (Gilman, *Living,* 260).

4. A similar but slightly later diary entry reads, "Bad night. This is really a very low time—worst since England. . . . Go to see Father" (Diary, 3 November 1897, AESL).

Later, when she was feeling better, the visits with her father apparently did not bother her so much. A December diary entry reads: "He fades gradually. I find him sitting dully in his chair—alone. He gets very bright and interested when I talk. . . . But he can say very little now, connectedly" (Diary, 26 November 1897, AESL). And two days later, she matter of factly noted, "[Houghton] draws up my 'will'—is to be executor. Give him list of my debts" (Diary, 28 November 1897, AESL). Or some weeks later. "Write in morning. Go to see father in afternoon. About the same—glad to see me and hear about progress of book etc." (Diary, 17 December 1897, AESL).

5. Gilman later noted that there were two books she carried with her when she traveled: Walt Whitman's *Leaves of Grass,* and Olive Schreiner's *Dreams.* "Having them, I had with me mountains and sunlight." In *Dreams,* Olive Schreiner showed "greater mastery of the allegorical than any writer since the ancient Hebrews; a range of vision that plays among eternities, a height of art which gives world visions in single sentences, the thought standing in naked beauty, the words unnoticed" (Forerunner II, no. 7 [July 1911], 197).

Gilman borrowed the "transition woman" image from Olive Schreiner's "Three Dreams in a Desert." In fact, Gilman quoted the work at length, though in emphasis and paragraph arrangement, her quotation differs slightly from the original. See Olive Schreiner, "Three Dreams in a Desert," in *Dreams,* 1895. Reprint, (Boston: Little, Brown, and Company, 1919), 52–70.

6. Gilman, *Women and Economics,* 168.

7. A number of years before, Alice Stone Blackwell had published and applauded one of Charlotte's early articles, and more recently, Charlotte had repeatedly visited the Blackwell home in Boston. Alice Stone Blackwell's parents, Lucy Stone and Henry Blackwell, had helped found the American Woman Suffrage Association and also had helped found, edit, and largely finance the Boston weekly Woman's Journal. For further discussion, see Hill, *Making of a Radical Feminist,* 137.

8. Gilman, *Women and Economics,* 167.

9. Various diary entries record Gilman's contacts with political reformers. Diary, 21 October 1897: Went to a "big political meeting in Carnegie Hall—Ratification of Seth Low for Mayor." 8 December 1897: "Social Reform Club. . . . Jane Addams speaks." 7 December 1897: "Go to call on Miss Addams. . . . Take Miss A. to see Mr. [William Dean] Howells" (Diary, 6 January 1898, AESL). After lecturing at the New York Social Reform club: "John Swinton guest of honor. I am the only woman speaker, and receive quite an ovation. Very good time."

10. Lillian Wald's "House on Henry Street" was in some ways parallel to Jane Addams's Hull House in Chicago. A home nursing center for the New York neighborhood, a pragmatic response to urban poverty, it was also "home environment" for a community of politically active women. See Blanche Wiesen Cook, "Female Support Networks and Political Activism: Lillian Wald, Crystal Eastman, Emma Goldman," in *Women's America: Refocusing the Past,* eds. Linda K. Kerber and Jane De Hart Mathews, (New York: Oxford University Press, 1982), 274–94.

11. In October she noted that there was some talk of her taking the editorship of the *American Fabian* for $25.00 a month, but because of other obligations, she decided to decline. (Diary, 5 October 1897, AESL.)

12. The final draft of *Women and Economics* was submitted in January 1898 and was published in early May 1898.

13. CPS, "Thoughts and Fingerings," 18 January 1898, AESL.

14. Gilman dealt with the issue of men's lack of political consciousness in several later fiction works. See, for example, "An Offender," *Forerunner* I, no. 4 (February 1910), 1–6; "Her Housekeeper," *Forerunner* I, no. 3 (January 1910), 2–8; and *Won Over,* serialized in Forerunner IV (1913).

Chapter 5. "Nearly Drowned in a Sea of Love"

1. The Gilman letters quoted in this introductory essay were written between 1 May and 30 May 1898, although they may not necessarily be included in the section that follows.

2. Although in her letters Gilman noted that the South "dislikes 'progressive women'"(CPS to GHG, 18 May 1898), her autobiography is more appreciative of the Southerners' perspectives. "I have spoken in every one of the Southern States, and was struck from the first by the vigor and efficiency of the women, as well as by their progressiveness" (Gilman, *Living,* 245).

3. Given her theories about women's need for economic independence, Gilman was pleased to be earning at least some money from her lectures, even though the amounts were always relatively modest. She would receive $42.50 at the end of her four-part lecture series, for example. "This is wealth," she wrote Houghton, "not bad a bit" (CPS to GHG, 3 May and 27 May 1898, AESL).

4. Gilman's later book, *Human Work,* argues that meaningful work was a basic human right and need. Gilman, *Human Work* (New York: McClure, Phillips, 1904), chapter XII.

5. CPS, Diary, 21 April 1898, AESL.

6. Harold Faulkner, *Politics, Reform, and Expansion: 1890–1900* (1959; reprint, New York: Harper & Row, 1963, 225.

7. *American Fabian* IV, no. 5 (May 1898), 4–5.

8. Alma Lutz, *Created Equal: A Biography of Elizabeth Cady Stanton* (New York: John Day, 1940), 310; Ray Ginger, *The Age of Excess* (New York: Macmillan, 1975), 193.

9. *American Fabian* IV, no. 5 (May 1898), 4–5. Although a number of reformers voiced their dissent from the very outset, many of the most rigorous critiques emerged after the war was over. In April 1898, for example, the *American Fabian* celebrated the "united" effort on behalf of our "helpless and oppressed neighbors" (*American Fabian* IV, no. 4 [April 1898], 4) yet some months later was incensed by the windfall profits to munition makers and by the "jobbery and inefficiency" that had been involved: "Capitalism . . . has again shown its murderous incapacity for dealing with any problems of public need" (*American Fabian* IV, no. 9 [September 1898], 4). Moreover, the Anti-Imperialist League (led by William Dean Howells, William Graham Sumner, Mark Twain, and others), was not founded until after the war had ended; and even then, unfortunately, their arguments were often couched in ethnocentric terms. Carl Schurtz, for instance, opposed annexation because is-landers were "incapable of becoming assimilated to the Anglo-Saxon." They were "utterly alien to us, not only in origin and language, but in habits, traditions, ways of thinking, principles, ambitions—in short, in most things that are of the greatest importance in human intercourse and especially in political cooperation" (Carl Schurtz, quoted in Ginger, *Age of Excess,* 290).

10. Gilman, *Women and Economics,* 126, 159; Gilman, *Herland,* 94.

11. Or, as Gilman put it in another letter, "So you are resisting the temptation to go kill Cubans—no Spaniards—are you? I don't think any less of your courage myself. But did you ever hear or dream of anything so ridiculous as these naval battles of ours?" (CPS to GHG, 7 July 1898, AESL).

12. Gilman, "War as a Socializer," *American Fabian* IV, no. 6 (June 1898), 5–6. In a later work entitled *The Man-Made World* (1911) Gilman was more critical of warfare than she was in 1898. Warfare, "at its best, retards human progress; at its worst, obliterates it." "It destroys the fruits of industry and progress," "lowers the standard of the non-combatants," and worst of all, intensifies the "psychic effects of military standards of thought and feeling." "Deceit, trickery, lying, every kind of skulking underhand effort to get information; ceaseless endeavor to outwit and over-come 'the enemy'; these, with cruelty and destruction are characteristic of the mili-tary process." Or again, "civilized warfare"—"we might as well speak of 'civilized

cannibalism!'" War "may prove which of two peoples is the better fighter, but it does not prove it therefore the fittest to survive" (Gilman, *Man-Made World*, 3d ed. [New York: Charlton Company, 1911] 215–18). See also. Hill, *Making of a Radical Feminist*, 279.

Despite her socialist convictions, Gilman's letters show a striking insensitivity to the racial issue, and at times a racist and xenophobic bias, which tragically was all too widely shared. She expressed no discomfort, for example, that the Royall family's aristocratic, leisured lifestyle resulted from the work of the "pleasant and quiet" "colored servants" (CPS to GHG, 5 May 1898, AESL). Or, when "the colored folks" asked if she would "preach for them," she briefly quipped: "I will some time, not now" (CPS to GHG, 29 May 1898, AESL).

13. Houghton's volunteer Seventh Regiment had voted as a unit not to enlist for service, but the New York *Herald* had reported that orders were "expected within twenty four hours." See the New York *Herald*, 11 and 12 May 1898.

14. Some contemporary writers suggest that a daughter's desire for the maternal presence can be a "healthful regression," a "self-transcendence," and thus a source of artistic power. In her biography of Willa Cather, for example, Sharon O'Brien writes, "If such 'regressive' longings (to return to mother) are the 'motive force for art,' as they were for Willa Cather, then they are not, finally, regressive because they lead to active, fruitful endeavor in adult life" (Sharon O'Brien, *Willa Cather: The Emerging Voice* [New York: Oxford University Press, 1987], 211). See also, Anthony Storr, *The Dynamics of Creation* (New York: Antheneum, 1972), 81; Ernst Kris, *Psychoanalytic Explorations in Art* (New York: International Universities Press, 1952).

Moreover, it is now commonly believed that the mother-daughter bond is often closely interconnected with adult love relationships, and that sexual desire is in part often a search for the accepting maternal love one knew in childhood. As Gilman put it, "love of the mother for the child [is] at the base of all our higher love for one another. Indeed, even behind that lies the generous giving impulse of sex-love, the out-going force of sex-energy" (Gilman, *Women and Economics*, 260). But since most children, male and female alike, experience their earliest love relationships with mothers, Dorothy Dinnerstein and others suggest that male-female equality will not be possible until early nurturing roles are equally shared by men and women, until the ethic of caring is central in the lives of men and women both. See Dorothy Dinnerstein, *The Mermaid and the Minotaur: Sexual Arrangements and Human Malaise* (New York: Harper & Row, 1976). See also Carol Gilligan, *In a Different Voice*.

15. Ruth Perry, in *Mothering the Mind*, talks about the influence of lovers, husbands, etc., on writers' lives and work. They play many roles, "intercepting the world, conferring unconditional approval, regulating the environment, supplying missing psychic elements, and mirroring certain aspects of the self of the artist" (Ruth Perry quoted in *Willa Cather*, Sharon O'Brien, 244, fn. 43).

16. The struggles that are reflected in this chapter are in some respects similar to those described in Gilman's later novel, *What Diantha Did*. Gilman, *What Diantha Did* serialized in *Forerunner* I (1909–10).

17. Two of the men were Edwin Markham and Eugene Hough, and a third was probably Paul Tyner, co-worker with Gilman on *Impress* Magazine. Some months later Gilman wrote of Tyner, "Once I thought I should marry this worthy man. Then I found his weaknesses of character, and quite outgrew my love for him. Years and growth on my part however have made me feel very peaceful toward his life and work, though it is far from mine . . . he has bought *The Arena*—is owner and editor" (CPS to GHG, 12 October 1898, AESL).

Chapter 6. "What a Mother's Happiness Should Be"

1. Gilman, *Women and Economics,* 174, 268, 156, 184.

2. In the same article Gilman also wrote, "The mother, nervous, irritable, unfit for her work and not happy in it; a discontented person, her energies both exhausted and unused. What she wastes in uncongenial effort she might spend joyfully in work she was fit for" ("Genius, Domestic and Maternal," *Forerunner* I, no. 9 [10 July 1910], 6).

3. Gilman, "Coming Changes in Literature," *Forerunner* VI, no. 9 [September, 1915], 230.

4. Gilman, *Women and Economics,* 174, 181.

5. Grace Channing was one of Charlotte's closest confidantes since childhood and had later become Walter Stetson's second wife. Katharine went to live with Grace and Walter in May 1894. For a more extended discussion of the strains of these years and of the decision to send Katharine to Grace and Walter, see Hill, *Making of a Radical Feminist,* 194–202, 226–37, 256–57.

6. Although there is often a martyrlike tone in Gilman's letters—as though she blamed herself for unique motherhood deficiencies, or as though her suffering justified a decision that would have otherwise been unacceptable—her public writings show far more confidence. Repeatedly she would sympathize with children who were "encompassed and overwhelmed" by "exhausted, nervous" mothers, by "prematurely aged mothers" who inspired a "hot bed" of emotional intensity that Katharine was lucky to be spared. Gilman, *Women and Economics,* 184. See also Gilman's short story, "The Unnatural Mother," *Impress* 16 (February 1895), 4–5; as well as her later novel, *Mag-Marjorie* serialized in *Forerunner* III (1912). As Gilman later put it, "The 'natural' mother, of course, believes that her own care of her own child is better than any one's else. . . . The unnatural mother, who is possessed of enough intelligence and knowledge to recognize her own deficiencies, gladly intrusts her children to superior care for part of the time, and constantly learns by it herself" (Gilman, *Concerning Children* [Boston: Small, Maynard & Company, 1901], 273–74). For more discussion of this issue, see Hill, *Making of a Radical Feminist.*

7. The Gilman letters quoted in this introductory essay were written between 1 June and 22 September 1898, although they may not necessarily be included in the section that follows.

8. In an earlier letter, Gilman had quoted extensively from Olive Schreiner's "Three Dreams in a Desert" in order to affirm the pioneering nature of her efforts. Another part of that same poem, however, may have also helped her to come to terms with her separation from her daughter, Kate. When the heroine of the poem dreams of crossing to the "Land of Freedom," "Reason" tells her that she must leave her child:

> And Reason said, "Put him down."
> And she said, "He is asleep, and he is drinking! I will carry him to the Land of Freedom. . . ."
> He said, "Lay him down on the ground . . . you will forget to fight, you will think only of him. Lay him down." He said, "He will not die. When he finds you have left him alone he will open his wings and fly. He will be in the Land of Freedom before you. . . . In your breast he cannot thrive; put him down that he may grow." Olive Schreiner, "Three Dreams in a Desert," *Dreams,* 57–59.

9. Gilman's later novels often focus on daughters of this age.

10. The sensuous nature of Gilman's description of her love of Katharine in part may have inspired her later complaint that most literature talks only of Eros, "ignor-

ing that great goddess of mother-love in which service young Eros is but a running footman" ("Coming Changes in Literature," *Forerunner* VI, no. 9 [September 1915], 230).

11. Gilman routinely informed Houghton of her menstrual cycles—"x" days she called them—and in accordance with the common medical belief occasionally argued that her "brain trouble" was "ovarian." CPS to GHG, 14 September 1898, AESL.

12. Some of Gilman's efforts to deal with the separation from Katharine are reflected in her later fiction. In the novel *Mag-Marjorie,* for instance, the heroine's toughest challenge is the "plain duty of forgetting," of managing to control the "ceaseless heartache and remorse that motherhood had meant" (*Mag-Marjorie,* serialized in *Forerunner* III, no. 6 [June 1912], 154). She had to learn "how to hold down her grief, and use it as a spur. She rigidly closed her mind to thoughts of her child during the hours of work, and the hours of play" (Gilman, *Mag-Marjorie,* serialized in *Forerunner* III, no. 4, [April 1912], 101).

13. Gilman's diary entries during the summer of 1898 likewise reflect the debilitating mood. 8 July: "low all day. Can't write anything." 22 July: "Feel very weak & blue." 20 August: "All bad days and nothing in 'em." 23 August: "drag around generally."

14. Carolyn Heilbrun writes, "Marriage without children at its center . . . has largely been beyond the imaginative reach of either biographers or living women" (Carolyn Heilbrun, *Writing a Woman's Life,* 77).

15. Gilman, Diary quoted in *Living,* 248.

16. There are two consecutive letters dated 21 June 1898.

17. Commonwealth, Georgia.

Chapter 7. "Hope and Power"

1. Before the month-long visit with the Blackwell family, Gilman spent an autumn weekend with Houghton in Norwich, Connecticut, and also stopped for several days in New York, where she met with Lillian Wald at the Henry Street Nurses' Settlement House. Lillian Wald had recently invited her to visit, and although Gilman had enthusiastically responded—"it will do me lots of good to dip into their earnest brave lives—people who are living with others in frankest reality" (CPS to GHG, 18 September 1898, AESL). Nonetheless, her stay was very brief. Gilman's diary entries simply note: "Nice talk with Miss Wald. Lunch . . ., and more talk with Miss Wald" (Diary, 25–26 September 1898, AESL). Given Gilman's preference for lecturing and writing and her reluctance to involve herself in pragmatic, organizational reform, it is more than likely that she felt some discomfort with the Henry Street reformers. In one letter she had noted that no one in New York had "wanted" her, and yet in another letter she suggested that the secrecy of her relationship with Houghton may have been an added reason for the briefness of her stay: "I don't want those hard-working women to see me wholly given over to cavorting about with desirable young men. Or even a desirable young man" (CPS to GHG, 28 May; 18, 22 September 1898, AESL). In her autobiography, Gilman referred to Lillian Wald as the "Jane Addams of New York" (Gilman, *Living,* 249). For Gilman's later negative perspectives on immigrants, see Hill, *Making of a Radical Feminist,* 172–74, 279; and Gary Scharnhorst, *Charlotte Perkins Gilman,* 108–10.

2. The Gilman letters quoted in this introductory essay were written between 4 October and 15 November 1898, although they may not necessarily be included in the section that follows.

3. Geoffrey Blodgett, "Alice Stone Blackwell," in *Notable American Women,*

1607–1950: A Biographical Dictionary, ed. Edward T. James, et. al. (Cambridge, Mass.: Belknap Press, 1971) 1:157.

4. Gilman, *Living,* 216–17. In her brief sketch of the Blackwell family, Alice Rossi notes that in spite of Lucy Stone's extraordinary active history of political involvement, she nonetheless was plagued by periodic depressions emerging from the strains of family life. The conflicts between domestic and political responsibilities that Gilman persistently experienced unfortunately are ones that can be found in the lives of many nineteenth-century women. See Alice Rossi, *Feminist Papers,* 323–46. Lucy Stone died in 1893. See also Phyllis Chestler, *Women and Madness*; and Susan Gilbert and Sandra Gubar, *Mad Woman in the Attic.*

5. Boston *Advertiser,* 10 November 1899, AESL.

6. About the first edition of her *In This Our World* anthology, Gilman noted: "I don't call it a book of poems. . . . I call it a tool box. It was written to drive nails with." An interview with CPS quoted in the *Topeka State Journal,* 18 June 1896.

7. *Harper's Weekly* (25 January 1896), 79; *Dial* 25 (1 September 1898), 134; *American Fabian* IV, no. 6 (June 1898), 11–12. Although the *American Fabian* review was mostly positive, it noted an occasional inelegant and ponderous technique: "When she grows serious, indeed, the attention flags" (*American Fabian* IV, no. 6 [June 1898], 11–12). A reviewer for the *Bookman,* however, was considerably more negative: "To listen too seriously to Mrs. Stetson's raging dithyrambs about the washtub and her denunciations of the 'Holy Stove' might make one believe that she had often been obliged to rise betimes and light the fire, while her liege lord was smoking that *ne plus ultra* of Boheminanism, a cigar before breakfast" (*Bookman* I [June 1895], 335–37).

8. Gilman loved playing the numbers game with the figures Small and Maynard gave her or speculating about the income future books or articles would bring. In her later fiction, in *What Diantha Did,* for example, Gilman repeated the head-spinning financial calculations but made her fictional heroines far more economically successful than she ever would be herself.

9. Alicia Ostriker writes, "For a woman, perhaps the most decisively difficult act is to think of herself as powerful, or as more powerful than a man, and capable of influencing the outward world without sacrificing femaleness" (Alicia Ostriker, *Stealing the Language,* 113). Or, as Carol Gilligan points out, women are most likely to allow themselves to be assertive only when they can explain their actions in terms of the benefit to others. See Carol Gilligan, *In A Different Voice: Psychological Theory and Women's Development.*

10. Although Gilman had strong spiritual and religious commitments, she never found organized religion to her liking. In fact, she often chided Houghton for his church-going habits, particularly because he often went simply out of kindness to his father. Apply that principle "to all people," she quipped, "and I think you would see the world wag backward pretty fast if we all went to the church of our fathers continually" (CPS to GHG, 3 January 1899, AESL). Or in an earlier letter, she noted her reaction to a church service in Goldsboro, North Carolina: It was "a foreign mission sermon—salvation & damnation—I quite suffered. To think that 'Christianity' still obtains among us in such a guise" (CPS to GHG, 22 May 1898, AESL).

11. See the work of Nelle Morton and Carol Christ, for example. They point out that in a patriarchal culture, the emphasis on sin and selfishness had, in fact, significant religious value for those in positions of power and authority. Dominant groups clearly *need* spiritual reminders of the dangers of their search for power. But the message has a considerably different impact on women and minorities or others who have been traditionally oppressed. It tends to encourage their already well-developed sense of powerlessness, their training in humility and self-sacrifice, and thus discour-

ages the growth of strength and self-respect. See Carol Christ, *The Laughter of Aphrodite: Reflections on a Journey to the Goddess* (San Francisco: Harper & Row, 1987), 127 ff; Carol Christ, "Why Women Need the Goddess," in *The Politics of Women's Spirituality,* ed. Charlene Spretnik, (Garden City, N.Y.: Anchor Books, 1982); Rita Nakashima Brock, *Journeys of the Heart: A Christology of Erotic Power* (New York: Crossroads Publishers, 1988), xii; Rosemary Reuther, *Religion and Sexism: Images of Women in the Jewish and Christian Traditions* (New York: Simon and Schuster, 1974) 166–68; Letty M. Russell, ed., *Feminist Interpretations of the Bible* (Philadephia: Westminster Press, 1985).

12. Gilman's emphasis on love rather than sin is rather different from the perspective suggested in an earlier poem entitled "A Prayer":

> O God! I cannot ask thee to forgive;
> I have done wrong.
> Thy law is just; thy law must live,—
> Whoso doth wrong must suffer pain.
> But help me to do right again,—
> Again be strong.

Gilman, In This Our World, 50.

13. Some might argue that Gilman's emphasis on love, her insistence that "there is no evil," reflects a disquieting naivete, a "female sentimentalism," or even an excessive optimism characteristic of many reformers of her generation. Enjoying a privileged middle-class position like that of many of her socialist and feminist contemporaries, Gilman clearly did not experience the poverty or survival struggle that many minorities and working-class people had to face. Contemporary feminist theory suggests another more psychological interpretation: women are far less likely than men to see evil as an aggressive force within themselves. As Nelle Morton and other theorists have noted, women are more likely to fear their own passivity and powerlessness.

14. Charlotte Perkins Stetson, "Economic Basis of the Woman Question," *Woman's Journal* XXIX, no. 40 (1 October 1898) 313–14. Gilman argued that women, far more than men, were "naturally" inclined toward useful and productive work. As she wrote in a *Woman's Journal* article at about this time, "The female of any species, having the larger share in reproductive processes, naturally inclines to those activities we call economic. She, by nature, works. There are species in which the male helps the female in her labors of nest-building, food-getting, etc.; but the main line of economic energy in the world is the female line. . . . The labor of the animal world is all for the young; it is reproductive energy, finding its expression in economic activity through the mother" (Charlotte Perkins Stetson, "Causes and Uses of the Subjection of Women," *Woman's Journal* XXIX, no. 53 [24 December 1898], 410).

15. Charlotte Perkins Stetson, "Economic Basis of the Woman Question," *Woman's Journal* XXIX, no. 40 (1 October 1898) 313–14.

16. Charlotte Perkins Stetson, "Causes and Uses of the Subjection of Women," *Woman's Journal* XXIX, no. 53 (24 December 1898), 410.

17. Later Gilman would do precisely that, of course, in a book entitled *The Home: Its Work and Influence* (New York: McClure, Phillips and Company, 1903). She would later describe it as the "most heretical—and the most amusing—of anything" she had ever done (Gilman, *Living,* 286).

18. In the 1890s, Gilman was still using standard patriarchal images. She was still speaking of God as "He" our "Father," still seeing *His* "Kingdom, Power and Glory" as the goal. In her later writings, however, Gilman wrote far more extensively about the need for more female-affirming religious imagery, and about the destruc-

tiveness of the male monopoly on religious truth. She argued that while traditional religions provide no conflict for men between their public and private responsibilities, for women they create a split. Encouraging women on the one hand to believe in themselves and their own value, traditional religions also teach women to believe that their major purpose is to offer loving service to their families. A "healing" religion must therefore work to unify the divided self. See Gilman's later book entitled *His Religion and Hers*. See also the religious perspectives, particularly the goddess worship, in her utopian novel, *Herland*, 1915.

19. Several years before, when Gilman was working on the *Impress Magazine*, she did a "Studies in Style" series that was intended to imitate the literary methods of a number of contemporary authors. According to her autobiography, her literary imitation of Maurice Maaterlinck was later reprinted by Small and Maynard publishers. Gilman, *Living*, 241.

20. There are two consecutive letters dated 5 October 1898.

21. Higginson, considered by some to be an avid woman's rights supporter, was bothered by Gilman's "attack" on motherhood. She is "doing more than a hundred clubs of 'remonstrants' to check the course of development for true womanhood," and in utter disrespect for the "the natural instinct of the high-minded woman to give herself the pleasure of tending her baby herself." After all, Higginson continued, "The foundation of all human progress must surely be that close personal tie between parent and child. . . . I have few sweeter pictures in my memory than that of one fair-haired young mother guiding me silently, with shaded lamp, from room to room, to see her four sturdy boys stretched in the deeper silence of sleep." Thomas Wentworth Higginson, "Women and Men," *Harper's Bazaar* (1 October 1888), 831. Higginson is also often cited as an early and important "supporter" of the works of Emily Dickinson.

22. Although several reviews of *Women and Economics* had been published by this time (in the *New York Times Saturday Review* and the *American Fabian*), the majority had not yet appeared. I therefore assume that the "scrapbook" primarily contained reviews of her *In This Our World* poetry anthology. Reviews of *Women and Economics* will be discussed in a later chapter.

23. Gilman may or may not have read the review of *In This Our World* by Harry Thurston Peck. It begins with a standard antiwoman complement, a proverbial tribute to masculine literary supremacy, and gradually emerges into a full-scale defense of masculine supremacy in almost every field of work. Because of "the terseness of her phrase, Peck condescendingly asserts, and the general compactness of her style," Gilman "stands head and shoulders above any of the other minor poets of her sex. In fact, did we not know the author's name, we should have selected many of the poems collected in this volume as having been written by a man." But like the "slovenly and sluttish" types of women "who would snarl and complain over anything," she complains too much about married women's "inferior position" as cook-stove slaves when the "majority" actually hire domestic servants, and those who can't afford to are no worse off than millions of "hustling for a living" men. Obviously, "the household must have food." And because obviously "some one must cook that food," "we are forced to the conclusion that there is really no way out of it but just the same old way; that the husband should go out and earn the money, and the wife stay home and attend to her domestic duties. Which, when you come to think of it, seems pretty sensible after all." In Peck's view, Gilman should advise women to buy a "well-built serviceable Cook-Stove," to read cookbooks instead of Browning poetry, to refrain from Women's Clubs and University Extension Lectures, to greet their husbands with "dainty looks" and "equally dainty dinner[s]," and, above all, to stop "yawping" about the woman's suffrage cause. Harry Thurston

Peck, "The Cook-Stove in Poetry," *Bookman* VIII (September 1898), 50–53. A full discussion of Gilman's response to Harry Thurston Peck's will be included in a later chapter.

24. In his review of *In This Our World* for the *Conservator,* Horace Traubel wrote: "She is neither past nor present master of phrases and verbal dress suitings. But the effect she achieves is wonderful. What is it that makes the poem? Not your skill in verbal legerdemain but the burning conviction within that is not forced to but enforces its escape. . . . *In This Our World* touches at some point every problem of our time—now and then didactically or argumentatively, perhaps, but with an art which eludes and subdues the schoolmaster" (Horace Traubel, Review of *In This Our World, Conservator* IX [September 1898]).

25. For a time Gilman hoped that Annie Russell would be interested in performing in the play she would write some months later in collaboration with Hervey White. According to the letters, Annie Russell had been encouraging for a time.

Chapter 8. "My Business First Last and Always Is to Serve"

1. The Gilman letters quoted in this introductory essay were written between 16 November 1898 and 25 January 1899, although they may not necessarily be included in the section that follows.

2. In the late 1890s, ex-governor Altgeld was considered one of the most prominent reform-oriented leaders in the Democratic party, and according to historian Charles Beard, he was particularly indebted to the Hull House women's efforts. Not only had their work inspired the public sentiment that elected him to office, but as Beard explained it, "Nearly everything in his program" was initially inspired and sponsored at Hull House: the "extension of child-labor legislation from mines to factories, extermination of sweatshops in cities, introduction of factory inspection, arbitration of labor disputes, regulation of public utilities, abolition of the exploitation of convict labor by private contractors, enlargement and improvement of state welfare institutions, lifting the state University to a high position as center of learning in the public service, and advancement of popular education in every department" (Charles Beard, *The American Spirit: A Study of the Idea of Civilization in the United States* [New York: The Macmillan Company, 1942], 479).

3. Gilman, *Living,* 184; Beard, *The American Spirit,* 478. Although at Hull House Gilman was meeting some of the most nationally prominent women's movement leaders, her letters, unfortunately, note them only occasionally and very briefly. She mentioned having a discussion with Florence Kelley, for example, but described nothing of its content. On Alice Hamilton, she simply stated: "I sat and talked, pleasantly and profitably, with a fair frail little woman—Dr. Hamilton by name" (CPS to GHG, 8 December 1898, AESL). About "the Great" Jane Addams, Charlotte's letter simply reads: "I don't feel at all near her" (CPS to GHG, 19 November 1898; 9 December 1898, AESL).

4. Many were writers and editors for various reform-oriented journals, for example, for Joseph Wayland's *The Coming Nation,* for Prestonia Mann's *American Fabian,* and for Paul Tyner's *Arena.* Many were also supporters of like-minded political associations: the National Christian League, for instance, or the American Institute of Christian Sociology at Chautauqua, or the Union League, which would later be reorganized into the Social Reform Union. And although each had a separate base of operations, they were interconnected through their journal writing, through their mutually supportive lecture invitations, and through their pragmatic efforts to integrate politics with their Christian Socialist beliefs.

5. James Dombrowski, *The Early Days of Christian Socialism in America* (New York: Columbia University Press, 1936), 14, 10.

6. Some historians note the "easy optimism" of the Christian Socialists' perspective. Largely middle class in background and experience, they maintained a naive "conception of man's inherent goodness and perfectibility," and an overly simplistic faith that evolutionary law would promote economic equality and social justice. Dombrowski, for example, criticizes the Christian socialists' optimistic faith that there was an "underlying harmony of interests between the working class and the owning class," and that the "cooperative commonwealth" could thus be easily achieved by peaceful means. Dombrowski, *Early Days of Christian Socialism in America*, 19–28.

What historians have less frequently acknowledged, however, is that there was also a disturbing gender-based bias to the Christian Socialist perspective. Their religion of love and human service meant different things to men and women. Because women were expected to give self-sacrificing devotion to their private families while simultaneously pursuing public social service, they experienced deeply troubling conflicts that were rarely shared or understood by men.

7. *St. Louis Post Dispatch;* 18 January 1899, AESL; Charlotte Perkins Stetson, "Economic Basis of the Woman Question," *Woman's Journal* XXIX (1 October 1898) 313–14.

8. *St. Louis Post Dispatch;* 18 January 1899, AESL.

9. Charlotte Perkins Stetson, "Economic Basis of the Woman Question," *Woman's Journal* XXIX (1 October 1898), 313–14. Whereas Gilman most frequently emphasized social conditioning as the major cause for gender differences, like most of her contemporaries she was not consistent on this point and sometimes blurred the distinction between acquired and inherited characteristics.

10. *St. Louis Post Dispatch;* 18 January 1899, AESL.

11. One of the most common themes in women's literary writings is the struggle to believe their work has value. Women confront the divided or fragmented self who is, on the one hand, proud and forceful and on the other desperately insecure. As Alicia Ostriker describes it, "self-division is culturally prescribed, wholeness culturally forbidden," and then the "cleavage in the brain" inherited from so many women writers is labeled schizophrenia. Ostriker writes, "It is ironic that an analysis designed to describe a psychotic personality resembles so closely a normal woman's dilemma." In the divided self, the two sides conflict with one another, but also reinforce each other. For the public person is so strong, so forceful, that insecurities are necessarily driven back to secrecy. The mask or armor needs to be effectively secured. The outer self appears "narcissistic and exhibitionistic" simply because of trying to insure that inner insecurities will not be publicly revealed. Yet to speak of a "true self" and a "false self" does not capture the dilemma. Both selves are true, both false—"or rather their truth or falsity is not the issue. The issue is division: that the halves do not combine to a whole, as if a tree had roots and leaves but no trunk. The issue is that the left foot is cut off from the right, the right from the left, and that the division reflects and is reinforced by our culture's limited images of feminine personality" (Alicia Suskin Ostriker, *Stealing the Language,* 83–84).

12. The words "husband" and "wife" frequently appear in Gilman's correspondence, even though the formal wedding date was not until 11 June 1900.

13. A number of feminist writers point out that women often present themselves as powerless, as diminutive, in order to avert attack or pain.

14. In *No Man's Land,* Sandra Gilbert and Susan Gubar note that women's rebellion against the norms of femininity was almost always secretive and indirect.

Sandra Gilbert and Susan Gubar, *No Man's Land: The Place of the Woman Writer in the Twentieth Century* (New Haven: Yale University Press, 1988).

15. In the late 1890s, Gilman was at least attempting, though not consistently, to share her Hull House contemporaries' respectful attitude toward immigrants. And yet her comment several days before—that she was "dreading that dreary settlement audience"—suggests some considerable ambivalence. CPS to GHG, 2 December 1898, AESL. Gilman's later writings, however, are far more ethnocentric. In an article entitled "Let Sleeping Forefathers Lie" (1915), she wrote: "Let us by all means welcome and help a steady stream of incoming new-made Americans; but let us, before it is too late, . . . protect ourselves from such a stream of non-assimiable stuff as shall dilute and drown out the current of our life, and leave this country to be occupied by groups of different stock and traditions, preserving their own nationality, and making of our great land merely another Europe" (Gilman, "Let Sleeping Forefathers Lie," *Forerunner* VI [October 1915], 216). See also Gilman, "A Suggestion on the Negro Problem," *American Journal of Sociology* XIV (July 1908), 78–85; Gilman, "Is America Too Hospitable," *Forum* (October 1923). See also Hill, *Making of a Radical Feminist*, 172–74, 279.

16. Unfortunately, the letter of 7 January is too badly torn to be legible.

17. Although Gilman was certainly proud of her Beecher ancestry and her ministry abilities, her religious and political perspectives differed considerably from those of the famed Henry Ward Beecher. Whereas he had encouraged the more conservative inclinations of the churches—"God has intended the great to be great and the little to be little" (Dombrowski, *The Early Days of Christian Socialism in America*, 5)—Gilman was preaching socialism as the law of God.

18. She is staying with F.M. Crunden and family.

Chapter 9. "An Endless Love for Women"

1. The Gilman letters quoted in this introductory essay were written between 1 February and 26 April 1899, although they may not necessarily be included in the section that follows.

2. Howard Quint, *The Forging of American Socialism: Origins of the Modern Movement* (New York: Bobbs-Merrill, 1953), 189–90.

3. Eltweed Pomeroy, "A Sketch of the Socialist Colony in Tennessee," *American Fabian* III, no. 4 (April 1897), 1–3.

4. *American Fabian* III, no. 4 (April 1897), 3. The members were particularly concerned about the free-love charge, which in the popular mind was thought to be an "evil" synonymous with socialism.

5. Gilman, *Living,* 252–53. Convinced "of the hopelessness of colony life" (CPS to GHG, 1 February 1899, AESL) and of the ineffectiveness of cooperative models, Gilman later argued that domestic work should be put on a professional basis in order to ensure equality. In her private letters about the Ruskin community, however, she did not focus on the women's issue, or on some glaring contradictions of its "equality" ideal. Ranking "brotherly love" as one's highest calling, Ruskin was owned and controlled exclusively by male reformers. Women were expected to ensure the colony's practical survival—purchasing, preparing, cooking, and serving food—while the men not only retained exclusive economic ownership of the Ruskin joint stock company, but also had exclusive access to most of the politically and intellectually satisfying jobs. See J. W. Braam, "The Ruskin Co-operative Colony," *The American Journal of Sociology* VIII (March 1903), 667–80.

A number of other writers have also criticized the Ruskin "brotherly community":—its "worthless" lands, its "laughing-stock" farming efforts, its "defective" accounting system, its "cheaply constructed" buildings (Raymond Lee Muncy, *Sex and Marriage in Utopian Communities: 19th Century America* [Bloomington: Indiana University Press, 1973], 118, 254, 667–71). See also J. W. Braam, "Ruskin Cooperative Colony," *The American Journal of Sociology* VIII (March 1903), 667–80.

According to one contemporary, some financial dishonesty also was involved. He wrote that the Ruskin founder, Joseph Wayland, had "sent money down to a few people who were first to arrive on the ground, and one of them who was a sort of self-constituted agent kept writing for more, alleging that various work was under way. . . . When Wayland appeared on the scene he found nothing had been done, but that the pioneers were quartered at a hotel at Tennessee City, living in luxury on the money he forwarded" (Quoted from Wayfarer, "A Trip to Girard," *Socialism and American Life* I, ed. Donald Drew Egbert and Stow Persons. bibliographer T. D. Bassett [Princeton: Princeton University Press, 1952], 259).

For the most hostile account of the Ruskin experiment, see Isaac Braam, *The Last Days of the Ruskin Co-operative Association* (Chicago: Charles H. Kerr & Company, 1902). See also, Francelia Butler, "The Ruskin Commonwealth: A Unique Experiment in Marxian Socialism," *Tennessee Historical Quarterly* XXII (December 1964), 333–42; and Earl Miller, "Recollections of the Ruskin Cooperative Association," in *American Communities and Cooperative Colonies,* ed. William Alfred Hinds (Chicago: C. H. Kerr & Company, 1902).

6. See the *Atlanta Constitution,* 27 February 1899; 22 February 1899; 23 February 1899; 25 February 1899.

7. In later short stories and novels, Gilman described heroines who delight in using "psychic tricks and methods" to outwit unconventional or unsuspecting foes. In the novel *Benigna Machiavelli,* for example, not only does the heroine want to become strong and skillful but also to develop an armory of concealed weapons to help her with her tasks. See *Benigna Machiavelli,* serialized in *Forerunner* V (1914).

8. For further discussion of Gilman's relationship with Adeline Knapp, and the reasons for its failure, see Hill, *The Making of a Radical Feminist,* 187–209. See also Lane, *To Herland and Beyond,* chapter VII.

9. Carroll Smith-Rosenberg, "The Female World of Love and Ritual: Relations between Women in Nineteenth-Century America," *Signs* I, no. 1 (Autumn 1975), 1–29.

10. Charlotte Anna Perkins to Martha Luther, 15 August 1881, RIHS. The fact that women's love for one another is sometimes motivated by "pity," as well as by "reverence," is one of the more destructive effects of the "institution of heterosexuality." As Janice Raymond points out, women are taught to be "*not lovable* to their Selves and to other women," and thus "identify with other women out of a shared pain and not out of a shared strength" (Janice Raymond, *A Passion for Friends* [Boston: Beacon Press, 1986], 23).

11. Charlotte Anna Perkins to Martha Luther, 13 August 1881, RIHS.

12. Immediately before Grace and Walter's wedding, Charlotte wrote to Grace:

> Do you know I think I suffer more in giving you up than in Walter—for you were all joy to me. . . .
>
> It is awful to be a man inside and not able to marry the woman you love!
>
> When Martha married it cracked my heart a good deal—your loss will finish it.
>
> I think of Walter with some pain, more pleasure, and a glorious sense of rightness—escape triumph.
>
> I think of you with a great howling selfish heartache. *I* want you—*I* love you—*I* need you myself!

(CPS to GEC, 3 December 1890, AESL).

13. Gilman, *Living,* 143.

14. Gilman had already experienced the pain of public scandal. Not only had the press rigorously condemned her divorce from Walter Stetson but also her separation from her daughter. As the San Francisco *Examiner* put it, "There are not many women, fortunately for humanity, who agree with Mrs. Stetson that any 'work,' literary, philanthropic, or political, is higher than that of being a good wife and mother. . . . Either all her reasons have not been made public (which is probable), or she is wanting in those powerful instincts which render the love of husband and children necessary to woman's happiness" (San Francisco *Examiner*, 25 December 1892).

15. Smith-Rosenberg, "The Female World of Love and Ritual," 1–29.

16. Gilman, *Women and Economics*, 37.

17. Although in many of Gilman's novels, the most empowering relationships are women's friendships with each other, she did not directly discuss the issue of lesbian relationships; nor, of course, did most writers of her generation. Commenting on the banning and prosecution of Radclyffe Hall's 1928 novel, *The Well of Loneliness*, Virginia Woolf and E. M. Foster point out that while "murder and adultery" were "officially acceptable" in novels, the subject of homosexuality was not. Quoted in Rachel Blau DuPlessis, *Writing Beyond the Ending: Narrative Strategies of Twentieth-Century Women Writers* (Bloomington: Indiana University Press, 1985), 2.

In recent years, however, women writers have been far more assertive in claiming the empowering force of lesbian relationships. Janice Raymond argues, for example, that women must be first in importance to each other: "first in claims of attention, affection, and activity; first in not allowing men to interfere with or encroach on female friendship; first meaning . . . that which shapes the finest fabric of female existence; and first in the sense of re-possessing the memory of an original attraction to women that belongs to the initial state of Gyn/affective growth and development" (Raymond, *A Passion for Friends*, 35).

18. As a number of feminists recently have argued, one of the functions of the "institution of heterosexuality" is to teach women to reject precisely the kind of relationships that might have helped to heal their cycles of self-doubt. As Adrienne Rich puts it, "the institution of heterosexuality" is "a major buttress of male power. It is high time that the institution receive the same searching scrutiny that class and race have received and are receiving, and that the indoctrination of women toward heterosexuality be challenged" (Adrienne Rich, *On Lies, Secrets, and Silence* [New York: W. W. Norton, 1979], 17).

19. In my view, this comment suggests more about Gilman's negative response to Lydia Commander than it does about her view of women's affectionate relationships with one another. It seems likely, however, that this unhappy incident, followed by a similar but more affectionate experience with Clara Royall, precipitated Gilman's open discussion of her former love relationship with Adeline Knapp.

20. Gilman's father, Frederick Perkins, had been seriously ill for the last several years, and had been staying in a nursing home in Delaware Water Gap. Although his approaching death may have contributed to the recent emotional depression, her recent letters had not mentioned him at all. For further discussion of Charlotte's relationship with Frederick Perkins, see Hill, *Making of a Radical Feminist*, 1–43, 61–62, 102–4, 132, 200, 221–24, 291.

21. The reference here is to Charlotte's stepmother, Frankie Beecher Johnson Perkins. Mary Perkins, Charlotte's mother, died in 1893.

22. After Joseph Wayland left the colony, Lydia Commander was largely responsible for editing the Ruskin journal, *The Coming Nation*, though typically historians credit Herbert Casson for the work.

23. Herbert Newton Casson's energetic support of socialist experiments was

later matched by an energetic admiration of businessmen's expertise: "If I were asked—'Who was the most competent, generous, original and independent man in the world?' I would be obliged to answer, 'Andrew Carnegie.'" Likewise, note the chapter titles in Casson's later work, *How to Keep Your Money and Make It Earn More* (1923): "Speculate on Properties, not Schemes," "Buy Only what Can Be Resold without a Loss"; "Take Your Profits"; "Buy at the Bottom and Sell at the Top." Herbert Casson, *How to Keep Your Money and Make it Earn More* (New York: B. C. Forbes Publishing Company, 1923). See also, Herbert Casson, *Tips on Leadership: Life Stories of Twenty-five Leaders* (New York: B. C. Forbes Publishing Company, 1927), 87.

24. Gilman's discussion of the need for professional housekeeping service was already reflected in her public writing. For instance, a 1898 *Woman's Journal* article noted: "Mrs. Stetson predicted that the time would come when families could hire flats with . . . the services of professional cleaners thrown in as part of the bargain, as janitors' services are now; that every neighborhood would have a kindergarten where children of nursery age could be taken care of for some hours of each day by skilled kindergartners; and that well-cooked meals would be furnished to all who wished by professional caterers, instead of each family being compelled either to have its own cook-stove, or else to live in a boarding-house. . . . Mrs. Stetson said: 'We are coming to the end of mistress and servant, and the beginning of employer and employee'" (*Woman's Journal* XXXI, no. 43 [22 October 1898], 340).

25. In her later utopian novel, *Herland,* Gilman wrote that "Eternal life" was "a singularly foolish idea, . . . And if true, most disagreeable" (Gilman, *Herland,* 116).

Gilman only quoted the first stanza in this letter, but later included the entire poem as a separate enclosure. The subsequent stanzas read:

> Done with the varying distress
> Of retroactive consciousness;
> Set free to feel the joy unknown
> Of Life and Love beyond my own.
>
> Why should I long to have John Smith
> Eternally to struggle with?
> I'm John—but somehow cherubim
> Seem quite incongruous with him.
>
> It would not seem so queer to dwell
> Eternally as John Smith in Hell
> To be one man forever seems
> Most fit in purgatorial dreams.
>
> But Heaven! Rest and Power and Peace
> Must surely mean the soul's release
> From this small labelled entity
> This passing limitation—me!

(CPS to GHG, 21 March 1899)

Chapter 10. London

1. Gilman, *Living,* 258.

2. The Gilman letters quoted in this introductory essay were written between 16 May and 19 August 1899, although they may not necessarily be included in the section that follows.

3. C. P. Stetson, "The Woman's Congress of 1899," *Arena* XXII (August 1899), 342–50.

4. Gilman's diaries and letters note that the following organizations sponsored meetings and entertainments: the Sesame Club, the Governor Crescent Club, the Conservative Club, the Fabian Society of American Women in London, the Writers' Club, the Bureau for the Employment of Women, the Pioneer Club, the Considerers, the Grovenor Club, and the Woman's Institute. For the most part she was pleased with the enthusiastic welcome she received.

5. *Women in a Changing World: The Dynamic Story of the International Council of Women since 1888* (London: Routledge & Kegan Paul, 1966), 3.

6. C. P. Stetson, "The Woman's Congress of 1899," *Arena* XXII (August 1899), 342–50; May Wright Sewall, "The International Council of Women," *Fortnightly Review* 72, no. 66 (July 1899), 151–59; London *Times,* July 1, 1899; *Women in a Changing World*, 20.

Although the organizers of the conference had agreed that they would allow speakers for both sides of any controversy, when Susan B. Anthony was invited to be the key-note speaker, the antisuffragist opponents were denied equal time. The result was that the Anthony lecture, the largest and most enthusiastically attended, was sponsored independently by the National Union of Women's Suffrage Societies of Great Britain. See *Women in a Changing World*, 22.

One of the important controversies of the Congress was on the "Protective Legislation" issue. Some delegates emphasized women's double-jeopardy position, their need for pragmatic assistance on hours, wages, and factory conditions. Others, often those less sensitive to factory work conditions, felt that protective legislation was in the long-run discriminatory, and thus perpetuated women's status as the second sex. See C. P. Stetson, "The International Congress of Women," *Ainslee's* IV, no. 2 (September 1899), 145–152.

7. *Women in a Changing World*, 23.

8. For further discussion of Gilman's contributions to the 1899 convention, see International Council of Women, *Report of Transactions of Second Quinquennial Meeting Held in London July 1899,* ed. Countess of Aberdeen, 7 vols. (London: T. Fisher Unwin, 1900). See also Gilman's diary, 27, 28, and 30 June 1899, AESL.

9. London *Times,* July 1, 1899.

10. Although the *New York Times* published several respectful accounts of the conference proceedings, others were quite hostile. As one reporter claimed, "Anything more futile or purposeless has seldom been seen in this city than the Woman's International Congress. . . . The audience arrived unpunctually, and the incessant coming and going of agitated, weirdly clad delegates was an unbroken interruption. Except in the case of actresses the voices, diction, and delivery of most of the speakers were bad. . . . In many cases there was no discussion after the papers, which were simply rattled off one after another like so many shots from a cannon. Even Mrs. Charlotte Perkins Stetson, who said some trenchant things, appalled her English hearers by advocating highly trained, well-paid women as substitutes for mothers. In fact, English women of advanced views who attended are asking was it worth while gathering women together from the ends of the earth to gabble platitudes of precisely ten minutes' duration. The effect of the congress upon public opinion here is nil" (*New York Times,* 2 July 1899).

11. Frances H. Low, "A Woman's Criticism of the Women's Congress," *The Nineteenth Century* 46 (August 1899), 192–202.

12. Low, "A Woman's Criticism of the Women's Congress," 192; Kassandra Vivaria, "On the International Congress of Women," *North American Review* 169 (August 1899), 145–64.

13. Vivaria, "On the International Congress of Women," 159.

14. Lady Aberdeen was active in the Canadian Victorian Order of Nurses, the Women's National Health Association, and also served on the executive board of a women's committee associated with the Liberal party. She was the second president of the National Women's Liberal Federation, and from 1894 until 1936 served periodically as president of the International Council of Women. See Renate Bridenthal and Claudia Koonz, eds., *Becoming Visible: Women in European History* (Boston: Houghton Mifflin Company, 1977), 332. In Gilman's view, Lady Aberdeen was among the most impressive women at the convention. An "able woman, an advanced woman, a woman capable of planning and executing large measures of public good," she "touched a high note in her opening address to the delegates, and held it steadily through all the wearing work of the crowded week" (C. P. Stetson, "The International Congress of Women," 150).

15. C. P. Stetson, "The International Congress of Women," 145–152; C. P. Stetson, "The Woman's Congress of 1899," Arena XXII (August 1899), 342–50.

16. Alice Stone Blackwell, letter to the editor, *New York Times*, 25 July 1899; *New York Times*, 8 July 1899. In a later account of the convention, Susan B. Anthony suggested she had helped to "contrive" the reception herself: "When all sorts of notables were giving us receptions, I said to Lady Aberdeen: 'If this great Council of Women . . . were meeting in Washington, we would be invited to the White House. Can't you contrive an interview with the Queen?" See Susan B. Anthony and Ida Husted Harper, eds., *The History of Woman Suffrage*, vol. 4 (Indianapolis: Hollenbeck Press, 1902), 354.

17. Diary entry quoted in Gilman, *Living*, 260. According to her autobiography, Gilman was in fact rather proud of her nonaristocratic dress. "I never had any impressive clothes, and in England it makes far more difference than it does here. I trotted about in my very ordinary raiment, with my everlasting little black bag, just as I would at home" (Gilman, *Living*, 267). Or on the Dutchess of Sutherland's reception Gilman wrote, "Here was mighty Stafford House, here were long lines of knee-breeched liveries, and here was I, giving my waterproof and rubbers to these functionaries as if it were the coatroom at a church fair" (Gilman, *Living*, 263). In fact, Gilman always was annoyed by social snobbery, by women parading about in their "jeweled glory," or ostentatiously wearing their newest and very best (Gilman, *Living*, 260). In later years she would write a book about the "gross excesses" and "jarring contradictions" of woman's fashion (Gilman, *Dress of Women*, serialized in *Forerunner* VI, no. 5 [May 1915], 138). They show "more visibly, more constantly, than any words, how exclusively she is considered as a female; how negligible has been her relation to society as a whole" (Gilman, *Dress of Women*, serialized in *Forerunner* VI, no. 3 [March 1915], 77). Not only were most fashions extravagantly wasteful, they were degrading to women's dignity as well. The "conspicuous idiocies," the "grovelling slavishness," the "brainless submissiveness"—no wonder women were "the butt of humorists and satirists" (Gilman, *Dress of Women*, serialized in *Forerunner* VI, no. 11 [November 1915], 304–7). The corset is "as idiotic as a snug rubber band around a pair of shears" (*Forerunner* VI, no. 3, 79), or as to the peculiar display of women's hats, Saint Paul might appropriately say: "Let your women's hats be covered in the churches" (Gilman, *The Dress of Women*, serialized in *Forerunner* VI, no. 6 [June 1915], 164).

Although Gilman's 1899 published articles were positive about the conference, she later wrote that she had been annoyed by a number of social incidents at the conference: the whispered slurs, the patronizing of "budding celebrities," and the arrogance toward the timid and more plainly dressed. And as for that eagerly awaited queen's reception, Gilman later wrote, the women "had to stand about for two hours in a stone courtyard"—a "serious tax" on the older ones—and all for only a momentary glimpse of royalty. Queen Victoria appeared briefly in her carriage; Lady Aberdeen "knelt . . . and kissed her hand"; a conference delegate (one out of five hundred) was formally presented; and then the queen "calmly" drove away. Subsequently "tea was served by flunkies," Gilman quipped, the delegates "could proudly state that they had been to tea with the Queen," and "I could proudly state that I'd been asked and wouldn't go" (Gilman, *Living,* 264–65).

Although Gilman would flaunt her indifference to the Windsor Castle spectacle in her autobiography, at the time she regretted having failed to go: "Think I made a mistake in not going to Win[d]sor to see the Queen" (Diary, 7 July 1899, AESL).

18. Susan B. Anthony and Ida Husted Harper, eds., *The History of Woman Suffrage,* 352)

19. Stetson, "Woman's Congress of 1899," 342–50; Stetson, "International Congress of Women," 145–152; Gilman, *Living,* 257–60.

20. Stetson, "International Congress of Women," 145–152.

21. From 16 May to 27 July, Gilman stayed in Hammersmith and London. For most of August, she visited various friends and associates in Eltham, Kent, Edinburgh, and Newcastle.

22. Gilman, *Living,* 265–66.

23. Gilman wrote a series of reports on the International Council of Women for the *Arena* and *Ainslee's* and also a number of articles for the *Philadelphia Saturday Evening Post:* "The Flagstone Method," "The Fear of Want," and "American Children." In "The Flagstone Method," she wrote, "Mushrooms, we are told, can lift a flagstone in a single night. Perhaps they can; but we do not therefore recommend the cultivator to put flagstones on his mushroom beds. . . . It is observed also that transcendent genius can surmount difficulties. . . . But as we do not know how many mute, inglorious mushrooms have not lifted flagstones, but perished miserably thereunder, so we cannot estimate the number of geniuses who have failed to transcend their difficulties" (*Philadelphia Saturday Evening Post* 172, no. 3 [15 July 1899], 42).

24. At first Gilman was annoyed with her publishers because *Women and Economics* was not available during her first weeks in England. The book's delay "has spoiled all my fine plans for making an impression in England. I have neither lectured nor written as I should have if they had been here, out, reviewed and discussed" (CPS to GHG, 20 June 1899, AESL). As it turned out, however, there would be a number of reviews in the English papers—in the *London Daily Chronicle,* the *Manchester Chronicle,* the Westminster *Gazette*—so that in her autobiography Gilman would later write: "The book was warmly received in London, with long, respectful reviews in the papers. What with my former reputation, based on the poems, this new and impressive book, and my addresses at the Congress and elsewhere, I became quite a lion" (Gilman, *Living,* 260).

25. Gilman thought that Mrs. Muriel Norman was one of her most important London contacts: Her "letter is worth a lot to me. It 'opens' London in exactly the way I wanted—through the thinking people—not the 'social reformers' alone" (CPS to GHG, 11 February 1899, AESL). Mrs. Norman, with whom Gilman stayed temporarily, was the daughter of Annie Dowie, Gilman's Edinburgh friend. Gilman, *Living,* 258.

26. A number of the letters of May 1899 are too badly torn to be legible.

27. Daughter of Elizabeth Cady Stanton and suffragist organizer and activist, Harriot Stanton Blatch made her home in England for a number of years and later returned to the United States to organize the more militant Women's Political Union.

28. It is likely this letter is misdated, and that it is in fact a continuation of the 15 June letter.

29. In her autobiography, Gilman was also essentially positive about her visit at the home of Hubert and Edith Nesbit Bland, and she focused mostly on the "delightful" aristocratic Georgian setting: the moat-surrounded out-door parlor, the badminton and tennis courts, the jolly "little plays and fairy-tales" with "lovely . . . barefoot" children. And yet Hubert Bland's Manchester *Chronicle* review of *Women and Economics* ("A Sane Word in a Mad Controversy," AESL, #299), was one of the most hostile that Gilman received. Moreover, according to one commentator, the poet and novelist Edith Nesbit Bland was a "restless, moody" hostess, and her husband, Hubert Bland, was so busy with "persistent and flagrant infidelities" that he kept the household in "continuous emotional turmoil" (Howard Haycraft and Stanley J. Kunitz, eds., *Twentieth Century Authors: A Biographical Dictionary of Modern Literature* [New York: The H. W. Wilson Company, 1942], 1011–12).

Chapter 11. "To Eat and Drink So Largely of Human Life"

1. The Gilman letters quoted in this introductory essay were written between 26 September and 6 December 1899, although they may not necessarily be included in the section that follows.

2. *Toledo Sunday Journal,* November 1899.

3. Susa Young Gates later wrote privately to Gilman, "While I was ill this winter I read your wonderful book. It is truly wonderful. I shall never be quite the same woman, never look at life in the same way as in the former days. My views and impressions are still somewhat chaotic, the change was so sudden and startling," and yet "there is such a mass of truth of pure inspiration in it that I am overwhelmed with its stupendous force. . . . Oh, if you had only left out the Darwinism and the occasional touch of materialism[;] how gladly would I have put the book into the hands of every girl and boy I could reach. As it is we are to have a Mother's Class to meet each week and read, study, and discuss its pages" (Susa Young Gates to CPS, 20 March 1900, AESL).

In her autobiography, Gilman would refer to Susa Young Gates as a "remarkable woman, herself a writer and speaker, an organizer, an editor," a "mother of eleven children" and also a "lasting friend" (Gilman, *Living,* 264).

4. *Minneapolis Journal,* 14 November 1899; *Deseret Evening News,* Salt Lake City, 2 December 1899.

5. *Deseret Evening News,* Salt Lake City, 1 December 1899.

6. *St. Louis Post Dispatch,* 18 January 1899; Toledo *Sunday Journal,* November 1899; Minneapolis *Sunday Times,* 19 November 1899; Chicago *Daily News,* 16 November 1899.

7. *Salt Lake Herald,* Sunday, 26 November 1899.

8. *St. Louis Post Dispatch,* 18 January 1899.

9. In late September, Gilman noted that she had stopped by the Small and Maynard office and had read a collection of positive reviews of *Women and Economics.* "I am getting a world hearing by my beloved book, and that promptly" (CPS to GHG, 13 October 1899, AESL). In spite of the impressive reviews, however, *Women and Economics* would never be financially rewarding. Gilman later wrote, "The discrepancy between its really enormous vogue and its very meager returns I have never understood" (Gilman, *Living,* 270). Since she had returned from England with one dollar in her pocket, she continued to write short pieces that were financially rewarding. She was currently working on several editorials for the Philadelphia *Sat-*

urday Evening Post, for example, "Supply & Demand in Literature," "Education & Punishment," "Ethics in Schools," "Children & Flats," "Is Man's Nature Dual?"

10. *St. Louis Post Dispatch,* 18 January 1899.

11. Gilman, Diary, 18 September 1899, AESL.

12. Gilman was always more concerned that one's work have a social value than she was about one's moneymaking skills. In a later story entitled "An Offender," the heroine falls in love with the owner of a city street car company who was economically successful but who lacked social conscience about the public dangers his street cars caused. When a child was accidentally killed by one of his fenderless street cars, the heroine was so horrified and angered that she rejected his proposal of marriage. "An Offender," *Forerunner* I, no. 4 (Feb. 1910), 1–6.

13. Gilman had of course been applying these self-improvement strategies to herself for years, as well as offering them to other women in novels, articles, and lectures as a means of enhancing their self-respect. For a fictional version of her intellectual and physical fitness resolutions, see *What Diantha Did* (1909), *Benigna Machiavelli* (1914), and "A Coincidence," *Forerunner* I, no. 9 (July 1910), 1–4.

14. Gilman was staying at the home of Alice Stone Blackwell.

15. Amy Wellington, a close friend of Gilman's for many years, would later publish her biographical reflections in *Women Have Told: Studies in the Feminist Tradition* (1930). Wellington was particularly disturbed by the public opposition Gilman faced, by the "storm of criticism, ridicule, caricature and consternation," the "persistent and even scurrilous hostility," the "misunderstanding, ridicule or insult," the "years of lonely and courageous thinking." Gilman was regarded as a "disrupter of family life and destroyer of the home," a "dangerous," "erratic" writer of "queer," "revolting" doctrines. She was a woman of "religious passion," of "wit and forcefulness," Wellington continued, a "genuine creative thinker" who was able "to see further and suggest more than any other American woman of her day." Wellington would acclaim not only the "scourging civic satire" of Gilman's poetry, the "uncanny art" and "startling expression" of the "Yellow Wall-paper," but also the brilliance of her "revolutionary" and "epoch-marking" *Women and Economics.* As Wellington summarized the central Gilman message, "*We* have pushed sex distinction to such a point that it has reached the very soul, . . . and *we* suffer mortally under the consequences without knowing what is the matter" (*Women Have Told: Studies in the Feminist Tradition* [Boston: Little Brown, and Company, 1930], 115–31).

16. *Women and Economics* would eventually be translated into seven languages, including Hungarian, Russian, and Japanese.

17. Although Samuel Jones lost the election for governor of Ohio in 1899, he was reelected four times as mayor of Toledo, serving until his death in 1904. A nonpartisan, socialist progressive, he was a "Tolstoyan anarchist," according to one critic, who "took Christ" as his living "model," and preached the "Golden Rule" as a principal of business "success." Starting out as the son of a tenant farmer and a drill pump worker in the Pennsylvania oil fields, he subsequently became an organizer and owner of the Acme Sucker Rod Company and a firm advocate of workers' basic rights. In his 1899 publication, *The New Right: A Plea for Fair Play Through a More Just Social Order,* Jones called for a socialist, cooperative society in which "every man would be guaranteed the right to labor and to the full fruit of his toil". As mayor of Toledo, he introduced the merit system in the police and public works departments, an eight-hour day for city employees, and kindergartens and playgrounds for the children. In response he won the "thundering condemnation" of the more "respectable" and the thundering applause of workers and economic underdogs (Howe quoted in Harold U. Faulkner, *Politics, Reform, and Expansion* 45). See also

Frederic C. Howe, *The Confessions of a Reformer* (New York: Charles Scribner's Sons, 1925), 185.

18. In Indianapolis, Gilman stayed with May Wright Sewell, currently president of the International Congress of Women.

19. Gilman would incorporate her reflections about appropriate child-rearing techniques in a later work entitled *Concerning Children* (1900).

20. According to the Chicago *Times Herald* reporter, Gilman had gone "through convolutions that for ease and grace might make a contortionist envious. 'Do you know, said the imperturbable performer in parting, with my toes I can lift a cup of coffee from the floor to my lips.' What won't Mrs. Charlotte Perkins Stetson do next, pray tell?" *Times Herald,* 12 November 1899.

21. Having worked closely with Gilman in the West Coast Women's Press Association, in Nationalist Clubs, and among California protest groups, Harriet Howe later would insist that she had always been an admirer of Gilman. "It is perhaps no exaggeration to say that she saved my life," Howe later noted. She was "the greatest personality that I had ever seen. . . . And she had given me the greatest of all gifts,— the courage of my convictions" (Harriet Howe quoted in Hill, *Making of a Radical Feminist,* 184). Yet, in the 1899 private correspondence, Howe conveyed some irritations and reactivated memories of some unpleasant experiences in California.(Harriet Howe to CPS, 25 November 1899, AESL).

22. *Denver Evening News,* 1 December 1899:

> There is probably no woman in America today who commands more attention from the best minds of Europe and America than Mrs. Stetson. Her book, *Women and Economics* is recognized as one of the brightest, most original and readable on women ever written. It is selling all over the United States and England, and is being translated into French, German, Dutch and Swedish.
>
> In addition to this work, Mrs. Stetson has written a volume of verse, "In This Our World," which has been very much sought after, and her other work, "The Yellow Wall Paper," is regarded as an American classic. While Mrs. Stetson is brilliant as a writer, she is yet stronger as a public speaker. She comes from that kind of stock, being the great granddaughter of Lyman Beecher therefore a grand niece to Henry Ward Beecher and Harriet Beecher Stowe.
>
> Mrs. Stetson speaks as she thinks, clearly, distinctly and in a perfectly straightforward and simple manner, but with something in her utterance so magnetic that she wins attention from her hearers.

Chapter 12. The Blessed Joy of Natural Beauty

1. Gilman, *Living,* 274.

2. The Gilman letters quoted in this introductory essay were written between 10 December 1899 and 16 April 1900, although they may not necessarily be included in the section that follows.

3. According to Gilman's autobiography, *Human Work* was her most important and ambitious effort: "Here was an enormous change of thought, altering the relationships of all sociological knowledge . . . from the ego-centric to the socio-centric system." "This was the greatest book I have ever done," she wrote, and yet it also was "the poorest—that is, the least adequately done." In fact, "in the four times I did it over I never knew where to begin" (Gilman, *Living,* 275, 285). Although Gilman worked most of the winter of 1900 on *Human Work,* it did not appear until 1904.

4. Gilman, *Human Work,* 9, 197. Many contemporary reformers believed that industrialization was inherently a progressive force. Veblen argued, for example, that science and industry promoted regard for the "impersonal standpoint," for "quantitative relation, mechanical efficiency or use." Although Veblen was sometimes re-

garded as a cynic, he not only optimistically affirmed his belief in the "instinct of workmanship," but he also argued that the leisure class inevitably would disappear because of their isolation from productive labor and because of the "decline of war, the obsolescence of proprietary government, and the decay of the priestly office." Whatever the perceived self-interest of the leisured class, the "instinct of workmanship" was so prominent and compelling that even the most resistent would feel compelled to engage in socially productive work. (See Thorstein Veblen, *Theory of the Leisure Class* [New York: American Library, 1953], 29, 220, 161.) For a more extended discussion of the implications of this argument, particularly the endorsement of industrialization on the military model, see Hill, *Making of a Radical Feminist*, 169–74.

5. Gilman, *Human Work*, 345, 285, 206, 172–73.

6. Gilman, *Human Work*, 356.

7. Gilman, *Human Work*, 151–53, 221, 179. Gilman found Veblen's *Theory of the Leisure Class* a "valuable, interesting, and occasionally delightful work." "There is a lot of truth in that," she noted. She also would meet Veblen in Chicago in the spring of 1900. "Interesting man," she noted. Diary, 1 February 1900; 17 November 1900, AESL; CPS to CHG, 27 January 1900, AESL.

8. Gilman, *Human Work*, 207, 171, 315, 133. *Human Work* was fairly well received by some reviewers. According to the *Boston Literary World*, it was "a subtle and thorough analysis." The Chicago *Tribune* said that it was the "best thing that Mrs. Gilman had done." With this book she "places herself among the foremost students and elucidators of the problem of social economies." According to the *Atlantic Monthly*, however, "An impatient habit of generalization compromises the effectiveness of the book both from the literary point of view and as a scientific study." Quotations from the reviews of *Human Work* are in Gary Scharnhorst, *Charlotte Perkins Gilman* (Boston: Twayne Publishers, 1985), 63–64. Scharnhorst notes that *Human Work* is "poorly organized, ponderous, redundant, and discursive" (61).

9. Diary entries are quoted from Gilman, *Living*, 276. One of Gilman's New Year's resolutions was to pay back her outstanding debts, the largest of which ($775.00) was to Adeline Knapp. The total was $2,030. "Little by little, I was clearing things off," she later wrote, paying the gas bill, the milk bill, and making cash returns to people she had not seen for years. Gilman, *Living*, 275.

10. Harriet Howe later admired Charlotte's stamina during these early California years: "To support and nurse a dying mother would be enough for many women; to support and rear a child would be enough for almost any woman; to take over a house full of boarders would be more than enough for the majority of women. Yet she cheerfully assumed all three of these responsibilities, because they were necessary" (Harriet Howe, "Charlotte Perkins Gilman—As I Knew Her," *Equal Rights: Independent Feminist Weekly* II, no. 27 [5 September 1936], 211–16). For more discussion of the Gilman-Howe relationship, see Hill, *Making of a Radical Feminist*, particularly pages 178, 183–84, 194–95, 201–7, 216.

11. Gilman, *Living*, 274.

12. As Gilman was making plans for Katharine to live with her, she was also writing about possible arrangements for isolated mothers. In an article entitled "Six Mothers," for example, she suggested that mothers "divide the working days of the week among them, agreeing that each shall on her chosen day take charge of the children of the other five." Not only would such sharing benefit the children, but as the mothers developed patterns of "mutual helpfulness" and systematic study, they would be a "help to uncounted thousands of ungrouped mothers who are struggling on alone" (C. P. Stetson, "Six Mothers," *Harper's Bazaar* 33, no. 22 [June 2, 1900], 282–84).

13. In her later years, Gilman would call for a literature that would "give mother-hood its place," that would explore the "comedy and tragedy," the "humor, pathos, patience, despair, and a silent grandeur both of failure and success" (Gilman, "Coming Changes in Literature," *Forerunner* VI, no. 9 [September 1915], 231–34). Moreover, in her novel, *Mag Marjorie*, (1912) she tried a fictional recreation of her strains with Kate, the years of separation, the "ceaseless heartache and remorse" (Gilman, *Mag-Marjorie*, serialized in *Forerunner* III, no. 6 [June 1912], 154), the need to learn "how to hold down her grief, and use it as a spur" (Gilman, *Mag-Marjorie*, serialized in *Forerunner* III, no. 4 [April 1912], 101).

Hers was a hunger unknown to most mothers; a stored, accumulated hunger; a hunger that had unconsciously absorbed such other longings as these growing years might else have known. The self-reproach which she bore always within gave a desperate bitterness to her longing (*Mag-Marjorie*, serialized in *Forerunner* III, no. 10 [October 1912], 265).

On the one hand, Gilman's heroine, Margaret Wentworth, was fighting for "a principle" (*Mag-Marjorie*, serialized in *Forerunner* III, no. 4 [April 1912], 99)—to "prove that there's something more to a woman than this one performance" (*Mag-Marjorie*, serialized in *Forerunner* III, no. 2 [February 1912], 48). But on the other hand, the problem for the fictional heroine, and for Gilman as well, was that she also had to approach her daughter cautiously; in fact she had to "fight" to win her daughter's love. The heroine found she had to lay "siege" to her daughter's "young affections with careful skill. She must not go too far—too fast. . . . She must tempt—withdraw—be always kind, but not always within reach." She must conduct her "bitter-sweet campaign . . . with patience—the wooing of her own child's heart" (*Mag-Marjorie*, serialized in *Forerunner* III, no. 10 [October 1912], 265). Or, as Gilman had recently described her own efforts with Katherine, "I am going to woo that damsel with all arts I can compass." "Great plot—the Traitorous and Seductive Mother—secretly wooing her Child! . . . What a delightful lot of 'Good Villain' stories I can write when I get at it! Nice book it would make!" (CPG to GHG, 15 October 1899, AESL; 10 November 1899, AESL).

14. Gilman, Diary, 16 February 1900. AESL.

15. In this letter, she calculates that her remaining debt is $2,030.00.

16. Likewise in her public writings Gilman expressed a patriotic pride in American democracy. In *Women and Economics*, for example, she argued that the freeing of the slaves had resulted from the "same impulse" that "set in motion the long struggle toward securing woman's fuller equality," and "more prominently in this country than in any other." Moreover, America's "Federal Democracy"—though "politically expressed by men alone"—had "strengthened, freed, [and] emboldened, the human soul." Gilman, *Women and Economics*, 146–48. There are, of course, some powerfully destructive aspects of our history. We "have cheated the Indian, oppressed the African, robbed the Mexican and childishly wasted our great resources." Gilman, "Race Pride," *Forerunner* IV, no. 4 (April 1913), 90. And yet overall our "democracy has brought to us the fullest individualization that the world has ever seen." Gilman, *Women and Economics*, 146–48. In fact, Americans "are the kind of people who have made a country that every other kind of people wants to get into!" Gilman, *Living*, 317.

17. Grace Channing had suffered a miscarriage.

18. Louisa May Alcott, *Work: A Story of Experience* (New York: Schocken Books, 1977).

19. When Charlotte's brother Thomas learned about the marriage he wrote to Charlotte:

I read my letter mail upon the sunlit snow with a background of dark Murry pines and mountain slopes and a foreground of Smith's snow-shoe tracks, while the creek and river joined their waters and united their voices.

And I was duly and sufficiently surprised at the news of your intended matrimonial adventure, and snow-shoed persuasively back to my cabin with many of my cherished schemes for your advantage (heretofore mainly 'floating in the air') now "nipped in the bud."

Nevertheless I'm no wise blame you for becoming victim to the Perkins matrimonial habit, which seems to claim its own irrespective of age or circumstances, myself believing that its advantages are manifold. . . .

Your loving brother, T. A. Perkins. 3 April 1900.

(Thomas Perkins to CPS, 3 April 1900, AESL.)

20. In another letter Charlotte suggested that Small and Maynard may not have paid her adequately. "I shall be polite—but I am going to urge further inquiry—it don't seem possible it is right—so little income from so much sales." CPS to GHG, 18 March 1900, AESL.

21. As it turned out, a California friend lent her money so that she was able to give several hundred dollars to Grace and Walter and also cover her own current expenses.

22. The letters of early April also include mention of various women's club contacts and of financial calculations in connection with her spring lecture tour. As it turned out, the Oakland group could not pay the fifty dollars that Charlotte requested for her lecture, and as she put it in later letter, "I won't work for less." CPS to GHG, 10 April 1900, AESL.

23. Although Gilman had some political concerns about the 7th Regiment's strike-breaking activities, her current letters speak only about her fear for Houghton's safety. As she put it in another letter, "And tomorrow I shall know about that strike—in which my only interest is to know if you are hurt! There's a humanitarian for you!" CPS to GHG, 25 April 1900, AESL.

Chapter 13. "With Thanks for Life and Love"

1. The Gilman letters quoted in this introductory essay were written between 26 April and 7 June 1900, although they may not necessarily be included in the section that follows.

2. According to the letters, Gilman only occasionally went to Hull-House on this visit. She wrote Houghton, "wonderful Miss Addams handling it all so well and meeting the thousand calls upon her so gently and effectually—it is magnificent, but it tires me very much" (CPS to GHG, 15 May 1900, AESL).

3. Several of Gilman's later short stories, particularly those portraying maiden aunts who are pious, disapproving, and self-righteous, suggest some lingering resentments toward Houghton's relatives. See, for example, "The Boy and the Butter," *Forerunner* I, no. 12 (October 1910), 1–5. Alternately, however, Gilman offered sympathetic explanations for the unmarried woman's narrow life: "If she does not succeed in being chosen, she becomes a thing of mild popular contempt, a human being with no further place in life save as an attachee, a dependent upon more fortunate relatives, an old maid" (Gilman, *Women and Economics,* 88).

4. Because Houghton and Charlotte were first cousins, the family connections were particularly intense. Emily Perkins Hale, for example, was the sister of his mother, Katherine Beecher Perkins Gilman, and her father, Frederick Beecher Perkins.

5. For all of her feminist convictions, Gilman rarely spoke of men's fathering responsibilities. If she and Houghton were to have more children for their own, for

example, she wrote him: "I won't turn them loose on you—even at night—not if I have to hire two relays of nurses!" (CPS to GHG, 2 November 1898, AESL).

6. Gilman also read her poem entitled "Heroism" at the convention. It reads in part:

> It takes great love to stir a human heart
> To live beyond the others and apart.
> A love that is not shallow, is not small,
> Is not for one, or two, but for them all.
> Love that can wound love, for its higher need;
> Love that can leave love though the heart may bleed;
> Love that can lose love; family, and friend;
> Yet steadfastly live, loving, to the end.
> A love that asks no answer, that can live
> Moved by the one burning, deathless force—to give.
> Love, strength, and courage. Courage, strength, and love,
> The heroics of all time are built thereof.
>
> (Gilman "Heroism," in *In This Our World*, 14–15.)

7. Charlotte and Houghton were married in Detroit on 11 June 1900. Her diary entry reads: "Arrive at 6 [in Detroit]. Houghton in the station. . . . Unitarian Minister, arrives about 7:30, and we are married. Very short and reasonable service. Then a very nice little dinner—far too long, and then we go" (Diary, 11 June 1900). The service was held at the home of Mr. and Mrs. Sidney Corbett, Jr.

8. Louisa Gilman was the sister of Katherine Beecher Gilman, Houghton Gilman's mother.

9. In Denver, Colorado, Gilman had stayed for several days with her close friend and surrogate mother, Helen Campbell. She had heard that Helen Campbell's health was failing, and that, "temporarily affected in her mind," she was considering marrying a "crank." Gilman decided, however, that instead of being ill, Helen Campbell was simply lonely and thus invited her to live with the Gilmans in New York. As it turned out, Helen Campbell did not remarry. And although she stayed with the Gilmans periodically, for the most part she made her home with other friends. CPS to GHG, 3 November 1899, AESL.

Afterword

1. Charlotte's letters unfortunately indicate that she purposely destroyed them.

2. That is not to say that Gilman's theories were without their weaknesses. As I have noted before, her arguments were often seriously weakened by her inattention to issues of race and class, and by a perspective that too often was racist, classist, and ethnocentric.

3. Charlotte Gilman, like many other women, often tried to credit Houghton with her success and happiness. As Carolyn Heilbrun puts it, women's identity is often "grounded through relation to the chosen other. Without such relation, women do not feel able to write openly about themselves; even with it, they do not feel entitled to credit for their own accomplishments, spiritual or not" (Heilbrun, *Writing a Woman's Life*, 24).

4. Carolyn Heilbrun suggests the need for "a new plot of marriage." Virginia Woolf "wrote one with her life," Heilbrun notes, "but never with her fiction; nor did George Eliot, or Beatrice Webb—nor has anyone" (Heilbrun, *Writing a Woman's Life*, 89).

5. Except for the "Yellow Wallpaper," many of Gilman's fictional pieces likewise portray heroines who are rationally astute but who lack emotional complexity and depth.

6. Katharine Beecher Stetson went to live with Houghton and Charlotte at the end of July 1900, thereafter dividing her time between the Gilmans and Stetsons. Katharine later married F. Tolles Chamberlin, became a sculptor and a painter, and raised two children, Dorothy and Walter Chamberlin.

Bibliography

Major Works by Charlotte Perkins Gilman

Benigna Machiavelli. Serialized in *Forerunner* II (1914).

The Charlotte Perkins Reader. Edited, with introduction by Ann J. Lane. New York: Pantheon, 1980.

Concerning Children. Boston: Small, Maynard, 1900.

Forerunner 1–7 (1909–16). Reprint. New York: Greenwood, 1968.

Herland. Serialized in *Forerunner* VI (1915). Reprint, with introduction by Ann J. Lane. New York: Pantheon, 1979.

His Religion and Hers: A Study of the Faith of Our Fathers and the Work of Our Mothers. 1923. Reprint, Westport, Conn.: Hyperion Press, 1976.

The Home: Its Work and Influence. 1903. Reprint, Urbana: University of Illinois Press, 1972.

Human Work. New York: McClure, Phillips, 1904.

In This Our World. 1893. Reprint, New York: Arno, 1974.

The Living of Charlotte Perkins Gilman: An Autobiography. With a foreword by Zona Gale. 1935. Reprint, New York: Harper & Row, 1975.

Mag-Marjorie. Serialized in *Forerunner* III (1912).

The Man-Made World: Our Androcentric Culture. *Forerunner* I (1909–10). Reprint. New York: Charlton, 1911.

Moving the Mountain. Serialized in the *Forerunner* II (1911). Reprint. New York: Charlton, 1911.

*What Diantha Did.*Serialized in the *Forerunner* I (1909–10). Reprint. New York: Charlton, 1910.

With Her in Ourland. Serialized in the *Forerunner* VII (1916).

Women and Economics: A Study of the Economic Relation between Men and Women as a Factor in Social Evolution. With introduction by Carl Degler. 1898. Reprint, New York: Harper & Row, 1966.

"The Yellow Wall-paper." *New England Magazine* 5 (January 1892): 647–59.

Selected Secondary Sources

Allen, Polly Wynn. *Building Domestic Liberty: Charlotte Perkins Gilman's Architectural Feminism.* Amherst: University of Massachusetts Press, 1988.

Barry, Kathleen. *Susan B. Anthony: A Biography of a Singular Feminist.* New York: New York: New York University Press, 1988.

Belenky, Mary Field. *Women's Ways of Knowing: The Development of Self, Voice, and Mind.* New York: Basic Books, 1986.

Berkin, Carol. "Private Woman, Public Woman: The Contradictions of Charlotte Perkins Gilman." In *Women in America: A History*. Boston: Houghton Mifflin, 1979, 150–73.

Black, Alexander. "The Woman Who Saw It First." *Century* 107 (November 1923): 33–42.

Brownley, Martine Watson, and Ruth Perry, eds. *Mothering the Mind*. New York: Holmes & Meier, 1984.

Chesler, Phyllis. *Women and Madness*. Garden City, N.Y.: Doubleday, 1972.

Chodorow, Nancy. *The Reproduction of Mothering*. Berkeley: University of California Press, 1978.

Christ, Carol. *Diving Deep and Surfacing: Women Writers on Spiritual Quest*. Boston: Beacon Press, 1980.

———. *Laughter of Aphrodite: Reflections on a Journey to the Goddess*. San Francisco: Harper & Row, 1987.

Cott, Nancy F. *The Grounding of Modern Feminism*. New Haven: Yale University Press, 1987.

Degler, Carl N. "Charlotte Perkins Gilman on the Theory and Practice of Feminism." *American Quarterly* 8 (Spring 1956): 21–39.

Dell, Floyd. *Women as World Builders*. Chicago: Forbes, 1913.

Dinnerstein, Dorothy. *The Mermaid and the Minotaur: Sexual Arrangements and Human Malaise*. New York: Harper & Row, 1976.

Dombrowski, James. *The Early Days of Christian Socialism in America*. 1936. Reprint, New York: Octagon, 1966.

DuPlessis, Rachel Blau. *Writing Beyond the Ending: Narrative Strategies of Twentieth-Century Women Writers*. Bloomington: Indiana University Press, 1985.

Egbert, Donald Drew, and Stow Persons, eds. *Socialism and American Life*. T. D. Bassett, Bibliographer. Vols. I–II. Princeton: Princeton University Press, 1952.

Eisler, Riane. *The Chalice and the Blade: Our History, Our Future*. San Francisco: Harper & Row, 1988.

Faulkner, Harold. *Politics, Reform, and Expansion: 1890–1900*. 1959. Reprint, New York: Harper & Row, 1963.

Friedman, Susan Stanford. "Creativity and the Childbirth Mataphor: Gender Difference in Literary Discourse." In *Speaking of Gender*. Edited by Elaine Showalter, 73–100. New York: Routledge, 1989.

Gale, Zona. "Charlotte Perkins Gilman." *Nation* (25 September 1935): 350–51.

Gilbert, Sandra M., and Susan Gubar. *The Madwoman in the Attic: The Woman Writer and the Nineteenth-Century Literary Imagination*. New Haven: Yale University Press, 1979.

———. *No Man's Land: The Place of the Woman Writer in the Twentieth Century*. New Haven: Yale University Press, 1988.

Gilligan, Carol. *In a Different Voice: Psychological theory and Women's Development*. Cambridge, Mass.: Harvard University Press, 1982.

Ginger, Ray. *The Age of Excess: The United States from 1877 to 1914*. New York: Macmillan, 1975.

Gornick, Vivian. "Twice-Told Tales." *Nation* (23 September 1978): 278–81.

Hall, Radclyffe. *The Well of Loneliness*. 1928. Reprint, Garden City, N.Y.: Blue Ribbon Books, 1936.

Hayden, Dolores. "Charlotte Perkins Gilman and the Kitchenless House." *Radical History Review* 21 (Fall 1979): 225–47.

———. *The Grand Domestic Revolution: A History of Feminist Designs for American Homes, Neighborhoods, and Cities,* especially Part V, "Charlotte Perkins Gilman and Her Influence," Chaps. 9–12. Cambridge: MIT Press, 1981.

Hedges, Elaine. Afterword to *The Yellow Wall-paper.* Old Westbury, N.Y.: Feminist Press, 1973.

Heilbrun, Carolyn. *Writing a Woman's Life.* New York: Norton, 1988.

Heyward, Carter. *Touching Our Strength: The Erotic as Power and the Love of God.* San Francisco: Harper & Row, 1989.

Hill, Mary Armfield. "Charlotte Perkins Gilman: A Feminist's Struggle with Womanhood." *Massachusetts Review* 21 (1980): 503–26.

———. *Charlotte Perkins Gilman: The Making of a Radical Feminist.* Philadelphia: Temple University Press, 1980.

———. *Endure: The Diaries of Charles Walter Stetson.* Philadelphia: Temple University Press, 1985.

History of Woman Suffrage, Vols. I–III. Elizabeth Cady Stanton, Susan B. Anthony, and Matilda J. Gage, eds.. Rochester, N.Y.: Charles Mann, 1881, 1882, 1886. Vol. IV ed. Susan B. Anthony and Ida Husted Harper. Indianapolis: Hollenbeck Press, 1902. Vols. V and VI ed. Ida Husted Harper. New York: J. J. Little & Ives, 1922.

Hite, Shire. *The Hite Report: Women and Love: A Cultural Revolution in Progress.* New York: Knopf, 1987.

Howe, Harriet. "Charlotte Perkins Gilman—As I Knew Her." *Equal Rights: Independent Feminist Weekly* II, no. 27 (5 Sept. 1936): 211–16.

Hoy, Pat C., II, Esther H. Schor, and Robert DiYanni eds. *Women's Voices: Visions and Perspectives.* New York: McGraw-Hill, 1990.

Karpinski, Joanne B. "When the Marriage of True Minds Admits Impediments: Charlotte Perkins Gilman and William Dean Howells." *Patrons and Proteges: Gender, Friendship, and Writing in Nineteenth-Century America.* Edited by Shirley Marchalonis. New Brunswick, N.J.: Rutgers University Press, 1988.

Kelly, Mary. *Private Woman, Public Stage: Literary Domesticity in Nineteenth-Century America.* New York: Oxford University Press, 1984.

Kennard, Jean K. "Convention Coverage or How to Read Your Own Life." *New Literary History* 13 (Autumn 1981): 69–88.

Kerber, Linda K., and Jane DeHart Mathews. *Women's America: Refocusing the Past.* New York: Oxford University Press, 1991.

Kessler, Carol Farley. "Brittle Jars and Bitter Jangles: Light Verse by Charlotte Perkins Gilman." *Regionalism and the Female Imagination* 4 (1979): 35–43.

Kessler-Harris, Alice. *Out to Work: A History of Wage-Earning Women in the United States.* New York: Oxford University Press, 1982.

Kolodny, Annette. "A Map for Rereading: Or, Gender and the Interpretation of Literary Texts." *New Literary History* 11 (Spring 1980): 451–67, esp. 455–60.

Lane, Ann J., ed. *The Charlotte Perkins Gilman Reader: "The Yellow Wallpaper" and Other Fiction.* New York: Pantheon Books, 1980.

———. *To Herland and Beyond: The Life and Work of Charlotte Perkins Gilman.* New York: Pantheon Books, 1990.

Langley, Juliet A. "'Audacious Fancies': A Collection of Letters from Charlotte Perkins Gilman to Martha Luther." *Trivia* 6 (Winter 1985): 52–69.

Lerner, Gerda. "Placing Women in History: Definitions and Challenges." *Feminist Studies* III, no. 1/2 (Fall 1975): 5.

Lutz, Alma. *Created Equal: A Biography of Elizabeth Cady Stanton.* New York: John Day, 1940.

MacPike, Loralee. "Environment as Psychopathological Symbolism in "The Yellow Wallpaper." *American Literary Realism* 8 (Summer 1975): 286–88.

Magner, Lois N. "Women and the Scientific Idion: Textual Episodes from Wollstonecraft, Fuller, Gilman, and Firestone." *Signs* 4 (Autumn 1978): 61–80, esp. 68–77.

Meyering, Sheryl L. ed. *Charlotte Perkins Gilman: The Woman and Her Work.* With a foreword by Cathy N. Davidson. Ann Arbor, Mich.: UMI Research Press, 1989.

Morton, Nelle. *The Journey Is Home.* Boston: Beacon Press, 1985.

Muncy, Raymond Lee. *Sex and Marriage in Utopian Communities: 19th Century America.* Bloomington: Indiana University Press, 1973.

Nicolson, Nigel, and Joanne Trautmann, eds. *The Letters of Virginia Woolf.* New York: Harcourt Brace Jovanovich, 1979.

Nies, Judith. *Seven Women.* New York: Viking, 1977.

O'Brien, Sharon. *Willa Cather: The Emerging Voice.* New York: Oxford University Press, 1987.

Olsen, Tillie. *Silences.* New York: Delacorte Press, 1978.

O'Neill, William L. *Everyone Was Brave.* New York: Quadrangle, 1969, 38–44, 130–33.

Ostricker, Alicia. *Stealing the Language: The Emergence of Women's Poetry in America.* Boston: Beacon Press, 1986.

Pagels, Elaine. *Gnostic Gospels.* New York: Random House, 1979.

Palmeri, Ann. "Charlotte Perkins Gilman: Forerunner of a Feminist Social Science." In *Discovering Reality: Feminist Perspectives on Epistemology, Metaphysics, Methodology, and Philosophy of Science.* Edited by Sandra Harding and Merill B. Hintikka. Boston: D. Reidel, 1983.

Peck, Mary Gray. *Carrie Chapman Catt: A Biography.* New York: H. W. Wilson Company, 1944.

Plaskow, Judith and Christ, Carol P., eds. *Weaving the Visions: New Patterns in Feminist Spirituality.* San Francisco: Harper & Row, 1989.

Quint, Howard. *The Forging of American Socialism: Origins of the Modern Movement.* New York: Bobbs-Merrill, 1953.

Radway, Janice A. *Reading the Romance: Women, Patriarchy, and Popular Literature.* Chapel Hill: University of North Carolina Press, 1984.

Raymond, Janice. *A Passion for Friends.* Boston: Beacon Press, 1986.

Rich, Adrienne. "Compulsory Heterosexuality." In *Women's Voices.* Edited by Pat C. Hoy, Esther H. Schor, and Robert DiYanni. New York: McGraw-Hill Publishing Company, 1990.

——. *On Lies, Secrets, and Silence.* New York: W. W. Norton, 1979.

——. *Of Woman Born: Motherhood as Experience and Institution.* New York: Norton, 1976.

Rose, Phyllis. *Women of Letters: A Life of Virginia Woolf.* New York: Oxford University Press, 1978.

Rossi, Alice, ed. *The Feminist Papers: From Adams to de Beauvoir.* 1973. Reprint, New York: Bantam, 1978.

Ruether, Rosemary Radford. *Religion and Sexism: Images of Women in the Jewish and Christian Traditions.* Edited by Rosemary Radford Ruether. New York: Simon and Schuster, 1974.

Russell, Letty M., ed. *Feminist Interpretation of the Bible.* Philadelphia: Westminster Press, 1985.

Scharnhorst, Gary. *Charlotte Perkins Gilman.* Boston: Twayne Publishers, 1985.

———. *Charlotte Perkins Gilman: A Bibliography.* Metuchen, New Jersey: Scarecrow Press, 1985.

———. "Making Her Fame: Charlotte Perkins Gilman in California." *California History* 64 (Summer 1985): 192–201.

Schopp-Schilling, Beate. "The Yellow Wallpaper: A Rediscovered 'Realistic' Story." *American Literary Realism* 8 (Summer 1975): 284–86.

Schreiner, Olive. "Three Dreams in a Desert." In *Dreams,* 1895, Reprint, Boston: Little, Brown, and Co., 1919.

Scott, Anne Firor. "A New-Model Woman." *Review in American History* 8 (December 1980): 442–47.

Smith-Rosenberg, Carroll. "The Female World of Love and Ritual: Relations between Women in Nineteenth-Century America." *Signs* I, no. 1 (Autumn 1975): 1–29.

Spacks, Patricia Meyer. *The Female Imagination.* New York: Knopf, 1975.

Storr, Anthony. *The Dynamics of Creation.* New York: Atheneum, 1972.

Veblen, Thorstein. *The Theory of the Leisure Class.* 1899. Reprint, New York: American Library, 1953.

Wood, Ann Douglas. "'The Fashionable Diseases: Women's Complaints and Their Treatment in Nineteenth-Century America." *Journal of Interdisciplinary History* 4 (Summer 1973): 25–52.

Woolf, Virginia. *A Room of One's Own.* 1929. Reprint, New York: Harvest Edition, 1981.

Index